Twelve Days in May

Brian Cull, Bruce Lander and
Heinrich Weiss

GRUB STREET · LONDON

Published by
Grub Street
The Basement
10 Chivalry Road
London SW11 1HT

A catalogue record is available on request from the British Library

ISBN 1-898697-20-5

Typeset by Pearl Graphics, Hemel Hempstead

Printed and bound in Great Britain by
Biddles Ltd, Guildford and King's Lynn

Brian Cull is the author of the following Grub Street titles:

AIR WAR FOR YUGOSLAVIA, GREECE & CRETE, 1940-41 with Christopher
Shores and Nicola Malizia
MALTA: THE HURRICANE YEARS, 1940-41 with Christopher Shores and
Nicola Malizia
MALTA: THE SPITFIRE YEAR, 1942 with Christopher Shores and Nicola
Malizia
BLOODY SHAMBLES, Volume 1 with Christopher Shores and Yasuho Izawa
BLOODY SHAMBLES, Volume 2 with Christopher Shores and Yasuho Izawa
SPITFIRES OVER ISRAEL with Shlomo Aloni and David Nicolle

CONTENTS

ACKNOWLEDGEMENTS

First and foremost, Brian Cull wishes to thank Val not only for continued patience but for her practical help and encouragement while working on this book—his seventh in almost as many years—which has left little time for anything else! Similarly, Bruce Lander wishes to acknowledge June's support over the three years of research involved, while Heinrich Weiss—co-opted at the eleventh hour—has laboured diligently to supply information for inclusion, and he offers his thanks to Margret for being so understanding during this difficult period.

A number of veterans have been contacted whose contributions have proved invaluable, including Wg Cdr Joe Kayll DSO OBE DFC, former commander of 615 Squadron, who kindly agreed to read the manuscript and write the Foreword.

Others who have provided information and photographs include Sqn Ldr A.H.B. Friendship DFM (3 Squadron), Wg Cdr P.L. Parrott DFC AFC (607 Squadron), Flg Off C.E. Hampshire (85 Squadron), Grp Capt J.A. Hemingway DFC (85 Squadron), Flt Lt T.C. Jackson (615 Squadron), Wg Cdr P.C.P. Farnes DFM (501 Squadron), Sqn Ldr K.N.T. Lee DFC (501 Squadron), Wg Cdr W.H.R. Whitty DFC (607 Squadron), Air Marshal Sir Denis Crowley-Milling KCB CBE DSO DFC AFC (615 Squadron), Mr Bill Bowman (607 Squadron); Mrs Alan Brooks on behalf of her husband; also the late Sqn Ldr A.G. Lewis DFC (85 Squadron), the late Grp Capt F.B. Sutton DFC (56 Squadron), the late Flt Lt A.H. Deacon (85 Squadron); the late Wg Cdr C.A.C. Stone DFC (3 Squadron); Mr Brian Courtney, son of the late Grp Capt R.N.H. Courtney DFC, 151 Squadron. Others who have contributed in various ways include Mr G.I. Smith Hon Sec 615 Squadron Association; Mr Fred Beacon Hon Sec 607 Squadron Association; Mr Fred McMillan, Registrar of The Aircrew Association; Mr John Banfield, Hon Sec of the RAF Ex-Prisoner of War Association. Our sincere thanks to you all.

We also acknowledge the fine work of Chris Thomas in producing the excellent cover illustration; and we thank Cynrik De Dekker and Jean-Louis Roba, Belgian air historians and authors of *Mei 1940: Boven Belgie* for their generous assistance and loan of photographs.

Our gratitude is offered to fellow aviation historians Norman Franks (for his comments on the first draft and for the loan of photographs; his *Valiant Wings* should be read in conjunction with this account); to Jack Foreman (for information, translations, the loan of photographs and for taking time to read the first draft); to John Vasco (for information); to Chris Shores (for information); to Andy Saunders (for information); to Simon Muggleton (for information and the loan of photographs); to Flt Lt Andy Thomas (for the loan of photographs); to Paul Sortehaug

(New Zealand) and Australians Lex McAulay, Dennis Newton and Ian Primmer (for their respective contributions of information and for the loan of photographs); to Kenneth Nelson (Canada) (for the loan of the relevant part of his manuscript of *Spitfire RCW*); and to Winfried Bock (Germany). Also, our thanks to the staff of the PRO, RAF Hendon, British Newspaper Library, Bury St Edmunds Public Library, Commonwealth War Graves Commission, the Air Historical Branch of the Ministry of Defence, and the RAF Personnel Management Centre. And last but not least, to Stuart Uster of Thetford Micros for practical help, my old friend Barry Baddock for help with translations, and Mr Jack Lee.

Finally, the authors wish to thank Mr John Davies of Grub Street for another excellent production.

AUTHORS' NOTE

The authors have endeavoured to provide a comprehensive account of operations undertaken by Hurricanes of the RAF's Advanced Air Striking Force and Air Component during the fateful twelve days, 10-21 May 1940, following the German invasion of Northern France and the Low Countries. However, few detailed records survived the RAF's withdrawal from France: some squadrons were ordered to destroy their records, others lost their records due to enemy action or during the confusion of the retreat. The Air Ministry's Air Historical Branch summary covering the period revealed:

> 'From the historical viewpoint what mattered... was the destruction of practically all records... Many unit records were burnt before moving. Others, including those of Headquarters, were stacked ready for loading on the leave quay at Boulogne, but were then dumped into the harbour, presumably from an absence of shipping, time or forethought.'

In addition, the majority of records and documents that did survive the débâcle have, in many cases, proved to be wanting, since most were compiled many days, even weeks, after the events took place, often by persons who were not directly involved.

The authors herewith attempt to unravel the confusion of those twelve days, the story retold mainly in the pilots' own words extracted from combat reports and squadron Operations Record Books, contemporary reports and published works, private interviews and correspondence. Much invaluable detail has been made available from German records, some of which has helped to determine the fates of a number of Hurricane pilots who were listed previously in official records simply as killed in France or Belgium.

Several veterans have been contacted and while some gaps in the records have thus been filled, memories are fallible, particularly at a distance of 55 years, and whilst efforts have been made to record events and incidents as they occurred, inaccuracies will inevitably remain. For example, times and even dates of certain incidents recorded within may prove to be incorrect, while the serial numbers of Hurricanes entered in pilots' personal logbooks and squadron records are often found to be inaccurate. Therefore, the authors will be delighted to hear from those with additional or corrected information, and may be contacted via the publisher.

BRIAN CULL
BRUCE LANDER
HEINRICH WEISS

FOREWORD

Reading the manuscript of *Twelve Days in May* has brought back many memories, probably because it is factually written and, for the first time, I have been able to read German pilots' reports of their victories and escapes. This book emphasises what a superb aircraft the Hurricane was and also the magnificent work performed by the ground crews who were operating from very temporary accommodation in most cases, and had frequently to move to other aerodromes at short notice, while their aircraft were constantly flying, as can be seen by the number of sorties flown.

One of the many interesting facts recalled in the book was the variety of aircraft flown during this short period, so that it was hardly surprising that occasionally unfortunate mistakes in identification were made.

Reading the Chapter Summaries brings home the speed of the German Army's advance and the ease with which it was able to conquer three countries, Belgium, Holland and France. One can understand the pleas from the heads of these countries for more Hurricanes from Britain, which were the only really effective weapon against the Luftwaffe. Air Chief Marshal Dowding's resistance to what must have been impassioned pleas was absolutely correct as, had he let them go, it would have left this country very short of suitable aircraft for the Battle of Britain.

This is an historical account of a little known period of Fighter Command's war effort.

WG CDR JOE KAYLL, DSO OBE DFC
COMMANDING OFFICER 615 SQUADRON, MAY 1940

DEDICATION

This book is dedicated to airmen of all nationalities who participated in those fateful twelve days in May 1940—a small tribute to those who gave their lives and to those who survived; however, for survivors of such conflict the stress inflicted on their minds and bodies is often overlooked. One veteran wrote:

> 'I took part in the battles of 1940 (France, Dunkirk and Britain) continuously from 10 May until September. I was then taken off flying by the Medical Officer, suffering from a mental condition now called Reactive Depression. Recently I had a recurrence of that dreadful affliction which put me out of circulation for a year or more and back into the hands of the psychiatrists. Just as I was being given up as lost, I made a sudden miraculous recovery—God said I would stay—and resumed a normal life of quality. The result of all this is that I am now more than ever determined to keep my mind facing forwards and refuse to allow it to delve into the stressful events of years ago.'

They should not be forgotten.

CHAPTER I

INTRODUCTION AND PREAMBLE

'I have to tell you . . . this country is at war with Germany.'

Prime Minister Neville Chamberlain, in a broadcast to the nation on the morning of 3 September 1939.

Within a few days of Chamberlain's dramatic announcement to the British public, the RAF found itself in France for the second time in 25 years. A token force of Hurricane fighters (four squadrons)—designated the Air Component—together with Blenheim and Battle light bombers of the Advanced Air Striking Force (AASF), was hurriedly dispatched across the Channel as a show of solidarity and support for the French, who faced an immediate threat as German military forces and air units assembled on her border. Thus began the stand-off period which became known as the Phoney War.*

Air Officer Commanding the RAF in France was Air Marshal A.S. Barratt CB CMG MC. His deputies were Air Vice-Marshal P.H.L. Playfair CB CVO MC, AOC the Advanced Air Striking Force, and Air Vice-Marshal C.H.B. Blount OBE MC, AOC the Air Component, with Grp Capt P.F. Fullard DSO MC AFC (a Great War fighter ace) as OC Air Component fighters. Many of the RAF's senior officers—some recalled from retirement were veterans of the Great War—were found to be wanting when the shooting war started, as epitomised by the recollections of the newly appointed Air Officer in charge of Administration of the Air Component, Acting Air Commodore Victor Goddard, who wrote later:

'The Air Force in 1939, struggling with its own expansion, was hopelessly overstretched. There had been no time to find out

---

* For coverage of the Phoney War period, the authors recommend *Fledgling Eagles* by Christopher Shores et al, published by Grub Street.

1

whether officers in the Reserve List of group captains were, in fact, the men they once were. Thus when it came about that the war plan was dramatically changed, a certain once famous officer of World War I was appointed by the Air Ministry to be SASO in the HQ of the Air Component. This particular officer was holding the rank of Acting Brigadier-General in the RFC. When this man turned up at Farnborough, his flame had died. No flair for the task, shrunken in his khaki uniform of World War I and carrying the red tabs of a brigadier-general, he was unaware that 20 years previously the title brigadier-general had been abolished by the Army; he was unaware, too, that Army rank titles could no longer be used by Air Force officers. Nothing could persuade this one-time gallant warrior to accept the fact that he was not a general but a group captain, and that the appropriate dress was a blue uniform with four stripes on the cuff. Charles Blount [AOC Air Component] was told by the Member of the Air Council for Personnel to make best use he could of the man.'

Originally, the four RAF fighter squadrons (1, 73, 85 and 87 Squadrons) had been grouped into 60 Fighter Wing Servicing Unit, commanded by Wg Cdr J.A. Boret MC DFC, and were based in the Rouen-Boos and Le Havre-Octeville areas, although this was a temporary disposition as their intended use was for the protection of the concentration of BEF forces. However, the Advanced Air Striking Force had no attached fighter squadrons, and when 1 and 73 Squadrons were detached from the Air Component for this purpose, they came under the administrative control of the newly established 67 Fighter Wing Servicing Unit, commanded by Wg Cdr C. Walter, with its headquarters at Bussy-la-Cote. To replace these two squadrons, two more were transferred from England, 607 and 615 Squadrons, both Gladiator-equipped Auxiliary Air Force units, which were placed under the control of 61 Fighter Wing Servicing Unit, commanded by Wg Cdr R.J. Eccles.

At about the same time 62 Fighter Wing Servicing Unit was formed at Rouen-Boos, for the protection of the lower Seine area at the request of the French. The organization was put in place to receive two further RAF Hurricane squadrons in an emergency. It had been the original intention to send 46 and 501 Squadrons to fill this role should the need arise, but events elsewhere dictated that 46 Squadron be dispatched to Norway. Yet another administrative wing—63 Fighter Wing Servicing Unit—was set up at Lille/Seclin in March, where it was to be available to control two further Hurricane units should they be required (3 and 79 Squadrons were earmarked for dispatch).

'It was impossible, in the Air Staff view, to lock up skilled personnel in such units for possible needs, at a moment when actual commitments such as the Norwegian campaign existed. Accordingly, Air Marshal Barratt was told that should events in France imperatively demand the presence of fighter squadrons beyond the additional four already contemplated and prepared for by the dispatch of 62 and 63 Fighter Wing Servicing Units, such reinforcements could be made by attaching further initial aircraft to the existing squadrons in France.'

Although the RAF squadrons were grouped into wings, these were not tactical formations but merely administrative organizations, designed to control two fighter squadrons and to hold essential equipment. The officers in command were not wing leaders (like those of 1941 and onwards), but were senior officers of wing commander rank who had to deal with the administration of the wing they commanded rather than any tactical or operational activities.

The AASF Hurricane Squadrons

1 Squadron

1 Squadron was led by a forceful commander—Sqn Ldr P.J.H. Halahan. It was Halahan who instigated the re-harmonisation of the Hurricanes' eight guns from 400 yards to 250 yards, ensuring more hitting power at closer range, and it was Halahan who quickly realised the need for seat armour to be fitted to his unit's aircraft—and made sure his pilots got it. The Squadron possessed two capable Flight Commanders in Flt Lt P.R. Walker (A Flight) and Flt Lt P.P. Hanks (B Flight) and had amassed a score of 26 victories during the Phoney War period; the first of these achieved by Plt Off P.W.O. Mould on 30 October 1939, the RAF's first victory in France, for which he received a DFC. On the eve of the invasion it was based at Vassincourt, west of Nancy. The Squadron had been allotted the code letters NA in 1938, but these were dropped on arrival in France.

73 Squadron

Sqn Ldr J.W.C. More commanded 73 Squadron, which saw a fair amount of action during the Phoney War period. The Flight Commanders were Flt Lt R.E. Lovett (A Flight) and Flt Lt J.E. Scoular (B Flight) and its pilots had claimed some 30 victories by the beginning of May 1940, and had produced the RAF's first fighter ace of the war, Flg Off E.J. Kain, who was awarded a DFC. The Squadron was based at Rouvres, in defence of the Maginot Line. Although allocated the code letters TP at the outbreak of the war, the use of such code letters was dropped soon after joining the AASF.

The Air Component Hurricane Squadrons

Various moves had been made by the Air Component fighter squadrons during the Phoney War period. In the Northern Sector, facing the Belgian border, were 85 and 87 Squadrons under the control of 60 Wing, based at Lille/Seclin, although the latter unit was operating temporarily from Senon, near Nancy. 607 and 615 Squadrons, comprising 61 Wing, were based at Vitry-en-Artois and Abbeville respectively, and were in the throes of exchanging their Gladiators for Hurricanes. One of 607 Squadron's three regular pilots was Plt Off Peter Parrott, who recalled:

> 'Re-equipment with Hurricanes started on 8 April, when I ferried the first one from Rouen to Vitry-en-Artois (the unit's first two Hurricanes were P2753 and P2754). I was the only pilot in the Squadron who had flown a Hurricane. A Miles Master had been issued to us for initial training on a low-wing monoplane with flaps and retractable undercarriage. So the Squadron had only a bare four weeks with the Hurricane before we were embroiled in the most disorganised, chaotic week or ten days of action. Few, if any, of our pilots had sufficient experience on type to be classed as operational.'

85 Squadron

85 Squadron was commanded by Sqn Ldr J.O.W. Oliver and was based at Lille/Seclin; it had been concerned mainly with sector patrols and fighter affiliation with the Armée de l'Air. The Squadron's first victory had been achieved on 21 November 1939 by B Flight Commander Flt Lt R.H.A. Lee, who was awarded a DFC. A Flight was commanded by Flt Lt J.R.M. Boothby and the Squadron's Hurricanes carried the code letters VY.

87 Squadron

During April 1940 a dozen Hurricanes of 87 Squadron had been detached from the Air Component to operate from Senon, where they co-operated with the Lysander reconnaissance aircraft of 2 Squadron; the remainder of the unit was attached to 85 Squadron at Lille/Seclin. The Squadron had been in the Northern Sector since 1939 and had seen little action, despite its move to Senon, and was under orders to return to Lille/Seclin if and when the Germans attacked. Sqn Ldr J.S. Dewar was in command and the Flight Commanders were Flt Lt R. Voase Jeff DFC, who had achieved the Air Component's first victory on 2 November 1939, and Flt Lt M.L. Robinson, although the latter was injured in a flying accident on the eve of the German onslaught. The Squadron's Hurricanes bore the code letters LK.

607 Squadron

607 (County of Durham) Squadron arrived in France with its Gladiators in November 1939, based initially at Merville before moving to Vitry-en-Artois. Hurricanes began arriving in April and by the eve of the invasion the Squadron was fully equipped under the command of Sqn Ldr L.E. Smith. Only one victory had been claimed by the unit's Gladiators and that was before leaving England; one of those involved in that combat was Flt Lt J. Sample, who commanded B Flight, while A Flight's commander was Flg Off W.F. Blackadder. The Squadron's Gladiators and Hurricanes carried the code letters AF.

615 Squadron

615 (County of Surrey) Squadron arrived in France at the same time as 607 Squadron, being based at Vitry-en-Artois before moving to Abbeville for re-equipping. B Flight was still in the process of converting from Gladiators when the Blitzkrieg started. The CO, Sqn Ldr J.R. Kayll, had been posted in from 607 Squadron in April, succeeding Sqn Ldr A. Vere-Harvey; the Flight Commanders were Flt Lt J.G. Sanders and Flt Lt L.T.W. Thornley. Squadron aircraft bore the code letters KW.

At this period of the war, as in the Great War, squadron commanders were not encouraged or even required to fly at the head of their units in action. Many of the squadron leaders of the fighter units in France—indeed throughout the RAF—were peacetime regular career officers, mostly over 30 years of age and with extremely varied flying experience gained not only on fighters but on bombers and flyingboats. As squadron commanders their responsibilities were not only for flying operations and their pilots, but for their squadron as a whole: for unit discipline, for ground personnel—mechanics, clerks, cooks—for supplies, spares, quarters and all the other hundreds of duties involved in the day to day running of an operational unit.

Nonetheless, some squadron commanders decided to lead their units in the air, leaving the less exciting duties to their adjutants. However, to underline the then current procedure, officially the CO flew only under exceptional circumstances and the squadron was led in the air by the flight commanders. As squadrons usually operated on a one Flight on, one Flight off duty—and even more frequently in sections of three—the squadron commander's decision to fly could upset the normal Flight roster! It was soon realised that many of the squadron commanders were by age and experience totally unsuited to flying in fighter versus fighter combat.

Whereas in 1914 both the Allied and German air forces were completely new to the concept of aerial warfare, by 1939 the Germans had not only built on their experience gained in the Great War, but they had updated this experience with recent actual combat in the Spanish Civil War. In the RAF it was a different story. Not only had past lessons been forgotten or ignored, but conservatism had gained a firm hold and a theory of aerial warfare based on a totally false appreciation of the realities had been adopted.

At the beginning of the Second World War the belief that the 'bomber will always get through', as envisaged by aviation theorists and certain RAF—and indeed Luftwaffe—leaders in the 1920s and 1930s, was a major factor in influencing strategical concepts of how future wars should and would be fought. Such thinking was based partly on the success of Germany's He111 bomber in the Spanish Civil War, when it out-performed the fighters of the day. It seems incomprehensible, on reflection, that the tactical experts responsible for the training of RAF fighter pilots should ever have devised the set of aerial evolutions known as Fighting Area Attacks—but they did, on the assumption that any attack against the United Kingdom would be made from Germany, and that fighters would not have the range to provide escort.

'Fighter Command's tactical training was based on the theory that the air threat to Britain would be hordes of German bombers flying in close formation, and not escorted by fighters, since the Messerschmitt 109 could not reach our shores from airfields in Germany. Apparently those who assessed the nature of the threat did not take into account the possibility of more adjacent airfields becoming available to the Luftwaffe.'

The three main Fighting Area Attacks, as practised, were, basically:

No 1 Attack: A succession of fighter aircraft—usually three or six— attacking from astern, against a single bomber aircraft.
No 2 Attack: Two or more fighter aircraft attacking in line abreast, against a single bomber aircraft.
No 3 Attack: Three fighter aircraft attacking a single bomber simultaneously from the rear, beam and rear quarter.

Such manoeuvres could be effective only if enemy bombers flew straight and level, thus allowing themselves to be attacked by fighters in line abreast, line astern or some other variation. In practice, these tactics were a recipe for disaster. Even unescorted bomber formations usually proved to be a tough proposition, with the top speed of attacking fighters being barely greater than that of the bombers, particularly when the latter were in a shallow dive. The stern attack was usually the only option open to the fighter pilot, which allowed the bomber's rear gunner the opportunity to test his mettle.

Even single bombers could prove a difficult prey to attacking fighters, which were concentrating more on maintaining formation than watching their tails. Most squadron commanders and flight leaders soon learned to ignore these set-piece tactics, often as a result of bitter experience, although some were still using them during the Battle of Britain. To have tried to impose such rigid formality on what must be the most fluid informality—flight—demonstrates the depth of mis-understanding then prevalent in the executive ranks of the peacetime RAF. Another fallacy of the inter-war thinking seems to have been that fighter versus fighter combat was impossible with 300 mph monoplane fighters.

Throughout the twelve fateful days of the battle covered by this account—10 to 21 May 1940, which saw the virtual demise of the AASF and Air Component Hurricane squadrons, together with many of the reinforcing units—no serious attempt was made to co-ordinate the operations of the fighters: squadrons continued to operate in small formations of three or six aircraft, while patrols were carried out in the hope of seeing the enemy—usually they did, but at a great disadvantage. Briefings were in the main non-existent and attempts to organize escorts for bombers were woefully unsuccessful; ground control was rare while most of the Hurricanes had unreliable R/T systems.

The peacetime RAF had been likened to a very exclusive flying club—and in many ways it was. Sadly, many of the members were to pay the extreme price, thanks mainly to the short-sightedness of the training which produced superb pilots but did not prepare them for the demands and ruthlessness of modern warfare.

The Allied Air Forces

The French Armée de l'Air on paper looked impressive—1,145 combat aircraft—but in reality it was an unbalanced air force. Records show that aircraft available on the eve of the invasion numbered 490 modern single-engined fighters, 28 obsolete single-engined and 67 modern twin-engined fighters; 75 modern and 65 obsolete bombers; and 270 modern and 150 obsolete reconnaissance aircraft. These were divided among the four area commands of the Armée de l'Air (the North, East, South and the Alps), the bulk of the fighters being concentrated in the first three of these Zones and subsequently participating in the initial German assault. Overall Air Force commander was Général Joseph Vuillemin, Chief of the Air Staff, although he was subordinate to Général Maurice Gamelin, Commander-in-Chief of the French Armée.

Mention must be made of the other links in the French air defence system, none of which however were to make much impression in the air battles that followed the invasion. The basis of the French air raid reporting system was a series of observer posts, which used the public telephone system to relay sightings to the various command centres. It was not very efficient or effective. In addition, there were a series of Army observation posts and these reported by W/T to the local air unit, supplemented by 25 British W/T observer units, normally manned by two RAF operators and four Army observers, together with a driver where the set was mobile.

The French had been admitted to the embryonic RDF (radar) secret before the war. Impressed with the possibilities, they contemplated a widespread adoption of the system, but by the eve of the invasion only six mobile sets had been made available by Britain. The original siting comprised four locations in the north, one at Calais and one for the BEF at Bar-le-Duc, and centres to filter and process reports were planned; only the centre at Arras was operational when the shooting started in earnest, although a temporary filter centre in the north, at Allonville, was in use. The effectiveness of the system was arguable: 'The whole system of detecting and reporting movements of hostile aircraft was in such a state of transition that it was hardly possible for a high degree of effectiveness to be obtained by the time of the German attack.'

Since the outbreak of hostilities in Europe, both Belgium and the Netherlands had maintained their neutrality, although this was about to be violated by the imminent German invasion. Neither country possessed a large or modern air force. Aeronautique Militaire Belge was the air echelon of the Belgian Army and was equipped with mainly obsolete biplanes of British manufacture, and consisted of only 180 serviceable aircraft on the eve of the invasion, of which only 33 were monoplanes. Its 1st Regiment (Army Co-operation) was dispersed between Bierset, Deurne and Gossoncourt with 40 Fairey Fox biplanes and ten Renard 31 biplanes. The 2nd Regiment (Fighters) was divided between Schaffen-Diest and Nivelles with 30 Fairey Fox biplanes, 25 Fiat CR42 biplanes, 15 Gladiator biplanes and 11 serviceable Hurricanes, while 3rd Regiment (Reconnaissance and bombers) was based at Evère with 27 Fairey Fox biplanes and 13 Battles.

Of the 11 Hurricanes immediately available to Escadrille 2/I/2 on the eve of the invasion, most were survivors from the 20 supplied from RAF stocks to Belgium in 1939 (ex-RAF serials L1918-L1920, L1993-1997, L2040-2044, L2105-2111) and were allocated serials H-1 to H-20; the others were mainly from a batch of about 20 built under licence in Belgium by Avions Fairey, while one (serialled H-21), fitted with a Rotol three-blade propeller, was undoubtedly an RAF Hurricane which had been force-landed in Belgium by a pilot of 87 Squadron on 10 December 1939 and consequently impounded; the Belgians had by then already received three other RAF Hurricanes in this manner, all courtesy of 87 Squadron, since L1619 LK-P, L1628 LK-H and L1813 LK-O had earlier force-landed in their territory.

Belgian fighters had already made news. Six days into the war, a small force of RAF Whitleys had carried out a leaflet raid over Germany, and two of the bombers strayed into neutral Belgium's airspace. Fairey Fox and Firefly biplanes scrambled to intercept. The result of the ensuing series of skirmishes was that one Whitley was forced to land on a Belgian airfield (where the crew was interned) and another crash-landed in France. In return, one Fox was shot down and a Firefly crash-landed. A second major incident occurred on 2 March 1940, when a Luftwaffe Do17P of 1(F)/22, having evaded attacks by French Hawk H-75As, flew into Belgian airspace and was intercepted by three Hurricanes of Escadrille 2/I/2. The Hurricane leader led a line astern attack, which resulted in his death when his aircraft was shot down, while the other two Hurricanes were also hit and obliged to force-land, one of which overturned when so doing. The Dornier escaped with minor damage.

The Royal Netherlands Army Air Division (Nederlandse Militaire Luchtvaart) was in the main an indigenous force and similarly small, comprising 29 Fokker DXXI fighters in three squadrons (1e JaVA and 2e JaVA at De Kooy and Schiphol respectively, and 5e JaVA at Ypenburg) and two squadrons totalling 23 Fokker G-1 twin-boom fighters (3e JaVA and 4e JaVA at Waalhaven and Bergen respectively); there were also a dozen Fokker TV medium bombers and nine Fokker CX biplane bombers of the 1st Air Regiment, and a miscellaneous collection of reconnaissance machines—Fokker CVs and Fokker FK51s, a few American-built Douglas 8As and a handful of Fokker DXVII seaplanes. Dutch fighters had also been responsible for the destruction of an RAF Whitley, the bomber having been shot down by a Fokker G-1 when returning from a leaflet raid over Germany on 27 March 1940. The Whitley crashed near Parnis, with the death of one member of the crew and the internment of the other four.

The Luftwaffe

Across the frontier, awaiting the command to strike, was the might of the Generalfeldmarschall Hermann Göring's Luftwaffe: 3,500 modern, front-line aircraft of Luftflotte 2 and 3, their crews confident and raring to go—many already blooded in Spain and Poland. The Luftwaffe had commanders with experience of how to conduct an aerial offensive to support a land campaign. Equipped with the excellent Messerschmitt Bf109E and the much-vaunted twin-engined Bf110C Zerstörer (Destroyer), Luftwaffe units could expect to meet little opposition from fighters of equal or superior performance, while bomber units flying Ju88s, He111s and Do17s could expect to fly at least as high and almost as fast as most of the defending fighters they might encounter over the

Continent. The Luftwaffe also possessed a unique weapon in the guise of the Ju87 dive-bomber, which was in a class of its own. Commonly known as the Stuka, it had already achieved a certain notoriety in Poland.

Luftflotte 2 (HQ Münster: General der Flieger Albert Kesselring)

Bomber Unit	Aircraft Type	Aircraft on Strength/Serviceable	Location
Stab/KG4	He111P	8/7 ⎱	Fassberg
	He111D	1/0 ⎰	
I/KG4	He111H	36/24	Gütersloh
II/KG4	He111P	35/18	Fassberg
III/KG4	He111P	23/12	Delmenhorst
	Ju88A	37/21	Delmenhorst
Stab/KG27	He111P	5/4 ⎱	Hannover-Langenhagen
	He111D	1/1 ⎰	
I/KG27	He111P	36/25	Hannover-Langenhagen
II/KG27	He111P	35/25	Delmenhorst
III/KG27	He111P	38/32	Wunstorf
Stab/KG30	Ju88A	2/2 ⎱	Oldenburg
	He111H	1/0 ⎰	
I/KG30	Ju88A	34/25	Oldenburg
II/KG30	Ju88A	38/25	Oldenburg
III/KG30	Ju88A	30/20	Marx
Stab/KG54	He111P	6/4 ⎱	Quakenbrück
	He111D	1/0 ⎰	
I/KG54	He111P	36/33	Quakenbrück
II/KG54	He111P	29/26	Varrelbusch
III/KG54	He111P	35/27	Vechta
Auklarungs-	Do17M	5/4 ⎱	Bremen
staffel zbV	He111H	2/1 ⎰	
Stab/KG77	Do17Z	8/6	Düsseldorf
I/KG77	Do17Z	35/28	Werl
II/KG77	Do17Z	35/28 ⎱	Düsseldorf
	Do17U	1/1 ⎰	
III/KG77	Do17Z	34/21	Düsseldorf
Stab/LG1	He111H	5/4 ⎱	Düsseldorf
	Ju88A	1/0 ⎰	
I/LG1	He111H	30/22	Düsseldorf
II/LG1	He111H	26/18 ⎱	Düsseldorf
	Ju88A	32/4 ⎰	
III/LG1	He111H	12/5 ⎱	Düsseldorf
	Ju88A	37/12 ⎰	

Ground Attack Unit	Aircraft type	Aircraft on Strength/Serviceable	Location
Stab/StG2	Ju87B	3/3 ⎱	Köln-Ostheim
	Do17M	6/5 ⎰	
I/StG2	Ju87B	40/33	Köln-Ostheim
III/StG2	Ju87B	38/27	Nörvenich
I/StG76	Ju87B	39/34	Köln-Ostheim

Stab/StG77	Ju87B	4/3 ⎫	Köln-Butzweilerhof
	Do17M	6/5 ⎭	
I/StG77	Ju87B	39/31	Köln-Butzweilerhof
II/StG77	Ju87B	39/30	Köln-Butzweilerhof
IV(St)/LG1	Ju87B	39/37	Duisburg
II(S)/LG2	Hs123	49/38	Lauffenberg

Reconnaissance Unit	Aircraft Type	Aircraft on Strength/Serviceable	Location
1(F)/121	He111H	9/7 ⎫	Münster-Handorf
	Ju88A	3/2 ⎭	
2(F)/122	He111H	7/5 ⎫	Münster-Loddenheide
	Ju88A	5/4 ⎭	
3(F)/122	He111H	10/7 ⎫	Münster-Loddenheide
	Ju88A	2/2 ⎭	
4(F)/122	He111H	7/5 ⎫	Goslar
	Ju88A	5/2 ⎭	
2(F)/123	Do17P	12/10	München-Gladbach
Wekusta 26	Do17Z	6/3 ⎫	Münster-Loddenheide
	He111H	4/3 ⎭	

Fighter Unit	Aircraft Type	Aircraft on Strength/Serviceable	Location
Stab/JG1	Bf109E	4/4	Jever
I/JG1	Bf109E	46/24	Gymnich
II/JG2	Bf109	47/35	Nordholz
IV(N)/JG2	Bf109D	31/30 ⎫	Hopsten
	Ar68	36/13 ⎭	
III/JG3	Bf109E	37/25	Hopsten
I/JG20	Bf109E	48/36	Bönninghardt
I/JG21	Bf109E	46/34	München-Gladbach
Stab/JG26	Bf109E	4/3	Dortmund
I/JG26	Bf109E	44/35	Bönninghardt
II/JG26	Bf109E	47/36	Dortmund
III/JG26	Bf109E	42/22	Essen-Mühlheim
Stab/JG27	Bf109E	4/4	München-Gladbach
I/JG27	Bf109E	39/28	München-Gladbach
II/JG27	Bf109E	43/33 ⎫	Bönninghardt
	Bf109C	1/0 ⎭	
Stab/JG51	Bf109E	4/3	Bönninghardt
I/JG51	Bf109E	47/38	Krefeld
II(J)/TrGr186	Bf109E	48/35	Wangerooge
I(J)/LG2	Bf109E	48/32	Wyk-auf-Föhr (one Staffel at Esbjerg)
I/ZG1	Bf110C/D	35/22	Kirchenhellen
II/ZG1	Bf110C/D	36/26	Gelsenkirchen-Buer
Stab/ZG26	Bf110C/D	3/3	Dortmund
I/ZG26	Bf110C/D	34/11	Niedermendig
III/ZG26	Bf110C/D	37/30	Krefeld

Luftflotte 2 therefore had a total of 730 twin-engined bombers (485 serviceable), 302/246 ground attack aircraft, 70/55 reconnaissance machines and 811 fighters, of which 630/457 were Bf109Es and 145/82 were Bf110s.

Luftflotte 3 (HQ Bad Orb: General der Flieger Hugo Sperrle)

Bombers Unit	Aircraft Type	Aircraft on Strength/Serviceable	Location
Stab/KG1	He111H	5/3	Giessen
I/KG1	He111H	34/25	Giessen
II/KG1	He111H	35/23	Kirtorf
III/KG1	He111H	33/27	Ettinghausen
Stab/KG2	Do17Z	7/5 ⎫	Ansbach
	Do17U	1/1 ⎭	
I/KG2	Do17Z	36/22	Giebelstadt
II/KG2	Do17Z	36/28	Ansbach
III/KG2	Do17Z	36/30	Illesheim
Stab/KG3	Do17Z	6/6	Würzburg
I/KG3	Do17Z	35/31	Aschaffenburg
II/KG3	Do17Z	36/27	Schweinfurt
III/KG3	Do17Z	35/28	Würzburg
III/KG28 (attached)	He111P	36/30	Bracht
Stab/KG51	He111H	1/1 ⎫	Landsberg/Lech
	Ju88A	1/0 ⎭	
I/KG51	He111H	36/18 ⎫	Lechfeld
	Ju88A	23/7 ⎭	
II/KG51	Ju88A	38/15	München-Riem
III/KG51	He111H	39/29	Landsberg/Lech
Stab/KG53	He111H	7/4	Roth
I/KG53	He111H	36/21	Roth
II/KG53	He111H	36/24	Oedheim
III/KG53	He111H	36/26	Schwäbisch Hall
Stab/KG55	He111P	6/5	Leipheim
I/KG55	He111P	35/25	Neuburg-Donau
II/KG55	He111P	36/24	Leipheim
III/KG55	He111P	36/17	Gablingen
Stab/KG76	Do17Z	4/4 ⎫	Nidda
	Do17U	1/0 ⎭	
I/KG76	Do17Z	36/32	Nidda
II/KG76	Do17Z	34/25	Nidda
III/KG76	Do17Z	35/26	Nidda

Ground Attack Unit	Aircraft Type	Aircraft on Strength/Serviceable	Location
Stab/StG1	Ju87B	3/3 ⎫	Siegburg
	Do17M	6/5 ⎭	
II/StG2	Ju87B	38/33	Siegburg
I(St)/TrGr186	Ju87B	39/36	Hemweiler
III/StG51	Ju87B	39/31	Köln-Wahn

Reconnaissance Unit	Aircraft type	Aircraft on Strength/Serviceable	Location
3(F)/121	He111H	8/3 ⎫	Frankfurt/Main
	Ju88A	3/2 ⎭	
4(F)/121	Do17P	10/7 ⎫	Gablingen
	Ju88A	2/1 ⎭	
5(F)/122	Do17P	11/9	Köln-Wahn
1(F)/123	Do17P	8/6 ⎫	Langendiebach
	Ju88A	6/3 ⎭	

3(F)/123	Do17P	9/7 ⎫	Gelnhausen
	Ju88A	3/2 ⎬	
Wekusta 51	Do17U	1/1 ⎫	Langendiebach
	He111H	4/3 ⎭	

Fighters Unit	Aircraft Type	Aircraft on Strength/Serviceable	Location
Stab/JG2	Bf109E	4/4	Frankfurt-Rebstock
I/JG2	Bf109E	45/33	Frankfurt-Rebstock
III/JG2	Bf109E	42/11	Frankfurt-Rebstock
I/JG3	Bf109E	48/38	Vogelsang
II/JG51	Bf109E	42/30	Böblingen
Stab/JG52	Bf109E	3/3	Mannheim-Sandhofen
I/JG52	Bf109E	46/33	Lachen/Speyerdorf
II/JG52	Bf109E	42/28	Speyer
III/JG52	Bf109E	48/39	Mannheim-Sandhofen
Stab/JG53	Bf109E	4/4	Wiesbaden-Erbenheim
I/JG53	Bf109E	46/33	Wiesbaden-Erbenheim
II/JG53	Bf109E	45/37	Wiesbaden-Erbenheim
III/JG53	Bf109E	44/33	Wiesbaden-Erbenheim
Stab/JG54	Bf109E	4/4	Böblingen
I/JG54	Bf109E	42/27	Böblingen
I/JG76	Bf109E	46/39	Ober-Olm
Stab/JG77	Bf109E	4/3	Peppenhoven
I/JG77	Bf109E	46/28	Odendorf
Stab/ZG2	Bf110C/D	3/2	Darmstadt-Griesheim
I/ZG2	Bf110C/D	32/22	Darmstadt-Griesheim
II/ZG26	Bf110C/D	35/25	Kaarst/Neuss
I/ZG52	Bf110C/D	35/23	Neuhausen ob Eck
Stab/ZG76	Bf110C/D	3/3	Köln-Wahn
II/ZG76	Bf110C/D	33/25	Köln-Wahn
V(Z)/LG1	Bf110C/D	33/27	Mannheim-Sandhofen

Luftflotte 3 had on its establishment 847 (579 serviceable) twin-engined bombers, 125/110 ground attack aircraft, 65/44 reconnaissance machines and 775 fighters, of which 601/427 were Bf109Es and 174/127 were Bf110s.

In addition, there were 340 Armée Co-operation Hs126s of (H)/10, (H)/11, (H)/12, (H)/13, (H)/14, (H)/21 (although 3 Staffel operated Fi156s), (H)/22, (H)/23, (H)/31, (H)/41 and (H)/LG2; at least one of the above units still operated a few antiquated He46s in this role. There were also the Armée's long-range reconnaissance Do17Ps and Bf110Cs of 2(F), 3(F) and 4(F)/11, 4(F)/14, 1(F), 2(F) and 3(F)/22, and 3(F)/31. The Luftwaffe also had available 475 Ju52 transport/troop-carriers of KGzbv 1 and KGzbv 2, together with 45 DFS230 gliders, many of which would be used in the initial strike against the Dutch and Belgian defences. Finally, there were 1,000 front-line aircraft effectively in reserve, aircraft tasked ostensibly for defence of the Reich, most of which could be called upon if the need arose.

For several days before the German invasion was launched, rumours of its imminence were rife. There had been such scares before, but this time it was for real and at 0215 on 9 May, Air Marshal Barratt received a call from Air Ministry advising of Germany's ultimatum to Holland. One of Barratt's first actions was to recall 87 Squadron from Senon, although this order was subsequently rescinded. However, all RAF units were put on 'Readiness No 1'. The scene was set for the start of the greatest and bloodiest conflict the world has ever seen.

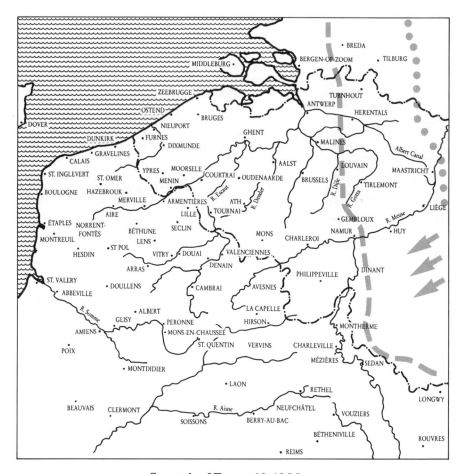

Synopsis of Events 10-12 May

10 May As German forces advanced into Holland and Belgium, the French and British Armies moved forward to join with the forces of the neutrals to meet the attack. 1 Squadron was based at Vassincourt, 73 Squadron at Rouvres, 85 Squadron at Lille/Seclin, 87 Squadron at Senon, 607 Squadron at Vitry-en-Artois; 615 Squadron's A Flight was at Le Touquet, while B Flight was at Abbeville. During the afternoon, 1 Squadron moved to Berry-au-Bac, 73 Squadron to Reims-Champagne and 87 Squadron to Lille/Seclin, while 615 Squadron's A Flight moved to Merville with its Hurricanes. Reinforcements in the guise of 3 and 79 Squadrons arrived at Merville from their UK bases, and 501 Squadron landed at Betheniville.

11 May On the left the French 7th Armée engaged the German forces in an attempt to break through to the Dutch. In the centre, the BEF and the Belgian Army took up defensive positions along the River Dijle.

12 May As the line Antwerp-Louvain-Gembloux held, the main German thrust approached between Dinant and Sedan. During the morning 615 Squadron's A Flight moved to Vitry while 79 Squadron's B Flight operated from Mons-en-Chaussée, although the whole Squadron moved to Norrent-Fontès that evening, while 504 Squadron arrived from the UK, with A Flight going to Bapaume and B Flight to Vitry.

●   German advance   — Allied line

CHAPTER II

FRIDAY 10 MAY
THE BLITZKRIEG

'Soldiers of the Western Front, your time has come. The fight, which begins today, will determine Germany's future for the next 1,000 years.'

German Chancellor Adolf Hitler.

The ambitious and audacious German plan of attack called for three simultaneous assaults on its neighbours to the west: an air and ground attack aimed at speedily subjugating Holland, thereby protecting the northern flank of the proposed advance into Belgium and Northern France; air and ground attacks on Belgium in an attempt to draw the French and British armies forward from their main positions in Northern France; and a sweep through the Ardennes and Luxembourg to seize the bridgeheads across the Meuse in the Sedan area, bypassing the much-vaunted French Maginot Line defence system and thus opening up the whole of Northern France. Hitler sent an eleventh hour message to his troops:

'For 300 years the rulers of England and France have made it their aim to prevent any consolidation in Europe, and above all to weaken Germany. France has declared war on Germany 31 times in two centuries, while it has been the aim of the British rulers to prevent the unification of Germany at all costs, and to deny the Reich the means of life. After a gigantic manoeuvre in the south-east of Europe, Britain and France have attempted to attack the Ruhr District through Belgium and Holland. Soldiers of the Western Front, your time has come. The fight, which begins today, will determine Germany's future for the next 1,000 years.'

Air Operations Over Holland

At Schiphol, the nine serviceable Fokker TV bombers of the Neder-landse Militaire Luchvaart were ordered off at 0350 in an attempt to escape being attacked on the ground by reported approaching raiders. As they were taxiing, two low-flying He111Ps of III/KG4 swept across the airfield and one Dutch aircraft suffered damage. The remaining eight managed to get airborne and several became involved with other He111s, two of which were claimed shot down by Dutch air gunners. Following the attack on Schiphol, one TV returned to base but the others dispersed to airfields elsewhere, four landing at Ruigenhoek; one of these suffered engine damage. Another crashed while attempting to land at De Kooy and a third was damaged later by Dutch AA fire as it made its way back to Schiphol from Flushing, where it had landed initially.

Simultaneous with the attack on Schiphol, He111Hs of I/KG4 raided Waalhaven airfield near Rotterdam, from where only two Fokker G-1s of the resident 3e JaVA were able to get airborne, these claiming three of the raiders shot down. One of the G-1s suffered damage from return fire while, on the airfield, three more were destroyed. Ten minutes later a second wave of Heinkels arrived, but not before another G-1 had scrambled, its pilot engaging and claiming two of the bombers shot down and a third damaged, his own aircraft being hit by return fire. Following the bombing attack, Waalhaven was then subjected to a paratroop assault, Ju52s of III/KGrzbV 1 disgorging parachutists of III/Fallschirmjaegerrgt 1 (III/FJR 1) over the airfield, four more G-1s being scrambled on their approach. One of these claimed a He111 and a Do17 before being shot down by escorting Bf109s, while the others claimed a total of three Bf109s, two Ju52s, a He111 and a Ju87. Believing the airfield to have been captured, the G-1s landed on a beach near Oostvoorne (where they were destroyed four days later by strafing Bf109s).

Meanwhile, at Bergen, 4e JaVA had been virtually wiped out by the Luftwaffe's dawn attack, only one G-1 having been able to take off to pursue the raiders. Unable to make contact, the pilot instead strafed three Ju52s of KGrzbV 1 on a beach near Katwijk.

An hour later (at 0630), one TV bomber was sent to attack the Ockenburg sports field, south of The Hague, where Ju52s of KGrzbV 2 were landing troops of III/FJR 2, but this aircraft was shot down by Bf109s following its attack. Three more TVs were dispatched to Ockenburg and carried out a reportedly successful attack, then returned safely to Schiphol to refuel and rearm. As soon as they were ready, they were sent to bomb Ju52s landing at Waalhaven, escorted this time by seven DXXIs, but these were unable to prevent Bf109s shooting down two of the bombers on the way back to Schiphol.

Only one Fokker DXXI of 5e JaVA survived the morning's combats, although pilots of this unit claimed three Ju52s, a Bf109, a Bf110C (of 4/ZG1) and a He111. Meanwhile, eight DXXIs of 8e JaVA claimed four

Bf109s shot down in the vicinity of De Kooy for two losses. In fact two Messerschmitts were lost in this engagement, one of which was flown by the Staffelkapitän of 5(J)/TrGr186, who crash-landed his aircraft near De Kooy and was captured by British troops, while another pilot from this unit was killed. South of Rotterdam, Bf109s of II/JG27 shot down two Fokker CX biplane light bombers.

The RAF lost one of its reconnaissance Blenheims over Holland during the morning, the 40 Squadron machine from RAF Wyton falling to Bf109s of 5/JG27; the crew survived to be taken prisoner. A second aircraft from this unit returned safely and reported the German attack on Waalhaven.

In a futile attempt to aid the Dutch, six Blenheim IFs of 600 Squadron's B Flight departed from RAF Manston at 1230 to attack Waalhaven, where they encountered troop-laden Ju52s escorted by Bf110Cs of I/ZG1; one of the transports was claimed destroyed on the ground jointly by two of the Blenheims before the escort was able to react, but when they did, five of the Blenheims were speedily shot down; the sole returning crew reported the probable destruction of an airborne Ju52. One of the Blenheims shot down was able to force-land, and its crew managed to evade capture and returned to England aboard the destroyer evacuating the Dutch Royal Family. This crew claimed to have shot down a Bf110 and damaged two Ju52s before their own aircraft was hit. Of the other missing Blenheims, only the pilot of one and the observer of another survived.

An hour later, at 1330, 600 Squadron's A Flight Blenheim IFs were ordered to patrol the line Middelkerke-Zeebrugge-Flushing, a He111 seen on the ground being strafed and claimed destroyed. During the afternoon, the crew of a French Potez 631 of the Aeronvale's AC1 reported shooting down a Ju52 over Ijmuiden then, at 1415, nine Blenheim bombers of 15 Squadron set out from RAF Wyton to attack Waalhaven, where they claimed at least a dozen Ju52s destroyed on the ground by bombing. All returned safely, several showing signs of Flak damage. Although Bf109s were seen by some of the crews, the German fighters failed to sight the low-flying Blenheims on this occasion.

Schiphol, De Kooy and Ypenburg airfields were evacuated during the afternoon, the latter having fallen to paratroops of I/FJR 2. A German report of this operation reveals that not all went according to plan:

'As the 41 machines [Ju52s] approached the Ypenburg airfield, heavy AA fire caused the formation to split up. The jumping began much too early—60 men dropped south of Delft, others right on top of the airfield and into the Dutch defensive positions to the east. Our airborne troops eventually managed to occupy the airport buildings, but only half an hour remained before the 22nd Division was due to arrive—not enough time to clear the airfield of the enemy. As the aircraft came into land they were met by fire from several enemy machine-guns, light Flak and even some light tanks. 17 Ju52s burst into flames, but more kept coming in. Collisions occurred while taxiing and still more aircraft went up in flames.'

In response to RAF France HQ's urgent request for an air strike to be launched against Ypenburg, 40 Squadron at RAF Wyton was ordered to dispatch a dozen Blenheims at 1545, although in the meantime Dutch forces had actually recaptured the airfield. On approaching Ypenburg, Bf109s of 6/JG27 were encountered and two Blenheims were shot down with a third seriously damaged. An hour later, a further dozen Blenheims of 110 Squadron from RAF Wattisham followed, escorted by Blenheim IFs of 604 Squadron, and attacked Ju52s which had landed on the beaches near The Hague, when bombs were seen to fall among the many abandoned troop-carriers. The accompanying Blenheim fighters also strafed the grounded Ju52s, of which at least four were claimed destroyed and others damaged, although one Blenheim was obliged to force-land on a beach near Scheveningen. The crew survived and were able to return to England.

Air Operations over Belgium

The attack on Belgium erupted soon after 0430 and, some 40 minutes later, Ju87s of III/StG2 commenced dive-bombing attacks on the frontier fortress at Eben-Emael, their task to soften up the defences before an assault by paratroops who were on their way from Germany aboard a fleet of Ju52s. At 0430, 40 Ju52s—each towing a DFS230 glider carrying between eight and twelve highly trained assault troops of Detachment Koch—had taken off from Ostheim and Butzweilerhof airfields near Köln. Apart from capturing the fortress, the airborne troops were also to seize the three bridges leading over the Albert Canal, the keypoints of the Belgian defence system to the east.

The paratroops started landing at 0530 and fierce fighting erupted between these and the defenders of Eben-Emael. Overhead, He111s dropped supplies of explosives to the assault troops while 88mm Flak batteries provided covering fire and Hs123s of II(S)/LG2 and Ju87s of III/StG2 and I/StG77 attacked continuously. The bridges at Vroen-hoven and Veldwezelt were captured intact, although the bridgeheads remained under heavy Belgian fire throughout the day.

The Ju52 glider-tugs returned to Germany, refuelled, reloaded, and then set out for their second mission. When some 25 miles west of the Albert Canal they descended and released 200 'paratroops'. When Belgian troops, diverted from the Canal area, arrived to confront the new threat, the 'paratroops' were found to be 'straw dummies in German uniform armed with self-igniting charges of explosives to imitate the sound of firing'.

Meantime, in the Belgian Ardennes, 400 German troops were airlifted aboard 98 Fi156 Armée Co-operation aircraft to an area near Witry, where they were to capture and hold vital roads and commanding heights, essential for the success of the German advance on Sedan. The Fi156s set out in two groups in sections of three, some inevitably becoming lost and at least one crashed and burned; others were damaged when landing in rough terrain.* Witry was duly captured by early afternoon and the approaches to Neufchâteau, on the road to Sedan, were open.

Over half the aircraft of the Aeronautique Militaire Belge had been destroyed on the ground during the early morning blitz on its main airfields. At Schaffen-Diest waves of He111s bombed and destroyed three of Escadrille 2/I/2's Hurricanes, badly damaged six others and also destroyed a further two under repair in a hangar. Most of these had been preparing for take-off when the raiders struck, several pilots suffering burns and other injuries. A taxiing Gladiator collided with a burning Hurricane, although three others managed to get airborne, as did two of the Hurricanes, the latter flown by Capitaine Albert Van den Hove d'Ertsenrijck (in H-23) and Caporal Jacobs. Near Louvain, the Hurricane pilots engaged a Heinkel, which Van den Hove d'Ertsenrijck claimed shot down, a second being claimed by one of the Gladiator pilots, but one of the biplanes, hit by return fire, crash-landed. The Belgian fighters landed at Le Culot, to where they had been ordered, and were joined later by a third Hurricane from Schaffen-Diest. It was no better at Nivelles where 13 CR42s were written off, although others had been flown to Brustem before the raid commenced and these were able to engage the raiders, claiming two Do17s and a Bf109 shot down.

Foxes of the 1st and 3rd Regiments also suffered heavy losses on the ground, although an aircraft of the 2nd Regiment succeeded in bringing down a Bf109 before being shot down itself. Other Foxes were shot down in unequal air battles over or near the airfields: Bf109s of JG51 claimed three east of Brussels and a CR42 west of Tirlemont (Tienen), while I/JG1 claimed a Fox near St Trond (Sint-Truiden). Bf109s escorting Ju52s encountered five Belgian Gladiators in the area St Trond-Tongeren at about 0915 and claimed all shot down, three by pilots of I/JG21 and the other two by 3/JG27. One Messerschmitt was badly hit in the engagement, but the pilot was able to reach German

---

* German records show that 22 Fi156s had been lost or written off by the end of the day, due mainly to heavy landings.

territory before baling out. Two more Gladiators were claimed at 1000 by pilots of I/JG21 whilst escorting Ju87s in the Tirlemont area.

The RAF's 18 Squadron dispatched a Blenheim at 0930 to reconnoitre the Maastricht area, but it failed to return and was reported later to have crash-landed at Celles, having been damaged by Bf109s of II/JG27. The same unit sent out another Blenheim at 1600, but this too failed to return. By the end of the day Luftwaffe units operating over Belgium had claimed the destruction of about 30 Belgian aircraft on the ground, at least 14 (plus two RAF Blenheims) in the air, at a cost of about ten of its own.

Air Operations over Luxembourg

At 0725 the French 2nd Armée reported that German troops were advancing into Luxembourg. Shortly afterwards, a French reconnaissance machine confirmed that a mechanised column, some ten miles long, was on the road from Echternach. In a plan to capture the vital communication centre at Esch-sur-Alzette on the Franco-Luxembourg border, 125 German volunteers were airlifted to the area by a fleet of 25 Fi156s. There was little opposition.

During this traumatic morning, AASF Battle squadron commanders pressed Air HQ for permission to seek out the advancing German spearhead, but General Gamelin would not allow Air Marshal Barratt to dispatch his bombers, nor would he allow his own forces to attack. He was apparently fearful of an all-out bombing war, for which the Armée de l'Air was ill-equipped, and instead authorized only reconnaissance and fighter sorties; thus Potez 637s and Bloch 174s of GRII/33 from Athies-sous-Laon undertook reconnaissance flights in advance of the French 1st and 9th Armées.

By midday a frustrated Barratt had taken matters into his own hands and unleashed his bomber force, heedless of French argument and authorization, and instructed Air Vice-Marshal Playfair to send the Battles to attack the German advance through Luxembourg. The first attack was made by 32 aircraft drawn from 12, 103, 105, 142, 150, 218 and 226 Squadrons, but no fighter escort was made available and 13 of the bombers failed to return, shot down by fighters and mobile AA defences. Apparently one Battle encountered a Hs126 over the Grand Duchy and in the ensuing engagement both machines were shot down, the German crew being killed. At 1530 a further AASF strike was ordered and 12, 105, 150 and 226 Squadrons each dispatched sections of four aircraft, again without fighter escort, and this time nine were shot down by fighters and Flak, whilst a further four returned badly damaged.

Air Operations over Northern France

The main German thrust towards Northern France came via Maastricht, Tongeren and Gembloux, while Panzer units moved forward to strike through to Sedan. To meet the German advance, BEF and French Armée forces between the northern end of the Maginot Line and the coast moved across the frontier to take up their pre-determined positions along the line River Meuse-Namur-Wavre-River Dijle-Antwerp.

In addition to the raids on airfields in Holland and Belgium, German bombers struck at no fewer than 47 airfields in France, some of which suffered severe damage, although the majority escaped remarkably lightly. The Armée de l'Air reported about 35 aircraft damaged beyond repair, mainly Potez 63s and Vought 156s, while RAF units suffered the loss of two Hurricanes (of 615 Squadron) and three Battles. Inevitably, with such large-scale and diversified air operations, errors and mistakes were bound to be made. One such incident occurred during the morning when a He111 inadvertently intruded Swiss airspace and was intercepted near Butschwil by Bf109s of the Swiss Air Force. The Heinkel's gunners opened fire, but were soon silenced and the bomber was last seen crossing the frontier near Altenrhein, smoking heavily from a damaged engine. Another incident occurred during the early afternoon, when nine He111Hs of 8/KG51 from Landsberg set out to bomb the airfield at Dijon-Longvic; however, one section bombed the German border town of Freiburg in error, causing 57 civilian casualties. As a cover-up, first the French, then the RAF, were blamed for what became known to the Germans as the 'Freiburg massacre'.

Over the Channel during the morning a patrolling Blenheim IF of 600 Squadron was ordered to investigate aircraft off the coast of France. A He111 was sighted, but as the Blenheim closed in, four more Heinkels were seen and the nearest aircraft was then engaged and claimed damaged.

Meanwhile, the AASF and Air Component Hurricane squadrons had been in contact with the raiders since first light, most patrols finding no shortage of targets—mainly formations of unescorted He111s and Do17s.

67 Wing, AASF

From Vassincourt, at 0400, Hurricanes of 1 Squadron's B Flight took off to patrol the Maginot Line where, an hour later, a formation of Do17Zs of III/KG3 was sighted. Flt Lt Prosser Hanks (N2380/S), leading the Hurricanes, selected a vic of three from 8 Staffel at the rear, shooting down Fw Helmut Hoffmann's aircraft, while Flg Off Peter 'Boy' Mould (possibly P2649/T) attacked the starboard aircraft of the trio. This he overshot and, as a consequence, was hit by return fire, one bullet puncturing a tyre while another ripped through the right leg of his flying suit.

The Wing's other unit, 73 Squadron at Rouvres, was also in action at an early hour when three bombers were seen orbiting the aerodrome at 0400, two Hurricanes being scrambled to investigate. At the same time the airfield defences opened fire. Avoiding this, Flt Lt Reg Lovett (P2804/E) and Flg Off Newell 'Fanny' Orton (P2575/J) engaged one Do17Z of 5/KG2 over the airfield, but the latter's aircraft was hit by return fire, forcing him to break away and force-land near Conflans. Lovett was unable to shoot down the bomber which was however left in a damaged condition; it returned to its base with one crew member killed and another wounded.

An hour later (at 0500), Sqn Ldr More led off four more Hurricanes when eleven Do17Zs of 4/KG2 were sighted approaching the airfield. Only Flt Lt Lovett and Sgt Humphries made contact, selecting a bomber near the rear of the formation and each pilot carried out an attack. Lovett's Hurricane (P2804/E) was hit by return fire and fell away in flames; unable to open the hood due to badly burned hands, Lovett was forced to stay with his burning aircraft and subsequently crash-landed in a field near Conflans. He sustained facial burns and a bad cut over his left eye in the process and was dragged from the burning aircraft shortly before it exploded. Meanwhile, Humphries' aircraft also suffered serious damage by return fire, although he was able to return to base. With Lovett thus incapacitated, command of A Flight passed to Flg Off Fanny Orton.

At 0525, Flg Offs Harold 'Ginger' Paul and Edgar 'Cobber' Kain (P2535/K) scrambled, the former flying around Rouvres where he met at 18,000 feet the same Dornier formation (4/KG2) north-east of the aerodrome. Paul engaged one at the rear (probably that flown by Uffz Karl Schiwek) which spiralled down inverted, and observed one of the crew bale out. On the return flight to Rouvres he encountered five more Dorniers but was unable to engage these as he had exhausted his ammunition. Kain, meanwhile, patrolled at 20,000 feet over Metz and at 0600 met nine Do17Zs of 9/KG3 which he attacked. He overshot the first one but engaged Oblt Gottfried Hagen's aircraft, seeing his bullets enter its engines and fuselage. It began to burn and he followed it down, firing several bursts until he saw it crash east of Metz. Kain also came across a small formation of Dorniers as he made his way back to base, but, like Paul, he had by then used all his ammunition.

Half an hour later Sqn Ldr More took off at the head of five Hurricanes. A lone He111H of 3(F)/121, on a reconnaissance sortie to Metz and Thionville, was spotted and More attacked. The aircraft exploded in mid-air and fell to the ground in pieces, killing Oblt Kaspar Scheurich and his crew. One of the Flight, Sgt Humphries, failed to return but had only lost his way and landed at Athiés, from where he returned later.

At about 0530, Hurricanes of 1 Squadron's A Flight—Flt Lt Peter 'Johnny' Walker, Flg Off Mark 'Hilly' Brown, Flg Off Paul Richey (L1679/G), Flg Off John 'Iggy' Kilmartin and Sgt Frank Soper (L1905/H)—were scrambled to patrol at 20,000 feet over Metz where they encountered a lone Do17Z of 7/KG3, flown by Uffz Wolfgang Gräfe, which all five attacked; Richey wrote later:

> 'We watched Johnny [Walker] go down, his little Hurricane looking graceful and deadly. We watched him open fire . . . then break away to the left and go down in a steep glide. Looks as though he's hit! Hilly [Brown] got on to the Hun next and then it was my turn. I got in some good long bursts at close range. The Hun did some magnificent flying; it seemed almost a pity to smack him down. We saw him make a slow half circuit round a large field and then go in to crash-land. He hit a ridge, bounced in the air, came down again and slithered along the ground. We continued circling for five minutes, diving down to look at him, before anyone appeared. Some French soldiers at last strolled over and as they did so the roof of the Dornier's cockpit opened and a figure stood up in it, waving both arms at us as we circled overhead.'

The bomber had come down near Dun-sur-Meuse, but Walker's aircraft (N2382/B) had indeed been hit by return fire, necessitating a belly landing east of Verdun. Once the returning Hurricanes had been refuelled and rearmed they were ordered into the air again with instructions to circle the aerodrome in case of an attack; all flyable Hurricanes were sent off, including one with inoperable guns.

Shortly before midday, 73 Squadron's B Flight was in action against a small formation of Ju88s (possibly from KG51) between Senon and Reims. Flt Lt John Scoular (Hurricane P) claimed two shot down, one of which was apparently seen to fall in flames, although no Ju88s were recorded as being lost. At midday came orders for 73 Squadron to evacuate Rouvres and move to Reims-Champagne, so all flyable Hurricanes left for that destination. Ground personnel worked feverishly to make two unserviceable Hurricanes airworthy and Sgts George Dibden and Donald Sewell stayed behind to fly them, together with Flg Off Ginger Paul who remained (with his Hurricane) in order to accompany them to the new base. A formation of German bombers paid a visit to Rouvres soon after the Squadron had departed although little damage resulted.

At about the same time 1 Squadron was advised of an imminent move to Berry-au-Bac and, subsequently, B Flight departed at 1430. En route they ran into a formation of bombers—apparently He111Hs of 5/KG53

—although Flt Lt Prosser Hanks and Plt Off Richard Lewis reported engaging and shooting down a Do17; however Flg Off Boy Mould and Flg Off Billy Drake (Hurricane P) each claimed a Heinkel. Two of the latter were indeed lost, one flown by Oblt Willy Partl (in which all the crew were killed), and another from which the crew were captured, two by British forces and the other three by French troops. A third machine suffered damage and a wounded crew member. The Squadron lost a Hurricane in this engagement when Flg Off Lawrie Lorimer's aircraft (L1689) was hit by return fire, forcing the pilot to bale out near Châlons-sur-Marne. He was unhurt and was collected by car and returned to the airfield, as was Walker. A Flight followed B Flight to Berry-au-Bac, led by Sqn Ldr Halahan. Half an hour after their arrival, the airfield was raided and three French labourers, together with their horses, were killed.

Just after 1500, Dorniers raided Reims-Champagne, 73 Squadron's new base. A hangar was demolished and three French soldiers killed and a further 30 suffered injuries. Kain told war correspondent Charles Gardner later:

> 'We all lay under the wings of our planes and we could hear the whine of the bombs coming down—and then crumps on the airfield. I've never been so scared in my life.'

67 Wing had been strengthened during the afternoon by the arrival of 501 Squadron from England, when 16 Hurricanes from RAF Tangmere landed at Bétheniville at 1610. The Squadron had been under orders to stand by to reinforce the RAF in Norway, so when the CO, Sqn Ldr A.V. Clube, received a telephone call from Group instructing him to make ready his unit to fly to France, he initially questioned the movement order. But France it was to be and, immediately on arrival at Bétheniville, Clube sent off his pilots to familiarize themselves with the area. The unit was soon in action when, at about 1800, Flg Off Derrick Pickup (L2037 SD-L) and his No 2 set off on a reconnaissance patrol. The two became separated before Pickup sighted a Do17, probably a reconnaissance aircraft, 15 miles north of Vouziers:

> 'I saw this German aircraft minding his own business, on a recce I should think, slightly below. So, pulling myself together and remembering what I was there for, I had a go. Having pulled up and come around, I noticed that smoke was pouring from him and parachutes began to appear. I did not see him crash. It was later confirmed that the Do17 had crashed.'

During a broadcast for the BBC from the front towards the end of the day, Charles Gardner commented on the activities of the AASF Hurricane squadrons:

'The first day of what I'm almost tempted to call the start of war here has, so far, been in our favour. The Germans have sent over waves of their bombers—and practically all they have done is to lose ten of them to our fighters and AA guns, and six at least to the French. Just after sunrise the first German raiders came flying over the frontier—they crossed it at great height—and then came down lower in an attempt to find their targets. Soon after it became obvious that these targets were the aerodromes of the RAF—and attacks were made on a number of them. A very large number of bombs was dropped—though they were mainly small ones—and the Air Force reported critically that the bombing was bad and inaccurate, and that it had no casualties.

By six o'clock there was a series of air fights going on over a wide area. In these, five Dorniers were shot down and another four were so badly knocked about that it is unlikely they got home. By this time our Hurricane fighter patrols were right in the thick of it—only coming down to rearm, refuel and take off again. Two Hurricanes caught up with a lone Heinkel and put burst after burst into its engines, and raked the pilot's cockpit from back to front. The Heinkel crashed and two of its crew were dead and the other three were taken prisoner by the French. Later in the morning our fighters attacked a section of Ju88s and set one on fire—while one other Hurricane took on five Dorniers and split up the formation before he ran out of ammunition and had to come back.

The latest news I have is that a patrol of Hurricanes not long ago fought three separate battles with formations of Dorniers—and they claim that three of them were brought down. I take a little comfort from the sight and sound, through the window, of Hurricanes which are still patrolling round here—waiting for the next raid, or a continuation of this one.'

Gardner added later:

'The fuller reports that are now available about our activity here show that the Allies shot down 44 German planes. These are the definite victories—machines whose wreckage has been found on French territory.'

60 Wing, Air Component
Pilots of 85 Squadron at Lille/Seclin were also in action very early, as noted by the Squadron's diarist:

'0410 hours. At the marginally noted hour, the Blitzkrieg started, and the first intimation the Squadron received was the sound of innumerable Hun aircraft overhead and the sound of anti-aircraft fire both light and heavy. Within a few minutes one section of A Flight and one of B Flight were in the air after the Hun, and inside 40 minutes the two sections had landed to refuel and rearm.'

The trio from B Flight—Flt Lt Dickie Lee (N2388 VY-R), Flg Off Derek Allen and Plt Off Pat Woods-Scawen—encountered a formation of Hs126s, and although each pilot claimed one shot down it seems that none were actually lost in this engagement. However, the German pilots may have been forced to land their aircraft abruptly, possibly with some damage having been inflicted. Meanwhile, Flt Lt Bob Boothby, leading the A Flight section (Plt Off David Mawhood and Flg Off Ken Blair), reported sighting two Ju88s—aircraft from 8/LG1—at 12,000 feet near Grammont:

'I was leading my section and as I approached e/a they turned into the sun and I was unable to attack from astern. I attacked left-hand machine, firing long burst. E/a's engine stopped and oil poured out. Broke away and delivered another attack. This e/a suddenly shuddered and began to fall. I followed him and fired until I ran out of ammunition. E/a went into steep dive. No 1 of my section [Mawhood] followed e/a down and verified destruction.'

Plt Off Mawhood added:

'Leader attacked left-hand e/a, firing long bursts. E/a's engine stopped and poured out oil over leader's aircraft. The other e/a attacked my aircraft, immediately hitting my machine in the tail. I returned the attack, gave it four bursts and followed e/a down although blinded in one eye.'

Fortunately for Mawhood, he was able to land his damaged aircraft (VY-S) in spite of near blindness caused by perspex splinters entering his eye. Blair mistakenly believed the bomber attacked by the section to have been a Heinkel:

'E/a opened fire at about 1,000 yards. I closed to 400 yards and gave e/a three bursts of four seconds each. Heavy smoke from starboard engine and e/a dived steeply and I lost sight of it in ground mist.'

The Ju88, flown by Fw Ernst Schade, crashed near Mons. The crew managed to bale out and were handed over by their Belgian captors to the British.*

Another section had taken off on the heels of the others, Sqn Ldr Oliver, Plt Off John Lecky and Sgt Geoffrey 'Sammy' Allard (N2319) meeting a bomber at 10,000 feet north of Lille; Sqn Ldr Oliver (P2821) reported:

> 'Mistook e/a north of Lille for Hurricane, but on following AA bursts, recognized either Heinkel or Ju88. Could not overhaul it until I pulled the plug. Fired two bursts from astern and rear gunner, who had been firing tracer, ceased fire. My windscreen was covered in oil, but cleared as I pulled out for third attack. E/a started to spiral and slowed right down, descending slowly and steeply. I fired three long bursts, 45° deflection, at pilot. Had to pull out to avoid collision and e/a passed into steep dive underneath me, and on turning I lost sight of him in the darkness.'

Plt Off Lecky added:

> 'Climbed to 16,000 feet, forming on section leader. Saw e/a. Over-hauled him from astern and opened fire. After second burst rear gunner of e/a ceased to fire. I closed to 50 yards, firing long burst. Followed e/a, which was smoking heavily from both engines, down to 2,000 feet. Lost e/a in darkness (most likely a Do17).'

Sgt Allard reported:

> 'Saw e/a over Armentières. Closed with e/a. He immediately opened fire with tracers from rear gun. I opened fire at 300 yards range, diving down on him. I continued to close until a cloud of oil and black smoke covered my own aircraft. Saw him go down in a steep spiral and was about to follow when I saw another fighter engage him. I broke off the engagement near Ypres.'

Thus, all three had apparently attacked the same aircraft and had claimed it to have been a Ju88, a He111 and a Do17!

Flt Lt Dickie Lee (L1779) was back on patrol with a section of B Flight (Flg Off Allan Angus and Plt Off Pat Woods-Scawen) at 0730 when a twin-engined aircraft identified as a Ju88 was sighted at 15,000 feet between Armentières and the Forêt-de-Nieppe. Lee reported:

---

* The crew of the Ju88 were sent later by the British authorities to a prisoner of war camp in Canada, but during the crossing of the Atlantic, the gunner, Gfr Heinrich Maibom, fell overboard from the transport vessel and drowned.

'After being sighted, e/a dived to very low height. I could only overhaul from astern very slowly. From 500 yards to 700 yards enemy rear gunner fired continuously. I fired short bursts and finished ammunition on closing to 200 yards. No apparent results except black smoke from one engine. My own aircraft shot badly.'

Flg Off Angus added:

'Witnessed three e/a approaching from the north-east and informed Flt Lt Lee by R/T. Gave chase and e/a dived to tree-top level. Flt Lt Lee fired, then I came into attack, and closed to 50 yards; after two bursts saw rear gunner disintegrate. Starboard engine of e/a cut out. Last I saw of the e/a it was diving to ground near Gand [Ghent]. As I was out of ammunition and had no oil pressure, I returned home. Engine seized and I force-landed at Celles.'

Angus was obliged to abandon his aircraft (N2472) at Celles, but from there was given a lift back to Lille/Seclin, rejoining his unit within a few hours, none the worse for the experience. The third member of the section, Plt Off Woods-Scawen, failed to engage. It seems that their opponent was in fact a He111P of Stab II/KG27 flown by Lt Hans-Wilhelm Hover, on an armed reconnaissance, which was attacked east of Armentières. Badly damaged, it force-landed east of Courtrai. Two of the crew were wounded in the encounter and were admitted to hospital (from where they were soon liberated by German troops); the other two were handed over to British forces.

The raids and interceptions continued throughout the day, Sgt Sammy Allard (N2319) encountering a He111H of III/KG1 at 1445:

'Returning from Vimy on north-east course when I saw a He111 on left. Climbed into sun to 8,000 feet and aligned quarter attack. Each time I closed to within 50 yards. As I closed in, e/a dived into ground in flames 1 mile off Condcourt [Contescourt]. Nothing of e/a remains.'

During the course of the afternoon's hectic operations Plt Off John Ashton claimed two He111s—probably aircraft of III/KG1—although the times of his engagements are unknown.

A section of B Flight, on patrol between Helchin and Courtrai at 1820, sighted He111Ps of III/KG54 at 11,000 feet and immediately attacked; Flg Off Bill Lepine reported:

'On seeing bombers at Hellvin [sic] flew there and saw nine He111s flying in formation. Attacked left rear aircraft. By the time I was in range, this e/a was ahead of others. I fired burst of 150 rounds. Had to break away. When I returned to attack, e/a was diving east, emitting smoke from both engines. I attacked another aircraft and fired a burst of 150 rounds per gun. This e/a had already been engaged by other Hurricanes and port engine was out of action.'

His companion, Plt Off John 'Paddy' Hemingway (L1979 VY-X), also claimed one shot down:

'I was on patrol when I observed AA shell bursts which attracted my attention to nine He111s. I left formation and attacked nearest Heinkel in stern attack. I opened fire at 250 yards and closed to 50 yards. Broke away to left and downwards. Saw clouds of smoke and flame coming from e/a. I was so close that my engine was covered in enemy oil. E/a fell to earth in slow spiral and then dived in at between Desselgem and Wakken. Noted when e/a shot down it passed parachutist on his way down.'

Red Section of A Flight, led by Flt Lt Bob Boothby, patrolled over the airfield at 1830 and also engaged the Heinkels of III/KG54; Boothby recalled:

'Leading Red Section on patrol over base. I was ordered to land, then told to orbit north of base at 15,000 feet. On way up sighted large formation of twin-engined aircraft and reported facts to Ops. E/a were circling so waited to find place to join in with section. Ring broke upon far side and some six other Hurricanes got in first. Brought section into action and attacked already smoking aircraft. This went into steep dive so I left it, breaking out of the dogfight to the right.'

Plt Off John Lecky took up the attack, reporting that the Heinkel was shot down. Meanwhile, Boothby attacked another:

'I then spotted two aircraft of the leading enemy formation diving low for cover. I dived on one and used the rest of my ammunition, leaving it smoking, wheels down.'

A third He111 was engaged by Flg Off Tom Pace:

'On patrol at 15,000 feet over aerodrome with two others. Followed leader to attack. Picked out one escaping and delivered stern attack, quarter attack and a final stern attack. E/a dived steeply to ground.'

Flg Off Pace was off again at 2015, flying as No 2 to Sgt Sammy Allard, when two He111s (stragglers from either I/LG1 or KG27) were reported south of Cambrai. Allard (N2319):

> 'As Red leader I took off with Red 2 and climbed up to the enemy at 10,000 feet. When in position I attacked the right-hand aircraft and Red 2 the left-hand one. We closed to attack to 50 yards. I found that it was essential to break away upwards and in front. I then delivered an attack from the quarter. Both aircraft were losing oil and black smoke came from the e/a. I carried on the attack after Red 2 ran out of ammunition and breaking away saw both aircraft losing height. The undercarriage of the port e/a was hanging down.'

Flg Off Pace:

> 'Took off with Red 1 and overhauled and engaged two He111s. Red 1 attacked right-hand one and I attacked the one on the left. Opened fire at 200 yards and closed to 50 yards and was forced to break up and to left. Delivered a quarter attack and used remaining ammunition. When last seen e/a had undercarriage down and starboard engine stopped and smoke issued from it. Rear gunner stopped firing after first attack. I noticed black smoke coming from machine Red 1 was attacking.'

Two more Heinkels (also stragglers from LG1 or KG27) were claimed shot down just after 2040, between Arras and Vitry. Flg Off Ken Blair reported:

> 'I attacked two e/a flying in formation at 8,000 feet between Arras-Vitry. The first e/a's starboard engine caught fire and black smoke poured out of it. Another fighter attacked the first e/a and I attacked once more when fighter had finished. Black smoke and oil completely obscured the target after my second burst of fire and it began to descend. I then turned my attention to the other, who had been firing at me. In my second burst, black smoke appeared from the engine and fuselage and e/a appeared to be gliding to the ground. As darkness was approaching rapidly I returned to my aerodrome and landed in the dark.'

Plt Off Michael Rawlinson:

> 'Enemy (five He111s at about 1,500 feet) in sight all the time, flying in two sections of three and two. Followed section of two. Flg Off Blair opened fire on No 1. When he broke away, smoke poured

from both engines. Rear gunner was still alive, shooting at him. Closed and overshot e/a before ammunition was expended, but rear gunner was out of action. When last seen, e/a was in a shallow dive with oil and smoke pouring from both engines.'

Ten minutes later Flt Lt Dickie Lee's section (Flg Off Derek Allen and Plt Off Pat Woods-Scawen) sighted what was believed to be a Ju88, but was almost certainly another Heinkel of LG1 or KG27, at 7,000 feet, five miles north-west of St Amand. Lee:

'Section attacked in line astern. After first aircraft attacked, starboard engine caught fire and one member of the crew jumped by parachute. Second and third aircraft attacked and set e/a completely on fire and it crashed in flames.'

The raiders continued the onslaught after dark, 85 Squadron's diarist noting that:

'Two bombing attacks were made on the aerodrome which proved inaccurate, the bombs dropping to the north and south-east of the Squadron HQ.'

Bombs also fell near 85 Squadron's quarters, one exploding 20 yards from where Flg Off Ken Blair was sleeping, although he was unhurt.

87 Squadron, temporarily based at Senon, was also in the thick of the action, as the unit's diarist noted:

'Dawn. Nine Do17s raided Senon at 10,000 feet—we brought down two. 0700: lone Do17 over Senon at ten feet and machine-gunned some Potez on the opposite side of the airfield. Shot down by Brownings and crashed two miles outside airfield.'

In the air, Flg Off Harry Mitchell, a Canadian from Ontario, opened the Squadron's account:

'At 0430 I intercepted 14 Do17s south-west of Senon at 14,000 feet. I attacked one of the machines which had lagged behind and shot it down ten miles north-east of Metz. The remaining machines headed east and had disappeared by the time I had finished.'

The Dorniers were from 8/KG3 and one of the bombers suffered 30% damage during Mitchell's attack and two members of the crew were wounded. An hour later four more 87 Squadron Hurricanes scrambled in pursuit of an estimated 60 raiders; Flt Lt Voase Jeff attacked a formation of a dozen Do17Zs (4/KG2, the unit engaged by 73 Squadron) bombing Thionville, Voase Jeff also reporting an escort of three Bf110s:

> 'Picked outside flank e/a in rear section. Delivered one quarter and four stern attacks. On final attack the e/a wobbled badly. At same time my aircraft was hit. I carried out these attacks as e/a were bombing Thionville on north-west run. I force-landed at Doncourt. Do17 crashed at Boulages—four prisoners.'

Flg Off Mitchell attacked a second Dornier:

> 'I attacked outside e/a of rear formation and made one quarter and two stern attacks. E/a went into steep spiral and I broke off to attack another e/a. I finished ammunition but saw no result. [First] e/a crashed at Audun-le-Roman; three prisoners.'

The other two members of the Flight, Plt Off Trevor 'Taffy' Edwards and Plt Off John Cock (N2383), engaged a Heinkel at 12,000 feet over Luxembourg, but it escaped after Edwards had inflicted some damage:

> 'E/a [Heinkel] sighted north of aerodrome at 4,000 feet. Attacked by another Hurricane [Cock]. Evasive action. Opened fire from 400 yards, closing in slowly. Four bursts. No 2 Heinkel broke away with glycol leak.'

An estimated 14 Do17Zs—probably 4/KG2 again—were then seen at 15,000 feet, one of which Edwards attacked, reporting that it went down and crashed after a four second burst. Cock—from Renmark, South Australia—reported damaging one before it escaped in cloud. It seems that 4 Staffel lost two of its aircraft to 87 Squadron in this engagement: Fw Franz Schmidt and his crew were taken prisoner by French forces, but the fate of Uffz Hermann Veit and his crew is uncertain.

At 0600, a section of 87 Squadron was joined by a section from 607 Squadron from Vitry, the latter flying as top cover. A few minutes later, Sgt Gareth Nowell (of the former unit) sighted two Hs126s of 3(H)/14 (spotting for 7 Pz Division) south of the Luxembourg border:

> 'I saw two aircraft, which I took to be Lysanders, but coming below them I realised they were Henschel 126s. I attacked but the aircraft at which I was aiming turned steeply. I followed and blacked out; when I came round I saw an aircraft almost immediately in front of me. I fired and saw strikes on the aircraft which dived towards the ground and blew up. The second Henschel was still turning above

when I attacked it in the same way and shot it down. Both aircraft crashed in woods, bursting into flame.'

Flg Off Bill Whitty of 607 Squadron recalled:

'We joined up with 87 Squadron and caught some aircraft doing circular bombing of a road junction—all were shot down. I am not sure of the type; I think they were either a high-wing mono or biplane.'

Both Henschels were totally destroyed with the death of at least one crew member, observer Lt Paul Koll. Just after midday nine aircraft—identified from the ground as Do17s—attempted to bomb Metz airfield but none of the bombs found their target. However, when Plt Offs Dennis David (L1630) and Gordon Saunders—the latter a New Zealander from Wellington—reached altitude at 1220, they engaged four He111Hs of II/KG53 five miles south of Thionville. Both made stern attacks and saw 'parts falling away' from one machine and another 'diving with smoke streaming from it'. Saunders attacked a third but was hit by return fire, although he was able to return to base and reported:

'Climbed from aerodrome with Plt Off David and went into attack first, from rear. After attack, broke away to left and downwards. Enemy lost height then turned over to port and dived steeply. After breaking from first attack, saw Plt Off David follow a diving e/a with smoke streaming from it. Renewed attack on remaining e/a from the rear, under severe fire from each machine. Put long burst of fire into enemy and saw him break away downwards to the left. As my radiator burst, the glycol blinded me. The engine checked so I broke away and made the airfield (numerous bullet holes in aircraft).'

The Heinkels were also attacked by other members of the Flight, Sgt Frank Howell claiming the probable destruction of two and Plt Off Chris Darwin one more. Two Heinkels crash-landed as a result of this action and amongst the wounded was the Gruppenkommandeur, Obstlt Wilhelm Kohlbach. As Plt Off David touched down on his return to Senon, he noticed that the airfield was being bombed:

'I took off and was joined by Sgt Nowell in another Hurricane (he had not landed). We climbed above clouds and sighted six e/a [Do17Zs of III/KG2] in two sections of three. We each attacked one e/a of left section and delivered stern attacks. My e/a started on fire after my second burst and crashed in flames approximately ten

miles south-east of Thionville. I saw the aircraft attacked by Sgt
Nowell crash near the same place.'

Nowell added:

'My e/a went down in flames after I opened fire and crashed about
15 miles south-east of Thionville. I then attacked another but am
uncertain as to result.'

Nowell's aircraft was hit by two bullets in the radiator, although he was
able to land back at base with a seized engine. Records suggest that only
one Dornier, Lt Josef Mumb's 7 Staffel aircraft, was damaged when it
crash-landed near Trier with three wounded on board, although a
second damaged machine from the same Staffel returned to base with
two wounded crewmen.

With the return of the patrol, 87 Squadron was ordered to proceed to
Lille/Seclin, from where it was to join 85 Squadron in combating small
raids over Belgium. At 1450, a patrol of six Hurricanes, led by Flg Off
Jack Campbell (who had assumed command of B Flight following the
injury to Flt Lt Michael Robinson), met four Do17Zs of 7/KG76 over
Mézières at 9,000 feet. Campbell (L1970) claimed that 'one went down
with both engines stopped' and then caused smoke to pour from the
engines of two others:

'I attacked a formation of four Dorniers (which had just attacked
the aerodrome) with my Flight of six. I attacked the port side
aircraft and when he went down with both engines stopped, I
finished my ammunition on two others, both of which poured white
then black smoke from their engines, also oil.'

Fw Walter Reiske's aircraft crash-landed near the French/Belgian
border and the crew were taken prisoner by French troops. Meanwhile,
Plt Off John Cock (N2353) identified the aircraft he attacked as 'five
Messerschmitt 110s' and claimed 'one damaged slightly'. He may have
misidentified the Dorniers as Messerschmitts or possibly the bombers
had been provided with an escort of Bf110s.

At 1855, Cock was in action again when he and Plt Off Taffy Edwards
intercepted over Lille a lone twin-engined bomber reported to have
been a Ju88, but was almost certainly a He111P of III/KG54. Edwards
reported:

'E/a sighted flying north-east over Lille at 3,000 feet. Dived to
attack. Enemy continued on its course but dived to ground level on
crossing frontier. Stern chase for 20 miles into Belgium, flying very

low (50 feet). Fired short burst and starboard engine seen to catch fire (own aircraft hit by two bullets).'

Cock (again flying N2353) added:

'I continued the attack and the port engine began to run inter-mittently and smoke came from it. The e/a was having great difficulty in maintaining height and was flying starboard wing very low. The position would be 50 miles north-east of Lille.'

By the end of the day 87 Squadron had claimed 17 victories (of which five were considered to have been probably destroyed) for two Hurricanes force-landed and two others rendered temporarily unserviceable.

61 Wing, Air Component

At Vitry-en-Artois, three pilots of 607 Squadron's Red Section were on readiness 30 minutes before dawn, one of whom was Plt Off Peter Parrott:

'Our Mess was in the village and our dispersal point on the airfield was about a half to three-quarters of a mile away. We were in the Mess having a cup of tea waiting for the transport to pick us up. We heard it pull up and then the driver came running into the Mess (an unheard of breach of discipline!) shouting that German aeroplanes were flying over the airfield. We made all speed as we indeed saw several He111s in ones and twos passing over in a north-easterly direction (they had been attacking Army and RAF HQ at Arras). Discipline again went by the board as we piled into our aircraft and took off individually. I think I was first off.'

The Hurricanes, flown by Flg Off Francis Blackadder (P3535 AF-C), Plt Off Tony Dini* (P2572 AF-B) and Parrott (P2574 AF-F), roared into the air and climbed after the He111Hs—aircraft from II/KG1— which were by then over Conde; Parrott continued:

'The e/a were flying at about 5-7,000 feet. Take-off had been to the east and I started to climb at full throttle in pursuit of two He111s. It was a long stern chase and I was still out of range when I realised that we were nearing the Belgian border. We had been repeatedly

---

* Plt Off Antonio 'Tony' Simmons Dini was a New Zealander born in Christchurch of Italian ancestry, whose father was well known in civil aviation in New Zealand. Plt Off Dini joined 607 Squadron in April 1940.

warned not to cross into Belgium because of the risk of internment should we be forced down. I therefore opened fire at long-range on the rearmost aircraft, and was rewarded with a return of tracer from the dorsal air gunner. Before I had finished my ammunition, the air gunner had stopped firing, but whether this was a hit by me, or he was reloading his gun, I shall never know. All I could claim was "possibly damaged". On the way back I passed several more Heinkels making their way home, but could do nothing about them, being out of ammunition. Thus ended my first combat. It taught me to look all round before selecting a target.'

Plt Off Dini reported:

'Lost section leader. First attack at 300 yards down to 200 yards— ten seconds. Silenced rear gunner and black smoke from port engine. Second attack, smoke from starboard engine. E/a fell away, but now over Belgian border. Centre aircraft registered one hit (on own aircraft). On return to aerodrome, AA opened fire and Hurricane damaged.'

By 0500 Green Section of B Flight was airborne and met a lone He111H north of Douai. Flg Off Jim Bazin led the attack:

'E/a attacked from 250 yards. No 1 [Bazin] gave one burst of 15 seconds—rear gunner put out of action and one or both engines stopped. Attack continued by No 2. E/a observed to land on or near the Belgian border. One of crew landed by parachute.'

Sgt Ken Townsend (Green 2) added:

'Leader attacked e/a and his burst observed to converge on tail of e/a and traverse longitudinally. I continued attack after leader broke away. E/a observed to lose height. One of crew landed by parachute and e/a landed close to Belgian border.'

Flg Off Monty Thompson reported:

'A few seconds after No 1 had started firing, my windscreen was covered in oil, making it impossible to see anything. I therefore broke away. I was attempting to ascertain my position when I saw e/a about 3,000 feet above me. I climbed up and attacked e/a from astern. No return fire experienced. Vision was partly obscured but e/a appeared to leave thin trail of black smoke before I broke away.'

The Heinkel attacked by the three pilots was possibly Uffz Gerhard Kasten's aircraft of 6/KG1, returning from an attack on Cambrai. The pilot was able to bale out, but the remainder of his crew were killed when the aircraft crashed near Cambrai.

Fifteen minutes later Yellow Section of A Flight encountered a number of He111Hs east-north-east of Douai, also aircraft from II/KG1; Flg Off Bill Gore (P2573 AF-A) reported:

> 'When attacked, e/a turned into sun and remained so. Defensive fire from dustbin put out of action in third attack. E/a dropped what appeared to be a string of black balls. Action broken off with e/a pouring oil from both engines.'

These bombers were also intercepted by Flg Off Bill Whitty of B Flight:

> 'I had just arrived [at dispersal] when my Flight Sergeant pointed out aircraft bombing Cambrai. I took off and caught two flying together and got one He111—which crashed near Mons—and got a burst at the second on his port motor before he got into cloud.'

7/KG1 lost an aircraft in this engagement when it crashed near Hinacourt, about seven miles south of St Quentin; Ofw Kurt Buchholz, the pilot, was captured by French forces, but the remainder of his crew were killed. Meanwhile, Blue Section of B Flight met three more He111s at 17,000 feet near Le Quesnoy; Flt Lt John Sample (Blue 1 in P2615) reported:

> 'While patrolling Douai sighted three aircraft to south-west of base, flying east. Opened to full throttle and climbed up, but was left behind by Blue 3 whose aircraft was faster. Blue 3 carried out one attack, followed by Blue 2, during which I climbed above e/a to identify them, as I was not entirely satisfied as to their identity. Having satisfied myself they were Heinkels, I carried out attack from astern on a single aircraft, flying about 500 yards behind and to one side of the other two. I fired four bursts, commencing at 350 yards and broke away at about 50 yards. During my fourth burst the e/a banked over to starboard slowly. After I broke away I could no longer see him. Oil appeareed to come from the e/a as my windscreen was covered with it.'

Flg Off Charles Bowen (Blue 3):

> 'There were three e/a, two in close formation and one about 500 yards to the right and behind. I carried out No 1 attack on the single

aircraft, opening fire at about 200 yards. After a very short burst I was covered in oil and could not see target ahead. I broke away and saw the other aircraft attacking the enemy. The e/a commenced to lose height rapidly, smoke or steam pouring from his starboard engine. I followed this aircraft for about a minute until it vanished in the ground haze. Throughout this, I was following the two remaining aircraft from about 1,000 yards astern, until my windscreen cleared. I closed in to about 300 yards and opened fire on the starboard aircraft and closed in to about 200 yards, firing until all ammunition was exhausted. The bullets appeared to be entering the aircraft, which broke formation and appeared to drop back, but as I was well into Belgium I broke away without watching further.'

Flg Off John Humpherson, who had been the Squadron's pre-war flying instructor and adjutant, was flying as Blue 2:

'I attacked No 2 after Blue 3. This aircraft was about seven spans from leader of the enemy formation. I experienced a lot of difficulty with oil on the windscreen which was evidently thrown back from the e/a. After expending my ammunition I returned to base.'

At 0540 Yellow Section was off again when an unidentified aircraft was seen in the vicinity of the airfield; Flt Lt George Plinston* who led the section in P2536 AF-R, reported:

'Took off on sight of one aircraft. Climbed and chased e/a which went into Belgium. Broke off when another aircraft attacked. Observed AA fire bursts at three aircraft (identified as Ju88s) flying south, then east. Attacked. No visible results except that rear gunners did not fire after first two or three bursts. E/a flew straight into the sun.'

Plinston's aircraft suffered a few bullet strikes in this action, although he was able to return to base and land safely. By 0730 the Squadron believed it had shot down seven enemy aircraft.

At 1000 a Heinkel was engaged by Flg Off Bob Weatherill (P2571 AF-G) when on patrol with Yellow Section of A Flight, but it managed to evade his attack and got away. In the early afternoon, He111Hs of III/KG1 attacked, in squadron formation, the Potez factory near Albert, about 15 miles north-east of Amiens, but the advance element

---

* Flt Lt George Plinston, a former Flight Commander with 1 Squadron—with which he had seen some action earlier in the year—was officially on ground duties with 607 Squadron, but managed to fly several sorties during the first few days of operations.

was intercepted during the outward journey by Yellow Section of 607 Squadron. Five Heinkels were sighted at 10,000 feet, 15 miles east of Mons and were engaged, Flg Off Anthony 'Bunny' Forster (P3448 AF-H) reporting one shot down and a second probably destroyed.

Yellow Section was airborne again at 1330, meeting another Staffel of He111Hs from III/KG1 15 minutes later. These were engaged and three claimed shot down, one each by Flg Off Weatherill (P2574 AF-F), Flg Off Forster (P2573 AF-A) and Plt Off Parrott (P2536 AF-R). The leader (Weatherill) reported:

> 'Scrambled after smoke trail. Chased trail 30 miles east of Mons. Saw four He111s in scattered formation. Attacked individually. Port engines of two Heinkels exploded. The third Heinkel's under-carriage dropped down and starboard engine belched smoke and petrol.'

At 1430, 607 Squadron scrambled nine Hurricanes—including Yellow Section, which had just refuelled and rearmed—on the approach of more Heinkels of III/KG1. Seven of the bombers were encountered north-west of St Quentin at 12,000 feet and Flt Lt John Sample (Blue 1 in P2615) led the attack:

> 'Spotted formation of seven He111s over Albert, orbiting, with one straggler 300 yards behind others which were in close vic formation. Ordered line astern and proceeded to attack the straggler. After the first burst of fire from my guns, I noticed that he was closed up with the rest of his formation. I received crossfire from all the aircraft in the formation. During my second burst of fire I saw my incendiary bullets entering the fuselage and wings of e/a and the port engine gave off light coloured smoke. The e/a began to turn away from his formation. At this moment my engine was hit by several bullets and began pouring out oil, blinding me. I broke away and escaped by parachute, as I could not have seen well enough to land.'

Sample sprained both ankles severely on landing. Thereafter, until recovery, he was obliged to wear carpet slippers at all times, even when flying. Meanwhile his No 2, Sgt Ken Townsend, attacked another Heinkel:

> 'Centre straggler attacked. Starboard engine tank appeared to be pierced for my machine was covered in oil and that engine stopped. Machine descended slowly. Made an individual attack on [another] straggler due to losing section leader. Apparently engines stopped so I discontinued attack and e/a landed at French airfield (Castres).'

Fifteen minutes later Townsend encountered another Heinkel, south of Cambrai:

> 'A Hurricane from A Flight [Plt Off Peter Parrott] and self made attack and e/a descended slowly. French base at Castres said two e/a descended slowly in flames. One of these was shot down by A Flight Hurricanes, but the other was the one mentioned in this report.'

Meanwhile, Flg Off Monty Thompson (Blue 3) engaged a number of the bombers:

> 'After a burst of about seven seconds, a burst of smoke appeared from e/a's starboard engine. This e/a, on extreme right of formation, turned right just before I fired. After short burst at next inner e/a, I broke away, as range too close. Coming out of my dive, I sighted another e/a below and a mile away from the formation. This I followed round a small cloud and attacked from about 400 yards with the remainder of my ammunition. As the e/a went into a cloud, smoke could be seen coming from its starboard engine.'

Flg Off Bill Gore (Yellow 1, P3448 AF-H) led his section after a vic of three Heinkels heading south-west:

> 'Outside aircraft attacked first (No 3 Attack with two Hurricanes). Engines put out of action. Attacked No 1 bomber with similar results.'

Yellow 2, Flg Off Bunny Forster (P2573 AF-A), followed his leader closely:

> 'Yellow leader put starboard engine out of action. E/a attacked by Yellow 2. Emitted large amount of oil from starboard engine. Formation shadowed by Yellow Section and only four remained.'

The same Heinkel was attacked by Flg Off Bob Weatherill (Yellow 3, P2574 AF-F):

> 'Attacks carried out on two near aircraft. Both aircraft starboard engines belching smoke. Followed one down to ground, 15 miles east of St Quentin. Aircraft burst into flames about 200-300 feet above the ground.'

French Moranes were also in the vicinity, as noticed by Plt Off Peter

Parrott (Red 2, P2536 AF-R):

'Lost Section leader. Joined B Flight section. At 15,000 feet sighted several e/a below being attacked by Morane fighters. Gave chase and joined two Moranes attacking formation of three e/a. Port engine appeared to blow up. Enemy went into slow dive with smoke pouring from both engines. Followed e/a down to 2,000 feet then lost it. Fire returned from rear gunner but no hits recorded. E/a, on being attacked, dropped several black balls.'

With the battle at its height, another trio of 607 Squadron Hurricanes— Green Section of B Flight—were scrambled and encountered three He111s at 4,000 feet. Flg Off John Humpherson reported:

'Three e/a were sighted flying west. I and the rest of Green Section went into the attack and, on seeing us, the enemy began violent evasive action and the fight developed into individual attacks. At this point, three more Hurricanes arrived on the scene and went into attack before we could close with the enemy. I waited for the other Hurricanes to break away from the machine I intended to attack, then I went in. I closed to about 250 yards before opening fire. After about eight seconds the enemy machine jettisoned about 30 bombs. I continued firing and about ten seconds later both engines of the machine appeared to explode and stop. The machine then rolled over on to its back and disappeared below me. This was the last I saw of it as I had to break away over it to avoid a collision.'

The Heinkels of III/KG1 had suffered serious losses during their foray over Northern France, losing five aircraft shot down to the Hurricanes of 85 and 607 Squadrons, plus two others seriously damaged, both of which crash-landed. Amongst those killed was the Gruppenkommandeur, Maj Otto Schnelle:

He111H of Stab III/KG1 flown by Maj Schnelle crashed two miles east of St Quentin: crew killed.

He111H of 8/KG1 flown by Oblt Kurt Schnaase crashed eight miles south of Lille: crew killed.

He111H of 9/KG1 flown by Oblt Hermann Braune crash-landed near Albert: crew captured and handed over to British forces.*

---

* The Heinkel (V4+DT) came down near a Great War military cemetery, the German crew scampering clear of the wreck. They were challenged by the unarmed British wargrave keeper, who told them to hand over their weapons. One airman threatened to shoot, but obviously thought better of it and all five surrendered.

He111H of 9/KG1 flown by Lt Kurt Neumann crash-landed near Albert: crew evaded capture.

He111H of 9/KG1 flown by Uffz Hermann Heintze crashed near Albert: one killed, three baled out.

He111H of 9/KG1 crash-landed at Bonn-Hangelar on return, 65% damaged and with one crewman wounded.

He111H of 9/KG1 crash-landed at Giessen on return, 40% damaged: crew unhurt.

During the afternoon, sections of Heinkels from both I/LG1 and II and III/KG27 set out, at regular intervals, to attack aerodromes, probable military headquarters and important rail and road targets, as well as concentrations of troops and transport in the area of Ghent-Brussels-Antwerp. On the reported approach of the advance echelons, Red Section of 607 Squadron was sent off to patrol the Ath-Leuze area, where they met four He111Hs at 1510. Plt Off Trevor Jay was leading the section in P2571 AF-G and reported:

'Section sighted enemy and executed No 3 Attack during which we split up. I delivered two attacks on the second. The undercarriage of the enemy dropped, the port engine blew up and black smoke came out. I followed the enemy down and it crashed near a village.'

Plt Off Tony Dini (Red 2, AF-P):

'Carried out attack with Red 3 and both e/a's engines gave out great quantities of oil and smoke, covering my windscreen and I had to return to base. When last seen, e/a was diving for the ground (near Lille).'

Plt Off Peter Dixon (Red 3, P3448 AF-H):

'On patrol when four He111s sighted being attacked by three Hurricanes. One dropped back with starboard engine revving slowly. Attacked and stopped port engine. Aircraft then released bomb load in fields and was seen gliding down for ground with both engines stopped.'

Three patrolling Hurricanes of Green Section met a similar number of He111Hs of I/LG1 at 5,000 feet north of Ath at 1710, Flg Off Arthur Le Breuilly (Green 1) leading the attack:

'Being 3,000 feet above the enemy, I dived to attack the formation and selected No 3. After a short burst smoke was emitted from the starboard engine. Breaking away and turning to attack for a second time, I again selected No 3 and emptied my guns. As I broke away, the enemy began to lose height and I followed it down and watched it crash into a house in attempting to force-land.'

Plt Off Charles Rowe (Green 2):

'There was a thin haze and 6/10 cloud—the enemy took refuge in this. I was able to get about five short bursts in and a cloud of smoke issued from No 3 in the formation. Almost at once my machine was hit and began to falter. I fired remaining shots at same Heinkel but was falling back fast and observed no effect.'

Rowe's aircraft (P2697), having been hit by return fire, was crash-landed and the pilot suffered injuries. Meanwhile, Plt Off Johnny Ashton (Green 3), a Canadian from Winnipeg, reported:

'Approached from beam and swung into line astern, closing to 200 yards. Emptied my guns with result the e/a's motors belched smoke and began to drop behind. No return fire from rear gunner. Saw e/a fire on accompanying aircraft—two holes in leading edge from which either petrol or oil came streaming out. Last seen by me breaking away to the right. Two aircraft approached from opposite direction; looked like Messerschmitt 110s but couldn't be sure. As I was out of ammunition evaded them by flying in cloud.'

At 1730 it was the turn of Red Section to see further action when they met seven He111Ps of 6/KG27 at 10,000 feet near Oudenaarde. Plt Off Tony Dini (P2572 AF-B) lost sight of his leader and attacked alone:

'Attacked last aircraft of formation, first from rear then from quarter. E/a broke away, dived and crashed (in flames) at Hundel-gem, six miles east-north-east of Oudenaarde. Lost rest of formation and returned alone.'

Uffz Walter Zimmermann and his crew perished in the crash. Red Leader, Flg Off Bob Weatherill, meanwhile engaged a second Heinkel which he believed he shot down, but his own aircraft, P2574 AF-F, was hit by return fire and he was obliged to carry out a force-landing near Oudenaarde. The third member of the section, Plt Off Trevor Jay (P2571 AF-G), gained strikes on the bomber he selected, hitting its fuel tank, noting that it had 'burst'.

Yellow Section scrambled at 1830, meeting an estimated 27 He111Ps from III/KG54 near Roeselare, which they proceeded to attack. Plt Off Trevor Jay (P2536 AF-R), who was leading the section, claimed two of the bombers shot down while Plt Off Peter Parrott (P3535 AF-C), flying his fifth sortie of the day, reported shooting down one Heinkel and damaging another. Yellow 2, Plt Off Peter Dixon (P2573 AF-A), was unable initially to make much of an impression on the tightly-packed bomber formation:

'Sighted AA fire. Headed toward it and saw enemy bombers— attacked individually owing to scattered enemy formation. Five attacked—inconclusive.'

He then attacked another, which he claimed shot down after noting that one of its engines had stopped, but not before his own aircraft had suffered a bullet strike in its oil tank.

The final operation of the day for 607 Squadron was again flown by Red Section, taking off at 2015. The trio of Hurricanes met three He111Ps (III/KG54 stragglers) near Orchies, but only Plt Off Tony Dini (P3535 AF-C) was able to carry out an attack:

'Attacked starboard aircraft and fired one-second bursts from 300- 150 yards. Engines smoked but oil on windscreen prevented seeing what happened to e/a in bad light.'

The successful action against the III/KG54 Heinkels brought 607 Squadron's claims for the day to an impressive 18 'confirmed', six probables and a dozen damaged—all He111s. None of the bomber formations encountered had been provided with fighter cover and had paid the price accordingly.

The Wing's other unit, 615 Squadron, was still in the throes of re-equipping with Hurricanes, A Flight at Le Touquet having already lost the services of three of its new aircraft when the airfield was raided by He111s (believed from II/KG27) at dawn. A member of the ground crew, LAC Alan Brooks, suffered burns to his hands when trying to extinguish a fire in one of the Hurricanes. However, one of the damaged aircraft was considered repairable. Sqn Ldr Kayll, the CO, commented:

'We were bombed very early in the morning. The pilots were billeted at an unoccupied château a few miles from the aerodrome and we were woken up by the bombs. As we had received no warning of any kind we assumed that it was the French practising. It wasn't until we received a call from the aerodrome that we realised the war had started.'

One of his pilots, Plt Off Tom Jackson, recalled:

> 'Woke at dawn to huge thumps. Looked out of hotel window and saw smoke from airfield half a mile away. Leapt out of bed and put uniform over pyjamas. Commandeered a car and drove back to hotel but others did not join me, so drove to the airfield and found two aircraft on fire. Got Hurricane started and took off. Saw Heinkel in distance and higher. Chased, but could not get to it. Shot at and felt something on sleeve—thought I'd been hit, but it was oil. Nil oil pressure so returned and landed. We later put the engine from the damaged Hurricane into this one and it was soon operational again.'

Sqn Ldr Kayll added:

> 'The Squadron had been re-equipping for about a week and we should have had a further week's training but we returned to Abbeville that day, leaving our Gladiators behind. The Squadron had nine serviceable Hurricanes; five pilots were flown to England to collect more but returned without them. Three Hurricanes were collected from Glisy.'

A Flight returned to Merville in the afternoon, while B Flight, at Abbeville, had returned from St Inglevert the previous evening, in order to re-equip. One of the biplanes, in the hands of Flg Off Lewin Fredman, had taken off at 0500 in an attempt to engage a He111 at 20,000 feet, but was unable to shoot it down, although he had inflicted some damage, reporting:

> 'Port engine seen to emit black smoke and made off towards the west.'

63 Wing, Air Component

The Wing received its air echelon when 3 and 79 Squadrons arrived at Merville from England during the early afternoon. For the pilots of 3 Squadron at RAF Kenley, the day had dawned bright and clear, but the early peace was disturbed when a section of Hurricanes was scrambled to investigate an unidentified aircraft approaching the coast. In the event the chase proved fruitless, and as the returning Hurricanes landed back at their base they were greeted with the news of the German assault on the Low Countries and of their own impending departure to France. After a sketchy pep talk from Sqn Ldr Pat Gifford DFC*, the

---

* Sqn Ldr Pat Gifford DFC had received his award for services with 603 Squadron earlier in the year.

Commanding Officer, the pilots hurriedly packed their kit and shortly after lunch took off for France. As only a few maps were available, these were allocated to the senior pilots. Fortunately the trip was completed without mishap and the Squadron landed at Merville. Of the move, one of the 3 Squadron pilots, Plt Off Mike Stephens, recalled:

> 'Shortly after midday we were on our way to France. There were not sufficient maps for everyone; I, as the most junior member of the Squadron, was not one of the favoured few. We had therefore to content ourselves with following our leaders.'

For 79 Squadron at RAF Biggin Hill the orders for the transfer to France came in good time for the pilots to arrange the packing of their dress uniforms and off-duty gear, to take advantage of the supposed delights of France when the opportunity for leave arose. With their kit packed safely aboard the transport aircraft allocated to them, the Squadron bid a hurried farewell to wives and sweethearts and took off for France, arriving at Merville within a short time of 3 Squadron. Plt Off Don Stones (L1716) of 79 Squadron wrote:

> 'We crossed the Channel, calm as a lake with even a tinge of blue to grace this beautiful day, in tight peacetime formation as if we were going to an air display. In minutes we were over the foreign-looking fields of France. At once we were on patrol towards the fighting, but without our CO who was otherwise occupied with bowel trouble. We patrolled from Lille to Roubaix and Mons-en-Chaussée without seeing any German aircraft.'

The Commanding Officer, Sqn Ldr R.V. Alexander, was apparently taken ill on arrival and was seen only briefly by his pilots from then on and did not fly on operations.

The two new squadrons each had 16 Hurricanes. Spare pilots were transported to the new base aboard a Harrow transport (a converted Harrow bomber, fitted with seats) of 24 Squadron. Soon after arrival, the first patrol—by six Hurricanes of 3 Squadron—was led by Flt Lt Mark Carter to the Maastricht area, as noted by Stephens:

> 'Over the field telephone came an order for one Flight (six aircraft) to patrol between Maastricht and Bree. We saw nothing on the first patrol.'

At about 1930, Flt Lt Carter (N2333) was again at the head of Blue Section of B Flight when 20 to 25 He111Ps (part of the III/KG54 formation attacked by 85 and 607 Squadrons) were seen near Lille at

7,000 feet; Carter's Combat Report stated:

> 'Blue Section sighted e/a in four formations of five to seven aircraft and immediately chased them. E/a were being fired at by AA guns and were bombing when sighted. We were joined by at least four other Hurricanes from unknown squadron [probably 85 Squadron]. We attacked individually and mainly different aircraft each time. One aircraft was seen to crash some minutes later after being attacked by our aircraft and at least five others were very badly damaged and were gradually losing height on the way back due east. Blue Section returned individually to base.'

Plt Off Frank Carey DFM* (L1932) was credited with two of the Heinkels shot down and shared a third with his leader and Flg Off Dickie Ball (L1901), with two others inconclusive; Carter was uncertain of the fate of another bomber he attacked. Of his engagements, Carey reported:

> 'R/T being useless, we chased after the e/a independently. I attacked several e/a, taking a different one each time, but eventually settled on to one, which I attacked until both engines were put out of action and wheels were down, when it spun round to the right sharply and dived towards the ground. It eased out of the dive, but I observed what appeared to be a large cloud of dust as e/a apparently hit the ground. I resumed attack on other e/a until all ammunition was expended. During attacks, my fire was obviously damaging e/a as several were emitting black smoke or had wheels lowered. Other squadron and remainder of section were still attacking and many e/a observed losing height on easterly course and almost certainly did not reach their base.'

One of Carey's victims was the Heinkel flown by Uffz Walter Zenner, who was the only member of the crew able to bale out before the 8 Staffel aircraft crashed. The German pilot was saved from a mob of angry civilians, who wanted to lynch him, by the timely arrival of British troops.

Merville came under attack soon after 2100, Flg Off Ball (N2333) again being ordered off with Plt Offs Carey (L1932) and Stephens (L1901). The trio climbed to 18,000 feet and engaged three He111Hs (stragglers I/KG27) over Sillars. Flg Off Ball reported:

---

* Plt Off Frank Carey DFM had gained his award while serving with 43 Squadron earlier in the year.

'Blue 1 [Ball] attacked No 2 of enemy vic formation. Blue 2 [Carey] attacked No 3. Black smoke issued from both these aircraft and No 3's wheels went down. Air gunner of No 2—when I attacked— ceased firing shortly after I opened fire.'

Plt Off Carey (Blue 2) added:

'E/a seen almost immediately after take-off and chased. E/a flying in open vic formation at approximately 7,000 feet and climbing. E/a constantly changing direction and full use of this was made by Blue Section cutting corners. E/a eventually attacked at 15,000 feet and fire opened at 300 yards, using up to 20° deflection. Blue 1 [Ball] and 2 [Carey] concentrated on attacking wing aircraft and attack continued by Blue 2 until engines were very badly damaged and emitting clouds of smoke, with e/a losing height. Blue 2 imme- diately returned to base owing to failing light. Possibly two e/a shot down [one by Ball].'

Ball and Carey were each credited with a Heinkel shot down, but the former failed to return to Merville. Unable to make R/T contact or find the airfield in the dark, Ball set course for Dover but was similarly unable to find an aerodrome there, so baled out over St Margaret's Bay, near the Dover RDF Station. Unhurt and taken back to RAF Kenley in a Magister, he returned to Merville next day with a replacement Hurricane. Carey meanwhile landed safely at Merville at 2145 and Stephens ten minutes later. The latter had not seen the bombers and, without a map, had soon become separated and lost in the gathering darkness:

'We took off in whatever direction we happened to be pointing, hoping to catch the Heinkels. It was hopeless. There was no radar, no fighter control at all. We were just wasting effort and hazarding aircraft in the hope of finding our quarry in the gathering darkness.'

Fortunately, he saw another Hurricane silhouetted against the western sky and joined up with it, which turned out to be flown by Flt Lt Walter Churchill, who had taken off alone five minutes after Ball's section had scrambled. Hot on his tail was Flg Off Raymond Lines-Roberts' section, who sighted three bombers at 2115 near Lille at 12,000 feet and attacked, as Lines-Roberts (L1923) reported:

'E/a were flying in vic formation when first sighted. They were flying due west and later turned south-west. The only evasion tactics carried out by e/a were half turns to port and starboard. As No 2 and

3 of [my] formation were slightly ahead, they attacked the two outside aircraft. I then came into range and took No 1 position, attacking the leader of the e/a. I closed to 100 yards, firing four second bursts. I then broke away and immediately commenced No 1 Attack on the leading aircraft, as the rear gunners of the two outside aircraft had ceased firing. During my second attack I received a bullet in my engine and broke away. I then noticed oil pouring from the port engine of the leading aircraft and smoke coming from the starboard wing. My engine then stopped and I lost sight of e/a and Nos 2 and 3 of my formation. I attempted to force-land in a field (near Fieffes) but owing to a ditch which I could not see in the failing light, the aircraft crashed.'

As a result of the late afternoon/early evening operation over the Ghent-Brussels-Antwerp area, III/KG54's 8 Staffel had been virtually annihilated during attacks by 3, 85 and 607 Squadrons, losing six Heinkels shot down, while an aircraft of the Stabskette suffered damage; in addition, Stabsstaffel and I Gruppe of LG1 lost four aircraft and another damaged, while II and III/KG27 suffered two losses and four damaged, and I/KG1 lost a single aircraft, a total of 13 Heinkels totally destroyed and six damaged:

III/KG54

He111P of 8/KG54 flown by StKpt Hptm Fritz Stadelmayr crash-landed near Wevelgem: two killed, one PoW of the British, two PoW of the Belgians.

He111P of 8/KG54 flown by Oblt Volprecht Freiherr von Riedesel crash-landed near Wevelgem: one killed, three PoW of the Belgians.

He111P of 8/KG54 flown by Lt Alfred Jansen crash-landed near Ghent: three PoW of the Belgians, one PoW of the British.

He111P of 8/KG54 flown by Uffz Alfred Vogel crashed and burned near Ghent: one killed, three PoW of the Belgians.

He111P of 8/KG54 flown by Uffz Walter Zenner crashed and burned near Ghent: three killed, pilot baled out and PoW of the British.

He111P of 8/KG54 flown by Uffz Karl Reinhard crashed and burned near Ghent: crew baled out, two PoW of the British.

He111P of Stabskette III/KG54 10% damaged in combat near Ghent: three wounded.

I/LG1

He111H of Stabsstaffel I/LG1 flown by Lt Otto Dörwald failed to return Tournai-Louvain-Namur: two killed, one wounded and PoW of the French, one PoW of the British.

He111H of Stabsstaffel I/LG1 flown by Uffz Richard Bröer crashed ten miles north of Lille: one killed, two PoW of the British, one PoW of the Belgians.

He111H of 1/LG1 flown by Obfhr Hans-Hermann Thiessen crashed near Lille: one killed, one missing, two PoW of the British.

He111H of 3/LG1 flown by Fw Werner Hartmann crashed north of Orchies: all four PoW of the British, but one died in hospital and another, wounded, was released from hospital later by German troops.

He111H of 2/LG1 10% damaged in combat north of Lille: pilot and two crew wounded.

II/KG27

He111P of 6/KG27 flown by Uffz Heinz Zimmermann shot down near Oudenaarde and crashed south of Ghent: crew killed.

He111P of 9/KG27 flown by Fw Heinz Schmelz crashed south of Lille: crew killed.

He111P of 6/KG27 crash-landed Achmer, 35% damaged: one wounded.

He111P of 4/KG27 force-landed at Köln-Ostheim, 30% damaged: pilot and two crew wounded.

He111P of 7/KG27 10% damaged in combat six miles west of St Quentin: one wounded.

He111P of 9/KG27 10% damaged in combat north of Brussels: one wounded.

I/KG1

He111H of I/KG1 flown by Lt Wolfgang Seel crashed near St Quentin: two killed, one PoW of the British, one PoW of the French.

One of the KG54 pilots taken prisoner, Lt Alfred Jansen, wrote later of his experiences:

'The flight on 10 May was my first and also my last combat mission. The Heinkel flew very well, but our formation was attacked and dispersed by English fighters. So it was easy for them to destroy us. One engine was shot out and I tried at low level to reach our base. Unfortunately, we could not do so, because the second engine went out. I found a landing place. The capture was severe but humane. My wounded comrades were taken care of. They had very bad injuries, because the English used grenades. The soldiers were rougher to me. That day will remain a sad moment of my life for me.'

Summary

At close of play, when various intelligence reports and other scraps of information had been scrutinized by Allied Military HQ, the day's events were assessed and summarized as follows:

Holland: The Dutch were resisting the land invasion along the Maas and the Ijssel, but their fortifications on the latter river had already been breached, for the capture of Apeldoorn by the enemy was reported. The airborne forces, which had overleapt the Dutch defences and caused an immediate threat to the heart of the country, clung tenaciously to Waalhaven aerodrome, and had appeared in sufficient numbers throughout the day to cause the utmost confusion in the vital The Hague-Rotterdam area. The French 7th Armée had, according to plan, begun its race along the coast and the occupation of the island of Walcheren, not with the hope of saving the Dutch (whose resistance was never expected to last longer than a few days), but to secure the mouth of the Scheldt and the left flank of the Allied line.

Belgium: Demolitions had been carried out along the frontier, but had been prevented by parachutists at two bridges over the Albert Canal, west of Maastricht. This was to mean, in effect, that the first Belgian defence line was already pierced, for the enemy was very prompt to exploit the situation.

Luxembourg: The Germans had completely occupied the Duchy, whose southern frontier the French were, however, holding. The enemy was well set to advance into southern Belgium through the Ardennes.

A summary of the RAF's involvement concluded:

The strategical reconnaissance brought back information which was valuable, but not decisive. The bombing operations varied widely in the degree of successes achieved. Of these, the effect of the AASF attacks on German troops in Luxembourg was very temporary.

The work of the AASF and Air Component Hurricanes was undoubtedly magnificent. To provide anything like adequate protection for their allotted areas they were far too few, and had much too little in the way of an effective warning system; nevertheless they engaged the enemy ceaselessly and exacted a very high toll of his aircraft in proportion to the losses they themselves suffered. And in fact the BEF did—if not entirely due to this reason— advance into Belgium with very little unwelcome attention from the Luftwaffe.

So ended an exhausting and testing day for the RAF Hurricane pilots. Those with the AASF had flown 47 sorties and had been credited provisionally with six bombers shot down for the loss of five Hurricanes shot down or crash-landed; the squadrons of the Air Component flew 161 sorties, engaged in 81 combats and were officially credited with 36 bombers shot down for the loss of two Hurricanes, with a further eight damaged.

Claims by AASF and Air Component Hurricanes, 10 May

Type	Confirmed	Probable	Damaged	Total
He111	37	14	19	70
Do17	13	1	2	16
Ju88	5	1	—	6
Bf110	—	—	1	1
Hs126	5	—	—	5
	60	16	22	98

Luftwaffe Losses Attributed to AASF and Air Component Hurricanes, 10 May

Type	60% to 100%	Under 60%	Total
He111	25	10	35
Do17	7	4	11
Ju88	1	—	1
Hs126	2	—	2
	35	14	49

However, the Luftwaffe's total losses for the day over Holland, Belgium and Northern France amounted to 56 He111s, 22 Do17Zs, 16 Ju88s, ten Ju87s, 13 Bf109s and two Bf110s; three Do17P and two Do215 reconnaissance aircraft (from X Fliegerkorps), three Armée Co-operation Hs126s, four He59s and 22 Fi156s. In addition, 158 Ju52s were reported shot down or written off as a result of the assault on the Netherlands. German fighter pilots and bomber crews claimed a total of

64 victories during the day's fierce fighting, the majority in combat with French, Dutch and Belgian aircraft.

Although the RAF's Battle squadrons had suffered severe losses, for the fighters it had been a satisfying day; Grp Capt P.F. Fullard, OC Air Component fighters, commented:

> 'I have never seen squadrons so confident of success, so insensible to fatigue and so appreciative of their own aircraft.'

That night RAF Bomber Command dispatched a total of 36 Wellingtons to bomb Waalhaven, to help prepare the way for Dutch forces attempting to recapture the aerodrome. Fires were started and hits claimed on buildings, hangars and aircraft. All the Wellingtons returned safely.

Individual Claims—AASF and Air Component Hurricanes, 10 May

Time	Name	Squadron	Claim
0400-	Flt Lt R.E. Lovett / Flg Off N. Orton	73 Sqn	He111 damaged
0410-	Flt Lt R.H.A. Lee	85 Sqn	Hs126
	Flg Off D.H. Allen	85 Sqn	Hs126
	Plt Off P.P. Woods-Scawen	85 Sqn	Hs126
0410-	Flt Lt J.R.M. Boothby / Flg Off K.H. Blair	85 Sqn	Ju88
0415-	Plt Off A.S. Dini	607 Sqn	He111 damaged
	Plt Off P.L. Parrott	607 Sqn	He111 damaged
0430-	Sqn Ldr J.O.W. Oliver / Plt Off J.W. Lecky / Sgt G. Allard	85 Sqn	He111 probable
0430-	Flg Off H.T. Mitchell	87 Sqn	Do17
0500-	Flt Lt R.E. Lovett / Sgt L.J. Humphries	73 Sqn	Do17 damaged
0500-	Flt Lt P.P. Hanks	1 Sqn	He111
0500-	Flg Off J.M. Bazin / Flg Off M.H.B. Thompson / Sgt K.N.V. Townsend	607 Sqn	He111
0500-	Flg Off L. Fredman	615 Sqn (Gladiator)	He111 damaged
0515-	Flg Off W.E. Gore	607 Sqn	He111
	Flg Off W.H.R. Whitty	607 Sqn	He111, He111 damaged
0515-	Flt Lt J. Sample / Flg Off J.B.W. Humpherson / Flg Off C.E. Bowen	607 Sqn	He111 probable
	Flg Off C.E. Bowen	607 Sqn	He111 damaged
0525-	Flg Off H.G. Paul	73 Sqn	Do17
	Flg Off E.J. Kain	73 Sqn	Do17

Time	Pilot	Squadron	Claim
0530-	Flt Lt P.R. Walker		
	Flg Off M.H. Brown		
	Flg Off J.I. Kilmartin	1 Sqn	Do17
	Flg Off P.H.M. Richey		
	Sgt F.J. Soper		
0530-	Flt Lt R. Voase Jeff	87 Sqn	Do17
	Flg Off H.T. Mitchell	87 Sqn	Do17
	Plt Off T.J. Edwards	87 Sqn	Do17, He111 damaged
	Plt Off J.R. Cock	87 Sqn	He111 damaged
0600-	Sqn Ldr J.W.C. More	73 Sqn	He111
0612-	Sgt G.L. Nowell	87 Sqn	2 Hs126
0730-	Flt Lt R.H.A. Lee	85 Sqn	Ju88 probable
	Flg Off A.B. Angus		
1130-	Flg Off A.D. Forster	607 Sqn	He111, He111 probable
1130-	Flt Lt J.E. Scoular	73 Sqn	2 Ju88
1220-	Plt Off W.D. David	87 Sqn	He111
	Plt Off G.C. Saunders	87 Sqn	He111, He111 probable
	Sgt F.V. Howell	87 Sqn	2 He111 probable
	Plt Off C.W.W. Darwin	87 Sqn	He111 probable
1330-	Plt Off W.D. David	87 Sqn	Do17
	Sgt G.L. Nowell	87 Sqn	Do17, Do17 probable
1330-	Flg Off R.F. Weatherill	607 Sqn	He111
	Flg Off A.D. Forster	607 Sqn	He111
	Plt Off P.L. Parrott	607 Sqn	He111
1430-	Flt Lt P.P. Hanks	1 Sqn	Do17
	Plt Off R.G. Lewis		
	Flg Off P.W.O. Mould	1 Sqn	He111
	Flg Off B. Drake	1 Sqn	He111
1430-	Flt Lt J. Sample	607 Sqn	He111 damaged
	Sgt K.N.V. Townsend	607 Sqn	He111, He111 damaged
	Plt Off P.L. Parrott	607 Sqn	He111
	Sgt K.N.V. Townsend		
	Flg Off M.H.B. Thompson	607 Sqn	2 He111 damaged
	Flg Off W.E. Gore		
	Flg Off R.F. Weatherill	607 Sqn	He111 probable
	Flg Off J.B.W. Humpherson		
	Flg Off W.E. Gore		
	Flg Off A.D. Forster	607 Sqn	He111 probable
	Flg Off R.F. Weatherill		
	Plt Off P.L. Parrott		
	Two MS406 pilots	607 Sqn	He111 probable
1445-	Sgt G. Allard	85 Sqn	He111
	Plt Off J.H. Ashton	85 Sqn	2 He111
1450-	Flg Off J.A. Campbell	87 Sqn	Do17, 2 Do17 damaged
	Plt Off J.R. Cock	87 Sqn	Bf110 damaged
1535-	Plt Off D.T. Jay	607 Sqn	He111
	Plt Off A.S. Dini	607 Sqn	He111
	Plt Off H.P. Dixon		
1710-	Flg Off A.E. Le Breuilly	607 Sqn	He111
	Plt Off C.R. Rowe		
	Plt Off J.B. Ashton	607 Sqn	He111 damaged
1720-	Plt Off A.S. Dini	607 Sqn	He111

	Flg Off R.F. Weatherill	607 Sqn	He111 probable
	Plt Off D.T. Jay	607 Sqn	He111 damaged
1800-	Flg Off A.D. Pickup	501 Sqn	Do17
1820-	Flg Off W.N. Lepine	85 Sqn	He111
	Plt Off J.A. Hemingway	85 Sqn	He111
1830-	Flt Lt J.R.M. Boothby Plt Off J.W. Lecky	} 85 Sqn	He111
	Flg Off T.G. Pace	85 Sqn	He111
	Flt Lt J.R.M. Boothby	85 Sqn	He111 probable
1830-	Plt Off D.T. Jay	607 Sqn	2 He111
	Plt Off P.L. Parrott	607 Sqn	He111, He111 damaged
	Plt Off H.P. Dixon	607 Sqn	He111
1855-	Plt Off T.J. Edwards Plt Off J.R. Cock	} 87 Sqn	Ju88
1930-	Plt Off F.R. Carey	3 Sqn	2 He111, 2 He111 damaged
	Flt Lt M.M. Carter Flg Off A.R. Ball Plt Off F.R. Carey	} 3 Sqn	He111
	Flt Lt M.M. Carter	3 Sqn	He111 damaged
2025-	Flg Off T.G. Pace	85 Sqn	He111 probable
2035-	Sgt G. Allard	85 Sqn	He111 probable
2040-	Flg Off K.H. Blair	85 Sqn	He111
	Flg Off K.H. Blair Plt Off M.G.H. Rawlinson	} 85 Sqn	He111
2040-	Plt Off A.S. Dini	607 Sqn	He111 damaged
2050-	Flt Lt R.H.A. Lee Flg Off D.H. Allen Plt Off P.P. Woods-Scawen	} 85 Sqn	Ju88
2100-	Plt Off F.R. Carey	3 Sqn	He111
	Flg Off A.R. Ball	3 Sqn	He111
2115-	Flg Off R.B. Lines-Roberts	3 Sqn	He111

Losses—AASF and Air Component Hurricanes, 10 May

0400-	N2318	73 Sqn	Flg Off N. Orton: shot down by return fire from Do17Z of 5/KG2 and force-landed near Conflans; pilot unhurt, returned.
0415-	VY-S	85 Sqn	Plt Off D.V.G. Mawhood: aircraft damaged by return fire from Ju88 of 8/LG1 and force-landed at Mons-en-Chaussée; pilot wounded.
0500-	P2804	73 Sqn	Flt Lt R.E. Lovett: aircraft damaged by return fire from Do17Z of 4/KG2 and force-landed near Conflans; pilot wounded.
		73 Sqn	Sgt L.J. Humphries: aircraft damaged by return fire from Do17Z of 4/KG2 and force-landed at Rouvres; pilot unhurt.
0530-	N2382	1 Sqn	Flt Lt P.R. Walker: aircraft damaged by return fire from Do17Z of 7/KG3 and crash-landed near Verdun; pilot returned.
0530-		87 Sqn	Flt Lt R. Voase Jeff: aircraft damaged by return fire from Do17Z of 8/KG3 and force-landed at Doncourt; pilot unhurt.

0730-	L1779	85 Sqn	Flt Lt R.H.A. Lee: aircraft badly damaged by return fire from He111P of Stab II/KG27; pilot unhurt.
	N2472	85 Sqn	Flg Off A.B. Angus: aircraft damaged by return fire of He111P of Stab II/KG27 and force-landed at Celles; pilot unhurt.
1200-		87 Sqn	Plt Off G.C. Saunders: aircraft damaged by return fire from He111H of II/KG53 and force-landed; pilot unhurt.
1430-	L1689	1 Sqn	Flg Off R.L. Lorimer: shot down near Châlons-sur-Marne by return fire from He111H of 5/KG53; pilot baled out, unhurt.
1430-	P2615	607 Sqn	Flt Lt J. Sample: shot down over Albert by return fire from He111H of I/KG1; pilot baled out, slightly injured.
1710-	P2697	607 Sqn	Plt Off C.R. Rowe: aircraft damaged by return fire from He111H of I/LG1 and crash-landed near Ath; pilot unhurt.
1730-	P2574	607 Sqn	Flg Off R.F. Weatherill: aircraft damaged by return fire from He111P of 6/KG27 and force-landed near Oudenaarde; pilot unhurt.
2115-	L1923	3 Sqn	Flg Off R.B. Lines-Roberts: aircraft damaged by return fire from He111P of I/KG27 and force-landed near Lille; pilot unhurt.
2230-	N2333	3 Sqn	Flg Off A.R. Ball: became lost in darkness and baled out over St Margaret's Bay, Dover; pilot unhurt.

There had been dramatic happenings during the day in Britain with the resignation of Prime Minister Neville Chamberlain, following severe criticism of his apparent lack of appreciation of the worsening situation. Mr Winston Churchill was asked to form a new Administration to face the latest threat to world peace; he accepted and immediately established a War Cabinet, comprising members from all three main political parties. One of Chamberlain's last actions as Prime Minister had been to broadcast to the nation:

> 'This morning, without warning or excuse, Hitler added another to the horrible crimes which already disgrace his name by a sudden attack on Holland, Belgium and Luxembourg. In all history no other man has been responsible for such a hideous total of human suffering and misery.'

CHAPTER III

SATURDAY 11 MAY
ENTER THE MESSERSCHMITTS

'I glanced back to find a whole squadron of Messerschmitt 109s forming line astern behind me.'

Flg Off Gus Holden, 501 Squadron.

Air Operations over Holland

The Germans had overrun the frontier provinces on the north-east and were advancing steadily on the main Dutch positions, while German airborne forces were pressing towards The Hague and fighting continued in the Rotterdam area.

At 1000, the two remaining Fokker TVs of the Nederlandse Militaire Luchtvaart took off from Schiphol, escorted by three DXXIs, to bomb the bridges across the Maas. They reached the target undetected and attacked, but all the bombs missed. Having returned to Schiphol to refuel and rearm, the two bombers repeated the attack, but again failed to achieve any tangible results. On the return flight a dozen Bf110Cs of ZG1 intercepted and shot down one bomber, the tail gunner of which claimed the destruction of one of the attackers before baling out. Two more of the Messerschmitts were claimed by the escort, although one DXXI was shot down.

All surviving DXXIs were concentrated at Buiksloot, north of Amsterdam. During the day the Dutch pilots brought down a reconnaissance Do17M and a Bf109 of 4/JG27, but lost one of their number to the Messerschmitts. Meanwhile at 1600, two Fokker G-1s of 4e JaVA carried out a strafing attack on grounded Ju52s that had landed between Rotterdam and Delft. During one strafing operation by the Messerschmitts, the Staffelkapitän of 2/JG20 was shot down over Tiel, captured and handed over to the British.

In an effort to assist the hard-pressed Dutch forces, the RAF's 11 Group decided to dispatch squadron-strength patrols from UK bases.

Thus, a dozen Hurricanes of 32 Squadron from RAF Biggin Hill were sent to Ypenburg, where on arrival the pilots saw 15 Ju52s burning on the ground together with one undamaged machine, which they proceeded to strafe. Between 1540 and 1745, Hurricanes of 56 Squadron patrolled three miles out to sea off Flushing, but failed to sight any enemy aircraft. However, another patrol by a dozen Hurricanes from 17 Squadron, led by Sqn Ldr George Tomlinson (N2547), which departed RAF Martlesham Heath at 1630, met much opposition, as reported by Flt Lt Bill Toyne (N2662) of B Flight:

> 'We turned north and flew along the [Dutch] coastline to a point about one mile east of The Hague and then turned north again, and whilst doing so detached Blue and Green Sections with orders to patrol The Hague above cloud. A Flight, led by the CO, proceeded further south-east towards Rotterdam. I climbed away towards The Hague and whilst doing so heard somebody say on the R/T: "enemy aircraft behind you". I looked and saw about 3-4,000 feet above my section 12-16 109s coming in a loose line astern to attack Blue, Red and Yellow Sections. I immediately climbed for height and was able to get my sights on an e/a which was on the tail of a Hurricane. I gave two bursts of eight seconds each at full deflection at 150 yards range. The e/a fell out of my sight and stall-turned and I was about to follow him down, being confident he was out of control, when I saw two e/a on my tail. I immediately did a steep climbing turn to starboard, followed by a half roll, continuing my dive right down to the surface of the nearest canal and, since my ammunition was exhausted, I employed evasive tactics by steep turns in either direction.'

The Messerschmitts were from I/JG51 and had been patrolling The Hague-Rotterdam sector when the Hurricanes appeared. Sqn Ldr Tomlinson endeavoured to get on the tail of one which was attacking one of his pilots and, in doing so, his aircraft was hit from behind. At the same time four more approached from head-on. He reported:

> 'I attacked another Messerschmitt which was pulling out of a dive and gave him a five-second burst, closing from 300 to 100 yards. The machine was badly hit, staggered, dropped and turn-stalled to port and dropped to the ground.'

Tomlinson was again attacked by a Bf109 and this time his port petrol tank was punctured. With his engine coughing and spluttering he made for the Belgian coastal airfield at Knokke (as instructed in case of an emergency) but en route was attacked for a third time, which resulted in damage to his aircraft's starboard aileron and radio; however, he was able to force-land safely and made his way to Amiens, from where two days later he was flown back to England aboard DH86B N6246 of 24 Squadron.

The remainder of A Flight suffered mixed fortunes. Both Flt Lt Michael Donne (Red 1, flying N2403) and Sgt John Luck (P2758) were shot down; Donne was killed when his aircraft crashed near Numansdorp, south-west of Rotterdam, while Luck's aircraft was seen to fall in flames near Dordrecht; however, he managed to bale out and was taken prisoner. In return, Flg Off Dickie Meredith (Red 2) and Sgt Charles Pavey (Yellow 3) each claimed a Messerschmitt; Meredith (N2457) reported:

'I engaged three 109s and got into position on the tail of one of them and opened fire at about 350 yards—he dived down through the smoke to nearly ground level. I maintained position and gave him all I had. Black smoke was pouring out of his engine and oil was coming against my windscreen from him. I now broke away as I was being fired at. I received in all about 15 bullet holes, my port aileron being useless and the ASI damaged. I saw the e/a I had fired at continuing a steep dive and strike the ground and crumple up at a point about 15 miles south of The Hague.'

The other successful pilot, Sgt Pavey, stated:

'After the dogfight developed at 4-5,000 feet, I broke away from the section leader as a 109 got on my tail. I did a steep turn to the left and found he could not follow me. I eventually got on his tail and the e/a twisted and turned, diving down. I fired intermittently and finally gave him a deflection shot, finishing my ammunition. He then burst into flames, spinning down to the ground. I followed him down until he struck the ground.'

Yellow 2, Plt Off Richard Whittaker, claimed a highly questionable probable:

'A big dogfight developed and I broke away and saw three 109s on the tail of a Hurricane. I did a quarter attack [on one], giving a short burst but had to carry on past him. I then saw another 109 and we circled each other, feinting for position and I finally got on his tail. I gave him all I had. We had both been flying at very low speeds, trying to turn inside one another. At this point I commenced to stall and lost sight of the e/a temporarily. On coming out of the incipient stall, I saw a parachute descending where the e/a had been in the sky. I saw another 109 about to attack me so I broke away and flew

through the smoke which was over The Hague and Rotterdam, and
out to the coast. The Hague as a whole was on fire.'

B Flight fared little better and lost two of its six machines. Plt Off
George Slee (Blue 2, in N2405 YB-Y) was killed when his aircraft
crashed near Gravedeel, south of Dordrecht, although Plt Off Cyril
Hulton-Harrop (Blue 3 in N2407 YB-N) was able to bale out south-west
of Dordrecht and was taken prisoner*. Two Hurricanes were claimed
by Lt Ernst Terry of the Stabskette, two more by Oblt Heinrich Krafft
of 3 Staffel and another by Uffz Fritz Schreiter, also of 3 Staffel.
However, the latter was then shot down by another Hurricane and
baled out over Waalhaven, but his colleague, Uffz Franz Schild, was
killed when his aircraft crashed south of Rotterdam.

Flg Off Jerrard Jeffries (N2403), leading Green Section, enjoyed
better success when two Hs126 Armee reconnaissance machines were
encountered:

'I saw a machine at 2,000 feet above and I led my section after him.
The machine turned south and I caught up with him and he turned
back north; he dived to ground level, turning right and left. I gave
him three short bursts and e/a crashed in field and fell to pieces.'

Sgt Wynn, Green 3 in N2438 (who had been with the Squadron for five
years), reported:

'I followed Green 1 until after he had sighted e/a. I then sighted
another Hs126 and I flew straight towards it. When it dived down
towards the ground, I dived after it and on my first dive I overshot.
I throttled back and the e/a turned east. I then got behind it at a
range of about 200 yards. The e/a kept turning, first to one side and
then to the other. When it straightened up I gave it a short burst and
it dived down onto the ground and turned over at about a point six
miles south of The Hague.'

Fighter Command scored a further victory during the early afternoon,
when three Spitfires of 19 Squadron encountered a Ju88 of 3(F)/122 off
the Dutch coast and shot it down into the sea, ten miles east of the East
Dudgeon lightship. However, during the course of a patrol by Spitfires
of 54 Squadron north-west of Rotterdam, Bf109s of 5/JG27 engaged
and shot down one Spitfire into the sea, with the loss of its pilot.

---

* Plt Off Cyril Hulton-Harrop's brother Montague was killed on 6 September 1939,
when his 56 Squadron Hurricane was one of two shot down in error by Spitfires of 74
Squadron over East Anglia.

Air Operations over Belgium and Northern France

The RAF's 18 and 53 Squadrons were again asked to dispatch Blenheims at dawn to reconnoitre the Albert Canal/Maastricht area. Four of these failed to return to their bases: one was shot down over the target area by Bf109s of 3/JG1, another fell to a Bf110C of II/ZG1 and the other two were victims of ground fire; one of the latter was hit by Belgian gunners and crash-landed at Châlons-sur-Marne on its return flight.

Shortly before 0700, nine Belgian Battles of 5/III/3, escorted by six Gladiators of 1/I/2, were dispatched to bomb the Albert Canal bridges. Only three badly damaged bombers returned to their base, the others having been shot down by Bf109s of 1/JG1 and 1/JG27 and intense ground fire in the vicinity of the target area. Four Gladiators of the escort were also shot down by Bf109s of 1/JG1, although the German pilots claimed seven of the biplanes in total. The Messerschmitt pilots also reported engaging and shooting down two Fairey Foxes over Maastricht during the day.

The Eben-Emael fortress finally surrendered at 1315, with 1,200 Belgian soldiers becoming prisoners, while 20 of their number had been killed; Detachment Koch suffered six dead and 20 wounded. Tongeren fell at about the same time.

Bf109s and Bf110s strafed airfields in Belgium during the morning and early afternoon; the remaining eight CR42s departed from Brustem for an emergency strip at Grimbergen near Brussels shortly before their arrival. However, the Messerschmitts succeeded in destroying seven Gladiators on the ground at Beauvechain at 1400 and He111s completed the destruction of the remaining Gladiators during a repeat attack at 1630; the last three Belgian Hurricanes were also badly damaged during a strafing attack against Le Culot airfield by Bf109s of I/JG27, when Capitaine Martin Charlier, Escadrille 2/I/2's commander, was slightly wounded in one foot.*

Eleven Blenheims of 110 Squadron set off at 1450 to attack concentrations in the Maastricht area, but two failed to return, one of which fell to a Bf109 of 3/JG27, the other to Flak. A follow-up raid by a dozen Blenheims of 21 Squadron also ran into a wall of Flak and most sustained damage. In addition, the Armée de l'Air launched its first day bombing mission of the war, an evening raid by a dozen LeO 451s of GBI/12 and GBII/12, escorted by 18 MS406s of GCIII/3 and GCII/6, directed against the bridges; one of the bombers was shot down by the

---

* Capitaine Charlier, although wounded, managed to reach France on 13 May, where he remained until January 1942, when he escaped to England via Spain and Gibraltar. Following a refresher course at 58 OTU, he was posted to 350 (Belgian) Squadron, flying Spitfires, but was killed on operations on 27 August 1942.

combined fire of Flak and fighters, while four Moranes fell to the Messerschmitts of I/JG1 and Bf110s. In return the French pilots claimed five of their attackers.

The Luftwaffe repeated its attacks against French airfields at first light, nine Do17Zs of 4/KG2 catching 114 Squadron's Blenheims on the ground at Conde/Vraux; six were left burning and all the others damaged by blast and debris. Ecury-sur-Coole was another airfield attacked; a Battle of 150 Squadron went up in flames there as a result and a second machine was damaged. The Armée de l'Air suffered even heavier losses, Luftwaffe bombers ranging far and wide in their quest for targets.

67 Wing, AASF

At 0500 Reims town and nearby Reims-Champagne aerodrome were bombed by nine Ju88s from 10,000 feet; it was a beautiful morning and the raiders were easily observed from the ground, but were greeted only by AA fire. On the airfield (where 73 Squadron was based), Sgt Lionel Pilkington noted:

> 'Two bombs whistle past my bedroom and drop 50 yards from my bedroom window. In a trench within minutes!'

Two Do17Zs of 1/KG2 then appeared and began circling the town, releasing bombs as they did so. A second bombing run was made by one Dornier from a height of 500 feet, when bombs fell near the Army HQ at Château-de-Polignac, while the other began machine-gunning the main street from low level. At that point a lone Hurricane from 73 Squadron arrived (one of three scrambled from Reims-Champagne) and Flg Off Fanny Orton (P2812/L) chased the bomber away, which was badly damaged and eventually crash-landed by Uffz Heinz Wolpers near his base at Geinsheim; two of the crew were wounded. Orton's aircraft was hit by return fire although he managed to land without further damage; he apparently identified his victim as a Ju88. The other two members of his section, Plt Offs Adrian Tucker and Hugh Eliot, failed to engage the raiders.

Flt Lt Prosser Hanks (N2380/S) and his section from 1 Squadron scrambled from Berry-au-Bac at 0540 on the approach of a raider. Having climbed to 15,000 feet the Hurricane pilots sighted a He111 which they pursued, but failed to engage. Pilots of 501 Squadron were also in action from Bétheniville during the early morning, when a patrol of three Hurricanes of B Flight, led by Flt Lt Williams, encountered a number of Do17Zs of 2/KG2 some 15 to 20 miles south-west of Reims. One of the bombers was claimed shot down by Williams and another by Sgt Bob Dafforn who, at 6ft 6in, was one of the tallest pilots in the RAF.

Uffz Paul Schuh and his crew were able to bale out of one of the stricken Dorniers, two being captured by British troops and two by French forces. The other bomber succeeded in returning to its base, having sustained only minor damage.

At 0800, Sqn Ldr Halahan led a dozen 1 Squadron Hurricanes into the air on the approach of a further raid. While A Flight was ordered to circle the airfield, Halahan led B Flight to intercept the bombers. The He111s turned back on sighting the Hurricanes and Halahan was obliged to recall his pursuing pilots; however, Flg Off Paul Richey encountered a lone Do17P of 3(F)/10, which he engaged:

> 'I attacked from astern. The Hun was going bloody fast and it was all I could do in my slow old wooden-blader to get within range. The Hun started turning, first one way then the other. I fired longish bursts following each other as rapidly as possible. Soon he was right down on the trees, slowing up but still going pretty fast. Every time I fired I saw whitish smoke come from one engine or the other— presumably it was glycol—but the bloody man kept on flying and I ran out of ammunition. I must have got his oil system too, for I got a lot of black oil on my windscreen.'

The crew of the reconnaissance Dornier were forced to bale out over Germany during the return flight when an engine caught fire. Meanwhile, having become separated from his companions and subsequently lost, Richey landed at Mézières, a French air base, where his Hurricane ran into a bomb crater and damaged its wingtip. The French obligingly flew him back to Berry-au-Bac in an ancient Mureaux parasol wing monoplane. Three days later, during a raid on Mézières by Do17s, Richey's abandoned Hurricane (L1679/G) was destroyed, as were 15 Potez 63s of the resident GAO 547.

Six Hurricanes of 73 Squadron set off from Reims-Champagne at 0930, Sqn Ldr More at their head. They were to escort eight Battles, four each from 88 and 218 Squadrons, which were to raid Wiltz, beyond Sedan. When about 15 miles north-east of Vouziers, a formation of seven Do17Zs was encountered by the Hurricanes although not attacked, since the Squadron's task was to protect the Battles. However, when flying below cloud, a lone Do17Z of II/KG76 was espied and chased at tree-top height by More and Plt Off Valcourt Roe; both claimed strikes on the fleeing bomber, which returned to its base with 30% damage, although both Hurricanes suffered damage from return fire, Sqn Ldr More's aircraft (P2813/H) being written off following his return to Reims-Champagne.

Meanwhile, the Battles attempted to attack their designated targets, but seven of the eight machines were shot down; four crash-landed in which two crew members were killed and the remaining ten were taken prisoner. The crew of another baled out at low level, but only the pilot and observer survived, both of whom were soon captured. All six crew members of the other two missing Battles were killed. The only machine to return, flown by an 88 Squadron crew, force-landed at Vassincourt, badly damaged. At least one Battle fell victim to German fighters, as a pilot of I/JG27 claimed one such bomber near Maastricht.

Shortly after midday two Bombays of 271 Squadron and an Imperial Airways Ensign arrived in the circuit at Bétheniville, the transport aircraft carrying personnel of 501 Squadron and spares for the unit. Two of the aircraft landed safely, but the second Bombay—L5183 piloted by Flg Off F.P.J. McGevor DFM—stalled on approach and crashed. Both McGevor and his co-pilot were injured, the latter seriously, while 501 Squadron's Adjutant, Flg Off A.C.J. Percy, was killed outright, as was one of the spare pilots, Sgt W.H. Whitfield, together with Sgt H.J. Barnwell of the ground crew. Those injured included four pilots: Plt Off B.L. Duckenfield, Plt Off B.J.R. Brady, Sgt D.B. Crabtree and Sgt H.C. Adams. Thus, at a stroke, 501 Squadron had been denied almost a quarter of its pilot strength. Sgt Paul Farnes, who was aboard the first Bombay, recalled:

'As a matter of interest I was originally put into the aircraft that crashed, but was taken out at the last minute and put into the other one. It certainly got us off to a pretty bad start.'

73 Squadron dispatched a section of three Hurricanes from Reims-Champagne at 1435, these meeting a formation of 30 He111Hs of II/KG53 plus an escort of Bf110Cs of I/ZG2 near Mourmelon. The trio of Hurricanes was quickly joined by another seven, together with others from 501 Squadron from Bétheniville. Five of the raiders were claimed as 'pretty certain' by 73 Squadron pilots, Flg Off Cobber Kain (P2535/K) variously identifying his victim as a Do215 or Bf110 (obviously the latter), while Flt Lt John Scoular (Hurricane P) claimed a Ju88. Three of the escorting fighters were credited to Flg Off Ginger Paul, Flg Off Fanny Orton (P2579/J) and Sgt Lionel Pilkington (P2569/D), with Kain claiming the probable destruction of another. In addition, Sgt Humphries reported damaging the port engine of a He111 and forcing it to jettison its bomb load, while Sgt Basil Pyne and Plt Off Hugh Eliot each claimed damage to Bf110s. Sgt Pilkington noted in his diary:

'I get a Messerschmitt 110 but one also gets me! A cannon shot in the tailplane passes through the fuselage and out the other side! Bullets in the engine, shot away throttle control; cannot close throttle and bullet hits in cockpit, beside rudder bar. Land on

[Rouvres] 'drome by cutting switches, rudder control wire practically sheared.'

Plt Off Aubrey McFadden's aircraft (P2811) was hit by a cannon shell in its radiator and force-landed in a field near Poilcourt, about three miles east of Neufchâtel-sur-Aisne, although McFadden was unhurt and was able to watch the air battle overhead. Meanwhile, the 501 Squadron formation, led by New Zealander Flg Off Cam Malfroy, engaged the same formation of He111s, two of these being claimed shot down, one by Malfroy and the other by Flt Sgt Alec 'Jammy' Payne, who pursued his victim to Mourmelon. Two escorting Bf110s were also claimed shot down, one each by Plt Off Dickie Hulse (near Cornay) and Sgt Percy 'Peter' Morfill (near Toureton).

At 1445, five Hurricanes of 1 Squadron's B Flight, led by Flt Lt Prosser Hanks (N2380/S), set off to escort Battles to targets north-east of Rethel. Near the target area the Hurricanes encountered I/ZG2's Bf110Cs; a subsequent report of the action stated:

'Three miles north-east of Rethel [the Hurricane pilots] saw enemy formation being attacked by unknown Hurricanes [obviously 73 and 501 Squadrons]. These broke off and 1 Squadron dived from the sun and attacked three e/a [Bf110s]. Flt Lt Hanks attacked first aircraft and starboard engine emitted white smoke. Flg Off Mould attacked the second aircraft and starboard engine put out of action. Flg Off Clisby attacked the same aircraft and put port engine out of action. Plt Off Stavert fired at the third aircraft and saw pieces falling from tailplane and fuselage. Hanks and Mould returned to attack the second machine, which dived towards the ground and force-landed one mile west of Chemery; crew taken prisoner. Clisby and Stavert then attacked the third aircraft—last seen with one engine stopped and other emitting white smoke. Crashed south-east of Rethel. Clisby then fired at the first aircraft—last seen diving with starboard engine and wings in flames.'

Following his combat, Flg Off Leslie Clisby, an aggressive Australian with two victories to his credit from the April skirmishing, had become disorientated and he landed at a French airfield to establish his position, only to be fired upon by the defences during his approach. However, the Hurricane was not hit and he returned later to Berry-au-Bac. War correspondent Charles Gardner, in his dispatch, wrote:

'The Hurricanes have been doing very well again today. Three of them, not so long ago, intercepted a mixed formation of 30 Ju88s [sic] and Messerschmitt 110s. For 20 minutes there was a terrific dogfight—after which other planes of the Hurricane Squadron came up—and the Germans turned back home. By this time they had lost five [sic] of the Messerschmitts—one of them to Cobber Kain. In that hectic 20 minutes, when the sky was full of warring planes, he was himself badly shot up by cannon shells and one tore a hole two feet square in his plane—but he managed to get it back safely.'

Although the pilots of 67 Wing had accurately reported shooting down three bombers, there was obviously a degree of over-claiming with regard to the damage inflicted on the escorting Bf110s. Two aircraft of I/ZG2 were lost whereas eight or nine successes were recorded by the Hurricane pilots:

He111H of 4/KG53 flown by Lt Walter Wellstein crashed near Ste Menehould: one killed, one missing and two PoW.

He111H of 4/KG53 flown by Uffz Paul Holz crashed near Ste Menehould: crew killed.

He111H of 4/KG53 crash-landed near Saarlautern: pilot and two injured.

Bf110C of 1/ZG2 crashed: Lt Dietrich Moeller baled out and returned, Gfr Günther Kergel killed.

Bf110C of 3/ZG2 crashed south of Charleville: Lt Walter Maurer* and Uffz Stefan Makera baled out and PoW.

1 Squadron's A Flight was in action at 1915, when five Hurricanes were scrambled on the approach of a raid directed against Reims, which comprised 30 Do17Zs of III/KG76 escorted by 15 Bf110Cs from I/ZG26. On sighting the enemy formation, Flt Lt Johnny Walker ordered his Flight to climb and then dived on the escort from astern. In a series of whirling dogfights, the Hurricanes outmanoeuvred their opponents and claimed no fewer than nine definitely shot down—two apiece by Flg Offs Hilly Brown, Iggy Kilmartin, Paul Richey and Sgt Frank Soper (L1905/H), while Walker claimed one and a probable. However, witnesses in the village of Romilly apparently reported seeing 'six

---

* At the time Lt Maurer had three victories to his credit, the first having been claimed during the brief Polish Campaign of September 1939. It would seem that he fell victim to Hurricanes of 1 Squadron; taken prisoner by the French as a result, he was released later. In 1941 he served in Russia, where he claimed three further victories, but by 1942 was flying a Me210 of 16/KG6 over the UK; he was shot down for a second time by 1 Squadron on 6 September 1942, one of the first victims of the Typhoon, and became a prisoner for the duration of the war.

Messerschmitts fall in flames' and allegedly 'ten wrecks were later found on the ground', thereby 'confirming' all ten claims. An official account of the action noted:

'No 1 [Walker] attacked first e/a from rear and fired bursts—no effect. One e/a got on to No 1's tail and our aircraft changed the position and got on e/a's tail and gave one burst and e/a did climbing turn. E/a burst into flames; pilot jumped by parachute and e/a was seen to crash in wood. No 1 then attacked second e/a and deflection shooting had no effect. No 1 then got in a second deflection shot with remaining ammunition and e/a was seen to go down on its back and directly towards the ground from 4,000 feet. E/a was not seen to hit the ground. Position east of Vervins.

Six e/a turned to form a right-hand circle. No 4 [Kilmartin] turned right, followed by No 2 [Brown], opening fire on circle and dogfight ensued. E/a appeared to form a steep climbing turn as an evasive tactic. No 2 picked out one e/a and followed it in a turn and on straightening out fired at the e/a; flames issued from forward and tail of e/a. No 2 broke away for further engagement and gave several short bursts into fourth e/a from rear and at the same time found an e/a on his tail. No 2 dived, pulled out and turned and reversed the position and got on to e/a's tail. No 2 opened fire and e/a continued down in a shallow diving turn from 500 feet. E/a disappeared into a wood, but was not actually seen to hit the ground. Having used up all his ammunition, No 2 returned [to Berry-au-Bac].

No 4 [Kilmartin] got on tail of fifth e/a and attacked on starboard bow and gave short burst and e/a broke into pieces in the air. No 4 then dived on the sixth e/a. After a good burst the e/a rolled over on its back and dived straight down into a wood. No 4 then climbed to gain height and then attacked e/a, out of a bunch of five, but a short burst appeared to have no effect. No 4 then saw four e/a round one Hurricane, so dived to assist the Hurricane and fired at one e/a, but ran out of ammunition.'

Flg Off Paul Richey failed to return from this engagement. He had been shot down and, although wounded, was safe; he wrote later of his experiences:

'I selected the rear one of two in line astern who was turning tightly to the left. He broke away from his No 1 when he had done a half-circle and steepened his turn, but I easily turned inside him, holding my fire until I was within 50 yards. To my surprise a whole lot of bits flew off him—bits of engine cowling and bits of his "glasshouse" [canopy]—and as I passed just over the top of him, I watched fascinated as he went into a spin, smoke pouring out of him; his tail suddenly swivelled sideways and came right off, while flames poured from his fuselage. Then I saw, with relief, a little white parachute open beside it. I looked quickly around me . . . I saw four other Huns going down. I had plenty of ammunition left . . . so I immediately started climbing after [three more]. I reached the rear Hun and shot him down in flames in a couple of bursts.'

Richey saw three more Messerschmitts climbing towards his aircraft, closely followed by two others. Having survived a series of attacks, the lone Hurricane (L1685) eventually suffered a fatal strike; he continued:

'There was a stunning explosion right in front of me. For a moment my brain did not work. My aircraft seemed to be falling, all limp on the controls. Then, as black smoke poured out of the nose and enveloped the hood, and a hot blast and a flicker of reflected flame came into the dark cockpit, I pulled the pin out of my harness, wrenched open the hood and hauled myself head-first out to the right.'

On reaching the ground, he was immediately confronted by two armed French soldiers. He had difficulty initially in persuading them he was British due to white flying overalls covering his uniform but, having done so, was taken to the nearby village of Romilly from where, later, he was collected and driven back to Berry-au-Bac, arriving next day.

Despite the multitude of claims by 1 Squadron, it would appear that only two Bf110Cs of I/ZG26 were totally lost in this action:

Bf110C of 1/ZG26 shot down near Romilly: Lt Friedrich Auinger (pilot) baled out and PoW of the French, Uffz Erich Ebrecht killed.

Bf110C of 1/ZG26 shot down near Romilly: Uffz Willi Weiss (pilot) baled out and PoW of the French, Ogfr Bernard Höfeler killed.

Although 501 Squadron had suffered no losses during the day's engagements, one of its pilots, Flg Off Gus Holden, narrowly missed being shot down while on a lone reconnaissance sortie to Sedan during the late afternoon. He recalled:

'I glanced back to find a whole squadron of Messerschmitt 109s forming line astern behind me, at which I felt the need for some immediate action. I turned on my back and went down vertically under maximum power.'

Following a tree-top chase, when the port wing of his aircraft (L2045 SD-A) was hit by a cannon shell, Holden managed to evade his pursuers and returned safely to Bétheniville.

60 Wing, Air Component

85 Squadron was also in action from Lille/Seclin during the morning, when Flt Lt Dickie Lee's section encountered a formation of Do17Zs of I/KG76, one of which Lee, Flg Off Derek Allen and Plt Off Pat Woods-Scawen claimed shot down before a second was attacked by Lee, which he also claimed. In fact only one Dornier (a 3 Staffel machine) was damaged in this engagement. During the latter combat however, Lee's aircraft (N2388 VY-R) was hit by Flak near Maastricht, obliging the slightly wounded pilot to bale out. He landed in a field near some tanks. There he encountered a peasant who told him the tanks were Belgian and, having obtained an old overcoat with which to cover his uniform, he approached the tanks, only to find they were German. The German troops apparently thought Lee was a civilian and locked him in a barn with several others, but he was able to climb out of a window and was soon on his way back to Lille.

Lille/Seclin airfield was on the receiving end of a sharp air raid at 1220 and five bombs hit the Officers' Quarters and Mess; a M/T driver was killed and a cook was injured. Although the Wing's other unit, 87 Squadron, carried out patrols, its pilots failed to engage any of the raiders seen. 85 Squadron was in action again during the afternoon when a formation of He111Ps of I and III/KG27 was encountered. Sgt Sammy Allard (N2319) claimed two shot down, as did (it is believed) Sqn Ldr Oliver (P2821). At least one aircraft of 2 Staffel was lost and its pilot, Fw Franz Ratzing, was taken prisoner by Belgian forces. A war correspondent wrote:

> 'The Squadron Leader [Oliver] came home slightly wounded, and at once went to sleep, but said that he would go up again on the dawn patrol. His squadron knew that it would be almost certain death for him to try to fight while in that state of exhaustion, so they put a guard on his quarters to see that nobody should disturb him until he woke naturally.'

Shortly afterwards Flg Off Ken Blair engaged two Bf109s during a patrol over Maastricht, although he did not make any claims. Meanwhile, Flg Off Derek Allen and his section (Plt Offs Paddy Hemingway and Pat Woods-Scawen) engaged a Do17P of 2(F)/123 which they claimed shot down, probably the aircraft flown by Oblt Hans Weiksel, which crashed south of Nivelles. Although Allen's aircraft was subsequently damaged by Flak, he was able to nurse it back to Lille/Seclin safely. However, Hemingway (L1979 VY-X) was not so fortunate, as he recalled later:

> 'Flew three sorties. On the third, after claiming one third of a Dornier 17, I attacked a Fieseler Störch [Fi156] at low level near Maastricht. The Störch dived to ground level as soon as it saw me and remained at that level throughout my five or six attacks, always keeping under me as I pulled up between attacks. I do not know if I damaged it.* The German AA opened up after my third or fourth attack, and during two attacks hit me a number of times, stopping my engine and covering me with oil and glycol. I turned west and crash-landed almost immediately. I got away from the aircraft as quickly as possible in case the Störch had followed me.
>
> I started to walk westward through the flat, seemingly deserted countryside until some time later I was picked up by a British Army scout car. The crew simply would not believe that the German Army was already well over the Maas, so I was quickly passed backwards and upwards to repeat my tale. By the end of the day I was believed. I spent that night somewhere under canvas, and had bits of shrapnel removed from my right knee and ankle. On the following day I was passed rearwards, mostly accompanied by Belgian civilians, and amongst refugees. I spent my second night in Brussels, mostly waiting on a bridge for transport. Eventually, a black Citroën turned up, driven by another Belgian, who saw me back as far as Lille. Squadron transport got me from Lille to Seclin. I carried my parachute with me throughout my return to Seclin.'

Sqn Ldr Dewar was at the head of six 87 Squadron Hurricanes patrolling over Brussels at 1500 when an estimated 60 Ju87s of Stabsstaffel and I/StG2 were seen dive-bombing the city. He ordered his Flight into the attack and is believed to have accounted for two of the dive-bombers himself, while others were claimed by Flg Off Harry Mitchell, Plt Off Dennis David (L1630), Plt Off Chris Mackworth and Sgt Gareth Nowell, whose aircraft was hit in the cooling system by the rear gunner. Mitchell reported:

> 'I was on patrol with five other aircraft when we spotted a great number of Ju87s dive-bombing over Brussels. We attacked them and I hit one which appeared to be put out of control and [to] go down in the forest south of Brussels.'

---

* Another pilot who encountered a Fieseler Störch, which he initially could only identify as a 'strange aircraft', reported: 'To my amazement the enemy aircraft appeared to stop and stand still in mid-air, forcing me to overshoot.'

On this occasion, the claims were remarkably accurate and StG2 lost six Ju87s shot down and one other damaged, in which the gunner was killed:

> Ju87B of Stab StG2 crashed south of Louvain: Oblt Arno Kädtler and gunner killed.
>
> Ju87B of 2/StG2 crashed near Tirlemont: Lt Siegfried Dryander killed and gunner PoW.
>
> Ju87B of 2/StG2 crash-landed: crew unhurt.
>
> Ju87B of 2/StG2 crashed near Tirlemont: crew unhurt and rescued by German troops.
>
> Ju87B of 2/StG2 crash-landed: one crew member wounded.
> Ju87B of 2/StG2 crash-landed: crew unhurt.

A trio of Do17Ms (also from Stabsstaffel StG2) was then sighted by the 87 Squadron pilots, one of which was claimed shot down by Plt Off David. Flg Off Mitchell shared another with his CO:

> 'Three Do17s escorted by Messerschmitt 109s appeared overhead. The 109s ran away and Sqn Ldr Dewar and I attacked one of the Dorniers. After chasing it across country on the deck we succeeded in shooting it down 15 miles north-east of Brussels.'

One Dornier, flown by Staffelkapitän Oblt Hans Metz, crashed near St Trond; one of the crew was killed and two taken prisoner. Meanwhile Sgt Nowell, his Hurricane streaming glycol, engaged one of the escorting Bf109s and claimed this shot down, but was then obliged to force-land when his engine seized.

61 Wing, Air Component
Further north, Hurricanes of 61 Wing carried out patrols during the morning. 615 Squadron operated uneventfully between Abbeville and Le Touquet. Meanwhile, 607 Squadron from Vitry failed to sight enemy aircraft until just after midday, when Yellow Section (Flg Off Bill Gore P3535 AF-C, Plt Off Trevor Jay P2571 AF-G and Plt Off Peter Parrott P2572 AF-B) encountered a He111H of 1/LG1 at 11,000 feet between Douai and Denain. Parrott (Yellow 3) recalled:

> 'We located and attacked a lone He111. We went into line astern, attacking the e/a from astern, breaking away to starboard, circling and going into a second attack. By the time I had finished my second attack, the e/a—which had been badly damaged from the first

attacks—was a mass of black smoke, with flames in the smoke, and was going down more and more steeply. Astonishingly, the gunner was still firing at us. At this juncture, Trevor Jay—having completed his second attack—flew up alongside and formated on the port side of the Heinkel. The gunner was still firing and fired at Jay, putting a bullet through his right knee. Seconds later one parachute appeared from the e/a and shortly after it crashed and exploded. Jay, to his credit, got his Hurricane back to base without further damage.'

An hour later Red Section (Flg Off Francis Blackadder P3448 AF-H, Plt Off Tony Dini P2536 AF-R and Plt Off Peter Dixon P2573 AF-A) and Blue Section (Flg Off Jim Bazin and Flg Off Monty Thompson) of 607 Squadron were in action, when another He111H of 1/LG1 was sighted at 4,000 feet 20 miles north-east of Brussels. Blackadder (Red 1):

'I was leading A Flight near Brussels. After a while a single aircraft was observed flying south-east some way off. We gave chase, found he was a Heinkel and after quite a battle shot him down in flames (the bomber fell onto a house which had been evacuated).'

Plt Off Dini (Red 3):

'E/a went into clouds. When emerging, I attacked from above and behind. Starboard engine exploded. Rear gunner fired short burst at beginning of the attack. E/a went down out of control and crashed—other Hurricanes attacked e/a unnecessarily.'

Flg Off Bazin (Blue 1):

'I attacked after one aircraft of Red Section. Starboard engine stopped after attack. Blue 2 attacked later with quarter attack (after several other aircraft had attacked). Flames seen coming from port wing root. E/a crashed and burst into flames.'

Flg Off Thompson (Blue 2):

'After one aircraft of Red Section and Blue 1 attacked, I carried out two attacks from astern and quarter. E/a appeared to be in difficulties before I attacked. As I broke away, e/a was seen to be on fire and exploded on crashing.'

Flg Off Blackadder continued:

'We circled round and I was just setting off back for the patrol line when Peter [Dixon], who had been flying on my right as No 2, called me up and talked of some more bandits. I did not receive the message but on looking round saw one machine setting off further east, so I followed. Soon I saw what he had seen, namely a score of black specks. We joined up and climbed up after them, and before we got near they had been joined by another large formation. Luckily two of the Heinkels [probably also from I/LG1] dropped slightly behind, so Peter and I each took one. That was the last I saw of him. I had seen a formation of single-seaters approaching and, imagining they were ours and having finished my ammunition, I pulled up towards them only to see the rude black crosses, so I hotly fled and eventually force-landed in a field (due to lack of fuel).'

Blackadder was able to find some petrol and managed to return to his airfield a few hours later. Meanwhile, Dixon continued chasing his victim in and out of clouds until his ammunition was exhausted; he finally left the bomber trailing black, oily smoke and then, with petrol dangerously low, he flew westwards. Through a gap in the clouds he sighted a town and dropped down to see if he could make out the name of the railway station, but was greeted by a hail of AA fire, so he climbed as quickly as he could (he ascertained later that the town was Aachen). With a fuel-starved engine coughing and spluttering, he looked for somewhere to land and saw a shell-cratered aerodrome, where he managed to land safely. Having taxied between shell craters to the other side of the aerodrome (near Tirlemont), he saw a main road along which a convoy of Belgian troops was passing. After some time a young officer approached and offered to take Dixon to his colonel. The Belgians apparently suspected he was a German because his French was considered too good for an Englishman! Having eventually established his identity, Dixon was allowed to return to his aircraft, still accompanied by the Belgian officer. However, while he was away the Luftwaffe had bombed the airfield and destroyed the Hurricane (P2573 AF-A). After a number of adventures, he eventually reached Brussels by road, from where he was transported back to Vitry.

During the course of another (or possibly the same) 607 Squadron patrol led by Flg Off Jim Bazin, a number of He111s were encountered, one of which Bazin reported shooting down. Sgt Ken Townsend claimed the probable destruction of two others. It would seem these were also part of the I/LG1 formation, as 1 Staffel reported the total loss of three aircraft during the operation north of Brussels, with a fourth aircraft damaged in which one crew member was killed:

He111H of 1/LG1 flown by Uffz Theodor Rothfuss crashed near Heist-op-den-Berg: crew killed.

He111H of 1/LG1 flown by Uffz Andreas Grünwald crashed north-east of Brussels: crew killed.

He111H of 1/LG1 flown by Uffz Kurt Fürstenberg crash-landed east of Brussels: two killed, one PoW of the French, one PoW of the British.

Meanwhile, Red and Blue Sections of 607 Squadron—four Hurricanes —departed Vitry at 1525 to escort three Battles of 88 Squadron to Maastricht; only one of the bombers returned. When patrolling over Maastricht at 1635, the Hurricanes were attacked by at least one of ten Ju87s of 8/StG2 seen bombing the village of Visé, south of Maastricht. The Hurricanes scattered and became separated in clouds, although Flt Lt George Plinston and Flg Off Dudley Craig of Blue Section jointly claimed their attacker shot down; Plinston reported:

'On patrol when attacked by a Ju87. Returned fire and e/a went into steep dive. No return fire from rear gunner.'

Flg Off Craig added:

'Three bursts and e/a seen to dive in deep spiral as if in trouble. Enemy formation broke up. No return fire but fairly heavy AA.'

The Ju87B, T6+MS flown by Oblt Karl Janke, crashed near Visé where the injured pilot was captured by French troops. Shortly after the skirmish with the dive-bomber, Plinston sighted some Hs123s of 5(S)/ LG2 bombing from 2,000 feet a village south-west of Arras:

'E/a were spotted bombing a village. I attacked one and got in four or five bursts after which it appeared to stall. AA fire was heavy so I turned and did not observe him strike.'

In fact the Henschel suffered 20% damage and managed to return to its base. At about the same time Flg Offs Bill Gore and Bunny Forster of Red Section engaged two Ju88s of 8/LG1 at 8,000 feet near Ath; Forster reported:

'Aircraft employed evasive tactics by turning and sideslipping. No 2 [Forster] attacked first. No 1 broke off attack due to gun failure. No 2 attacked second aircraft which disappeared in cloud.'

One of the two aircraft attacked by Forster suffered minor damage and the pilot, Fw Hans Peters, was wounded.

63 Wing, Air Component

Hurricanes of 63 Wing were also in action during the morning. From Merville, Yellow Section of 79 Squadron's A Flight engaged three He111Hs of Stabsstaffel KG1 at 0515, two miles north-west of Mons at 3-4,000 feet. Plt Off Lew Appleton (Yellow 2) reported:

'When flying on patrol in vicinity of La Louvière at 4,000 feet, three aircraft were sighted flying below us across our course. Leader [Flt Lt Edwards, L2068] ordered No 1 Attack. We were in a wide vic, the enemy in a vic. Leader opened fire on third aircraft and was under fire from all three until we came within range. I opened fire on No 2 e/a (starboard), drawing his fire from Yellow Leader. I made series of No 1 Attacks. After first attack black smoke trail appeared from port engine, also white smoke from fuselage or wing root. After second attack black smoke stopped. On approach for third attack, enemy lowered undercarriage and black smoke appeared from starboard engine. Final attack was made with e/a about 200 feet, attempting to land. E/a crashed into house and blew up on fire.'

His companion, Plt Off John Wood (Yellow 3) reported:

'On going into second attack on No 3, the enemy closed into the other two, so I closed up on the right of Yellow 1 and engaged enemy formation leader, while Yellow 1 engaged No 3. On breaking away downward, Yellow 1 burst into flames and was seen to dive almost vertically into a field, burning. On breaking away to the right, the e/a turned towards me, still firing. On continuing my turn I sighted No 2 and went to attack but Yellow 2 had already started the attack. The e/a began to lose height and ended by hitting the wall of a farmhouse and burst into flames (one hit on own aircraft behind cockpit).'

The Heinkel was V4+EA flown by Oblt Georg Schuster, and only one of the five crew members survived to be taken prisoner. Appleton continued:

'I last saw leader breaking away from his second attack, going into a vertical climb with sheets of flame from each side and later black smoke.'

Flt Lt Bob Edwards managed to bale out of his burning aircraft, having suffered severe burns to his arm, and returned to Merville next day. Meanwhile, Appleton was obliged to force-land his Hurricane (L2049) at Le Touquet, where it was damaged beyond repair.

3 Squadron continued to carry out patrols in the Lille area in the afternoon and early evening. During one of these patrols, at about 1730, Plt Off Frank Carey (L1932) intercepted and shot down a He111P of Stabsstaffel KG54. The pilot, Oblt Wilhelm Surborg, and two of his crew were captured by British troops; the other two crew members were killed in the crash.

Summary

AASF, Air Component and 11 Group Hurricane pilots claimed a total of 55 victories during the day—mainly He111s, Do17s and Bf110s—for the loss of 13 Hurricanes and five pilots (including one taken prisoner), a fair rate of success, but again the RAF bomber force had suffered considerably. However, there was an element of overclaiming against the Bf110s, 18 having been claimed for four actual losses! Although one RAF pilot commented: 'I don't recall seeing a French fighter in the air once the fighting started', Armée de l'Air fighters were active in the area covered by the AASF and Air Component during the day, and claimed ten He111s, three Do17s and two Bf109s.

Claims by AASF, Air Component and 11 Group Hurricanes, 11 May				
Type	Confirmed	Probable	Damaged	Total
He111	13	2	1	16
Do17	9	1	1	11
Ju88	1	—	2	3
Ju87	7	—	—	7
Hs123	1	—	—	1
Hs126	2	—	—	2
Bf109	4	1	—	5
Bf110	18	1	2	21
	55	5	6	66

Luftwaffe Losses Attributed to AASF, Air Component and 11 Group Hurricanes, 11 May			
Type	60% to 100%	Under 60%	Total
He111	9	1	10
Do17	5	2	7
Ju88	—	1	1
Ju87	7	1	8
Hs123	—	1	1
Hs126	1	—	1
Bf109	2	—	2
Bf110	4	—	4
	28	6	34

That night (11/12 May) 36 Whitley and Hampden bombers took off from their UK bases to bomb road and rail communications in the vicinity of München-Gladbach. Of the 18 Hampdens, three returned early because of mechanical problems. Two Whitleys and two Hampdens were lost. One of the missing Whitley pilots was the brother of 607 Squadron's Plt Off Peter Parrott.

Individual Claims—AASF and Air Component Hurricanes, 11 May

Time	Pilot	Squadron	Claim
0515-	Plt Off L.L. Appleton Plt Off J.E.R. Wood	79 Sqn	He111
0530-	Flg Off N. Orton	73 Sqn	Do17
0800-	Flg Off P.H.M. Richey	1 Sqn	Do17 probable
0930-	Sqn Ldr J.W.C. More Plt Off V.D.M. Roe	73 Sqn	Do17 damaged
AM-	Flt Lt E.S. Williams	501 Sqn	Do17
	Sgt R.C Dafforn	501 Sqn	Do17
AM-	Flt Lt R.H.A. Lee Flg Off D.H. Allen Plt Off P.P. Woods-Scawen	85 Sqn	Do17
	Flt Lt R.H.A. Lee	85 Sqn	Do17
Midday-	Flg Off W.E. Gore Plt Off T.D. Jay Plt Off P.L. Parrott	607 Sqn	He111
1300-	Plt Off A.S. Dini Flg Off J.M. Bazin Flg Off M.H.B. Thompson Flg Off W.F. Blackadder Plt Off H.P. Dixon	607 Sqn	He111
	Flg Off W.F. Blackadder	607 Sqn	He111
	Plt Off H.P. Dixon	607 Sqn	He111
	Flg Off J.M. Bazin	607 Sqn	He111
	Sgt K.N.V. Townsend	607 Sqn	2 He111 probable
c.1300-	Flg Off D.H. Allen Plt Off J.A. Hemingway Plt Off P.P. Woods-Scawen	85 Sqn	Do17
1435-	Flg Off E.J. Kain	73 Sqn	Do17, Bf110 probable
	Flt Lt J.E. Scoular	73 Sqn	Ju88
	Flg Off H.G. Paul	73 Sqn	Bf110
	Flg Off N. Orton	73 Sqn	Bf110
	Sgt L.S. Pilkington	73 Sqn	Bf110
	Sgt L.J. Humphries	73 Sqn	He111 damaged
	Sgt T.B.G. Pyne	73 Sqn	Bf110 damaged
	Plt Off H.W. Eliot	73 Sqn	Bf110 damaged
1440-	Flg Off C.E. Malfroy	501 Sqn	He111
	Flt Sgt A.D. Payne	501 Sqn	He111
	Plt Off C.S. Hulse	501 Sqn	Bf110
	Sgt P.F. Morfill	501 Sqn	Bf110
1445-	Flt Lt P.P. Hanks Flg Off L.R. Clisby	1 Sqn	Bf110

	Flt Lt P.P. Hanks		
	Flg Off P.W.O. Mould	1 Sqn	Bf110
	Flg Off L.R. Clisby		
	Flg Off L.R. Clisby	1 Sqn	Bf110
	Plt Off C.M. Stavert		
1500-	Flg Off H.T. Mitchell	87 Sqn	Ju87
	Sqn Ldr J.S. Dewar	87 Sqn	2 Ju87
	Plt Off W.D. David	87 Sqn	Do17, Ju87
	Plt Off C.C.D. Mackworth	87 Sqn	Ju87
	Sgt G.L. Nowell	87 Sqn	Ju87, Bf109
	Sqn Ldr J.S. Dewar	87 Sqn	Do17
	Flg Off H.T. Mitchell		
1525-	Flg Off G.D. Craig	607 Sqn	Ju87
	Flg Off G.H.F. Plinston		
	Flg Off G.H.F. Plinston	607 Sqn	Hs123
	Flg Off A.D. Forster	607 Sqn	2 Ju88 damaged
1915-	Flg Off M.H. Brown	1 Sqn	2 Bf110
	Flg Off J.I. Kilmartin	1 Sqn	2 Bf110
	Flg Off P.H.M. Richey	1 Sqn	2 Bf110
	Sgt F.J. Soper	1 Sqn	2 Bf110
	Flt Lt P.R. Walker	1 Sqn	2 Bf110
?	Sgt G. Allard	85 Sqn	2 He111s
	Sqn Ldr J.O.W. Oliver	85 Sqn	2 He111s
PM-	Plt Off F.R. Carey	3 Sqn	He111

Individual Claims—11 Group Hurricanes, 11 May

1630-	Sqn Ldr G.C. Tomlinson	17 Sqn	Bf109
	Flg Off R.V. Meredith	17 Sqn	Bf109
	Sgt C.W.J. Pavey	17 Sqn	Bf109
	Flt Lt J. Jeffries	17 Sqn	Hs126
	Sgt N.R. Wynn	17 Sqn	Hs126
	Plt Off R.C. Whittaker	17 Sqn	Bf109 probable

Losses—AASF and Air Component Hurricanes, 11 May

0515-	L2068	79 Sqn	Flt Lt R.S. Edwards: shot down by return fire from He111H of Stabsstaffel KG1; pilot baled out, burned.
	L2049	79 Sqn	Plt Off L.L. Appleton: aircraft damaged by return fire from He111H of Stabsstaffel KG1 and force-landed at Le Touquet; pilot unhurt.
0800-	L1679	1 Sqn	Flg Off P.H.M. Richey: aircraft damaged by return fire from Do17P of 3(F)/10 and force-landed at Mézières; pilot unhurt, returned.
AM-	N2388	85 Sqn	Flt Lt R.H.A. Lee: aircraft damaged by Flak and force-landed west of Maastricht; pilot unhurt, captured, escaped.
1200-	P2571	607 Sqn	Plt Off T.D. Jay: aircraft damaged by return fire from He111H of I/LG1; pilot wounded.
1300-	P2573	607 Sqn	Plt Off H.P. Dixon: force-landed near Tirlemont out of fuel; pilot unhurt, returned.
c.1300-	L1979	85 Sqn	Plt Off J.A. Hemingway: aircraft hit by Flak and force-landed; pilot unhurt, returned.

1435-	P2811	73 Sqn	Plt Off A. McFadden: shot down by Bf110C of I/ZG2 and force-landed near Poilcourt; pilot unhurt.
1500-		87 Sqn	Sgt G.L. Nowell: aircraft damaged by return fire from Ju87 of 2/StG2 and force-landed; pilot unhurt, returned.
1915-	L1685	1 Sqn	Flg Off P.H.M. Richey: shot down near Romilly by Bf110C of I/ZG26; pilot baled out unhurt, returned.

Losses—11 Group Hurricanes, 11 May

1550-	N2547	17 Sqn	Sqn Ldr G.C. Tomlinson: aircraft damaged by Bf109 of I/JG51 and force-landed at Knokke; pilot unhurt, returned.
	N2403	17 Sqn	Flt Lt M.S. Donne: shot down south-west of Rotterdam by Bf109 of I/JG51; pilot killed.
	N2405	17 Sqn	Plt Off G.W. Slee: shot down south of Dordrecht by Bf109 of I/JG51; pilot killed.
	N2407	17 Sqn	Plt Off C.P.L. Hulton-Harrop: shot down south-west of Dordrecht by Bf109 of I/JG51; pilot PoW.
	P2758	17 Sqn	Sgt J.A.A. Luck: shot down near Dordrecht by Bf109 of I/JG51; pilot PoW.

CHAPTER IV

SUNDAY 12 MAY
SLAUGHTER OF THE BATTLES

'My first kill was child's play. An excellent weapon and luck had been on my side. To be successful, the best fighter pilot needs both.'

Hptm Adolf Galland, Stab/JG27.

The Situation in Holland

The Germans landed further airborne forces in The Hague-Rotterdam area, the Dutch having failed to contain the situation there, although resistance continued to the north and south of the Waal.

The crew of the Nederlandse Militaire Luchtvaart's sole surviving Fokker TV was ordered to bomb German forces near Lake Ijssel and was given an escort of one DXXI but, on approaching Enkhuizen, a dozen Bf109s were encountered, forcing both Dutch aircraft to abort the mission and return to Schiphol at ground level, using available cloud cover. During the day a reconnaissance Do17 was claimed shot down by a DXXI west of Amsterdam. Pilots of II/JG27 reported shooting down two Fokker CX biplane bombers, but three Bf109s of 6(J)/TrGr186 were lost in the Den Helder-Texel area and the pilot of one was taken prisoner. The Dutch also lost two Fokker DXVII seaplanes to enemy action, and two others in accidents.

The RAF's 11 Group continued to fly patrols in support of the Dutch and in protection of naval operations off the coast of Holland. At 0510, three Hurricanes of 151 Squadron's Blue Section—piloted by Flt Lt Freddie Ives (P3319), Flg Off Derek Ward (L1747) and Sgt George Atkinson (L1654)—flew from RAF North Weald to RAF Martlesham Heath, from where an offensive patrol off The Hook was flown. En route they encountered three Blenheim IVs and patrolled with these over a cruiser, four destroyers and a patrol vessel. The Hurricane pilots noticed about 50 parachutes on the ground some three miles north of The Hook and, on a small aerodrome to the south-west, approximately

15 burnt-out Ju52s. However no enemy aircraft were sighted in the air and the section landed back at RAF Martlesham Heath at 0710.

On the next patrol by six Defiants of 264 Squadron and six Spitfires of 66 Squadron (flying in pairs), a Ju88 of 7/LG1 was encountered bombing a destroyer off the coast of Ijmuiden. It was chased inland by two of the Defiants and the Spitfires and claimed shot down, although it escaped with slight damage and one crew member wounded.

Blenheims of the Air Component continued to fly strategical reconnaissances over southern Holland, while three Blenheim IFs of 235 Squadron were dispatched from RAF Bircham Newton, at 0800, to escort a naval vessel off Texel, where a lone He111H of 2/LG1 was seen. This was attacked and slightly damaged, with one member of the crew being fatally wounded. Later, another patrol of three Blenheims was sent to cover a force of Royal Marines disembarking from destroyers at The Hague, but were attacked by eight Bf109s and two were shot down. The crew of the surviving machine claimed one of the attackers and reported seeing a second on the ground in flames, which they believed had been shot down by one of the missing crews. A later patrol by three Coastal Command Blenheims of 254 Squadron, briefed to protect an ammunition ship at Flushing, encountered some 20 Ju88s, Bf110s and He111s attacking the vessel and the jetty. The Blenheims engaged but were unable to report any definite successes.

By the end of the day the French 7th Armée had advanced to a line Breda-Turnhout, but was soon to retire again.

Air Operations over Belgium and Northern France

The rapidly advancing German Army had captured two vital bridges spanning the Maas at Maastricht, which allowed two Panzer divisions easy access from Holland into Belgium. Meanwhile, the Allied armies attempted to secure a defensive line encompassing the Dijle-Gembloux-Namur area, where they were to be supported by elements of the RAF and Armée de l'Air. It was considered vital by the Allies that the Vroenhoven and Veldwezelt bridges over the Albert Canal, three miles south-west of Maastricht, should be denied to the Germans and these were targeted for air attack. It was believed that by destroying the bridges the German advance would be slowed down.

Air Operations over Maastricht

Therefore, at first light three Battles from 103 Squadron were dispatched to attack columns west of Maastricht, which were advancing into Belgium, while a heavier assault was launched by nine Blenheims of 139 Squadron from Plivot, but these ran into Bf109s from Stab I/JG1,

2/JG1 and 3/JG27. Seven of the unescorted bombers were shot down, of which two were seen to fall in flames.

Six volunteer crews from the RAF's 12 Squadron at Amifontaine, also equipped with Battles, were briefed to attack the bridges during the morning, while Hurricanes of 1 Squadron were to provide cover over the target area. Thus, from Berry-au-Bac at 0820, eight Hurricanes led by Sqn Ldr Halahan (whose father had been the first commander of 12 Squadron when it was formed in 1914) set off to carry out a sweep of the target area in advance of the Battles, only five of which were able to take to the air, the sixth having developed a fault. However, by the time they reached Maastricht the Hurricanes were already engaged in combat.

As the Hurricanes approached Maastricht at 0915, five Bf109s were sighted by Sgt Frank Soper at 10,000 feet and two others by Flg Off Iggy Kilmartin, who identified them as He112s*. There were in fact 16 Bf109s of 2/JG27 in the area. An official report of the subsequent action revealed:

'The Hurricanes (except Kilmartin) engaged five of the Messerschmitt 109s. Flg Off Brown's aircraft was hit twice and dived into cloud and he made his way back to base. Flg Off Clisby saw a 109 crash after it had been attacked by Soper, then attacked another and saw it crash. Flg Off Lorimer and Soper attacked a 109 which dived to ground level and was last seen with smoke coming out. Plt Off Boot attacked two 109s and fired a long burst at one, but was then attacked by other and had his starboard wing damaged. Meanwhile, Kilmartin attacked two He112s [sic] as they dived on the Hurricanes—he fired at one and saw it roll and dive vertically through the clouds. Then attacked by two 109s and remaining He112, he did a few steep turns and fired a burst at the He112, but no damage noticed. Plt Off Lewis (L1688) was shot down in flames and was seen to bale out by Clisby and Soper.'

Sqn Ldr Halahan (L1671) reported:

'Fired short burst at a 109 which went down. Climbed and saw two large formations above—individual 109s from these formations dived singly on Hurricanes from the sun. In following one of these down, I was shot through the oil tank and on breaking cloud found one or two Henschels in sights. Fired few rounds and the Henschel disappeared—steered north-west and landed.'

---

* Despite repeated sightings of and claims against the He112 by RAF pilots, this type did not see service with the Luftwaffe, although for propaganda purposes photographs did appear in the aviation press during the Munich crisis of 1938, depicting the type in service with III/JG132; these aircraft were, in fact, a small batch of He112s destined for Japan.

Sqn Ldr Halahan was credited with shooting down the Bf109 and the possible destruction of the Hs126. Sgt Soper was also credited with a Bf109 and a second probably destroyed with Flg Off Lorimer; the former was obliged to force-land L1686 on returning to Berry-au-Bac. Flg Off Clisby was credited with a Bf109 destroyed while Flg Off Kilmartin was granted a He112 probable and Plt Off Peter Boot a Bf109 damaged. On the way back to base, Clisby emerged from cloud at 3,000 feet and encountered seven 'Arado biplanes' which he attacked immediately and claimed two shot down. On his return to base, Brown—whose aircraft had been hit by two cannon shells—reported having seen two Bf109s collide as he engaged them, although there is no evidence to support this incident.

As the Battles attempted to battle their way through to the target, two were shot down by Bf109s, one falling to a pilot of 2/JG27. One of the air gunners reported shooting down at least one of his attackers before he was forced to bale out of his burning aircraft.

Two of the remaining three Battles were promptly shot down by intense ground fire in the vicinity of the bridges, while the other badly damaged machine crash-landed on its way home. Of the four Hurricane pilots who remained to witness the Battles' plight, one was Clisby, who later told war correspondent Noel Monks:

'It gave me goose-pimples watching the bombers dive right down the muzzles of a hundred anti-aircraft guns.'

Of the 15 crew members who took part in the suicidal attack, six were killed and seven captured; both the leader, Flg Off Donald Garland, and his observer, Sgt Tom Gray, were awarded the Victoria Cross posthumously, although their gunner, LAC Lawrence Reynolds, received no recognition.

Pilots of 2/JG27 claimed four Hurricanes shot down during the morning's action, the first at 0915 by Lt Hans-Wedig von Weiher; two more were claimed five minutes later by Fw Erich Schröder (near Glons) and Gfr Emil Kaiser (near Tongeren), followed by another at 0935 by Oblt Gert Framm, who caught his victim about 15 miles west of Maastricht. One Bf109 was lost when Lt Friedrich Keller force-landed near Aachen, his aircraft 45% damaged.

When 1 Squadron's commander, Sqn Ldr Halahan, was returned to Berry-au-Bac by the Belgian Army having abandoned his damaged aircraft, he reported that his party had encountered a force-landed Heinkel at the side of the road. On questioning nearby French Senegalese troops, he was informed that the crew had been dragged clear of the wreck and killed. Meanwhile, the Squadron's other missing pilot, Plt Off Raymond Lewis, a Canadian from Saskatoon, had been captured but released again when the Belgians counter-attacked. Flg Off Paul Richey, who had not been flying, was sent to collect him from Maubeuge near the Belgian frontier. Lewis claimed that he had shot down a Bf109 and probably a second before he himself fell victim to a third.

Meanwhile, from RAF Wattisham two dozen Blenheims of the RAF's 2 Group had set out at first light to attack the bridges. The Blenheims, in four formations of six aircraft, were drawn equally from 15 and 107 Squadrons. On arrival over the coast they were to rendezvous with Hurricanes from both 85 and 87 Squadrons. Although the Hurricanes attempted to carry out their task, they were soon embroiled in a series of combats with a variety of German aircraft. One Flight of 85 Squadron engaged a formation of He111Ps (aircraft from KG54), two of which were claimed shot down by Sgt Sammy Allard (N2319) and one each by Sqn Ldr Oliver (VY-A) and Plt Off Lew Lewis (in VY-E); Oliver also reported shooting down a Do17. Another pilot claimed a Ju88 and Lewis reported shooting down a Bf109 over the target area. The 87 Squadron formation encountered Ju87s of 7/StG2 near Maastricht, two being claimed by Sqn Ldr Dewar and Flg Off Harry Mitchell (one only was lost and this crash-landed with both crew members slightly injured), while Plt Off Dennis David (L1870) and Flg Off Dick Glyde each reported shooting down He111s, probably part of the formation engaged by 85 Squadron.

Despite the multitude of claims, only one He111 failed to return, a Stabsstaffel machine flown by Lt Horst von Gundelach, which crashed near Tielt. The pilot and two of his crew were wounded and were taken to hospital; the other crew member was handed over to the British. A Ju88, 7A+CH of 1(F)/121, was also lost in the area and its pilot, Fw Kurt Denner, was killed, although the other members of the crew survived to be taken prisoner.

Two Hurricanes of 87 Squadron were shot down by the defending Bf109s, including that flown by Flg Off Jack Campbell. Two members of his section—Glyde and Cock—reported that they had managed to evade the attack from astern and had seen Campbell's aircraft (L1970) shot down; the Canadian from British Columbia was killed. Also shot down by the Bf109s was Sgt Frank Howell (L1632), who recalled later:

'They came from the sun with altitude advantage and I never saw them. Suddenly there was a shattering noise and the cockpit was full of burnt cordite.'

After a struggle Howell was able to bale out, but his parachute failed to open properly and he was rendered unconscious on hitting the ground. As he came to, he realised his parachute was dragging him across a field, although some peasant women were trying to release the harness. He was taken to Brussels for treatment where it was found that his injuries were mainly superficial—severe bruising and abrasions to the face and hands. Of the incident, Plt Off Chris Darwin noted later in his diary:

'Howell came back and gave us his story. An amazing escape by parachute. How he got out alive God only knows! His starboard wing was shot off by an Me109 and his aircraft went into a steep dive. He managed to bale out but his umbrella only half opened. He landed very heavily on his back. He is in hospital with a strained back.' *

It seems probable that the two 87 Squadron Hurricanes fell to pilots of Stab/JG27. One section, led by Hptm Adolf Galland, the Gruppe's operations staff officer, sighted a flight of eight Hurricanes about five miles west of Liège. Galland believed these to have been Belgian Hurricanes, but they had already been destroyed in the first two days of the invasion; of his first combat, Galland wrote:

'The Hurricanes had not yet spotted us. I was not excited nor did I feel any hunting fever. "Come on! Defend yourself!" I thought as soon as I had one of the eight in my gunsight. I closed in more and more without being noticed, thinking "Someone ought to warn him!" But that would have been even more stupid than the strange thoughts which ran through my head at that moment. I gave him my first burst from a range which, considering the situation, was still too great. I was dead on the target, and at last the poor devil noticed what was happening. He rather clumsily avoided action, which brought him into the fire of my companion. The other seven Hurricanes made no effort to come to the aid of their comrade in distress, but made off in all directions. After a second attack my opponent spun down in spirals, minus his rudder and with part of the wings flying off. A further burst would have been a waste of ammunition, so I immediately went after another of the scattered Hurricanes. This one tried to escape by diving, but I was soon on her tail at a distance of 100 yards. The Belgian [sic] did a half-roll and disappeared through a hole in the clouds. I did not lose track of him and attacked again from very close quarters. The plane zoomed for a second, stalled and dived vertically into the ground from a height of only 1,500 feet.'

A third Hurricane was credited to Galland's wingman, Lt Gustav

---

* Sgt Howell was transferred from Brussels to Ghent to recuperate, but two days later decided to try to get back to the Squadron, reaching Lille on 18 May.

Rödel, although it would seem in fact that he shared with Galland in shooting one down.

Despite the efforts of the Hurricane pilots, they had been unable to prevent the Blenheims from coming under attack. One machine from 107 Squadron had already been shot down by Flak, and a second badly damaged, before the target was reached. The defending fighters then pounced, a pilot of 2/JG27 shooting down two more. 15 Squadron fared no better, losing half its number to Flak, while all the remaining bombers suffered battle damage.

85 Squadron welcomed the return of Flt Lt Dickie Lee, who had been shot down the day before. The Squadron's diarist wrote:

> 'He had been shot down and had to bale out—he was only slightly wounded. He descended by parachute in or near a village in Belgium which was in the process of being re-occupied by German mechanized forces. He borrowed a peasant's smock and walked through the German lines and reported all he had seen to the first English unit he met; the information proved to be of the greatest value.'

It had been a disastrous morning for the RAF with the loss of six Battles, 19 Blenheims and five Hurricanes with no tangible results: the bridges at Vroenhoven and Veldwezelt remained intact and consequently the German advance had not been slowed. The French fared no better. Eighteen Bréguet 693s of GBA I/54 and II/54, escorted by a similar number of MS406s of GCIII/3, attacked columns in the Hasselt-St Trond-Liège-Maastricht area. Eight of the bombers were shot down, including that flown by the commander of GBA I/54.

67 Wing AASF
With 1 Squadron involved in the bomber support role over Maastricht, the brunt of the aerial combat in the AASF area fell to the pilots of 501 Squadron at Bétheniville, who were involved in constant action throughout the day. The entire KG53 flew a mass attack against Mourmelon airfield, south-east of Reims: the Heinkels of I Gruppe, escorted by Bf110Cs of I/ZG2, rendezvoused with Stab II and III Gruppen over Trier, these units already escorted by Bf110Cs of I/ZG52. East of Reims, I Gruppe was attacked by Hawk-75s of GCII/5 and lost three aircraft, while those of II Gruppe, a little further north, passed close to Bétheniville. On sighting the raiders, several of 501 Squadron's pilots scrambled to intercept, and four of the bombers were subsequently claimed by Flt Lt Gus Holden, Flg Off Peter Rayner, Plt Off John Sylvester and Flt Sgt Jammy Payne; Holden reported seeing his victim force-land near the Luxembourg border and that he

waved to the crew as they scrambled clear of the wreck. It would seem that this was an aircraft of 4 Staffel which force-landed near Birkenfeld, south-west of Idar-Oberstein; two of its crew were wounded.

A second aircraft from the same Staffel, flown by Oblt Karl Knorr, crashed west of Monthois; there was only one survivor and he was taken prisoner by French troops. Flg Off Peter Rayner's aircraft (L2054 SD-E) was believed to have been hit by return fire and crashed near Seuil, about five miles south-east of Rethel, killing the pilot, although he had been seen to shoot down a bomber first. However, the crew of an escorting Bf110C claimed a Hurricane shot down during the mission and it seems probable Rayner was their victim.

Noel Monks, the war correspondent, wrote:

> 'On the third day of the blitzkrieg, I was watching from my window 40 Heinkels and Dorniers pass overhead when I saw a lone Hurricane nosing into the sky after them. They were flying at about 5,000 feet, doubtless feeling secure in the knowledge that the few Hurricanes in the neighbourhood were badly needed for escort duty with our bombers. But soon this lone Hurricane was among them, and through my glasses I saw the Jerries break up their formations and scatter as though some great unseen power had jostled them. He [the Hurricane pilot] appeared to be playing leap-frog over them, diving under one, and up over on top of another, firing as he went. He was having the time of his life.'

Having rearmed and refuelled, Flg Off Holden took off in pursuit of a Do17Z seen over the airfield, the crew of which were apparently taking photographs. After climbing to 7,000 feet he intercepted the reconnaissance aircraft but, on closing in from astern, his Hurricane was hit by return fire. Despite the damage, Holden continued his attack 'sending bits off in all directions'. One engine started to pour volumes of smoke as he broke away. The Dornier was probably an aircraft of Stabsstaffel/KG3, the crew of which reported being attacked by a Hurricane west of Reims. The aircraft force-landed with a wounded crew member on board. Meanwhile, with a spluttering engine, Holden looked desperately for somewhere to force-land L2050 and was fortunate to find a large field, where a creditable wheels-up landing was achieved.

In the afternoon the main operational area for the Luftwaffe was Charleville-Mézières-Rethel, Fliegerkorps II's task being to support the thrust made by the Panzers of the German 12th Armee. Do17Zs of III/KG2 concentrated on Allied troop convoys south of Charleville-Signy-l'Abbaye; Do17Zs of I and II/KG3 operated in the Vouziers sector, while I/KG53 visited the Sedan area and He111Hs of II/KG55 were in action near Rethel. Escort to the various formations was provided by Bf110Cs of V(Z)/LG1 and I/ZG2. To the relief of the fatigued Hurricane pilots, French fighters put in an appearance when Moranes and Hawks from GCI/5, GCII/2 and GCIII/7 supported Hurricanes from 501 Squadron in combating the hordes of German bombers. However, it would seem that GCII/2 and GCIII/7 engaged the same formation of II/KG3 Dorniers as 501 Squadron. Two of the bombers were shot down, a third force-landed and two others suffered minor damage:

Stab II/KG3 Do17Z flown by Lt Rudolf Steingraber crashed: three killed, one PoW of the French.

5/KG3 Do17Z flown by Fw Wilhelm Brinkmann crashed near Reims: one killed, three PoW of the French.

4/KG3 Do17Z flown by Oblt Richard Martin crash-landed near Arzfeld, north-west of Bitburg: one wounded.

Stab II/KG3 Do17Z 5% damaged in combat near Poix: Gruppen-kommandeur Obst Albrecht Jahn wounded.

4/KG3 Do17Z 5% damaged in combat near Charleville: two wounded.

One Dornier was claimed by GCII/2 and two by GCIII/7. 501 Squadron also claimed two when a formation of the bombers was encountered by a section of Hurricanes 30 miles north-east of Bétheniville. One was claimed shot down by Sgt John Proctor, who also reported a successful engagement with one of the escorting Bf110Cs of I/ZG2. Another section of four Hurricanes, led by Flg Off Cam Malfroy, encountered four of the Do17s south of Sedan, but only Plt Off Kenneth Lee saw them in time to carry out an attack:

'I was ordered to fly rear cover (arse-end Charlie) and I observed bomb bursts below and then spotted four Dornier 17s flying 4,000 feet below. I flew up in front of the section and waggled my wings, pointing down (full radio silence was being maintained so as not to advertise our presence in France). I peeled off towards the enemy and followed the classic procedure: tighten straps, switch on gun button, lower seat, set sight with wingspan of target and range 300 yards. Whilst this was going on, the Dorniers assumed vic, with one in the box. I turned in towards them, looking confidently over my shoulders for my supporting friends, assuming a similar formation on me as practiced *ad infinitum* for No 2 Fighter Attack—but no one there!! I was committed and went on alone, with one Dornier down (as confirmed by French artillery) and one damaged—and 37 strikes on my own aircraft.'

While this engagement was taking place, Bf110Cs from I/ZG2 attacked the remainder of Malfroy's section and Flg Off Michael Smith (L2053) was shot down and killed when his aircraft crashed near Artaise-le-Vivier, about ten miles north of Sedan. Malfroy's aircraft (L1914) was also hit and was force-landed at Mourmelon. Plt Off Lee remarked:

> 'The survivors afterwards said they thought I was going back with engine trouble. I don't know why!'

Later, about ten miles south-west of St Hubert, three He111Ps of II/KG55 were intercepted by another 501 Squadron patrol, resulting in all three being claimed shot down by Sgts Paul Farnes (L2045 SD-A), Donald McKay and Peter Morfill, taking the Squadron's tally for the day to a round dozen. In fact, only one of the bombers crashed, although a second returned to base in a damaged condition:

> He111P of 4/KG55 flown by Lt Hans Junk shot down near Rethel: four killed, one PoW of the French.

> He111P of 5/KG55 30% damaged in combat near Rethel: one wounded.

73 Squadron at Reims-Champagne had a quieter day, having been stood down until 1300 to allow the pilots some rest. The only success was achieved during a patrol between 1645 and 1745, when Flg Off Cobber Kain encountered a Hs126 of 3(H)/21, spotting for the 12th Armee near Bouillon, which he promptly shot down; one member of the crew was killed. Sqn Ldr More returned from an afternoon patrol with a bad cut over his left eye, caused by a piece of shrapnel. He had the injury dressed and carried on with his duties as if nothing had happened. One of his senior pilots, Flg Off Ginger Paul, confided to one of the war correspondents that:

> 'Sqn Ldr More had fought like a demon for three days, until he could hardly stand.'

61 Wing, Air Component
A Flight of 615 Squadron was ordered to fly to Vitry, where it was to reinforce 607 Squadron; a section of the latter unit's Hurricanes was already up on dawn patrol by the time they arrived from Merville. Flg Off Bill Gore's section encountered a flight of three He111Hs from 4/LG1 at about 0500 and all three of the raiders were claimed shot down by Gore and his two Canadian companions—Flg Off Bob Weatherill (P2536 AF-R) and Plt Off Gordon Stewart (P2571 AF-G)—although

Gore's aircraft (P2572 AF-B) was hit by return fire and burst into flames. He was subsequently awarded a DFC for this action, the citation stating:

> 'Whilst leading his section on dawn patrol, he met three He111s. Due to his good leadership, a determined attack was delivered with the result that all three were shot down. Gore's aircraft burst into flames immediately after the attack but in spite of this he escaped successfully by parachute.'

Gore suffered burns, shock and bruising and, when recovered by Allied troops, was taken to a Field Service Hospital before being transferred back to England five days later. As a result of his combat, Weatherill's windscreen was covered in oil which forced him to land at the nearest airfield (Lille), thus only Stewart returned initially to Vitry to report the outcome of the engagement. Records show that 4/LG1 indeed lost three He111s in the Lille area, although it is believed that one of these was the victim of Plt Off John Cock (P3881) of 87 Squadron, who reported that he chased it through cloud before it crashed near Armentières. He was to learn later that its bomb load exploded after 35 minutes on the ground, killing three dozen bystanders.

> He111H of 4/LG1 flown by Staffelkapitän Oblt Kurt Söhler crashed north-west of Lille: three killed, one PoW of the British (possibly Cock's victim).
>
> He111H of 4/LG1 flown by Lt Wilhelm Fleckenstein crashed near Lille: two killed, two PoW of the British.
>
> He111H of 4/LG1 flown by Fw Erich Wolter crashed south-west of Lille: three PoW of the British, one PoW of the French.

Plt Off Peter Parrott had been allocated dawn patrol duty, but was the recipient of bad news, as he recalled:

> 'While waiting for transport to go up to the airfield, I was handed a signal from the Air Ministry advising me that my brother—who was a Whitley pilot—was posted missing. Stood down.'

However, eager to continue the fight, Parrott volunteered to carry out a test flight in Hurricane P2536 AF-R at 0845, once it had been serviced and cleaned, rearmed and refuelled following its earlier combat.

At about 0930, Flg Off Francis Blackadder (P3535 AF-C) set off at the head of two Hurricanes of A Flight, three from B Flight, and a section from 615 Squadron for a sector patrol. Just before 1000 they encountered a Staffel of Bf109s from I(J)/LG2. Blackadder—unable initially to shake off his attackers—did not get back to Vitry until an hour later, and was feared to have been shot down. Only two of the 615 Squadron section returned to Vitry. Flg Off Lewin Fredman was last seen chasing a section of Messerschmitts in the direction of Germany and was assumed to have been shot down by others. His Hurricane (P2564) crashed at Wihogne near Liège, from where his body was recovered from the wreck and buried in the nearby cemetery. During this engagement Flg Off Hedley 'Bill' Fowler (P2622) claimed a Bf109 shot down. The Messerschmitt pilots, who had been escorting He111s, reported meeting a squadron of Hurricanes near Tongeren, and claimed three shot down. Lt Helmut Mertens of 2 Staffel claimed one, while 1 Staffel's Oblt Hans-Erwin Jäger and Ofw Hermann Guhl were credited with the other two; one Messerschmitt of 2 Staffel crash-landed with 70% damage west of Tongeren (presumably Fowler's victim), although the pilot was reported later to be safe.

63 Wing, Air Component
Having put up a dawn patrol over Lille without sighting any enemy aircraft, 3 Squadron dispatched six Hurricanes of B Flight at 0725 to patrol between Diest and Louvain. Flg Off Walter Bowyer (N2339) led Blue Section—Sgt Ernie Ford (L1846/B) and Sgt Jimmy Sims (L1681) —while Green Section's Plt Offs Mike Stephens (L1610) and Frank Carey (L1932) were led by Flt Lt Carter. Stephens recalled:

> 'Suddenly we spotted about 60 tiny black dots in the sky, flying west like a storm of midges. The next moment we were among them— Stukas [of I/StG2] with an escort of about 20 Messerschmitt 109s. I got one [Ju87] lined up in my gunsight and opened fire from about 50 yards. After a short burst he blew up in an orange ball of flame, followed by a terrifying clatter as my Hurricane flew through the debris. Just then, from out of the cloud a few hundred yards away, emerged a Dornier 17. I gave him a short burst from short range, hitting his starboard engine which started smoking. I had the satisfaction of seeing the pilot belly-land the aircraft in a ploughed field.'

Stephens claimed a second Ju87 and Carey two more, one of which was unconfirmed. Carey then encountered a He111 and reported shooting this down also, although this may have been the same aircraft as that attacked by Stephens—probably a Do17Z of 8/KG77 flown by Lt Konrad Hengsbach which crash-landed with four of its crew wounded. Meantime, Blue Section's pilots claimed a further four of the Ju87s shot down—two each by Bowyer and Sims—and a fifth probably destroyed by Ford. Owing to lack of fuel Stephens landed at Grevillers, an airfield under construction, otherwise all Hurricanes returned safely to Lille/ Marcq, the escorting Messerschmitts having not interfered. Despite the multitude of claims, it seems that only two Ju87s of I/StG2 were lost, one of which crashed east of Louvain and the other crash-landed near Hasselt, with a wounded gunner.

At 1010 it was the turn of six Hurricanes of 3 Squadron's A Flight, the aircraft patrolling the Diest-St Trond area. At about 1100, two aircraft were seen below at low level and the Hurricanes dropped down to investigate; the aircraft were recognized as Hs126s, one of which Red Section—Flt Lt Walter Churchill (P3318), Flg Off Bunny Stone (N2351) and Sgt Roy Wilkinson (N2653)—attacked. The Henschel, from 1(H)/23, which had been spotting for the 6th Armee, crashed near Diest, killing both Uffz Wolfgang Ulbrich and his observer, Fw Johannes von Kienlin. Meantime, Yellow Section—Flg Off Wilfred Adams (N2654), Plt Off Noel Hallifax (L1899) and Sgt Basil Friendship (L1591)—pursued the other Henschel, a machine from 1(H)/41 (also a 6th Armee unit). Friendship recalled:

> 'The Henschel landed in a field between Louvain and St Trond. Our pilots flew round it at low level and the air gunner continued firing, but we didn't shoot him up.'

Both Uffz Heinz Kubik (the pilot) and Oblt Ulrich Strohm were captured by Belgian troops.

79 Squadron's A Flight was also in action during the morning, when Flt Lt Bob Roberts led five Hurricanes to operate from Mons-en-Chaussée, from where they encountered three He111s. Following a series of attacks, one of the Heinkels was claimed by the combined fire of Roberts, Plt Off Tom Parker, Flg Off Bob Herrick and Sgt Harry Cartwright; meanwhile Sgt Alf Whitby (N2384) engaged a Do17, which he also claimed shot down. This was possibly an aircraft of 4(F)/11, which came down in southern Luxembourg.

There were several other engagements during the day involving 79 Squadron, including a second success for Plt Off Parker who reported shooting down another Do17Z (an aircraft of 7/KG77), but his Hurricane (P2065) was hit by return fire; he baled out and landed behind German lines, but returned next day, having evaded capture. Flg Off Jimmy Davies (L2140) returned from a patrol during which he claimed a He111 and probably a second, while another section encountered 30 Bf109s, one of which Flg Off Bob Herrick claimed as probably destroyed. One of the Messerschmitts was flown by Hptm Adolf Galland of Stab/JG27, who claimed his third victory of the day:

> 'During a patrol flight that afternoon I shot down my third

opponent out of a formation of five Hurricanes near Tirlemont. I took this all quite naturally, for there was nothing special about it. I had not felt any excitement, and I was not particularly elated by my success. On that particular day I had something approaching a twinge of conscience, and the congratulations of my superiors and my comrades left an odd taste in my mouth.'

Later still, Flt Lt Bob Roberts and Sgt Alf Whitby (N2384) reported shooting down a reconnaissance Do17, to conclude a fairly successful day for the Squadron, which moved to Norrent-Fontès that evening.

Sqn Ldr Gifford led the next 3 Squadron patrol to the Diest-St Trond area, but no enemy aircraft were sighted. Not until an evening patrol by A Flight was there a further success, when Flg Off Bunny Stone (N2351) engaged and shot down another Hs126 near St Trond; he noted in his logbook:

'I got one—tail came off.'

This was another 6th Armee machine from 1(H)/41, which was reported missing from an observation sortie near Wavre. Both Fw Hans Poller and his observer, Fw Wilhelm Meyer, were killed. Sqn Ldr Gifford also led 3 Squadron's final patrol of the day, departing from Lille/Marcq at 1930, although no enemy aircraft were sighted on this occasion.

Reinforcements arrived for the Air Component during the evening, when 16 Hurricanes of 504 Squadron departed from RAF Debden at 1500, landing at RAF Tangmere en route to refuel, where Plt Off Ken Wendel, a New Zealander, broke his tailwheel when touching down and was not able to rejoin the Squadron until the following day. The remaining 15, led by Sqn Ldr J.B. Parnall, flew to Lille, from where A Flight continued to Bapaume and B Flight to Vitry.

Before the day was out there occurred a fatal accident when Flg Off John Brown, a pilot from 4 (Continental) Ferry Flight delivering a new Hurricane (P2807), crashed on landing in a field ten miles north of Aigle. He had apparently flown twice round the field and had then fired a flare before attempting to land.

The Air and Military summaries at the end of the day's fighting revealed that conflicting reports continued to come in from Holland and Belgium:

'Aerodromes were still attacked by the Luftwaffe, but on an evidently declining scale. About a dozen French and several Belgian aerodromes seem to have been bombed or machine-gunned during the day, aircraft on the ground (up to ten in number) being destroyed in two or three instances. Five of the AASF aerodromes and at least one of the RAF Component were also attacked by small enemy formations, but the damage seems to have been extraordinarily slight.

In general there is no doubt that the Luftwaffe was now turning its attention from aerodromes to communications, principally in the immediate rear of the Allied forces, coupled with intensive dive-bombing of forward Allied forces at selected points. The scale of attack was particularly heavy against Namur and the Belgian and French troops in the vicinity.

The Dutch, for all their efforts, failed to shake the increasing German hold, which was by now spreading to the district round Dordrecht. Resistance still continued both north and south of the Waal against the more orthodox German land attacks, the full extent of whose penetration was not clear.

In the north of Belgium the enemy pressed towards the Turnhout Canal, and by midday was reported to have occupied Mol. To the centre the Germans had passed through Tongeren and occupied St Trond and were moving towards the line of the Gotte from Tirlemont to Diest. Behind this the BEF had by the evening completed the first phase of their operations and had established themselves between Louvain and Wavre, along the main resistance line of the Dyle [Dijle]. To the south-east of this area Liège fortress was still holding out, but the Germans were well west of the town and in contact with the advance French Cavalry Corps between Hannut and Huy. Further to the south, in the Belgian Ardennes, German progress was very fast [and] had now in some places reached the Franco-Belgian border. In particular the direction of Sedan seemed to be threatened.'

Général François d'Astier de la Vigerie, Air Commander of the French 1st Armée, reported that fighters of the Armée de l'Air had carried out 250 sorties covering the French 2nd and 9th Armées, during which they claimed to have achieved 21 air victories, including a dozen Ju87s in a single engagement; but as one historian remarked:

'Considering the seriousness of the threat, one does get the impression that the French fighter squadrons, whose pilots were already short of sleep, did not press home their attacks with every ounce of vigour.'

Summary

AASF and Air Component Hurricanes continued to hold their own against the incursions of the Luftwaffe, although they were too few in number to prevent widespread bombing of selected targets. However, the appearance of Bf109s over the battle front had an immediate impact and at least six Hurricanes, of the dozen or so lost during the day, fell to their fire.

Claims by AASF and Air Component Hurricanes, 12 May

Type	Confirmed	Probable	Damaged	Total
He111	20	1	—	21
Do17	8	1	—	9
Ju88	1	—	—	1
Ju87	10	1	—	11
Hs126	6	1	—	7
Bf109	6	3	1	10
Bf110	1	—	—	1
	52	7	1	60

Luftwaffe Losses Attributed to AASF and Air Component Hurricanes, 12 May

Type	60% to 100%	Under 60%	Total
He111	7	1	8
Do17	7	2	9
Ju88	1	—	1
Ju87	3	—	3
Hs126	4	—	4
Bf109	1	1	2
	23	4	27

With the onset of darkness, six Coastal Command Beauforts of 22 Squadron set out from RAF Bircham Newton to attack Waalhaven airfield; they were joined in the night attack by nine bomb-carrying Swordfish biplanes of 815 Squadron (attached to Coastal Command), but 'nothing very spectacular in the way of results could be observed'. One Swordfish was hit by Flak and crash-landed, although its crew managed to reach the coast and were returned to England aboard a departing ship. Bomber Command dispatched six Whitleys to attack communications in Cleve, München-Gladbach and Wesel, although only four found their targets. Krefeld was also visited, the crews of the six Wellingtons involved reporting a successful attack. All the bombers returned safely.

Individual Claims—AASF and Air Component Hurricanes, 12 May

0500-	Flg Off W.E. Gore	607 Sqn	He111
	Flg Off R.F. Weatherill	607 Sqn	He111
	Plt Off G.McK. Stewart	607 Sqn	He111
0545-	Plt Off J.R. Cock	87 Sqn	He111
0700-	Flg Off E. Holden	501 Sqn	He111, Do17
	Flg Off P.H. Rayner	501 Sqn	He111
	Plt Off E.J.H. Sylvester	501 Sqn	He111

	Flt Sgt A.D. Payne	501 Sqn	He111
0725-	Plt Off M.M. Stephens	3 Sqn	2 Ju87, Do17
	Plt Off F.R. Carey	3 Sqn	2 Ju87, He111
	Flg Off W.S. Bowyer	3 Sqn	2 Ju87
	Sgt J.A. Sims	3 Sqn	2 Ju87
	Sgt E.G. Ford	3 Sqn	Ju87 probable
0900-	Sqn Ldr J.O.W. Oliver	85 Sqn	He111, Do17
	Plt Off A.G. Lewis	85 Sqn	He111, Bf109
	Sgt G. Allard	85 Sqn	2 He111
	Unknown pilot	85 Sqn	Ju88
0900-	Sqn Ldr J.S. Dewar	87 Sqn	Ju87
	Flg Off H.T. Mitchell	87 Sqn	Ju87
	Plt Off W.D. David	87 Sqn	He111
	Flg Off R.L. Glyde	87 Sqn	He111
0915-	Flg Off L.R. Clisby	1 Sqn	Bf109, 2 Hs126
	Sqn Ldr P.J.H. Halahan	1 Sqn	Bf109, Hs126 probable
	Plt Off R.G. Lewis	1 Sqn	Bf109, Bf109 probable
	Sgt F.J. Soper	1 Sqn	Bf109
	Flg Off R.L. Lorimer ⎫ Sgt F.J. Soper ⎭	1 Sqn	Bf109 probable
	Plt Off P.V. Boot	1 Sqn	Bf109 damaged
1000-	Flg Off H.N. Fowler	615 Sqn	Bf109
1100-	Flt Lt W.M. Churchill ⎫ Flg Off C.A.C. Stone ⎬ Sgt R.L. Wilkinson ⎭	3 Sqn	Hs126
	Flg Off W.S.C. Adams ⎫ Plt Off N.D. Hallifax ⎬ Sgt A.H.B. Friendship ⎭	3 Sqn	Hs126
AM-	Flt Lt C.L.C. Roberts ⎫ Plt Off T.C. Parker ⎬ Flg Off R. Herrick ⎪ Sgt H. Cartwright ⎭	79 Sqn	He111
	Sgt A.W. Whitby	79 Sqn	Do17
1645-	Flg Off E.J. Kain	73 Sqn	Hs126
PM-	Flg Off C.A.C. Stone	3 Sqn	Hs126
?	Sgt J.E. Proctor	501 Sqn	Do17, Bf110
?	Plt Off K.N.T. Lee	501 Sqn	Do17, Do17 probable
?	Sgt P.C.P. Farnes	501 Sqn	He111
	Sgt D.A.S. McKay	501 Sqn	He111
	Sgt P.F. Morfill	501 Sqn	He111
?	Plt Off T.C. Parker	79 Sqn	Do17
?	Flg Off J.W.E. Davies	79 Sqn	He111, He111 probable
?	Flg Off R. Herrick	79 Sqn	Bf109 probable
?	Flt Lt C.L.C. Roberts ⎫ Sgt A.W. Whitby ⎭	79 Sqn	Do17

Losses—AASF and Air Component Hurricanes, 12 May

0500-	P2572	607 Sqn	Flg Off W.E. Gore: shot down near Lille by return fire from He111H of 4/LG1; pilot baled out, wounded.
0700-	L2054	501 Sqn	Flg Off P.H. Rayner: shot down near Seuil by Bf110C of I/ZG52; pilot killed.

	L2050	501 Sqn	Flg Off E. Holden: shot down by return fire from Do17Z of Stab/KG3 and force-landed near Beauvillers; pilot unhurt, returned.
0900-	L1970	87 Sqn	Flg Off J.A. Campbell: shot down north of Liège by Bf109 of Stab/JG27; pilot killed.
	L1632	87 Sqn	Sgt F.V. Howell: shot down north of Liège by Bf109 of Stab/JG27; pilot baled out injured, returned.
0915-	L1688	1 Sqn	Plt Off R.G. Lewis: shot down by Bf109 of 2/JG27 and baled out; pilot unhurt, returned.
	L1671	1 Sqn	Sqn Ldr P.J.H. Halahan: shot down by Bf109 of 2/JG27 and force-landed west of Maastricht; pilot unhurt, returned.
	L1686	1 Sqn	Sgt F.J. Soper: aircraft damaged by Bf109 of 2/JG27 and force-landed at base; pilot unhurt.
		1 Sqn	Flg Off M.H. Brown: aircraft damaged by Bf109 of 2/JG27; pilot unhurt.
		1 Sqn	Plt Off P.V. Boot: aircraft damaged by Bf109 of 2/JG27; pilot unhurt.
1000-	P2564	615 Sqn	Flg Off L. Fredman: shot down north-west of Liège by Bf109 of I(J)/LG2; pilot killed.
?	L2053	501 Sqn	Flg Off M.F.C. Smith: shot down near Sedan by Bf110C of I/ZG2; pilot killed.
?	L1914	501 Sqn	Flg Off C.E. Malfroy: shot down by Bf110C of I/ZG2 and crash-landed west of Mézières; pilot unhurt, returned.
?	L2065	79 Sqn	Plt Off T.C. Parker: shot down west of Maastricht by return fire from Do17Z of 8/KG77; pilot baled out, unhurt.
?	P2807	4(C) Flt	Flg Off J.R. Brown: crashed, accident; pilot killed.

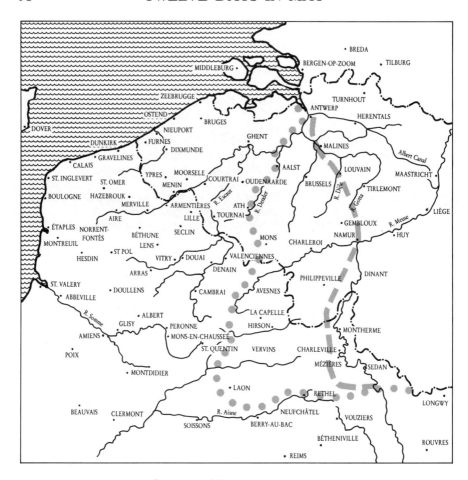

Synopsis of Events 13-16 May

13 May The Germans broke through the defences at Sedan and despite frantic efforts, both on the ground and in the air, from this moment on defeat for the Allies was inevitable. During the morning, 504 Squadron's A Flight moved to Lille/Marcq, where it was joined in the afternoon by B Flight.

14 May The German Panzers poured through the gap as the front was completely broken.

15 May Unco-ordinated counter attacks by French armour were swept aside as the German advance continued. In the north the Allies withdrew to the River Escaut. 87 Squadron moved to Lille/Marcq to make room for the imminent arrival of reinforcement Hurricanes from the UK.

16 May The Allies were powerless to stop the German advance. There was much movement during the day, with all three AASF Hurricane squadrons moving to airfields south of Reims: 1 Squadron transferred to Conde/Vraux, 73 Squadron to Villeneuve and 501 Squadron to Anglure. Within the Air Component, 615 Squadron moved to Moorsele, a small airfield in Belgium, where it was soon joined by 245/B Flight from the UK, its place at Vitry being taken by 56/B Flight, 229/B Flight and 253/B Flight from the UK; at the same time 242/A Flight joined 85 Squadron at Lille/Seclin.

• German advance   — Allied line

CHAPTER V

MONDAY 13 MAY
REINFORCEMENTS ARRIVE

'I followed the enemy aircraft until I saw it crash with wheels up. I then landed alongside and secured five prisoners—the entire crew —and handed them over to the French...'

Flg Off Leslie Clisby, 1 Squadron.

Mr Winston Churchill, Britain's newly installed Prime Minister, made one of his memorable speeches to the House of Commons on this day:

'I would say to the House, I have nothing to offer but blood, toil, tears and sweat. We have before us an ordeal of the most grievous kind. You ask, what is our policy? I will say: It is to wage war, by sea, land, and air, with all our might and with all the strength that God can give us: to wage war against a monstrous tyranny, never surpassed in the dark, lamentable catalogue of human crime. That is our policy. You ask, what is our aim? I can answer in one word: Victory—victory at all costs.'

Air Operations over Holland

The Germans continued to land airborne forces in the Rotterdam-The Hague area, while the Wehrmacht, advancing from the east, penetrated the Dutch defences at Wageningen, north of the Waal, and drove the French 7th Armée back through Breda to the general line Herentals-Bergen-op-Zoom. They were joined there by the retreating Belgian forces that had been defending the Turnhout area. The situation had become extremely serious:

'During the morning there were several indications that the Dutch were now thinking in terms of capitulation. The Dutch Prime Minister signalled London to the effect that if the German advances were not immediately stopped with the help of Allied support, the struggle would have to end. The Dutch Commander-in-Chief declared that the Dutch Air Force no longer existed, and that the position was hopeless unless complete air support was forthcoming.'

The Luftwaffe continued to attack Dutch airfields. For example, Bf110Cs of I and II/ZG1 strafed Haamstede, Flushing and Oostvoorne early in the morning and I Gruppe alone claimed the destruction of 26 aircraft on the ground. However, Dutch airmen endeavoured to fight back and at dawn two Fokker G-1s, five Fokker DXXIs and five Fokker CXs strafed German positions near Wageningen. Although the G-1s were attacked by Bf109s from I/JG26 and both damaged, they claimed one of the Messerschmitts in return. An hour later the Militaire Luchtvaart's last TV bomber set off with two G-1s as escort to bomb the Moerdijk bridges between Breda and Dordrecht, but the Dutch aircraft were attacked on the return flight by Bf109s of 4/JG26, the bomber and one G-1 being shot down.

RAF Fighter Command continued to send patrols across the Channel and, during the early morning, a flight of Spitfires from 66 Squadron accompanied a flight of 264 Squadron Defiants to attack grounded Ju52s along the coast north of The Hague. There they were greeted by both German and Dutch AA fire, but soon afterwards encountered and engaged a number of Ju87s from IV(St)/LG1 found bombing near Streefkerk. Four of the dive-bombers were claimed shot down before a Staffel of Bf109s (5/JG26) arrived and promptly shot down five of the Defiants and a Spitfire, for the loss of one their own. Later, three Coastal Command Blenheim IFs of 235 Squadron, patrolling off the Dutch coast, were engaged by Bf110s but were able to use cloud cover to escape.

At this point, the British and French commanders decided to abandon any further support for the retreating Dutch forces. Thus, the battle for the Netherlands was lost and the country was left to its inevitable fate.

Air Operations over Belgium and Northern France

The situation was not much better in Belgium, where the Belgian Army was retreating to positions between Louvain and Antwerp, effectively plugging the gap between the French and the BEF. The head of the British Military Mission signalled GHQ at Arras:

'I feel no confidence in [the Belgians] really fighting. The CGS is a fussy yes-man quite unfit for driving a partially unwilling army. I am certain that unless strongly supported by French or British troops, this army cannot be relied upon. The prevailing spirit denotes no wish for action if withdrawal can be effected.'

Meanwhile, the French 1st Armée was steadying itself to meet the German advance in the Namur-Gembloux-Wavre area, but to the south of Namur the Germans achieved a surprise crossing of the Maas at Houx, a few miles north of Dinant. A second, larger crossing was successfully carried out further to the south, on French territory. The feared but anticipated threat to Sedan had materialized:

'The Germans in fact had attacked this sector on a ten mile front between Douzy and Vrigne-sur-Meuse and had crossed the Meuse near Sedan to a depth of several miles. Thus began the penetration of the French defensive line which within a week allowed the Germans to sweep forward to the Channel at Abbeville, and to cut in twain the Allied armies.'

The Allied air response was pathetic. At 1020, seven Battles of 226 Squadron were sent to bomb an armoured column reported to be approaching the Boeimeer-Rijsbergen road junction. Six 11 Group Hurricanes of 56 Squadron, flying from RAF Martlesham Heath, were tasked to supply fighter cover. On arrival over southern Holland, they patrolled the Bergen-op-Zoom-Breda-Zundert-Turnhout line. Although they failed to meet any enemy aircraft during the patrol, heavy ground fire damaged Sqn Ldr Knowles' aircraft (N2402), together with that of Sgt Cliff Whitehead (N2398); however, both were able to fly back to England via Flushing and Ostend, landing at RAF Manston at 1150.

Meanwhile the Battle crews, although sighting German bombers in the vicinity, failed to discover any sign of troop movements on the road indicated, so bombed a factory at Boeimeer instead. Although one Battle suffered Flak damage and force-landed near Brussels, the returning crews reported a successful action. This was to be the only bombing raid dispatched by the RAF during the day. The French similarly mounted only one bomber strike against the Sedan area, when seven LeO 451s of GBI/12 and GBII/12, escorted by 27 Bloch 152s of GCI/1 and GCI/8, carried out an ineffectual attack on pontoons north of Dinant and columns of troops in the Dinant-Rochefort-Sorinnes area. All returned, although three or four of the bombers suffered Flak damage.

RAF Lysanders were again active over BEF positions, others being sent to observe enemy movement. One Lysander (P9063 of 4 Squadron) was shot down by a Bf109 of I/JG1 near Hoegaarden at 0945, with the loss of the crew, while two other Lysanders were fired on at Tirlemont.

An unarmed, photo-reconnaissance Spitfire of 212 Squadron, operating from Meaux, was sent to secure photographs of the Wageningen area, but was unable to do so due to low cloud. Five photographic and three strategical reconnaissance sorties were flown by Air Component Blenheims during the morning, four of the former returning early due to low cloud, while one of the latter, a machine of 59 Squadron from Poix, was lost. Another Blenheim, this from 57 Squadron, failed to return from an early evening sortie to Maastal, where it fell victim to Flak. The French also carried out several reconnaissances:

'It would seem that a French pilot who, for some unspecified reason, landed at Amifontaine [the base of 12 Squadron] was among the first to bring news to the British forces of the crossing of the Meuse north of Dinant.'

67 Wing, AASF

73 Squadron at Reims-Champagne experienced a fairly busy morning; the Squadron's activities were graphically recorded by war correspondent Charles Gardner, who wrote:

'The fighting started at 0530 when a Dornier flew over Reims aerodrome at 10,000 feet. Three Hurricanes [flown by Plt Off Dickie Martin, Plt Off Don Scott and Sgt Lionel Pilkington] immediately took off and went after it. The Dornier would probably have got away if it had carried on its course, but it turned—and this allowed the Hurricanes to make an attack. One after another the British fighters opened fire and the Dornier dived steeply, in obvious difficulties. As it flattened out a French Morane [probably an aircraft of GCI/5] came up and sat on its tail, so the Hurricanes returned at 0555.'

The Do17P—4N+FH of 1(F)/22 flown by Oblt Rudolf Sauer—crashed near Reims although the pilot, at least, survived to be taken prisoner by French troops. However, all three Hurricanes suffered strikes from the sharp-shooting Dornier rear gunner, as Pilkington noted in his diary:

'We all came back very riddled. Did not crash. Morane went in after me. Three got out by parachute.'

Gardner continued:

'Five minutes later, at six o'clock, another flight of Hurricanes took off to intercept nine Heinkels, nine Dorniers, three Messerschmitt 110s and 15 Ju88s [Gardner was, however, misinformed as to the identities of the raiders, as only He111Ps of KG55 and Bf110Cs were present] which were coming towards Reims. The Dorniers [sic] dispersed as soon as the Hurricanes were seen—so our pilots turned their attention to the Heinkels. They picked out the last one and [Flt Lt John Scoular, N2721/W] put both its engines out of action. They then went for the others in the formation and used up all their ammunition without getting any further victories. Meanwhile, the leader of the other Hurricane section [Flg Off Ginger Paul] was being attacked by three Messerschmitt 110s, which he dodged—while another lone Hurricane, flown by Plt Off Roy Marchand, went after one of the straying Dorniers [apparently a Bf110], attacking it from the rear. Marchand put in a burst at 250 yards, firing all the way until he was only 50 yards behind the Dornier's tail. The German rear gunner, however, still appeared to be operating because the Hurricane was hit in the oil tank and cooling system. Glycol fumes from the engine filled the cockpit, and oil came streaming back over the windscreen. Marchand fired a final burst and at the same time was hit in the shoulder. His final attack, however, apparently accounted for the Dornier's rear gunner and, when the plane was last seen, it was losing height at 6,500 feet and one engine was on fire.'

Marchand, wrestling with his crippled Hurricane (L1673), was immediately pounced on by a Bf110, which came up from behind. He managed to evade, but then crash-landed near Bétheniville, where his wound was dressed and clips put on a deep cut on his left cheek, caused by a splinter from his windscreen.

Gardner's final report of the morning's actions noted:

'By 0710, the Flight which had attacked the first lone Dornier was in the air again. This time two Heinkels had been seen near Vouziers and the Hurricanes were on them right away. The first Heinkel was forced down after three of the crew had jumped for it, and the second jettisoned its bombs and managed to escape. The first was shot down by Sqn Ldr More, and he saw the crew bale out. He watched them get down all right and saw French troops come out and capture them. What he didn't find out till afterwards was that the French, having no time for prisoners (especially parachute ones), immediately lined them up and shot them.'

At 0640, five Hurricanes of 1 Squadron's B Flight, led by Flt Lt Prosser Hanks (N2380/S), encountered about 30 KG55 He111Ps and their escort at 15,000 feet south-east of Vouziers, which Flg Off Boy Mould's section attacked from astern; Flg Off Les Clisby opened fire on one of the escort which was straggling and reported:

'I attacked Messerschmitt escort first and saw it crash in flames, then a He111 which gave out white smoke from both engines. But then I had to break off on account of an attack by a French Potez 63 [of ECMJ I/16]. On returning home, I sighted a He111 below and made an attack which used up my ammunition. Followed e/a until I saw it crash with wheels up (approximately 18 miles south-east of Vouziers). I then landed alongside and secured five prisoners—the entire crew—and handed them over to the French at Bourcq.'

Clisby's Hurricane (N2326) suffered damage in the landing and had to be abandoned. He arrived back at Berry-au-Bac a few hours later on board a refugee cart 'in the best of spirits, having shared a large bottle of red wine with the peasant and his family'. The Squadron's diarist added a touch of humour to Clisby's official report of the action when he wrote:

'Flg Off Clisby landed beside one of the machines and chased the startled crew all over the countryside, waving his revolver. He wanted their autographs!'

The Australian was credited with three victories in this action, giving him a total of seven and three shared in three successive days. Meanwhile, Mould also claimed a Bf110 shot down before similarly accounting for one of the bombers, which was 'estimated as an almost certain casualty'.

The other section, led by Flt Lt Hanks, attacked a vic of Heinkels, one of which he shot down jointly with Flg Off Lawrie Lorimer and Plt Off George Goodman, seeing it crash-land in the same field as a Bf110 which the Squadron had brought down two days earlier. Lorimer's Hurricane (L1681) was hit by return fire, obliging him to force-land at St Loup-Terrier, writing off his aircraft in the process.

The sixth member of B Flight, Flg Off Billy Drake, had been forced to leave the formation due to oxygen failure before contact with the bombers was achieved. However, his return flight to Berry-au-Bac was full of incident:

'I had been on patrol and was having to come back because of oxygen failure. On the way back I picked up a message addressed to some other Hurricanes saying there were some German bombers in the district. Naturally I looked round and just above me I saw some wings with black crosses on them—they were three Dorniers.

I went up to attack them and I had just got on to the tail of one when there was a terrible explosion in the cockpit. A Messerschmitt 110, which I had not seen, had come down out of the sun and was pumping cannon shells and explosive bullets into my aircraft [Hurricane P]. As the German hit me I pressed my own firing button and was lucky enough to hit the Dornier, causing it to burst into flames and crash. As the Messerschmitt shot me I felt a jar in my leg and in my back and gathered that I had been hit. But by that time my own cockpit was filled with flames and fumes, so I undid my straps and baled out. When I opened my parachute I heard the roar of engines and the noise of machine-guns and I saw tracer bullets passing all round me. The Messerschmitt had followed me down and was trying to shoot me up as I dangled on the end of my parachute. I tried to spill air out of my parachute to increase the rate of my descent and so avoid the bullets, but I found I couldn't raise my right arm because of the wounds in my back. But eventually the Messerschmitt joined his formation and left me to float gently to the ground—luckily not having hit me.'

Just after 1000, Sqn Ldr More of 73 Squadron was in the air again, this time after raiders were reported strafing the far side of the aerodrome, and was soon joined by Flg Off Cobber Kain and Sgt Basil Pyne. A twin-engined aircraft was seen and attacked by More, but on this occasion the intruder turned out to be a French Potez 637, flown by Cne Georges Escudier, who was returning from a reconnaissance sortie. The Potez, believed to have been an aircraft of Escadrille 5/2, suffered some damage before the error of identification was realised, although the French crew escaped injury.

As a result of the numerous engagements with RAF Hurricanes and French fighters (the latter alone claimed five Heinkels, three by MS406s of GCI/3 and GCI/5, and two by Potez 631s twin-engined fighters of ECMJ I/16), KG55 lost six of its bombers destroyed and four others damaged, one seriously:

He111P of Stabsstaffel KG55 flown by Oblt Dieter Clemm von Hohenberg crashed south of Charleville: three killed, two PoW of the French.

He111P of Stab II/KG55 flown by Gruppenkommandeur Maj Otto von Lachemair crash-landed north-east of Carignan (claimed by GCI/3): two wounded.

He111P of 6/KG55 flown by Lt Horst Köhler crashed near Charleville: two killed, three PoW of the French.

He111P of 6/KG55 flown by Lt Otto-Wilhelm Pöhler crashed near Charleville: three killed, two PoW of the French.

He111P of 6/KG55 flown by Lt Rudolf Bertelsmann crash-landed near Charleville: two killed, three PoW of the French.

He111P of 8/KG55 force-landed on fire west of Douzy on the west bank of the Maas: the five-man crew was captured (by Flg Off Clisby), but released that same afternoon by the advancing Panzer troops.

He111P of 8/KG55 crash-landed near Mannheim, 30% damaged: crew unhurt.

He111P of 3/KG55 5% damaged by AA fire: one wounded.

He111P of 6/KG55 5% damaged: one wounded.

He111P of 8/KG55 5% damaged (by Potez 631): three wounded.

During an afternoon patrol by a section of A Flight Hurricanes from 501 Squadron, Sgt Ginger Lacey became separated from his section leader, Flt Lt Charles Griffiths, and encountered a small formation of He111Hs of KG53 escorted by Bf109s. The Squadron's diarist wrote:

'One Hurricane [piloted by Sgt Lacey] intercepted one Messer-schmitt 109 and one Heinkel 111 at 1430 at 18,000 feet near Stenay, as a result of which both e/a were destroyed, being seen to crash in flames.'

Having landed, refuelled and rearmed, the section took off for a second patrol and met a Staffel of Bf110Cs near Le Chesne. In the ensuing series of dogfights, Sgt Lacey claimed his third victory of the day. Shortly afterwards, more Bf110s were encountered near Maubeuge and both Flt Lt Griffiths and Plt Off Kenneth Lee reported successful engagements.

60 Wing, Air Component
85 Squadron, joined by Moranes of GCI/4, was heavily engaged near Lille with He111Ps of II/KG4, escorted by Bf110s, and subsequently claimed a dozen of the bombers shot down or damaged in a series of actions; two were credited to Sqn Ldr Oliver, who shot down one north of Lille and another which crashed on the suburbs of Hazebrouck. Plt Off John Ashton reported shooting down two more, and it is believed that similar claims were submitted by Flt Lt Dickie Lee, Flg Off Derek Allen and Flg Off Ken Blair, two others probably falling to Flt Lt Bob Boothby and Plt Off John Lecky. A French pilot also claimed one Heinkel. There was a deal of over-claiming, obviously when two or more pilots attacked the same aircraft, as only three aircraft of II/KG4 were totally destroyed in this action:

He111P of Stab II/KG4 flown by Oblt Erich Freiherr von Werthern crashed between St-Lenaarts and Wuustwezel, north of Antwerp: pilot survived, remainder of crew killed.

He111P of 5/KG4 flown by Uffz Fritz Maas crash-landed north-east of Antwerp: crew PoW of the British.

He111P of 5/KG4 flown by Oblt von Talkmann crashed north-east of Antwerp (allegedly shot down by AA): crew baled out, returned.

During a later patrol, Bf109s of 8/JG3 were encountered near Tirlemont and Sqn Ldr Oliver (P2821) was forced to bale out over Belgium, shot down by Lt Winfried Schmidt; as he floated down he was fired at by Belgian troops, although not hit. He was returned to the Squadron in the afternoon. One of the Messerschmitts, flown by Obgfr Heinz Schlandt, was shot down by Sgt Albert Deacon and the pilot was killed.

87 Squadron had a much quieter day. During an early morning patrol in the Louvain-Wavre sector, Plt Off John Cock (P3887) reported that he 'intercepted ten Messerschmitt 109s over Louvain—and shot one down'. These were aircraft from 1/JG1 led by Hptm Wilhelm Balthasar, who claimed a Hurricane shot down near Jodoigne, south of Louvain. 1/JG1 suffered no losses in this engagement. That afternoon both Cock and Flg Off Harry Mitchell were taken off flying duties when they reported sick with dysentery. In the Sick Quarters they joined Plt Off Roland Beamont, who had been suffering from the virus since the eve of the Blitzkrieg.

61 Wing, Air Component
At 0435 Flg Off Francis Blackadder (P2571 AF-G) set out from Vitry at the head of a trio of Hurricanes of 607 Squadron, with Flg Off Bunny Forster (P3448 AF-H) and Plt Off Peter Parrott (P3535 AF-C) making up the section. Near Louvain they were bounced by a patrol of Bf109s from 1/JG21 and Parrott's aircraft was hit by a burst of fire; as he recalled later:

'Two loud bangs on the armour-plated seat-back was the first intimation I had of the attack, and I took immediate and violent evasive action, descending in a steep spiral. I pulled out of this descent, still turning steeply, and looked round for my assailant, but he was nowhere in sight, nor were any other aircraft, friendly or hostile. The two bangs I had heard were the only two bullets to have hit the aircraft. One had wrecked the radio and the other had broken a light strut in the fuselage. Repairs were quickly effected.'

Sgt Ken Townsend's aircraft (P2616) was also hit and he was obliged to bale out near Louvain and was taken prisoner; his aircraft crashed at Lens-St-Servais*. However, the other Hurricanes managed to evade their attackers although the Messerschmitts continued to harry them; Parrott became separated and eventually returned to base ten minutes after the other two had landed. Meanwhile, a worried Sqn Ldr Lance Smith (P2536 AF-R) had taken off at 0540 to cover the return of the overdue Hurricanes. Three Hurricanes were claimed by 1/JG21 during the day, one each being credited to Oblt Günther Schölz, Fw Karl Frentzel-Beyme and Uffz Max Clerico, although one of these related to a 3 Squadron Hurricane shot down later, during the early afternoon.

Sqn Ldr Smith (in P3448 AF-H) was airborne again at 0835, leading Flg Off Bob Weatherill (P2571 AF-G) and Plt Off Tony Dini (P2536 AF-R) on patrol in the Diest area. Messerschmitts (8/JG3) were again in evidence, but this time the 607 Squadron pilots got the upper hand and Dini claimed one shot down which was seen to crash near Diest, while Smith also reported a successful encounter, but identified his opponent as a He112 (sic). All three Hurricanes were back by 1000, Smith's aircraft having suffered some damage. One Messerschmitt crashed east of Brussels and its pilot was captured, probably the victim of Dini. Flg Off Bill Whitty recalled:

'We did two trips on successive days to Maastricht, fighting 109s over the bridges. We generally did about four flights a day of about one-and-a-half hours each, often running into 109s, without confirmed reports that those I fired at had been destroyed. After the third or fourth day we didn't see many He111s, just 109s.'

Meanwhile, pilots of 615 Squadron's B Flight at Merville were steadily gaining flying hours on the Hurricane, having been engaged in a number of bomber escort duties, as recalled by Sqn Ldr Kayll:

'The Squadron was ordered to escort a Blenheim [of 18 Squadron] on a low-level reconnaissance of the Albert Canal, to find out how many bridges were still standing. The Blenheim arrived at Merville and we took off together. A Blenheim at low level was just about as fast as a Hurricane and as he turned sharply several times, the outside aircraft were unable to keep up. Finally only myself and Flt Lt Thornley (in a bullet-damaged aircraft) were left as escort, one on each side. The Blenheim pilot was very skilled as he flew under the bridges when they were intact and the escort flew over the ends. The only trouble occurred on the way back when we flew low over a large German Army formation, who shot at us with everything they

---

* The engine of Sgt Ken Townsend's aircraft, P2616, was recovered during a dig in 1992.

had. The rear gunner of the Blenheim was wounded and I was saved by the armour plate behind my seat.'

Later during the afternoon, 615 Squadron carried out a further Blenheim escort, again without interference, but an evening patrol near Namur resulted in the loss of Flg Off Peter Murton-Neale (L2035), who was reported later to have been killed when his aircraft crashed at Courrière following a brief engagement with Bf110s. The victorious pilot was Lt Richard Marchfelder of Stab II/ZG1, who reported his victim however to have been a Spitfire.

Of this period, Plt Off Tom Jackson recalled:

> 'These few days were a jumble. We flew several sorties a day and seemed to land at a different airfield almost every night. We had no proper maps of the area, there were only three available; the CO had one and another was pinned on the door of the Nissen hut, which we had to study and memorize. The main point of reference was the Albert Canal. The weather was marvellous and everyone was happy—there was a picnic atmosphere. We felt lively in the air, but when we came down all we wanted to do was go to sleep.'

B Flight of 504 Squadron, the Wing's newcomers, joined A Flight at Lille/Marcq, although Plt Off Brian Van Mentz was obliged to stay behind with a broken tailwheel; he followed that evening as soon as the wheel had been replaced. Patrols were flown during the day but no enemy aircraft were seen.

63 Wing, Air Component

At 1120, Sqn Ldr Gifford (L1846 QO-B) set off at the head of six Hurricanes to patrol the Wavre-Louvain area. At about 1300, eight aircraft were seen by Red Section flying low down, variously identified as Arados or Henschels (they were in fact Hs123s of II(S)/LG2), one of which Sgt Roy Wilkinson (N2353) shot down in flames. Fw Hans Knerr and his gunner were reported missing. Sgt Dennis Allen (L1591) claimed a second Henschel shot down and this would seem to have been a Hs126 of 9(H)/LG2 (3 Pz Division), which crashed near Perwez, about 12 miles south of Wavre. The pilot survived but his observer, Oblt Hans Staudenraus, was killed.

A He111P of 3/KG54 was then sighted and engaged by Flt Lt Walter Churchill (N2351) and Sgt Allen who, together with Plt Off Frank Carey (L1932) of Blue Section, claimed that the bomber fell to their combined attack. A second Heinkel—or possibly the same aircraft—was intercepted by Wilkinson, who reported that its pilot took the aircraft through some very violent moves before he was able to shoot it down. No one was seen to leave the bomber before 'it crashed and exploded in a great orange flame'. Only one Heinkel was lost, from which Uffz Gustav Hoffmann and his crew baled out before it crashed near Namur. The German crew, however, believed they had been shot down by AA fire. Carey then joined Flg Off Dickie Ball (L1901) of Blue Section in pursuit of a Do17, but the latter was heard to call for help when attacked by five Bf109s. Ball, who hailed from Quebec, Canada, was seriously wounded in the thigh, crash-landed and was taken prisoner, but succumbed to his wounds on 4 June. His victor was from 1/JG21, the unit which had successfully engaged Hurricanes from 607 Squadron earlier that morning. Meanwhile, Carey reported shooting down the Dornier, an aircraft of 4(F)/14, from which the crew baled out.

At the request of Général d'Astier de la Vigerie (Air Commander of the French 1st Armée), a 3 Squadron patrol by six aircraft of Yellow and Green Sections was carried out forward of BEF positions, on a line stretching from Tirlemont, ten miles north of the town. Nothing was sighted, but when returning just before 1800 Flg Off Wilfred Adams (N2654) signalled Flg Off Raymond Line-Roberts (N2653) to close formation. For some unexplained reason, the two Hurricanes collided and exploded in mid-air, killing both pilots. The third member of the section, Flg Off Bunny Stone (L1946), landed safely and broke the news, following which Flt Lt Walter Churchill (N2351) took off immediately to search the crash area for signs of life.

79 Squadron at Norrent-Fontès was not engaged in action during the day, an early morning patrol having failed to sight three He111s clearly seen from ground in the vicinity of the aerodrome.

Air Chief Marshal Sir Hugh Dowding, AOC Fighter Command, had been authorized to dispatch a further 32 Hurricanes and their pilots to France to make good the losses, these being allocated to the squadrons as required. The majority were to depart England on the morrow, but nine arrived that evening at Reims-Champagne for 73 Squadron; these were Plt Offs F. Sydenham, R.D. Rutter, C.A. McGaw, N.C. Langham-Hobart, J.E.P. Thompson and B.P. Legge, Sgts A.E. Marshall and A.E. Scott—all woefully inexperienced since all had come direct from 6 OTU. Additionally, 1 Squadron was reinforced by the return of four pilots (Flg Off C.G.H. Crusoe, Sgt F.G. Berry, Sgt A.V. Clowes and Sgt R.A. Albonico) who had been recalled from leave in the UK.

Summary

Of the ten Hurricanes totally lost during the day, six had fallen to Messerschmitts and two in an accident. In return for these losses, Hurricane pilots believed they had accounted for five Bf109s and a similar number of Bf110s but had, in fact, shot down only five Messerschmitts.

Claims by AASF and Air Component Hurricanes, 13 May

Type	Confirmed	Probable	Damaged	Total
He111	11	10	—	21
Do17	3	1	—	4
Hs126	2	—	—	2
Bf109	5	—	—	5
Bf110	5	—	—	5
	26	11	—	37

Luftwaffe Losses Attributed to AASF and Air Component Hurricanes, 13 May

Type	60% to 100%	Under 60%	Total
He111	7	5	12
Do17	2	—	2
Hs123	1	—	1
Hs126	1	—	1
Bf109	2	—	2
Bf110	3	—	3
	16	5	21

Bombing operations during the night were on a small scale. Of the six Hampdens dispatched to attack Aachen and Eindhoven, only three found their target, while only two of the six Whitleys sent to Maesyck (Maaseik), Eindhoven and Maastricht (to interfere with the repair of the bridges) successfully bombed. One aircraft returned early with engine trouble and the other three failed to identify the target.

Individual Claims—AASF and Air Component Hurricanes, 13 May

Time	Pilot	Squadron	Claim
0555-	Plt Off R.F. Martin	73 Sqn	Do17
	Plt Off D.S. Scott		
	Sgt L.S. Pilkington		
	MS406 pilot		
0600-	Flt Lt J.E. Scoular	73 Sqn	He111
	Plt Off R.A. Marchand	73 Sqn	Do17 probable
0640-	Flg Off L.R. Clisby	1 Sqn	Bf110, 2 He111
	Flg Off P.W.O. Mould	1 Sqn	Bf110, He111
	Flt Lt P.P. Hanks	1 Sqn	He111
	Flg Off R.L. Lorimer		
	Plt Off G.E. Goodman		
	Flg Off B. Drake	1 Sqn	Do17
0710-	Sqn Ldr J.W.C. More	73 Sqn	He111
0900-	Plt Off A.S. Dini	607 Sqn	Bf109
	Sqn Ldr L.E. Smith	607 Sqn	Bf109
AM-	Plt Off J.R. Cock	87 Sqn	Bf109
AM-	Sqn Ldr J.O.W. Oliver	85 Sqn	2 He111
	Flt Lt R.H.A. Lee	85 Sqn	2 He111 (possibly)
	Flg Off K.H. Blair	85 Sqn	2 He111 (possibly)
	Plt Off J.H. Ashton	85 Sqn	2 He111 (possibly)
	Flg Off D.H. Allen	85 Sqn	2 He111 (possibly)

	Flt Lt J.R.M. Boothby	85 Sqn	He111 (possibly)
	Plt Off J.W. Lecky	85 Sqn	He111 (possibly)
1300-	Sgt R.C. Wilkinson	3 Sqn	Hs126, He111
	Sgt D.A. Allen	3 Sqn	Hs126
	Plt Off F.R. Carey	3 Sqn	Do17
	Flt Lt W.M. Churchill ⎫		
	Plt Off F.R. Carey ⎬	3 Sqn	He111
	Sgt D.A. Allen ⎭		
PM-	Sgt A.H. Deacon	85 Sqn	Bf109
PM-	Sgt J.H. Lacey	501 Sqn	Bf109, He111
PM-	Flt Lt C.D. Griffiths	501 Sqn	Bf110
	Plt Off K.N.T. Lee	501 Sqn	Bf110
	Sgt J.H. Lacey	501 Sqn	Bf110

Losses—AASF and Air Component Hurricanes, 13 May

0500-	P3535	607 Sqn	Plt Off P.L. Parrott: aircraft damaged near Louvain by Bf109 of 1/JG21; pilot unhurt.
	P2616	607 Sqn	Sgt K.N.V. Townsend: shot down near Louvain by Bf109 of 1/JG21; pilot baled out and PoW.
0600-	L1673	73 Sqn	Plt Off R.A. Marchand: aircraft damaged by Bf110C of I/ZG52 or V(Z)/LG1 and crash-landed near Bétheniville; pilot wounded.
0640-	N2326	1 Sqn	Flg Off L.R. Clisby: aircraft damaged when deliberately force-landed; pilot unhurt.
	L1681	1 Sqn	Flg Off L.R. Lorimer: aircraft damaged by He111P of KG55 and crash-landed near St Loup-Terrier; pilot unhurt.
	'P'	1 Sqn	Flg Off B. Drake: shot down by Bf110C of I/ZG52 or V(Z)/LG1; pilot baled out, wounded.
1300-	L1901	3 Sqn	Flg Off A.R. Ball: shot down by Bf109 of 1/JG21 and crash-landed near Wavre; pilot severely wounded and died 4 June 1940 as PoW.
PM-	P2821	85 Sqn	Sqn Ldr J.O.W. Oliver: shot down near Tirlemont by Bf109 of 8/JG3; pilot baled out, returned.
PM-	L2035	615 Sqn	Flg Off P.N. Murton-Neale: shot down near Courrière, south-west of Namur by Bf110C of II/ZG1; pilot killed.
1800-	N2653	3 Sqn	Flg Off R.B. Lines-Roberts: collided near Merville with Hurricane N2654 flown by Flg Off W.S.C. Adams; pilot killed.
	N2654	3 Sqn	Flg Off W.S.C. Adams: collided near Merville with Hurricane N2653 flown by Flg Off R.B. Lines-Roberts; pilot killed.

CHAPTER VI

TUESDAY 14 MAY
THE DAY OF THE FIGHTERS*

'We came across about 50 Ju87s. Then 20 Messerschmitt 109s dived
down from above. I engaged one in tight turns. I saw one go straight
down but couldn't follow—not conclusive.'

Sgt Basil Friendship, 3 Squadron.

The Situation in Holland

The resistance of the Dutch was now in its final stages. German troops
were pouring into the heart of the country, linking up with the airborne
forces. Then, at 1500, 57 He111Ps of KG54 raided the city of Rotterdam, ostensibly in an effort to aid German paratroopers trapped north
of the Willems Bridge over the Maas. Many fires were started which
burned unhindered and devastated a great part of the city, killing 913
of the inhabitants. The Rotterdam garrison surrendered two hours after
the raid.

The French 7th Armée had been thwarted in its attempt to join up
with Dutch forces and had been generally bested by the Germans in a
series of fiercely fought actions in the enclosed, canal-crossed countryside of north-west Belgium and southern Holland. The French forces
had lost heavily against the combination of ground and air attacks.
Accordingly, the French commander began to withdraw his battered
forces.

Meanwhile, the five remaining Fokker DXXIs of the Nederlandse
Militaire Luchtvaart at Buiksloot carried out a patrol above Dutch
troops withdrawing from the Valley position, all suffering damage from
the very troops they were attempting to protect and one crash-landed
near Utrecht as a result. The other four flew to Schiphol, where they

---

* With the conclusion of the day's air battles, which saw considerable success for the
Bf109 units, the Luftwaffe thereafter referred to 14 May as 'the day of the fighters'.

joined the last three Fokker G-1s to fly further patrols over the retreating troops. No German aircraft were encountered during the course of these patrols.

Seven Fokker CXs moved from Bergen via Schiphol to Ruigenhoek, from where reconnaissance flights were made south-east of Rotterdam. Two of the crews decided to head for France and landed safely at a French airfield. Later, both of the pilots and one observer escaped to England to continue the fight.

The Situation in Belgium and Northern France

On the right of the retreating French 7th Armée, the Belgian line began at Wijnegem, east of Antwerp, and continued through Lier to Louvain, from where the BEF line extended to the south of Wavre. There was very little contact in these sectors during the day, although south of the BEF positions the French 1st Armée had been heavily engaged by the advancing Germans in the Gembloux gap—between Gembloux and Namur—and the latter town was in danger of falling. Subjected to simultaneous attacks by both tanks and dive bombers, the French suffered heavy losses.

However, it was on the Meuse that the main German success occurred, at Sedan and Montherme, where the German bridgeheads overcame the weak defences of the French 2nd and 9th Armées and opened a gap through which the main armoured forces began to pour.

> 'The bridgehead over the Meuse at Houx (north of Dinant), captured in the early hours of 13 May, was maintained by the enemy, who was now across the river line on a ten mile front: and the left centre of the French 9th Armée, demoralised by dive-bombing and in any case of no great efficiency, was too disorganized to restore the situation.'

The Aeronautique Militaire Belge had by now almost ceased to exist. The last six CR42s were ordered to patrol over Fleurus, where troops of the French 7th Armée were entraining for the return journey to France. During the patrol, Messerschmitts of 8/JG3 attacked and shot down one of the Fiats, although another Belgian pilot reported shooting down a Do17.

To the south, the RAF's reinforcement Hurricanes and their pilots continued to arrive at various bases in France. Five landed at Merville for 615 Squadron; these were Plt Off V.B.S. Verity, Plt Off J.E.M. Collins and Plt Off M. Ravenhill of B Flight, 229 Squadron, Flg Off Leonid Ereminsky of 151 Squadron (the latter a White Russian) and Plt Off C.R. Young from 601 Squadron. In addition, Flg Off Tony Eyre returned from leave in England aboard a Hudson, rejoining 615 Squadron.

607 Squadron at Vitry also received an influx of reinforcement pilots to help make good its losses, as recalled by Flg Off Bill Whitty:

'The Squadron was kept up to strength by aircraft flown out and pilots sent us to stay, as well as flights from the UK for the day. We locals had to collect the visitor pilots and escort them to Vitry as they had no maps and neither had the other's crystals for R/T.'

Plt Off Peter Parrott added:

'Reinforcements arrived in the form of sections of three or six aircraft, but no extra ground crew, so our own people were hard pressed to service the new aircraft as well as ours, and to repair battle damage where it occurred. They worked magnificently.'

From 245 Squadron came Flg Off I.B.N. Russell (an Australian from Melbourne) and Plt Off J.S. Humphreys (from New Zealand). Two arrived from 601 Squadron, Flg Off G.I. Cuthbert and Plt Off R.S. Demetriadi (son of Sir Stephen), while 151 Squadron provided Flg Off K.E. Newton, another New Zealander, Plt Off D.H. Blomeley and Plt Off R.N.H. Courtney. All were inexperienced in terms of air fighting. Also attached to 607 Squadron for operations were four Canadian pilots from 242 Squadron's B Flight: Flt Lt J.L. Sullivan, Plt Off P.S. Turner, Plt Off R.D. Grassick and Plt Off W.L. McKnight. In addition, Flg Off R.E.W. Pumphrey, one of 607 Squadron's senior pilots, returned from leave in the UK.

3 Squadron at Merville received nine replacement pilots: Flg Off D.A.E. Jones, Plt Off P.M. Gardner, Plt Off J. Rose and Sgt R.T. Ware from 32 Squadron; Sgt P. Hillwood and Sgt J.L.C. Williams from 56 Squadron; and Plt Off D.L. Bisgood, Plt Off J.B. Hobbs and Plt Off C.D.St G. Jeffries from 253 Squadron. One of the new pilots, Plt Off Jack Rose, recalled:

'With three other volunteers from 32 Squadron, I flew to Merville. We were led by a Fairey Battle as we had no maps of France; I imagine that the pilot of the Battle must have been equipped with the right maps but he seemed a long time flying around France before we landed, for we were very short of fuel when we pitched up at Merville.'

The services of one of the new Hurricanes was immediately denied to the Squadron, as Sgt Jim Williams (of 56 Squadron) lost his way en route to Merville and attempted to land in a field to ask the way. On touching down, the aircraft (N2441) hit an unseen ridge and was badly damaged, although Williams was not hurt. Meanwhile, six new pilots arrived with their Hurricanes at Lille/Seclin for 85 Squadron—Plt Off R.W. Burton, Plt Off R.W. Shrewsbury and Sgt C.A. Rust from 145 Squadron, together with Plt Off H.D. Clark and Sgt H.N. Howes from 213 Squadron, and Sgt H.H. Allgood from OTU.

Despite the arrival of the reinforcing Hurricanes and pilots from England, the Air Component fighters were still hard pressed to provide adequate protection for the airfields:

> 'Some of the Gladiators recently discarded by 615 Squadron were distributed to other squadrons for the defence of aerodromes against low-flying attack. A few of the younger staff officers were withdrawn from RAF Component Headquarters to fly them.'

Air Operations over the Louvain-Tirlemont Area

At 0440, a section of 3 Squadron took off from Merville for a dawn patrol, led by Flt Lt Mark Carter. South of Louvain a Do17P of 3(F)/11, which was on a reconnaissance sortie for the 6th Armee, was sighted and pursued by Plt Off Frank Carey (L1932):

> 'I was attacking a Dornier 17 and it did a snap half-roll, which was an extraordinary thing for a kite of that size to do. I did the same and followed it closely down. It was nearly vertical; in fact, the pilot was dead, I think, because it just went straight on in. But before I'd realised that, the rear gunner fired and hit me well and truly.'

The Dornier pilot, Oblt Kopetsch, his observer and gunner all suffered wounds but survived the crash to be taken prisoner by French forces. Meanwhile, with his engine on fire and a slight leg wound, Carey endeavoured to bale out but was unable to do so due to the speed of his aircraft. Eventually he managed to crash-land the Hurricane in a large ploughed field in the neighbourhood of Hamme-Mille, about eight miles south of Louvain. After being picked up by a Belgian Army motorcyclist, Carey was taken to a village south of Brussels where his wounds were treated. From there he was driven by ambulance to a casualty clearing station just across the border into France, and from there to a hospital in Dieppe, before being transferred to La Baule*.

---

* Having made a speedy recovery from his injuries, Plt Off Frank Carey—with three other similarly indisposed RAF aircrew—was discharged to the nearest RAF unit, an aircraft stores depot near Nantes. They were still there by the second week in June when news reached them of an abandoned Bombay transport on the nearby airfield. Having checked this over and filled its tanks with petrol, the foursome departed for friendly shores, with Carey manning the rear gun. The English coast was reached safely, where they were investigated by RAF fighters, and landed finally at Hendon.

Some 20 minutes earlier a section of Hurricanes from 504 Squadron had encountered a Ju88 from 3(F)/122, which was attacked from astern by Sqn Ldr Parnall (L1639), Flg Off Michael Royce (L1950) and Plt Off Brian Van Mentz. The reconnaissance aircraft fell in flames and was followed down by Van Mentz, who saw it crash near the Albert Canal. All four members of Uffz Erwin Maxrath's crew managed to bale out and were handed over by their Belgian captors to British troops.

During another early morning patrol, a section of Hurricanes from 615 Squadron encountered what they believed was a Do17, which was claimed shot down by Flg Off Bill Fowler (P2622). In fact the aircraft was Ju88A 7A+BH of 1(F)/121, which failed to return from a recon-naissance of Brussels-Courtrai-Ghent-Antwerp; Oblt Heinz Spillmann and his crew were reported missing. Another Hurricane patrol—Yellow Section (Plt Off Lew Appleton, Plt Off John Wood and Sgt Len Pearce) of 79 Squadron, flying from Norrent-Fontès—shot down a Hs126 of the 6th Armee's 4(H)/22. Before it crash-landed near Louvain, the Henschel's gunner hit Pearce's aircraft in the windscreen although the pilot was able to return to base safely.

There were also losses during these early morning sorties however. A Lysander of 4 Squadron (L4742 TV-H) was shot down in the Louvain-Tirlemont area and two reconnaissance Blenheims—one each from 57 and 59 Squadrons—also failed to return:

> 'A special sortie was provided by 59 Squadron to cover the situation in the north; the fighters detailed to escort it, however, arrived at the appointed aerodrome without maps and were unable to take off at the same time as the Blenheim. It is not clear whether they regained contact, but the Blenheim failed to return.'

A large formation of German aircraft—Hs123s of II(S)/LG2 at low level and He111Ps of I and III/KG27 at a higher altitude, escorted by a swarm of Bf109s of II/JG2—was reported approaching the Louvain area at about 0900: 607 Squadron was ordered to dispatch all available Hurricanes, in company with 85 and 87 Squadrons from Lille. The 607 Squadron formation included at least three of the Canadian pilots of the 242 Squadron detachment, together with a number of the newly arrived replacement pilots. A contemporary newspaper reported Plt Off Courtney's involvement:

> 'Soon after landing at the base in France to which he is attached, he was obliged to leave the Hurricane in which he flew from this country and take off in a fuelled fighter with a patrol to intercept a flight of enemy bombers.'

Details of the ensuing action are somewhat sketchy due to lack of documentation, but it seems that a formation of 15 Hs123s, escorted by an estimated 45 Bf109s, was encountered near Louvain by 607 Squadron. According to a note in the logbook of Plt Off Willie McKnight (one of the Canadian pilots involved), ten German aircraft— Hs123s and Bf109s—were shot down (although McKnight probably meant ten claims for destroyed and damaged enemy aircraft were submitted) for the loss of four Hurricanes. McKnight (L2003 LE-A) himself did not claim, nor did his Canadian colleague, Plt Off Bob Grassick (LE-B), although both reported skirmishes with Bf109s.

Relevant records have not survived, but research would suggest that the Squadron's B Flight acting commander, Flg Off Jim Bazin, may have claimed one, and it seems probable that Flg Off Ian Russell submitted claims for four successes (in the light of his subsequent DFC award)*. In addition, Plt Off Buck Courtney was credited with one, Plt Off Jim Humphreys two (a Hs123 and a Bf109, both damaged) and Flg Off Ken Newton possibly two, since he is believed to have 'done well' in the fighting in France. Few, if any, of these victories were, or were considered, conclusive.

Only two Hs123s were lost during the engagement—aircraft of 5 Staffel—from which both Uffz Karl-Siegfried Lückel and Lt Georg Ritter were rescued by German troops. It is possible that other Henschels were damaged, or that they landed hurriedly and thus were believed to have been forced down by the attacking pilots.

However, the pilots of the four Hurricanes shot down were all killed. Flg Off Gerald Cuthbert's aircraft (P2618) crashed at Aische-en-Refail and Flg Off Monty Thompson's P2620 near Louvain, while Flt Lt John Sullivan, leader of the 242 Squadron detachment, was believed to have been caught in crossfire from two of the Henschels; his aircraft (P2621) crashed at Gorroy-le-Château, near Perwez, near where, it is believed Flg Off Arthur Le Breuilly's Hurricane (P2713) also crashed, having been shot down by the Messerschmitts. It was reported that Sullivan had baled out of his damaged machine, but was dead when found. The pilots of 4/JG2 submitted claims for four Hurricanes, three of these being credited to Oblt Hans Hahn, Fw Karl-Heinz Harbauer and Fw Siegfried Schnell. The Messerschmitts of II/JG2 suffered no losses.

Meanwhile, the other two Hurricane squadrons encountered the

---

* Flg Off Ian Russell was born in Melbourne, Australia and joined the RAF in 1936, where he trained at 11 FTS Wittering and was subsequently commissioned. However, he soon resigned his commission and went to the USA but, with the outbreak of war, returned to England, rejoined the RAF and was posted to 245 Squadron. The citation for his DFC mentioned that he had shot down ten plus six probables, but it is believed this should have been ten including six probables, which included several shared victories.

formation of He111Ps from I and III/KG27. 85 Squadron claimed four of these, including two (it is believed) by Flt Lt Dickie Lee and one by Flg Off Allan Angus, the latter pilot sharing another with Plt Off Dennis David (L1630) of 87 Squadron, who also claimed one on his own. I and III/KG27 sustained three losses:

> He111P of 2/KG27 flown by Lt Joachim Müller shot down and crash-landed near Tirlemont: three crew wounded.

> He111P of 7/KG27 flown by Fw Willi Biskupski shot down near Louvain: crew baled out, three PoW of the British, one PoW of the French.

> He111P of 9/KG27 flown by Oblt Konrad Häfele shot down (allegedly by AA fire) and crash-landed ten miles north of Hesselt: one crew member wounded, all rescued by German forces.

> He111P of 2/KG27 5% damaged in combat near Tirlemont: pilot killed and one other wounded.

87 Squadron lost two of its pilots in this action. Plt Off Paul Jarvis was last seen on the tail of a bomber (which was credited to him as probably destroyed) and was reported later as having been killed when his aircraft (L1616) crashed west of Maastricht. It would seem that he was shot down by Oblt Gert Framm of 2/JG27. Other pilots also encountered the Bf109s of JG27, which prevented them from reaching the bombers, as Plt Off John Cock noted:

> 'Patrol Louvain-Gembloux: patrol forced back owing to too much opposition (100 Messerschmitt 109s).'

Plt Off Gordon Saunders (L1612) also failed to return. The Squadron learned that he had been severely wounded when shot down near Mainvault, north-west of Ath, and died of his wounds five days later in Lille Hospital. It seems probable that he fell victim to a Bf110 of I or II/ZG1. On their return to Vitry, the remaining pilots of 607 Squadron discovered that, in their absence, the airfield had been bombed and at least one Hurricane had been destroyed:

> 'When he [Plt Off Courtney] returned after the successful flight, he found that his base had been bombed and the Hurricane he had flown a short time previously—in which were still his spare clothes and personal belongings—had been wrecked by a bomb.'

504 Squadron dispatched a section to the Louvain area at 1230. The three Hurricanes encountered heavy Flak east of Brussels, when Plt Off

Sam Sibley's aircraft (L1941) was apparently hit as he was seen to leave the formation; he was reported later to have been killed. A section of the Squadron's B Flight, led by Flt Lt William Royce, joined forces with a section from 87 Squadron during the afternoon for a patrol over Louvain. There, nine Blenheims were encountered (apparently 82 Squadron from RAF Watton, which had bombed roads on the outskirts of Breda and on the Tilburg-Breda railway line) and these were escorted to the coast, after which the Hurricanes made a wide circuit of Brussels and returned to base.

With the return of Flt Lt Royce's section, Sqn Ldr Parnall led another section of four aircraft of 504 Squadron to patrol the Louvain area, where six He111Hs from III/LG1 and a number of Bf109s of II and III/JG26 were sighted. The Hurricanes attacked the bombers in turn, before the Messerschmitts were able to react and Parnall was seen (by Flg Off Michael Royce) to damage badly a Heinkel but was then shot down himself, his aircraft (L1639) crashing at Hameau du Caillou; he was killed. Meanwhile, Royce claimed a Heinkel (probably the same aircraft as that attacked by Parnall, a machine of 9 Staffel in which one crew member was wounded) and damaged a Bf109, before another shot him down. He baled out of L1950 south-west of Brussels and was able to rejoin the Squadron later. Sgt Stan Hamblett was also shot down in the engagement and was killed when his aircraft (N2492) crashed near Ath. A fourth Hurricane was lost when a slightly wounded Plt Off Blair White crash-landed L1916. Two of the Hurricanes were claimed by Lt Gerhard Müller-Dühe and Lt Walter Blume of 7 Staffel, and the other two by Lt Joachim Müncheberg and Lt Hans-Jürgen Westphal of Stabsstaffel II Gruppe.

A section of 79 Squadron, led by Plt Off Lew Appleton, set out to cover a reconnaissance Blenheim operating in the Louvain-Namur area when three twin-engined bombers identified as Ju88s were sighted. However, it seems that these were in fact He111Hs of II/LG1 with an escort of Bf110s from I and II/ZG1. Appleton went after one bomber which had broken formation, while Plt Off Don Stones (L1716) and Sgt Harry Cartwright chased the other two. Stones damaged one which Cartwright finished off, then shot down the other. Appleton failed to return and it was reported later that his aircraft (P2537) crashed east of Renaix; he was killed. Stones recalled:

'Lew Appleton was leading the section, but we didn't see him go down—absolute mystery. I was his No 2 and No 3 was Sgt Harry Cartwright. Together we shared one and then got another, so one got away. However, the rear gunner of one of them drilled my port wing.'

II/LG1 lost three Heinkels, one of which possibly fell to Moranes of GCII/8 which also engaged the formation at this time:

He111H of Stab II/LG1 flown by Oblt Rupert Müllauer crash-landed south-west of Brussels: one killed, two PoW of the British, one PoW of the French.

He111H of Stab II/LG1 flown by Oblt Georg Preuss crash-landed south-west of Brussels: two killed, one wounded PoW of the French, one PoW of the British.

He111H of 5/LG1 flown by Fw Bruno Meininger crashed near Brussels: crew killed.

At 1900, 87 Squadron's Flg Off Frank Joyce and Plt Off Chris Mackworth were ordered to investigate enemy activity over Louvain. Mackworth was unable to start his engine, so Joyce went off alone and soon encountered a large formation of Bf110Cs from I and II/ZG1 south of Brussels. He attempted to bounce these, but his aircraft was seen by the Messerschmitts:

'An aircraft peeled off from the leading group in my direction. In reflex action I turned head-on to meet him and managed to get a good burst of fire on his nose before it was necessary to thrust smartly forward.'

He saw the Messerschmitt spiral downwards, so attacked a second and apparently silenced the rear gunner (possibly an aircraft of 1 Staffel in which the gunner was wounded) before his aircraft was hit by another, suffering severe wounds to his left leg and arm. Unable to bale out, he managed to level the aircraft (L1646) before it crashed into some trees; he was removed from the wreck by two Scottish soldiers and taken to a field dressing post. The soldiers told him they had seen one of the Messerschmitts crash and he subsequently claimed this. Eventually he was evacuated to the UK, where his leg was amputated. Meanwhile, Mackworth had managed to get his engine started and he followed. He too encountered the Bf110s, which were strafing the village of Bruyelles, and his aircraft (L1834) was shot down in flames, crashing at Ramegnies-Chin. Although he managed to bale out near Mainvault, it is believed his parachute caught fire and he was found to be dead when soldiers reached him.

Reconnaissance sorties by Lysanders of 4 Squadron in the area of Louvain-Tirlemont continued throughout the day, the unit suffering a second loss when P1711 failed to return from an early evening sortie.

Air Operations over the Sedan Battlefront

During the day the Allies made their first—and only—big effort to stem the German advance through Sedan. AASF HQ had passed a state of readiness to all units for 0400, following reports from various sources of the threat in and near Sedan. In the early morning hours, the commanding Général of the French 1st Armée called Air Marshal Barratt and advised him of the German breakthrough and demanded the full weight of the British bombers to destroy the important bridges over the Meuse. Thus, Air Vice-Marshal Playfair was ordered to carry out the attack with all available forces.

British and French air commanders hastily agreed upon a combined assault and laid plans to send four waves of bombers, at intervals of approximately three hours, with fighter escorts provided by both the RAF and Armée de l'Air. The plan of attack was:

Time	Strike Force	Target Area	Escort
0630 BST	6 Battles (103 Squadron)	Nouvion and Douzy	Hurricanes (73 Squadron)
0750	4 Battles (150 Squadron)	Douzy	None
0900	9 Bréguet 693s (GBA I + II/54)	Sedan and Maas	Bloch 152s (GCI/1) Bloch 152s (GCII/1) MS406s (GCII/6)
1245	13 Amiot 143s (GB I/34, GBII/34, GBII/38)	Bazeilles and Givonne	MS 406s (GCIII/7) D520s (GCI/3) Bloch 152s (GCI/10)
1300	8 LeO451s (GBI/12)	Bazeilles and Givonne	as above
1500	25 Battles (12, 142 and 226 Squadrons)	Gaulier, Romilly, Douzy, Mouzon, Villers, Bouillon, Givonne	Bloch 152s (GCI/1) Bloch 152s (GCII/1) MS406s (GCII/2) MS406s (GCIII/3)
1530	8 Blenheims (114/139 Squadrons) 23 Battles (105 and 150 Squadrons)	as above as above	Hurricanes (1 and 73 Squadrons) as above
1535	29 Battles (88, 103 and 218 Squadrons)	as above	Hurricanes (3, 87 and 607 Squadrons)
1820	28 Blenheims (21, 107 and 110 Squadrons)	Bouillon, Givonne and Sedan	Bloch 152s (GCI/1) Bloch 152s (GCII/1) Bloch 152s (GCII/10) Bloch 152s (GCIII/10) MS406s (GCI/3)

Thus, at 0630, six Hurricanes of 73 Squadron set off to provide cover for the six Battles of 103 from Bétheniville, the crews tasked to bomb the bridge at Romilly-Aillicourt. One hit was claimed on the bridge and several near misses, while one Battle was hit by ground fire and its pilot wounded. The aircraft force-landed near Bétheniville on return. Meanwhile, five Do17s of 3/KG76 were seen and the Hurricanes attacked with the advantage of height. The Dorniers immediately turned back towards Germany but at least two were claimed badly damaged by Flg Off Fanny Orton and Sgt Lionel Pilkington, the latter noting:

'I get [the] starboard engine. Large pieces fell off it and my windscreen covered in oil. Also damage port engine and get the gunner. He dives away and then tries to rejoin formation again on one engine. Shots in my plane and I fly home as I cannot use my gunsight owing to the oil on the windscreen.'

One of the Dorniers returned to its base slightly damaged with three of its crew wounded. During the attack, Plt Off Aubrey McFadden's aircraft (L1891) was hit by return fire and crash-landed, the pilot's second such crash in three days. He was taken off operational flying duties temporarily as a result.

At 0745, a large formation of Bf110s (possibly from I/ZG26) overflew Berry-au-Bac airfield at 15,000 feet, apparently part of the escort to bombers raiding Laon. Six Hurricanes of 1 Squadron's B Flight were scrambled, with Flt Lt Prosser Hanks (N2380/S) leading the chase, but they were unable to make contact until the Messerschmitt formation changed direction; Hanks recalled:

'We got above them and I dived vertically on the leader and fired a burst, allowing deflection, and he just blew up. Nothing left of him but a few small pieces. Then I pulled up in a climbing turn to the left and saw a bugger coming up at right angles towards me from the left and firing at me. He wasn't allowing enough deflection and all his shots were going behind me.'

Hanks was able to manoeuvre on to the tail of the Messerschmitt, which he reported was shot down in flames; he continued:

'I was just turning over him when my aeroplane was hit by some other bugger behind me and I was suddenly drenched in hot glycol. I didn't have my goggles down and the bloody stuff completely blinded me. I didn't know where I was and somehow got into a spin. I could see damn all and the cockpit was getting bloody hot, so I undid the straps and opened the hood to get out, but I couldn't. Every time I tried I was pressed back. I started to scream then, but stopped screaming and then somehow or other I got out.'

Flg Off Boy Mould (P2649/T) was the first to arrive back at Berry-au-Bac, his aircraft bearing the scars of battle, and was soon followed by Plt Off Peter Boot and Flg Off Peter Matthews. Although Mould claimed two of the Messerschmitts shot down before being chased back by two others, one of these had also been attacked by Boot, who claimed a share. Matthews apparently claimed one shot down and a second as probably destroyed. 2/ZG26 reported the loss of two Messerschmitts, one of which crashed near Vogelsang airfield on return with the death of Oblt Kurt Bruckner and his gunner (Gfr Eberhard König), while Lt Heribert Heisel was killed when the other crashed near Chimay. Of the other two members of B Flight, Flg Off Les Clisby (P2546) and Flg Off Lawrie Lorimer (L1676), there was no news:

> 'The Australian was hit by a cannon shell, and went into a dive with smoke and flames coming from his cockpit. No one actually saw him crash.'

Both were reported later to have been killed when French forces found the wrecks of their Hurricanes.

Next to attack were four Battles from 150 Squadron, their bombs aimed at the bridge near Douzy. From this operation all aircraft returned safely, German Flak gunners having experienced difficulty in sighting the bombers in the morning fog which covered the Meuse valley. At 0900, nine Bréguet 693s of GBA I and II/54 carried out a low-level attack on pontoons between Douzy and Vrigne-sur-Meuse and armoured columns in the Bazeilles area. Escort was provided by 15 Bloch 152s of GCI/1 and GCII/1 and 15 MS406s of GCII/6. One Bréguet was shot down by the Flak gunners and force-landed and five others returned with various degrees of damage.

Five Hurricanes of 73 Squadron scrambled at 1145, in pursuit of bombers reported attacking a convoy on the Givet-Namur road. Four Bf109s of I/JG76 were encountered and these were engaged by two of the Hurricanes. Of the action, Sqn Ldr More reported:

> 'One Hurricane [Flg Off Ginger Paul] attacked the rear Messerschmitt, but was itself attacked by a Messerschmitt which holed the Hurricane's oil tank. The Hurricane turned on the attacker and followed him down to 1,000 feet, firing all the while. Black smoke was pouring from the 109's engine when it was lost from sight, evidently very badly damaged, in a smoke-cloud above a small town which had just been severely bombarded. The second Hurricane [Flg Off Cobber Kain] succeeded in following his Messerschmitt through a series of steep diving and climbing turns; finally, by pulling his boost cut out, he kept up with him in a long steep dive

and got in a long burst as the enemy pulled out. The 109 went crashing into a field.'

The Messerschmitt crashed north of Sedan although the pilot, Lt Rudolf Ziegler, survived and was able to return to his unit. Meanwhile, the other Hurricanes—joined by Kain—engaged in a series of skirmishes with a large formation of Bf110Cs, estimated at about 50-strong (apparently from III/ZG26), which had been the escort for a bombing raid on a French convoy near Namur. Sqn Ldr More's report continued:

'One Hurricane, trying to get above the enemy aircraft, observed five layers of ten Messerschmitt 110s each, between 10,000 and 15,000 feet, and there was a sixth layer of ten more above him. The Hurricanes attacked. One Hurricane [Flt Lt John Scoular in C] silenced the rear gunner of one 110 and forced it to retire [believing that he had shot it down]. Another Hurricane [Flg Off Kain] spent about a quarter of an hour alternately dodging and flying in and out among the enemy layers, firing off its ammunition until it was nearly all gone. Then, coming down low over the hill-tops, it climbed back to 7,000 feet and fired what was left of its ammunition in an astern attack on three Junkers before setting off for his base.'

It would seem that the 'Junkers' attacked by Kain were, in fact, Potez 631s of ECMJ I/16 from Wez-Thuisy. The pilot of one of the French aircraft, Sgt Chef Roger Sauvage, reported being attacked by a Hurricane which opened fire, raking the wing and fuselage of his aircraft. One engine began to smoke and then belched flame. The air gunner, Sgt Simon, baled out but Sauvage could not open his canopy. Apparently the impact of bullets had twisted the fuselage, thus jamming his only means of escape. He was forced to use his head as a battering ram until the canopy smashed and he baled out only seconds before the Potez exploded. Sauvage* landed in the British sector, where he received treatment for cuts and bruises.

73 Squadron lost Plt Off Valcourt Roe in this engagement, his aircraft (P2856) last seen diving on the bottom layer of the Messerschmitts. It was presumed that he was shot down and he was reported later to have been killed.

Shortly before midday, 13 Amiot 143s—normally night bombers—of GBI/34 and GBII/34 were ordered to bomb in the Sedan area, but six others from GBII/38 failed to rendezvous and turned back. Escort was

---

* Roger Sauvage was credited with two victories with the Armée de l'Air in France, plus 14 and two probables with the Normandie-Niemen Air Regiment in Russia later in the war.

provided by a dozen MS406s of GCIII/7, a similar number of Bloch 152s of GCI/10 and nine D520s of GCI/3. On their approach to Sedan, one Amiot was hit by Flak and fell in flames. After releasing their bombs, the remaining bombers were attacked by Bf110Cs of III/ZG26 and a second fell in flames; another crash-landed and all the others returned badly damaged and were considered unfit for further operations. There occurred a simultaneous attack by eight LeO 451s of GBI/12, one of which was also shot down by Flak and all the others damaged.

A total of 77 Battles had been mustered from all ten squadrons of 71, 75 and 76 Wings, together with eight Blenheims from 114 and 139 Squadrons, for the afternoon assault. It was to prove to be a modern day charge into the valley of death for the bomber crews, as waiting for them were not only the formidable mobile Flak batteries, but an umbrella of Bf109s and Bf110s. At the planned time—around 1500—the 25 Battles of the first wave neared their targets, protected by the Bloch 152s and MS406s of the four French squadrons, and were immediately engaged by Bf109s from I/JG76. Within 15 minutes the Messerschmitt pilots had claimed two Battles, two Moranes and four Hawk-75s (in fact Bloch 152s), for the loss of two of their own, while Flak brought down more of the bombers. Almost 50% of the bombers failed to return, 12 and 142 Squadrons each reporting the loss of four aircraft, and 226 Squadron three more.

As cover for the second wave—23 Battles of 105 and 150 Squadrons, together with the eight Blenheims of the composite 114/139 Squadron—were the Hurricanes of 1 and 73 Squadrons. By now the bridges were being guarded by Bf109s of III/JG53, while those from I/JG53 circled Le Chesne, waiting for Stukas of StG77 which were tasked to bomb French troops near and around the town, but these were intercepted by 1 Squadron before the Messerschmitts could react. Five of the dive-bombers were claimed by Flg Off Iggy Kilmartin (two), Flg Off Hilly Brown, Flg Off Bill Stratton and Sgt Taffy Clowes. In fact six Ju87s were lost, although the Gruppenkommodore's aircraft was reported to have been shot down by French AA fire:

> Ju87B of Stab/StG77 shot down four miles south-east of Le Chesne (possibly by AA fire): Obst Günther Schwartzkopff and Fw Heinz Follmer killed.

> Ju87B of 2/StG77 shot down four miles south-west of Le Chesne: Lt Ludwig Kirchner and Gfr Reinhold Zeilinger killed.

> Ju87B of 2/StG77 shot down south-west of Le Chesne: Oblt Walter Scherzinger killed, Uffz Walter Rottländer wounded, baled out and rescued by German troops.

Ju87B of 2/StG77 shot down and crash-landed south of Le Chesne: Uffz Jakob Schneider and Uffz Fritz Wöllner both wounded and captured by the French.

Ju87B of 2/StG77 shot down and crash-landed south of Sedan: Lt Sinn and gunner rescued by German troops.

Ju87B of 2/StG77 shot down and crash-landed south of Sedan: Uffz Robert Munck and gunner unhurt, returned.

Ju87B of 2/StG77 5% damaged in combat: Gfr Hans Weidner (gunner) wounded.

By the time the Messerschmitt pilots of I/JG53 realised what was happening, the Hurricanes were in a good position to attack and claimed four shot down in a series of dogfights, one apiece being credited to Flg Off Hilly Brown, Flg Off Pussy Palmer, Sgt Taffy Clowes and Sgt Frank Soper. Indeed, four Messerschmitts were lost and two others damaged, although it was reported that one was destroyed when the Blenheim it was attacking exploded:

Bf109E of 1/JG53 shot down and crashed between Sedan and Bouillon: Ofw Walter Grimmling, victor of three combats including JG53's first of the war, was killed.

Bf109E of 1/JG53 shot down and crash-landed west of Sedan: Uffz Herbert Tzschoppe unhurt.

Bf109E of 1/JG53 shot down south of Bouillon: Lt Wolfgang Tonne baled out, wounded and on his return to his unit he reported that he had shot down a Blenheim first.

Bf109E of 1/JG53 flew into debris of exploding Blenheim: Fw Alfred Stark killed.

Bf109E of Stab I/JG53 5% damaged by Hurricane near Sedan: Oblt Wilfried Balfanz wounded and on his return to base he reported that he had shot down a Battle first.

Bf109E of I/JG53 10% damaged and force-landed near Niederbreisach on return: pilot safe.

South-west of Sedan the six Hurricanes of 73 Squadron also encountered Stukas—seven aircraft of I/StG76—which were engaged near Malmy. Sqn Ldr More's report of the action revealed:

'The leader of the Hurricanes [Plt Off Don Scott] attacked two machines, one of which dropped out of formation, while the second was last seen sinking at an angle of 45° with smoke and steam pouring out. Another Hurricane [Plt Off Dickie Martin] attacked three Ju87s in turn. A member of the crew was seen to jump out of the first with a parachute which was badly shot about. His aircraft was seen going down with the tail falling to pieces. The second Ju87 attacked by this pilot crashed into the ground and blew up. The third also dived to the ground. This pilot then attacked a Do17, which escaped into the clouds, leaving the Hurricane between two Messerschmitt 109s, which received the last of his ammunition. Another Hurricane [Sgt Lionel Pilkington] saw the Ju87 he attacked dive into the ground and explode. He thereupon engaged a Dornier, which turned for home. The survivors of the Ju87 squadron jettisoned their bombs and fled.'

Pilkington noted in his diary:

'Meet Ju87s, Do17s and Me109s—about 40. Fire a good burst into an 87, break away right into Messerschmitts and go right through them, jinking, then dive to the deck and fly home. Land at Bétheniville.'

I/StG76 lost two Stukas and a further two seriously damaged to the Hurricanes of 73 Squadron:

Ju87B of Stab I/StG76 30% damaged in combat south of Sedan, but returned: gunner wounded.

Ju87B of 2/StG76 shot down west of Malmy: Lt Kilian Olbert and Uffz Werner Günthert both wounded, rescued by German troops.

Ju87B of 2/StG76 shot down west of Malmy and crash-landed: crew unhurt and rescued by German troops.

Ju87B of 2/StG76 shot down south of Sedan and crash-landed (50% damaged): gunner wounded.

Before the Hurricanes could rendezvous with the bombers of 71 Wing however, the Bf109s of I and III/JG53 intercepted and, in the ensuing action, 73 Squadron lost two pilots when Sgt Basil Pyne (P2812) and Sgt George Dibden (P2689) failed to return. Both were reported later to have been killed. Of the day's losses, Pilkington noted in his diary:

'We lose Dibden, Roe and Pyne. This is a hell of a blow to me. Hell!'

It seems probable that Sgts Pyne and Dibden were shot down by Bf109s of I/JG53, although two Hurricanes were also claimed by pilots of III/

JG53, Hptm Werner Mölders and Lt Hans Kunert. However, Oblt Hans-Karl Mayer of 1 Staffel reported:

'The Staffel flew at 5,000 metres, crossing a Stuka formation that was at 3,500 metres. We were attacked from above by six Hurricanes and the covering Schwarm immediately engaged them. I myself went down over the Stuka formation, which had come under attack by various types of enemy fighter. I shot down a Hurricane, which burned.'

Mayer's No 2, Lt Hans Ohly, witnessed the action:

'The attack was in pairs, following the Staffel break. Oblt Mayer fired first. The Hurricane went down vertically after the first long burst of fire, crashed and burned.'

Within a minute of his victory over the Hurricane, Mayer shot down a Battle, followed by two Blenheims, before claiming a second Battle five minutes later. Mayer's Combat Report revealed that he used only 120 20mm rounds and 560 machine-gun bullets to achieve five kills. A second Hurricane was claimed by Uffz Heinrich Höhnisch, also of 1 Staffel:

'I flew as the third man in Lt [Alfred] Zeis' Schwarm. At 1520, enemy aircraft were sighted above us which at that moment were engaged by our aircraft. I broke and climbed above the engaged aircraft. I suddenly saw below me a Hurricane closing behind a Bf109 of our Staffel. I was in a very favourable attacking position and with only a slight turn got behind the Hurricane. I fired from 100-50 metres and shot it down in flames, spinning and burning.'

The No 2 pilot of Zeis' Schwarm, Uffz Gröten, had been the target of the Hurricane's attack:

'We were attacked at around 2,500 metres altitude. Because of the surprise, a Hurricane got behind me and opened fire, damaging my tail unit. I turned sharply to evade the attacker and the Hurricane overshot me, with a Bf109 behind it and firing. I could observe that the Hurricane burned, spun down and disappeared.'

Uffz Höhnisch went on to shoot down two Battles. Other pilots from I Gruppe claimed three more Battles plus two probables and five Blenheims. The two Battle squadrons lost a total of 11 aircraft shot down while four of the eight Blenheims also failed to return, three of which crash-landed; two others returned seriously damaged.

While the Hurricanes of 1 Squadron were away from Berry-au-Bac, a dozen more from 3 Squadron arrived at the airfield at 1545 to refuel before flying over Sedan battlefield area at 15,000 feet, as part of the cover for the 75 Wing attack—29 Battles of 88, 103 and 226 Squadrons. North-west of Sedan the Hurricanes, with Sqn Ldr Gifford (L1610) at their head, also encountered Ju87s, a large force in two waves. These were aircraft from I(St)/TrGr186, escorted by Bf109s of I/JG54. Sgt Basil Friendship (N2351) was Yellow 3 and recalled:

> 'We came across about 50 Ju87s. We went in line astern and picked off ones at the rear of the formation. Then 20 Messerschmitt 109s dived down from above. I got into a tight orbit and shot whatever passed through my sights; one went straight down and did not return, but as we were at about 20,000 feet I did not see it hit the ground.'

However, he was credited with one of each type, while the two other members of his section—Flg Off Bunny Stone (N2535) and Plt Off Noel Hallifax (L1609)—each claimed a Bf109. In addition, Stone claimed two Ju87s (one inconclusive) but Hallifax's aircraft was damaged by a Messerschmitt and he was obliged to force-land, although he was able to return, on foot, to the Squadron.

Flt Lt Walter Churchill's Red Section also successfully engaged the Stukas, four being claimed by Churchill (N2825) himself (one of which was credited as a probable). Meanwhile, Sgt Dennis Allen (L1591) was seen to shoot down a Stuka before he went missing, presumably a victim of one of the Messerschmitts engaged by Sgt Roy Wilkinson (N2422), who recalled:

> 'I was on to a Messerschmitt 109 and closing in. After a brief burst, I saw the pilot leave the aircraft and take to his parachute. At the same time I noticed tracer coming over my shoulder. I couldn't see the other aircraft, but because of the tracer I had a good idea where the enemy aircraft was, so I half-rolled and there was the 109 that had been doing the shooting. The 109 half-rolled and the chase was on. I started belting into him, then suddenly he hit the deck in front of me and blew up. I was so low I hauled back on the stick and passed out instantly unconscious. I regained consciousness at about 8,000 feet still going up under full boost.'

Sgt Ernie Ford (L1781) of Green Section claimed two Ju87s and Plt Off Mike Stephens reported shooting down a Ju87 and a Bf109 before forcing down a Hs126 (of 1(H)/11). His own aircraft (N2546) suffered some damage in the battle, obliging him to force-land near Maubeuge, from where he made his way back to the Squadron.

3 Squadron's total for the engagement was assessed to be 16, including the two probables, of which 11 were claims against the Stukas. In fact, I(St)/TrGr186 lost eight aircraft:

Ju87B of Stab I(St)/TrGr186 shot down and crashed near Chimay: Oblt Manfried Heyden and Lt Helmut Cords killed.

Ju87B of 1(St)/TrGr186 shot down and crashed in Florenville: Uffz Fritz Henken and Uffz Otto Kopania killed.

Ju87B of 1(St)/TrGr186 severely damaged and crash-landed (45% damaged) near Ferschweiler on return: crew unhurt.

Ju87B of 1(St)/TrGr186 shot down and crash-landed (40% damaged) near Malmedy: crew unhurt.

Ju87B of 2(St)/TrGr186 shot down and crashed south of Brevilly, six miles south-east of Sedan: Fw Walter Strehle and Gfr Heinrich Hüsch killed.

Ju87B of 2(St)/TrGr186 shot down and crash-landed south-west of Florenville: Uffz Otto Reuss wounded, returned, Uffz Ernst Hecht killed.

Ju87B of 2(St)/TrGr186 severely damaged and crash-landed (30% damaged) near Hemweiler on return: crew unhurt.

Ju87B of 3(St)/TrGr186 shot down near Prin, 12 miles east of Florenville: Obfhr Hans-Jürgen Ellerlage and Uffz Alfred Froese killed.

In addition to the Bf109s from the escorting I/JG54, Messerschmitts from II/JG52 and III/JG53 intervened, both Gruppes being on duty over the Meuse bridges. Pilots from these units claimed eight Battles shot down, while another two were claimed by two pilots from 2/JG2, which arrived on the scene as the bombers were withdrawing. A total of 14 Battles failed to return from this operation and one other was written off, while a Bf109 of 4/JG52 was hit by return fire and force-landed; a second aircraft from this Staffel nosed-over on landing at Wengerohr, killing Fw Hans Bauer. In addition, a Bf109 of 8/JG53 flown by Uffz Josef Kröschel crashed south-west of Sedan, killing the pilot, and was probably the victim of 3 Squadron as may have been Bauer. A pilot of 1/JG54, Lt Adolf Kinzinger, claimed an aircraft identified as a Spitfire, while Uffz Reinhold Thiel of 5/JG52 claimed a Morane; both were probably Hurricanes of 3 Squadron.

Meanwhile, 3 Squadron's Blue Section encountered Bf110s of I/ZG2, one of which shot down Plt Off Charles Jeffries (L1908):

'I, Blue 2, acting as bomber escort over Sedan, encountered twenty
Messerschmitt 110s—I was hit by their fire and started to burn. I
continued to attack one 110 and saw it dive towards the ground with
smoke pouring from the centre section. All my ammunition was
used up so I attempted to return to my base. My machine burst into
flames and I was forced to abandon it.'

Jeffries, a large man, came down in friendly territory and set out to walk
back to Merville, hitching lifts when he was able, and reached the
airfield in three days. Meanwhile, Flg Off Walter Bowyer (N2339)
apparently attacked the same aircraft as Jeffries, which was seen to
crash. Despite their belief that it was a Bf110, it would appear that it was
an accompanying Do17M of Stabsstaffel StG1, which was severely
damaged by a Hurricane north of Sedan during this operation and
crash-landed near Dockendorf with an injured crew member on board.

  607 Squadron had been ordered to provide six aircraft as escort for
the Battles of 105 Squadron. However, on arrival at Villeneuve, the
bombers' base, all was not well, as Plt Off Peter Parrott recalled:

'When we arrived the only Battle in sight was standing on its nose in
the middle of the landing area. We were told that the Battles had
already gone out on a raid but might fly another in the afternoon.
We waited until late in the afternoon, but no Battles returned. So
we flew back to Vitry.'

There was one final raid on the bridges, by RAF Blenheims from 2
Group, when a total of 28 aircraft drawn from 21, 107 and 110 Squadrons arrived in the Bouillon-Givonne-Sedan area at 1820. The promised
escort of 18 Hurricanes from 1 and 73 Squadrons failed to materialize
(due to earlier losses) although 79 Squadron provided a Flight of five
aircraft. Leading the Blenheims of 107 Squadron was Wg Cdr Basil
Embry, who wrote:

'About 40 miles from the target I saw flying below and to the side of
us a German light reconnaissance aeroplane, and attracted
Whiting's [Sgt Tom Whiting, navigator] attention to it. As I did so a
section of Hurricanes dived, firing their guns, and in a moment it
just disintegrated. Someone described it later as "bursting like an
electric light bulb".'

The Hs126 fell victim to the Hurricane leader, Flg Off Jimmy Davies
(L2140). Although Hurricanes were not available in great numbers, up
to 30 Bloch 152s (GCI/1, GCII/1, GCII/10 and GCIII/10), MS406s
(GCII/6) and D520s of GCI/3 were ordered to rendezvous with the

bombers instead, although these were unable to prevent Messerschmitts of III/JG2, I/JG53 and II/ZG26 from shooting down five of the bombers and causing two others to force-land. One of the attacking Bf109s from III/JG2 was hit by return fire and the pilot was forced to bale out west of Givonne.

Shortly after the successful engagement with the Henschel, the Hurricanes of 79 Squadron encountered about 15 Bf110Cs—part of the ZG1 formation engaged earlier by 87 Squadron—five miles north of Leuze at 6,000 feet. Plt Off John Wood (N2490) attacked two, without apparent result, and was about to engage a third when he saw tracers passing his cockpit from the rear:

> 'About five seconds later a bullet hit the back of my left hand, which was holding the throttle, and either it or another bullet punctured the reserve tank, the petrol pouring over the back of my head and body making it impossible to see out of the cockpit. The engine then cut dead and I pulled up the nose and climbed from 50 feet to 1,100 feet, where the aircraft stalled. I abandoned the aircraft, landing in a wood. I was picked up by a roving army patrol.'

However, his companions were more successful. The patrol leader, Flg Off Davies, claimed one of the Messerschmitts, while Sgt Harry Cartwright claimed a Ju88 and Sgt Alf Whitby (N2384) a Do17 inconclusive, although the latter two aircraft were probably also Bf110s.

As a result of the escort operation, pilots of ZG1 claimed a total of five Hurricanes shot down over Belgium (three of 87 Squadron and two of 79 Squadron), one of which was credited to the Gruppenkommandeur of I/ZG1, Hptm Wolfgang Falck, and another to Uffz Helmut Eberlein, both of whom identified their victims as Spitfires. Apparently pilots of II Gruppe claimed the other three Hurricanes.

It had been a field day for the German fighters. The Bf109 pilots of I and III/JG53 alone had claimed 13 Battles, seven Blenheims and four Hurricanes over Sedan during the mid-afternoon period, the Geschwader recording a total of 43 for the day, most of which were credited to I Gruppe. Of the 96 RAF bombers sent to Sedan during the day, 45—including 36 Battles—failed to return and a further three crash-landed in Allied territory, while at least eight more suffered battle damage. The majority of these fell to the Bf109s and Bf110s, although a number were victims of the deadly mobile Flak units.

67 Wing, AASF

501 Squadron at Bétheniville was tasked with providing protection for AASF aerodromes throughout the day, following Luftwaffe attacks on Mourmelon, Auberive and Berry-au-Bac during the morning. At the

latter airfield, 1 Squadron's diarist noted:

> 'Bombing raids were now of frequent occurrence and many people, who for the past six months had been wearing spurs to keep their feet from slipping on the desks, moved about with some alacrity. Wing HQ retired in a cloud of dust to a cellar due to a bomb dropping on the station opposite.'

One witness to the attack on Mourmelon was 501 Squadron's Sgt Ginger Lacey, who had been sent to the airfield to collect a Squadron Hurricane (L1914) which had been force-landed there. As he walked across the airfield towards the repaired aircraft, 20 Do17s (probably II/KG3) and 20 Ju87s appeared, as he recalled:

> 'I never felt so naked in my life as standing in the middle of that airfield. I didn't mind the hangars and camp which I had just left being bombed, but I did object to the sticks of bombs which were being dropped across the aerodrome, where I was standing. It felt as though every bomb was being aimed individually at me.'

Railways and communications were again the principal targets behind the lines for the German bombers, the railways at Vitry-le-François, Revigny and St Mihiel all coming under attack during the day. Important towns in the area were also bombed, including Vouziers, Etain and Varennes.

One patrol of three Hurricanes, led by Plt Off John Sylvester, encountered three Do17s near Auberive—possibly stragglers from the bombing of Mourmelon—one of which was claimed jointly by Sylvester and Sgt Paul Farnes (L2045 SD-A), while Plt Off Peter Hairs was granted 'one doubtful'. All three Hurricanes returned safely. During the course of another patrol, a formation of He111s (possibly aircraft of KG55) was intercepted and engaged and four claimed shot down—two by Sgt John Proctor and one apiece by Flt Sgt Jammy Payne and Sgt Bob Dafforn, while Flg Off Ryan Cridland reported shooting down a Do17. The Hurricanes suffered no losses. One of the Heinkels may have been one of the two which machine-gunned the main street at Reims and was engaged by a Hurricane, as witnessed by Charles Gardner:

> 'The Heinkel, in its panic, nearly turned into its companion, and in the resultant flap it was shot down. I saw it stall and turn over, and then it went out of sight behind the houses. Others who could see better say that it caught fire.'

The increased raids in the area compelled 67 Wing to move its headquarters to Cormicy.

Summary

It had been a disastrous day for the Hurricane pilots of the AASF and Air Component. Of the 27 Hurricanes shot down, 22 had fallen to the Messerschmitts, resulting in the deaths of 15 pilots; four others were wounded. Additionally, a further two pilots had been killed and one wounded in combat with bombers or had been shot down by ground fire.

Claims by AASF and Air Component Hurricanes, 14 May				
Type	Confirmed	Probable	Damaged	Total
He111	11	2	—	13
Do17	4	—	4	8
Ju88	4	—	—	4
Ju87	18	3	1	22
Hs123	—	—	1	1
Hs126	3	—	—	3
Bf109	11	—	3	14
Bf110	8	2	—	10
Bf109/Hs123*	1	7	—	8
	60	14	9	83

* See 607 Squadron's engagement in the morning.

Luftwaffe Losses Attributed to AASF and Air Component Hurricanes, 14 May		
Type	60% to 100%	Under 60%	Total
He111	6	2	8
Do17	2	—	2
Ju88	2	—	2
Ju87	15	4	19
Hs123	2	—	2
Hs126	2	—	2
Bf109	7	1	8
Bf110	2	1	3
	38	8	46

Forty-three sorties were flown by Bomber Command during the night of 14/15 May, 13 Hampdens bombing the Breda-Rotterdam and Breda-Rozendaal road junctions; two of the bombers were lost. Meanwhile, six Wellingtons attacked the railway station at Maastricht and a bridge over the Maas, and a further dozen raided the marshalling yards at Aachen. Finally, 12 Whitleys were sent to München-Gladbach, where troop concentrations and communications were bombed.

Individual Claims—AASF and Air Component Hurricanes, 14 May

AM-0420-	Flg Off H.N. Fowler	615 Sqn	Do17
	Sqn Ldr J.B. Parnall		
	Flg Off M.E.A. Royce	504 Sqn	Ju88
	Plt Off B. Van Mentz		
0440-	Plt Off F.R. Carey	3 Sqn	Do17
0445-	Flg Off N. Orton	73 Sqn	Do17 damaged
	Sgt L.S. Pilkington	73 Sqn	Do17 damaged
0800-	Flt Lt P.P. Hanks	1 Sqn	2 Bf110
	Flg Off P.W.O. Mould	1 Sqn	Bf110
	Flg Off P.G.H. Matthews	1 Sqn	Bf110, Bf110 probable
	Plt Off P.V. Boot	1 Sqn	Bf110
	Flg Off P.W.O. Mould		
0900-	Flg Off J.M. Bazin	607 Sqn	e/a destroyed/damaged (possibly)
	Flg Off I.B.N. Russell	607 Sqn	4 e/a destroyed/damaged (possibly)
	Plt Off R.N.H. Courtney	607 Sqn	e/a destroyed
	Plt Off J.S. Humphreys	607 Sqn	Bf109 damaged, Hs123 damaged
	Flg Off K.E. Newton	607 Sqn	2 e/a destroyed/damaged (possibly)
	Flt Lt R.H.A. Lee	85 Sqn	2 He111
	Flg Off A.B. Angus	85 Sqn	He111
	Unknown pilot	85 Sqn	He111
	Flg Off A.B. Angus	85 Sqn	He111
	Plt Off W.D. David	87 Sqn	
	Plt Off W.D. David	87 Sqn	He111
	Plt Off P.L. Jarvis	87 Sqn	He111 probable
1145-	Flg Off E.J. Kain	73 Sqn	Bf109
	Flg Off H.G. Paul	73 Sqn	Bf109 damaged
	Flt Lt J.E. Scoular	73 Sqn	Bf110
AM-	Plt Off L.L. Appleton		
	Plt Off J.E.R. Wood	79 Sqn	Hs126
	Sgt L.H.B. Pearce		
1530-	Plt Off D.S. Scott	73 Sqn	Ju87, Ju87 damaged
	Plt Off R.F. Martin	73 Sqn	2 Ju87, Ju87 probable
	Sgt L.S. Pilkington	73 Sqn	Ju87
	Flg Off M.H. Brown	1 Sqn	Ju87, Bf109
	Flg Off W.H. Stratton	1 Sqn	Ju87
	Sgt A.V. Clowes	1 Sqn	Ju87, Bf109
	Flg Off J.I. Kilmartin	1 Sqn	2 Ju87
	Flg Off C.D. Palmer	1 Sqn	Bf109
	Sgt F.J. Soper	1 Sqn	Bf109
1545-	Flt Lt W.M. Churchill	3 Sqn	3 Ju87, Ju87 probable
	Sgt D.A. Allen	3 Sqn	Ju87
	Sgt R.C. Wilkinson	3 Sqn	2 Bf109
	Plt Off M.M. Stephens	3 Sqn	Ju87, Bf109, Hs126
	Sgt E.G. Ford	3 Sqn	2 Ju87
	Flg Off C.A.C. Stone	3 Sqn	Ju87, Bf109, Ju87 probable

	Plt Off N.D. Hallifax	3 Sqn	Bf109
	Sgt A.H.B. Friendship	3 Sqn	Bf109, Ju87
	Flg Off W.S. Bowyer Plt Off C.G.St D. Jeffries	3 Sqn	Bf110
1900-	Flg Off F.P. Joyce	87 Sqn	Bf110 probable
1915-	Flg Off J.W.E. Davies	79 Sqn	Hs126, Bf110
	Sgt H. Cartwright	79 Sqn	Ju88
	Plt Off D.W.A. Stones	79 Sqn	Ju88
	Plt Off D.W.A. Stones Sgt H. Cartwright	79 Sqn	Ju88
?	Sgt A.W. Whitby	79 Sqn	Do17 damaged
PM-	Sqn Ldr J.B. Parnall	504 Sqn	He111 probable
	Flg Off M.E.A. Royce	504 Sqn	He111, Bf109 damaged
?	Plt Off E.J.H. Sylvester Sgt P.C.P. Farnes	501 Sqn	Do17
	Plt Off P.R. Hairs	501 Sqn	Do17 damaged
	Sgt J.E. Proctor	501 Sqn	2 He111
	Flg Off J.R. Cridland	501 Sqn	Do17
	Flt Sgt A.D. Payne	501 Sqn	He111
	Sgt R.C. Dafforn	501 Sqn	He111

Losses—AASF and Air Component Hurricanes, 14 May

0440-	L1932	3 Sqn	Plt Off F.R. Carey: aircraft hit by return fire from Do17P of 3(F)/11 and crash-landed near Hamme-Mille; pilot wounded.
0530-	L1891	73 Sqn	Plt Off A. McFadden: shot down by return fire from Do17Z of 3/KG76 and crash-landed; pilot unhurt, returned.
AM-	N2441	3 Sqn	Sgt J.L.C. Williams: landed in field—en route to Merville—aircraft w/o; pilot unhurt.
0800-	P2546	1 Sqn	Flg Off L.R. Clisby: shot down by Bf110C of I/ZG26 and crashed south of Sedan; pilot killed.
	L1676	1 Sqn	Flg Off L.R. Lorimer: shot down by Bf110C of I/ZG26 and crashed south of Sedan; pilot killed.
	N2380	1 Sqn	Flt Lt P.P. Hanks: shot down by Bf110C of I/ZG26 south of Sedan; pilot baled out, returned.
0900-	P2618	607 Sqn	Flg Off G.I. Cuthbert: shot down by Bf109 of 4/JG2 and crashed at Aische-en-Refail; pilot killed.
	P2620	607 Sqn	Flg Off M.H.B. Thompson: shot down by Bf109 of 4/JG2 and crashed near Gembloux; pilot killed.
	P2713	607 Sqn	Flg Off A.E. Le Breuilly: shot down by Bf109 of 4/JG2 and crashed near Gembloux; pilot killed.
	P2621	242 Sqn	Flt Lt J.L. Sullivan: believed shot down by return fire from Hs123s of II(S)/LG2 and crashed at Perwez; pilot killed.
0900-	L1616	87 Sqn	Plt Off P.L. Jarvis: shot down by Bf109 of 2/JG27 and crashed west of Maastricht; pilot killed.
	L1612	87 Sqn	Plt Off G.C. Saunders: shot down near Mainvault by Bf110C of ZG1; pilot severely wounded and died in Lille Hospital on 19 May.
1145-	P2813	73 Sqn	Plt Off V.D.M. Roe: shot down by Bf110C of III/ZG26 and crashed near Namur; pilot killed.

1230-	L1941	504 Sqn	Plt Off S.A.C. Sibley: shot down by Flak east of Brussels; pilot killed.
1530-	P2689	73 Sqn	Sgt G.M. Dibden: shot down by Bf109 (probably of I or III/JG53) and crashed near Sedan; pilot killed.
	P2812	73 Sqn	Sgt T.B.G. Pyne: shot down by Bf109 (probably of I or III/JG53) and crashed near Sedan; pilot killed.
1545-	L1591	3 Sqn	Sgt D.A. Allen: shot down by Bf109 (possibly I/JG54 or JG53) and crashed near Villers-Cernay; pilot killed.
	N2546	3 Sqn	Plt Off M.M. Stephens: aircraft damaged (possibly by Bf109 of I/JG54 or JG53) and force-landed near Maubeuge; pilot unhurt, returned.
	L1846	3 Sqn	Plt Off N.D. Hallifax: aircraft damaged by Bf109 (possibly I/JG54 or JG53) and force-landed; pilot unhurt, returned.
	L1908	3 Sqn	Plt Off C.G.St D. Jeffries: shot down by Bf110C of I/ZG2 west of Sedan; pilot baled out unhurt, returned.
1900-	L1646	87 Sqn	Flg Off F.P. Joyce: shot down by Bf110C of ZG1 south of Brussels; pilot wounded.
	L1834	87 Sqn	Plt Off C.C.D. Mackworth: shot down by Bf110C of ZG1 and crashed at Ramegnies-Chin; pilot baled out, died of wounds.
1915-	N2490	79 Sqn	Plt Off J.E.R. Wood: shot down by Bf110C of ZG1 near Frasnes, 5 miles north of Leuze; pilot wounded.
PM-	P2537	79 Sqn	Plt Off L.L. Appleton: shot down (believed by return fire from He111 of II/LG1 or by Bf110C of ZG1) and crashed east of Renaix; pilot killed.
PM-	L1639	504 Sqn	Sqn Ldr J.B. Parnall: shot down by Bf109 of II or III/JG26 and crashed at Hameau du Caillou; pilot killed.
	L1950	504 Sqn	Flg Off M.E.A. Royce: shot down by Bf109 of II or III/JG26 south of Brussels; pilot baled out, returned.
	N2492	504 Sqn	Sgt S. Hamblett: shot down by Bf109 of II or III/JG26 near Ath; pilot killed.
	L1916	504 Sqn	Plt Off B.E.G. White: aircraft damaged by Bf109 of II or III/JG26 and crash-landed; pilot injured.

CHAPTER VII

WEDNESDAY 15 MAY
THE SITUATION WORSENS

'We have been defeated. We are beaten; we have lost the battle. The front is broken near Sedan.'

French Prime Minister Paul Reynaud to British Prime Minister Winston Churchill.

The Situation in Holland and Belgium

The struggle had all but ceased to exist in Holland. Only in the province of Zeeland was there any real resistance, and there the Luftwaffe continued to support the ground forces in the area of South Beveland and Walcheren, where Flushing bore the brunt of the German attack. The Netherlands Government surrendered at 1100.

In northern Belgium, Antwerp was in grave danger. Although two divisions of the French 7th Armée were retained for the defence of Zeeland and two for the defence of Antwerp, the remainder steadily withdrew southwards. A BEF counter-attack in the neighbourhood of Louvain slowed the German advance, although the French 1st Armée was beginning 'a retirement to positions which would join the BEF at Charleroi'.

'It was in the sectors south of Namur, however, that the Germans continued to make really big headway. Although the French still clung to the Meuse at a point some five miles south of Namur, the line was then forced away in a big bulge which reached to Florennes, 15 miles west of the river at Dinant. Except at isolated points, the whole river defence was as good as lost between Namur and just above Stenay; the bulge west of Dinant was matched further south by even deeper penetrations. In particular, German progress was exceptionally fast west of the bypassed Mézières. This advance caused Air Marshal Barratt to issue orders, shortly before

midnight, that the AASF should begin a retirement in a southerly
direction. Thus, from Namur to some dozen miles south of Sedan an
enormous gap had opened.'

The Situation in Northern France

At about 0730 French Prime Minister Reynaud telephoned his British
counterpart, Winston Churchill:

> 'He spoke in English, and evidently under stress. "We have been
> defeated." As I did not immediately respond he said again: "We are
> beaten; we have lost the battle." I said: "Surely it can't have hap-
> pened so soon?" But he replied: "The front is broken near Sedan."
> I said I was willing to come over and have a talk.'

This message of doom followed one the previous day from M. Reynaud,
to the effect:

> 'You were kind enough to send four squadrons, which is more than
> you promised, but if we are to win this battle, which might be
> decisive for the whole war, it is necessary to send at once, if possible
> today, ten more squadrons.'

Churchill instructed the Chief of the Air Staff to take preparatory steps
for the early dispatch of ten additional Hurricane squadrons.

> 'The possibility of losing ten more squadrons (and possibly still
> more in the future) from the direct air defence of Great Britain was
> naturally most unwelcome to Air Chief Marshal Dowding [AOC
> Fighter Command] and he was given an opportunity to state his
> views on the subject before the War Cabinet. It so happened that
> the War Cabinet had decided to authorise attack on targets in the
> Ruhr, partly in an effort to force the enemy to attack British
> objectives in return, and thereby relieve France and Belgium. The
> prospect of immediate German retaliation therefore powerfully
> reinforced Dowding's normal viewpoint, and the War Cabinet
> decided, to his "inexpressible relief", that no further fighter
> squadrons should, for the present, be sent to France. Nevertheless,
> the following day [16 May] the War Cabinet decided to go some way
> towards meeting Reynaud's request.'

Air Operations over Belgium and Northern France

Four strategical and four photographic sorties were flown by the
Blenheims during the day. One of these was shot down by Bf109s and

another chased by the Messerschmitts. On occasions, the Blenheims had the luxury of fighter escort, as Flg Off Bill Whitty of 607 Squadron recalled:

'We were asked to escort Blenheims on recce flights but as they did these at nought feet we were of little help as AA was the main problem.'

However, on this occasion there lurked an unimagined danger. Having survived ground fire and evaded patrolling fighters, two of the photo-reconnaissance Blenheims were intercepted by Hurricanes on their return. One of these was shot down and the other was damaged (see later). The remaining Blenheims, together with a 212 Squadron photo-reconnaissance Spitfire, brought back information of movements on the roads up to 30 miles east of Louvain and Wavre, where refugees were said to be holding up columns of German transport. Of the ever-increasing problem of refugees, Plt Off Peter Parrott of 607 Squadron recalled:

'On the eastern boundary of the airfield [Vitry-en-Artois] there was a road crowded with refugees fleeing from the advancing Germans. A continual flow of families with their children, babies, pets, riding on farm carts, bicycles, pushing wheelbarrows; few cars because petrol was unobtainable. Our ground crews helped where they could, giving some their own rations. Petrol we could not spare.'

The main task for the Hurricane squadrons continued to be the protection of BEF and French 1st Armée forces along the Gembloux-Wavre-Louvain line.

67 Wing, AASF
The three AASF squadrons were all heavily engaged throughout the day in protection of their bases. At 0520, six Hurricanes of 73 Squadron were scrambled in an unsuccessful attempt to intercept five bombers flying north-west from Reims. At about 0730, six Hurricanes of 1 Squadron's A Flight were scrambled on the approach of a raid and met 40 Do17Zs of I and II/KG3 escorted by Bf110Cs of III/ZG26. In the ensuing series of dogfights, Messerschmitts were claimed by Flt Lt Johnny Walker, Flg Off Iggy Kilmartin, Sgt Frank Soper and Sgt Taffy Clowes. The Flight Commander, Walker, force-landed after his Hurricane (L1681) had been hit, while Flg Off Paul Richey's aircraft (L1943) was shot down in flames, although he claimed one and a probable, as he graphically recalled:

'The top squadron of Messerschmitts saw us as we reached their level astern of them . . . They immediately formed a defensive circle, flying round and round one behind the other. I lost sight of the other Hurricanes and climbed above the circle. Then I selected a Messerschmitt and dived on him from above, finishing in a quarter-attack. A lot of bits flew off him and flames leapt from his engines. I saw a Hurricane below being attacked by a Hun and I dived on the Hun's tail. He pulled up at about 60° with me still behind and firing long bursts savagely into him. Smoke suddenly poured from him and he fell away to the left with little flames shooting down his fuselage.'

Richey's aircraft was then attacked by another Bf110. With smoke pouring from its damaged engine, Richey put the Hurricane in a steep dive in an attempt to evade his attacker:

'The smoke suddenly increased and turned grey, then completely enveloped the nose and cockpit. I let go of the stick to dive over the side. I was so surprised to find myself in a state of suspension in space that I very nearly forgot to pull the ripcord!'

He came down near Bétheniville and was driven to Reims where he was collected by Squadron transport and taken back to Pontavert. III/ZG26 crews reported being attacked by Moranes (sic) and claimed nine shot down for the loss of two of their own aircraft, plus two others seriously damaged in crash-landings:

Bf110C of 7/ZG26 damaged in combat and crashed near Arlon, on the Belgian/Luxembourg border: crew baled out, unhurt and returned.

Bf110C of 8/ZG26 damaged in combat near Vouziers and crashed near Maitzborn when attempting to land with one engine out of action: Fw Josef Kistler and Gfr Kurt Wengler killed.

Bf110C of 9/ZG26 damaged in combat near Reims and crash-landed, 40% damaged: crew unhurt.

Bf110C of 9/ZG26 damaged in combat near Vouziers and crash-landed near Liège, 30% damaged: crew unhurt.

Despite the attention of the Hurricanes, some of the raiders got through and bombs dropped across the centre of Berry-au-Bac airfield, 1 Squadron's base. The Squadron's diarist wrote:

'Soper, who had just landed, flung himself flat on his tummy and the blast of the explosions lifted him clean off the ground and thumped him back again.'

Of the air battle, Charles Gardner recorded:

'There was a fight before breakfast when a section of Hurricanes ran into 15 Messerschmitt 110s—of which seven or eight straight away adopted circus tactics—that is, revolving on each other's tails.'

Although it was cloudy in the vicinity of Bétheniville, Flt Lt Charles Griffiths, Plt Off Peter Hairs and Sgt Peter Morfill of 501 Squadron were able to shoot down one of the raiders near the airfield at about 0815, and Flt Sgt Jammy Payne claimed a second, which crash-landed. Two Hurricanes force-landed on return, which rendered them temporarily unserviceable. A wounded crew member of the 5 Staffel Dornier brought down by Griffiths' section—Gfr Wolfgang Rohde, the air gunner—succeeded in baling out before the aircraft crashed. He was seen floating down by Plt Off Pat Hancock of 1 Squadron, who was being driven to Bétheniville with two others on attachment to 501 Squadron. He recalled:

'We saw a Dornier shot down and a parachute nearing the ground in a field not far from the road. An angry crowd of Frenchmen awaited his landing and, without any hesitation, Salmon [Flg Off Sammy Salmon, who was driving] used his very solid Bentley like a tank and we swept into the field. The Luftwaffe airman landed as we got there and I told him to get in the car and I put my RAF hat on his head as we drove through the crowd, who made it obvious that we were removing their intended victim.'

The critically wounded Dornier pilot, Uffz Fritz Frey, was recovered from the wreck, but died in the Station Sick Quarters next day. His aircraft was one of six aircraft engaged in bombing Auberive (where 75 Wing's HQ was located).

Just after 0900, one of the returning photo-reconnaissance Blenheims —L4847 of 53 Squadron—was slightly damaged following an attack by Flg Off Cobber Kain of 73 Squadron, who apparently misidentified his victim as a Do17, his second such act in consecutive days. In spite of the damage inflicted, the Blenheim pilot, Flt Lt B.B.St G. Daly, was able to return to Poix where a safe landing was carried out at 0940.

Another AASF airfield raided by the Luftwaffe was Rosières, home for 57 Squadron's Blenheims. Two of the ex-615 Squadron Gladiators, distributed the previous day for aerodrome defence, took off from Rosières to engage the raiders:

'Accounts of the incident vary: in its most favourable version, the two Gladiators shot down two Heinkels, caused the remaining seven to jettison their bombs, and landed shot-up but triumphant. Another version makes no positive claim of enemy aircraft destroyed, and implies that one of the two Gladiators was compelled to land again almost immediately, the other returning shot-up later.'

The identities of the two pilots concerned are not known.

At 1320, six Hurricanes of 73 Squadron engaged a formation of Bf110Cs from I/ZG2, as noted by Charles Gardner:

'On this occasion the Hurricanes climbed round into one turn and then broke into the German formation, one after the other. Two 110s went down—one without part of its tail and the other giving out smoke and steam. One Hurricane was attacked by four of the 110s which were outside the circle—but the pilot [Flg Off Kain] fought them off and damaged one seriously. Soon after this fight ended, eight more 110s were in the scrap with five Hurricanes and, after a long dogfight, one certain and two probable victories were recorded. Orton and Humphries failed to return. Orton had been wounded by three bullets in the right shoulder and his Hurricane had caught fire. He managed to bale out at 500 feet and was taken to hospital at Bétheniville. Humphries [L1693] was also shot down and wounded and was taken to a casualty clearing station.'

Flg Off Orton (P2579) claimed two of the Bf110s probably destroyed before being shot down by a third, and Plt Off Don Scott claimed another. Sgt Leon Friend's Hurricane suffered some damage during the engagement and was force-landed. An aircraft of 3/ZG2 was shot down, from which Lt Franz Mentzel and Gfr Wilhelm Oechsle baled out, to be taken prisoner. A second Bf110—an aircraft of Stab I/ZG2—crashlanded near Trier and was badly damaged.

1 Squadron's Flg Off Sammy Salmon witnessed the fight while returning to Berry-au-Bac from Bétheniville:

'Three [sic] 110s went down, also two Hurricanes. Flg Off Orton, cannon shell in his shoulder and his machine a mass of flames, jumped at 600 feet and landed safely.'

Salmon also saw another Hurricane (presumably that flown by Sgt Humphries) in an engagement with four Bf110s:

'The Almighty sure took over the controls. The Hurricane stayed in a tight vertical bank whilst the 110s took their time shooting bits off it. It finally got away and went at nought feet for Reims.'

Charles Gardner continued:

'There were several more fights during the day, mainly with 110s—
when a stray He111 was shot down with possibly one 110 and one
Dornier.'

The main skirmish later in the day occurred at 1820 when 73 and 501
Squadrons dispatched Hurricanes to operate south of Reims. Flg Off
Ryan Cridland and Plt Off Peter Hairs of the latter unit came upon
seven Do17Zs of 6/KG3, one of which Cridland shot down in flames
before the others escaped. The Dornier crashed in Luxembourg and
was totally destroyed. Sgt John Proctor reported shooting down one of
the escorting Bf110Cs of I/ZG52; it force-landed 35% damaged,
although the crew escaped injury. Meanwhile, Sqn Ldr More and Flt Lt
John Scoular (Hurricane H) of 73 Squadron accounted for the Heinkel
mentioned in Gardner's report. The aircraft—A1+LK of 2/KG53—
crashed near Grandpré, south-east of Vouziers, when Oblt Walter
Klaue and one other were killed, while the remaining three members of
the crew were captured. In addition, Sgt Lionel Pilkington damaged a
Do17 and noted:

'Panic take-off. First off, chase some Heinkels but do not catch
them. Come back to base and chase five Dorniers. Get starboard
engine then they all jettison bombs. Crossfire gets me in oil and
petrol tanks, also glycol. Get back to drome, glycol tank melted and
run into engine. Face slightly burnt and eyes sore from glycol. CO
says good show.'

A replacement Hurricane was denied to 73 Squadron during the day
when Plt Off R. Ferguson, of 4 (Continental) Ferry Flight, tipped P3279
onto its nose on landing at Reims-Champagne. The Hurricane's wheels
had caught a partially filled-in bomb crater, damaging the airscrew,
although Ferguson was unhurt.

60 Wing, Air Component
Flt Lt John Owen, Plt Off Edward Frisby and Plt Off Trevor Parsons of
504 Squadron were sent off on an early morning patrol, flying south of
Lille/Marcq and then over Douai and St Amand, before being ordered
to land at Seclin in order to reinforce 85 Squadron. Having landed, the
section was scrambled almost immediately when a warning of approaching aircraft was received. One twin-engined aircraft, identified as a
Ju88, was engaged by Owen and claimed severely damaged. His victim
was in fact the second photo-reconnaissance Blenheim to fall foul of a
Hurricane that morning, L9299 of 53 Squadron, which crashed in flames

near Tournai with the loss of Plt Off P.K. Bone and his crew, Sgt W.J. Cronin DFM and LAC J. Bromley.

The 504 Squadron section then reported meeting Messerschmitts, two of which were claimed damaged by Owen and Parsons. All three landed at Seclin, from where they returned later to Lille/Marcq. 85 Squadron also scrambled all available Hurricanes to engage the approaching bombers, as Sgt Cyril Hampshire recalled:

> 'I was plunged straight in at the deep end and my first sortie was behind Sam Allard. Sam went in behind a gaggle of He111s, then I followed and opened fire. Unfortunately, the oil seal in the front of the engine was leaking and I couldn't see the target. I got one damaged, for Sam said I hit it. I couldn't see it because the windscreen was covered in oil and was opaque.'

Two Heinkels were credited to Flg Off Allan Angus and possibly a third fell to Flt Lt Dickie Lee. One of these was apparently Lt Hans-Burkhard Eymer's aircraft from 1/KG54 which force-landed about 8 miles south-east of Brussels, from which the crew survived to be taken prisoner. A second Heinkel, a machine of 3/KG53, was slightly damaged and returned to base with two wounded crew members on board. It was reported that Sgt Sammy Allard's victim crashed near the aerodrome; having inspected the wreck, the Squadron's diarist wrote:

> 'Nothing of interest could be found except six unexploded 50 kilo bombs as the occupants and the plane were a smouldering mass of ruins.'

Meanwhile, another patrol of 504 Squadron from Lille/Marcq, led by Flt Lt William Royce, encountered a dozen Hs126s and a similar number of Ju87s from 2/StG2 between Wavre and Gembloux. Two of the Stukas were claimed shot down by Plt Off John Hardacre and Plt Off Brian Van Mentz (witnessed by each other) before the latter engaged and damaged one of the Henschels. One Ju87 crashed about two miles north-west of Gembloux, with the loss of the Staffelkapitän, Hptm Paul Metz, and his gunner, Fw Oskar Wagner; the other crashed in the same area, but both Lt Karl Brausch and Uffz Robert Borrmann survived, although injured. Nine escorting Bf109s attempted to intercept the Hurricanes and two were claimed probably destroyed by Flt Lt Royce and Sgt Gordon Spencer.

Shortly after midday, a patrol from 85 Squadron was ordered to fly a protection patrol for a Lysander of 13 Squadron. When east of Ath, the Hurricanes were bounced by Bf110s of 5/ZG26 and three were shot down: Flg Off Derek Allen promptly baled out of his burning machine

(P2828), returning to Seclin next day, as did Plt Off John Ashton (L1775), but the third pilot, Flg Off Tom Pace (L1964), suffered serious wounds and burns to his face and hands when he crash-landed his aircraft. Fortunately help was forthcoming and he was promptly evacuated to England. The Lysander (L6885) also failed to return and its crew were reported to have been killed. The Messerschmitt crews claimed three victories, one of which is believed to have been credited to Obfw Kurt Rochel and his gunner, Obfw Fritz Herber.

85 Squadron's sister unit, 87 Squadron, which had just moved to Lille/Marcq, also benefited from the arrival of 504 Squadron, pilots from this unit flying cover to a patrol of six Hurricanes led by Flt Lt Robert Voase Jeff. A formation of Bf110-escorted Do17Zs of I/KG76 was encountered at 1845 near Louvain, as Plt Off Roland Beamont (L1963) recalled:

> 'I got so excited, I opened fire well out of range. My Flight Commander tore me off a strip afterwards. He said he was in front of me and still out of range and there I was firing behind him and nearly hitting him. We closed in on the Dorniers. I hit one pretty hard. While I was wondering what was happening to everybody else, I suddenly noticed some stuff coming down past me, like bright rain. It was tracer bullets. There was a Messerschmitt 110 very close, doing a very tight turn on me from above.'

Both Beamont and Voase Jeff were credited with victories against the bombers, but only one bomber was seriously damaged and this returned to base with one dead and another wounded on board. The Squadron lost Plt Off Taffy Edwards (P2538), who was seen to be shot down in flames by an escorting Bf110C of II/ZG76 and was killed when his aircraft crashed south of Lille.

Meanwhile, a patrol of 87 Squadron's A Flight Hurricanes encountered the same formation of II/ZG76 Bf110s south of Lille, two being claimed by Flg Off Roddy Rayner and Plt Off Ken Tait, while Flg Off Rafael Watson claimed a probable. At about the same time, a patrol of 504 Squadron was on aerodrome defence when a lone He111 was encountered. On sighting the approaching Hurricanes, the Heinkel pilot dived his aircraft into cloud and was followed by Plt Off John Hardacre. Although he was unable to locate the bomber, on emerging from cloud Hardacre met what he believed to be four Ju88s, but were probably Bf110Cs of the II/ZG76 formation, and attacked one on the starboard flank, which he reported fell in flames. Having become lost, Hardacre was obliged to force-land at St Simon-le-Clastres, from where he rejoined Squadron two days later.

II/ZG76 lost two aircraft to the Hurricanes, both of which fell near Montcornet:

Bf110C of 6 Staffel shot down and crashed: Oblt Hans-Jochen Knop and his gunner, Uffz Jakob Neumayer, were both captured by French troops.

Bf110C of 6 Staffel shot down and crashed: Uffz Hans Obert baled out and returned; the gunner was wounded.

61 Wing, Air Component

Hurricanes from 61 Wing were also active in the morning: six aircraft of 615 Squadron's A Flight, led by Sqn Ldr Kayll, flew to Vitry, where they refuelled and awaited further orders. They learned that, in company with five Hurricanes of 607 Squadron's B Flight, to be led by Sqn Ldr Smith, they were to escort a dozen Blenheims (three of 15 Squadron and nine of 40 Squadron) which were to bomb the bridges over the Meuse. The Hurricanes set out for the target area but, when flying at 11,000 feet over Dinant, they encountered Bf110Cs plus Bf109s from Stab III/ JG53. Sqn Ldr Kayll recalled:

'The formation of Hurricanes was attacked by Messerschmitt 110s and 109s simultaneously. I did a head-on attack on the first 110, which afterwards force-landed, and a deflection shot on the second 110, which went into a dive and exploded in a wood.'

Flg Off Bill Fowler (P2622)—flying at the rear of the formation—saw a pair of Bf109s coming out of the sun. He shouted a warning over the R/T, but his Hurricane was hit at the same moment by a burst of fire from a Bf109 attacking from the other side. He pulled the Hurricane in a tight turn and almost blacked out, and on recovering his senses he saw a Messerschmitt flashing past on his port side. He got on to its tail and opened fire, reporting later that it 'turned over nose first and went straight down'. However, he was attacked again by another and the Hurricane burst into flame. He baled out with his flying boots on fire and landed in the Ardennes Forest. He met some French soldiers and joined forces with them, sleeping that night under the stars, but next day the group came under fire from a concealed machine-gun near a village. With no means of escape the survivors, including Fowler, were taken prisoner*.

The 607 Squadron Flight also came under attack and Sqn Ldr Lance Smith (P2870) was shot down and killed, although one report suggests he was lost to ground fire. Two Bf109s were claimed shot down, one by Flg Off Bill Whitty, who reported seeing the pilot bale out of the aircraft he attacked, and the other by newly attached Plt Off Bob Grassick of

---

* Flg Off Fowler escaped from Colditz in September 1942 and reached Spain via Gibraltar. On his return to the UK he was awarded the Military Cross and became a test pilot, but was killed flying a Typhoon on 26 March 1944.

242 Squadron's B Flight. Three Hurricanes were claimed by III/JG53 and were credited to Hptm Werner Molders, Oblt Heinz Wittenberg and Lt Georg Claus, while two of the Blenheims were shot down by Bf109s of 1/JG3 encountered when north-west of Charleroi.

Following the combined operation with 615 Squadron in the morning, 607 Squadron flew a further 14 sorties during the early afternoon, although it was not until about 1630 that a patrol of three Hurricanes, returning from Villeneuve via Reims, sighted a Staffel of He111Hs of 9/KG51. Two of the bombers were claimed shot down by Plt Off Peter Dixon (P2573 AF-A) and Flg Off Ian Russell, although the latter's aircraft (P2619 AF-D) was hit by return fire and the Australian was slightly wounded. Dixon continued chasing the remaining bombers until his oxygen supply suddenly failed when at 17,000 feet. Nevertheless, he continued the chase, gasping for breath, and only broke away when return fire hit his aircraft, a bullet narrowly missing his foot. On returning to Vitry, he landed at high speed without the use of flaps due to battle damage, and related later:

> 'If I had done this in peacetime, I would have radioed for the fire engine and ambulance to be in readiness.'

Meanwhile, the wounded Russell was taken to Paris, from where he was evacuated to England. The Squadron was not informed of his survival and his name was duly entered in the unit's records as 'missing, presumed killed'. It seems probable that the Heinkels were also attacked by a patrol of D520s from GCI/3, as a pilot of this unit claimed such a bomber in the area and, indeed, 9 Staffel lost three aircraft:

> He111H of 9/KG51 shot down north-east of Vitry, possibly by D520 of GCI/3: Fw Josef Straub and two killed, two baled out and PoW of the French.
>
> He111H of 9/KG51 shot down and crashed north of Vitry: Lt Helmuth Klischat and one killed, three PoW of the French.
>
> He111H of 9/KG51 damaged in combat and force-landed near Sedan with one engine on fire: crew survived.

During the afternoon, three patrols from 615 Squadron reported encounters with Hs126 reconnaissance machines. A section of Hurricanes, led by Flt Lt Leslie Thornley, carried out a low-level patrol north-west of Gembloux at 1500, when several German barrage balloons were seen and attacked, although they did not catch fire. Plt Off Tom Jackson reported:

'Flying around, we suddenly saw a Hs126 but only when it fired at me. Had a go and hit it and believed killed the gunner. I shot past it and the Flight Commander had a go. Turned round and it had gone into the ground.'

Flt Lt Thornley added:

'Aircraft first seen by Plt Off Jackson at fairly long range. E/a half-rolled and dived and I followed him down in the dive to 500 feet, firing all the way. E/a landed in ploughed field but did not crash. Assume engine was damaged.'

The third member of the section, Plt Off David Looker, also engaged the Henschel—an aircraft of 1(H)/23 (6th Armee)—but was apparently hit by ground fire. As he baled out he smashed his left leg against the aircraft's rudder, but made a safe landing, coming down on the battle-field at Waterloo. Having hobbled towards a farmhouse, he observed some soldiers who, luckily for him, turned out to be British and he was soon on his way to Brussels, from where he was flown back to the UK following treatment for his injuries. Although it was believed the crew of the Henschel survived the crash, both Lt Karl-Hermann Küster and his observer, Lt Felix Hach, were posted as missing.

At about the same time another Hs126 was sighted by Yellow Section of A Flight, five miles north of Gembloux, which Flg Off Peter Collard attacked:

'Saw Henschel flying low near wood at 100 feet. Diving quarter-attack. One short burst from rear gunner at 200 yards. Enemy pulled up and on its back at 50 feet as I went underneath. No sign of aircraft after.'

Fifteen minutes later, when near Wavre, Collard was attacked by a Bf109, which he identified as a He112 (sic):

'Enemy observed coming out of the sun, diving on two Hurricanes below. I came behind it but my reflector sight failed as I opened fire. E/a made a climbing turn to right, banking violently. Attack was broken off owing to running out of ammunition.'

At 1530 Red Section encountered another Hs126 (possibly an aircraft of 4(H)/22), two to three miles east of Gembloux, flying at 2,500 feet, which was attacked by Flg Off Horace Horne, a Canadian from Edmonton:

'The Henschel staggered after first attack and pancaked in a field. Unable to press home attack due to heavy AA fire. Attempted also to attack a balloon moored on ground but the latter was ringed with defences. Own aircraft hit four times.'

615 Squadron was at this stage instructed to move northwards into Belgium, following which Sqn Ldr Kayll and his senior Flight Commander departed Vitry to survey the area for a suitable landing ground, as Flt Lt Jim Sanders recalled:

'Joe Kayll and I had to fly up to locate an airfield in Belgium to operate from. I got into a Gladiator and he went off in a Hurricane. He flew to Moorsele while I went to Evère, on the east side of Brussels. I got into Evère and had just landed when I noticed it was full of Germans, so I rapidly shot off and, keeping on the deck, headed for home.'

63 Wing, Air Component

Hurricanes of 3 Squadron continued patrolling the Sedan-Dinant area. Sqn Ldr Pat Gifford, leading the dawn patrol personally, was obliged to force-land L1610 at Wevelgem, although he was unhurt and was soon returned to the Squadron. A second Hurricane was lost when Plt Off Mike Stephens force-landed N2546 QO-S when returning from a mid-morning patrol.

The next patrol, by Blue and Red Sections, set out at 1050 for the Namur-Dinant area, led by Flt Lt Mark Carter. Shortly before they were to return to base, seven Do17Zs of 8/KG76 escorted by Bf109s of III/JG26 were sighted at 12,000 feet. The bombers were engaged and one was claimed by Plt Off Peter Gardner (N2464) while Flt Lt Carter was seen to shoot down another. One of the Dorniers was damaged and its pilot wounded. Flg Off Bunny Stone (L1846 QO-B) also attacked the bombers and noted:

'Patrol Dinant, had crack at seven Do215s [sic]—no luck—force-landed at Vitry with bullet in starboard tank.'

The escorting Bf109s soon gained revenge and pursued the fleeing Hurricanes, Lt Joachim Müncheberg shooting down Sgt Jim Williams, who was killed when his aircraft (L1645) crashed near Overijse, about ten miles south of Brussels. Sgt Basil Friendship (N2351) recalled:

'Two 109s followed me on my way home. As they were faster than me I had to do a succession of orbits when they appeared to be within firing range to gain some more space, and I got one or two bursts. Almost certainly shot down one—other flew home after using up ammunition (presumably). My engine cut when I was just south of Brussels and thought I was in trouble until I realised that I had a reserve tank of petrol. Attacked one of two Heinkel 111s, but not enough ammo to bring it down.'

Sgt Roy Wilkinson's Hurricane (N2398) suffered some minor damage when:

'A bullet entered the cockpit on my port side, cutting my left wrist, then grazed my right arm before proceeding out the other side of the cockpit. The heat from the bullet cauterized the wounds, so there was very little bleeding.'

Flt Lt Carter (N2534) and Plt Off Noel Hallifax (N2422) were last seen heading north, pursued by fighters. Neither returned and it was learned later that the Flight Commander was killed when his aircraft was shot down north of Maubeuge, while Hallifax suffered injuries to his hands when shot down and was taken prisoner. Both Hurricanes apparently fell to Bf110Cs of II/ZG76.

Flt Lt Walter Churchill led the next patrol when, at 1620, the section met Bf109s of 9/JG26 at 12,000 feet near Lille. Churchill (L1899) claimed one shot down and another as probably destroyed, while Flg Off Denys Jones (L1609) shared a third with Plt Off Jack Rose (N2535), who reported:

'E/a seen 2,000 feet above and four miles away. They climbed through broken cloud and continued to climb. Flg Off Jones attacked a straggler and I attacked it from below and to one side. It was hit by both Flg Off Jones and myself. Just as I finished firing at him I saw the pilot bale out and his parachute open. As far as I know he landed safely. I then lost height and touch with e/a owing to loss of speed while climbing. While proceeding home alone, three 109s were engaged from long range but they dived and escaped.'

One of the Messerschmitts crashed near Louvain, from which the pilot survived, and was probably the victim of Jones and Rose.

Sgt Wilkinson (N2398) flew a lone patrol to Villeneuve at 1730 and, during the return leg to Merville, found himself flying through a formation of German bombers:

'It happened all too quickly to do anything, there was hardly time to blink. Suddenly a gunner opened fire from one of the German aircraft. As I hadn't done anything to him I thought he had a bloody cheek!'

above the clouds

Main fighter adversaries for the first few days of the Blitzkrieg, (top) Hurricanes of 73 Squadron, including P2569/D, P2575/J and N2334/Z and (bottom) Bfll0Cs of an unidentified unit over France.

Top: Sgt Basil Pyne of 73 Squadron watches as armourers load the .303 machine-guns of Hurricane A, probably L1578.
Bottom: German armourers watch in amusement a black cat as it mimics the styalized Black Cat insignia of an 8/JG51 Messerschmitt Bfl09E.

Top: Hurricane L1813 LK-O of 87 Squadron which force-landed in Belgium and was consequently impounded; it served later with Aéronautique Militaire Belge and was subsequently destroyed during the invasion.

Middle left: Hurricane H-31 of the Aéronautique Militaire's 2/I/2.

Middle right: Pilots of 2/I/2 with the Commanding Officer, Capitaine Martin Charlier, in flying suit.

Bottom: Capitaine Albert Van den Hove d'Etsenrijck of 2/I/2 immediately after landing at Le Culot having shot down a He111. (*All photographs via Jean-Louis Roba*)

Top: Group of 85 Squadron pilots at Lille/Seclin, 10 May. Back row, from left to right: Flt Lt Bob Boothby, Flg Off Tom Pace, Sqn Ldr Doggie Oliver, Plt Off John Ashton, Plt Off John Lecky, Flg Off Sam Stephenson, Sgt Sammy Allard, Sgt Len Crozier, Wt Off Newton;

Front, left to right: Flg Off Ken Blair, Sgt John Little.

Bottom: Sgt Sammy Allard returns from a successful combat, 10 May.

Top: Two successful pilots of 85 Squadron, Flt Lt Dickie Lee (left) and Plt Off Lew Lewis.

Bottom: Flg Off Dickie Martin of 73 Squadron.

Top: Pilots of 1 Squadron; from left to right:
Flg Off Billy Drake, Flg Off Leslie Clisby,
Flg Off Lawrie Lorimer, Flt Lt Prosser Hanks,
Flg Off Boy Mould, Sqn Ldr Bull Halahan,
Lt Moses Demozay (interpreter), Flt Lt Johnny
Walker, Squadron M.O., Flg Off Paul Richey,
Flg Off Iggy Kilmartin, Flg Off Bill Stratton,
Flg Off Pussy Palmer.

Bottom: Left to right: Sgt Lionel Pilkington,
Flg Off Ginger Paul, Flg Off Fanny Orton and
Flg Officer Cobber Kain of 73 Squadron.

Top: Pilots of 607 Squadron with a Gladiator prior to the outbreak of hostilities. Back row, from left to right: Flg Off Dudley Craig (2nd), Flg Off Bob Pumphrey (4th), Flg Off Bill Whitty (5th) Flg Off John Humpherson (7th), Flg Off Bunny Forster (l0th), Flg Off Monty Thompson (12th), Plt Off Peter Dixon (13th). Front row, left to right: Flg Off Francis Blackadder (1st), Flg Off Jim Bazin (2nd), Flt Lt John Sample (4th), Sqn Ldr Lance Smith (6th), Flt Lt Joe Kayll (8th), Flg Off Bill Gore (10th). *(via Simon Muggleton)*

Bottom: Pilots of 501 Squadron at Bétheniville, from left to right: Flg Off Gus Holden, Sgt Don McKay, Sgt Ginger Lacey, San Ldr A.V. Clube, Flg Off Michael Smith, Plt Off Kenneth Lee and Sgt Paul Farnes. *(via Wg Cdr P.C.P. Farnes)*

Top left: Plt Off John Cock, 87 Squadron. *(via Dennis Newton)*

Top centre: Plt Off Peter Parrott, 607 Squadron. *(via Norman Franks)*

Top right: Flg Off Dickie Glyde, 87 Squadron. *(via Dennis Newton)*

Middle left: Plt Off Tony Dillon, 229 Squadron. *(via Jean-Louis Roba)*

Middle right: Plt Off Buck Courtney, 151 Squadron attached to 607. *(via Brian Courtney)*

Bottom: Plt Off Tony Dini, 607 Squadron. *(via Paul Sortehaug)*

Top left: Hptm Günther Lützow of I/JG3.
(via Jack Foreman)

Top right: Oblt Hans Hahn of 4/JG2.
(via Jack Foreman)

Middle left: Hptm Karl Ebbinghausen of
4/JG26.

Middle right: Hptm Wilhelm Balthasar of
l/JGl. *(via Jack Foreman)*

Bottom left: Oblt Hans-Karl Mayer of l/JG53.
(via Jack Foreman)

Bottom right: Hptm Adolf Galland of
Stab/JG27. *(via Jack Foreman)*

Top: Pilots of 3 Squadron, from left to right: Sgt Denis Allen (back to camera), Flt Lt Walter Churchill, Sqn Ldr Pat Gifford, Flg Off Bunny Stone (with pipe), Plt Off Frank Carey (white overalls), Plt Off Noel Hallifax (sitting), Sgt Jim Sims (sitting on parachute), Sgt Ernie Ford. *(via Sqn Ldr A.H.B. Friendship)*

Bottom: Sgt Basil Friendship of 3 Squadron. *(via Sqn Ldr A.H.B. Friendship)*

Top: Sqn Ldr Joe Kayll (right) of 615 Squadron, with Plt Off Peter Dixon of 607 Squadron. *(via Flt Lt T.C. Jackson)*

Bottom: Pilots of 615 Squadron, from left to right sitting: Flg Off Brian Young, Flg Off Richard Gayner, Plt Off Tom Jackson, Flg Off Lewin Fredman; Standing: Flg Off Peter Collard, Flt Lt Jim Sanders. *(via Flt Lt T.C. Jackson)*

Top: Bf109E-3 White 11 of II/JG3 on a Belgian airfield.*(via Jean-Louis Roba)*

Middle left: Hurricane L2045 SD-A of 501 Squadron at Croydon en route to France, overshadowed by the wings of an Atlanta, with HP42 in background. *(via Flt Lt Andy Thomas)*

Middle right: Hurricane P2574 AF-F of 607 Squadron. *(via Flt Lt Andy Thomas)*

Bottom: Ju87B of I(St)/TrGrl86; Hurricanes claimed 18 Ju87s shot down on 14 May, and a further 11 on 17 May. *(via Jean-Louis Roba)*

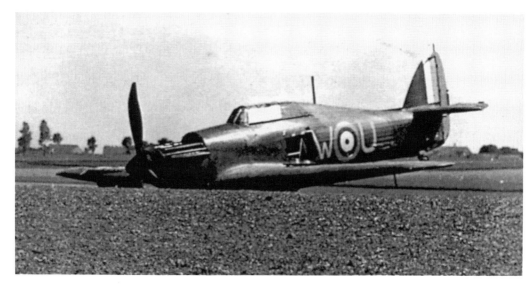

Top: Crash-landed Hurricane of 504 Squadron; note souvenir hunters have already secured fuselage roundel.

Middle left: Tattered tail unit of 151 Squadron Hurricane P3065 LZ-G; the pilot was able to fly back to England and landed safely.

Middle right: Burning remains of a Hurricane shot down over Belgium. *(via Jean-Louis Roba)*

Bottom: Force-landed Hurricane KW-U of 615 Squadron. *(via Flt Lt Andy Thomas)*

They did not return

Top: Oblt Hermann Braune's He111 V4+DT of l/KGl shot down near Albert on 10 May; the crew were captured by the unarmed British war grave keeper from the local cemetery.

Middle: Crash-landed He111, possibly of KG54, shot down over France.

Above: Another (or the same) crash-landed Heinkel, probably also from KG54.

Left: Remains of Do17P 4N+FH of 1(F)/22 flown by Oblt Rudolf Sauer near Reims, shot down by Hurricanes of 73 Squadron on 13 May.

Top: One of the Belgian Hurricanes destroyed during the attack on Schaffen-Diest airfield on the morning of 10 May.

Middle left: Unidentified crash-landed Hurricane stripped of fuselage roundel and squadron markings; note remains of Do17 in background.

Middle right: German troops pose with the remains of an RAF Hurricane destroyed on a French airfield at the time of the evacuation.

Bottom: German officers inspect a gutted Hurricane at Vitry-en-Artois; note the rear fuselage section of the 59 Squadron Blenheim (N6168 TR-A) shot down in error by a Hurricane on 16 May. *(All photographs via Jean-Louis Roba)*

Summary

Although it had been a quieter day for the AASF and Air Component Hurricane pilots overall, with less bomber activity, the German fighter sweeps had taken their toll. Of the 21 Hurricanes lost, half fell to the aggressive Bf110 crews and three others were shot down by Bf109s, with five pilots killed; two others were captured and four wounded.

Claims by AASF and Air Component Hurricanes, 15 May			
Type	Confirmed	Probable	Damaged	Total
He111	7	—	1	8
Do17	6	—	1	7
Ju88	1	—	1	2
Ju87	2	—	—	2
Hs126	2	—	2	4
Bf109	4	4	3	11
Bf110	13	3	—	16
	35	7	8	50

Luftwaffe Losses Attributed to AASF and Air Component Hurricanes, 15 May		
Type	60% to 100%	Under 60%	Total
He111	5	—	5
Do17	2	3	5
Ju87	2	—	2
Hs126	2	—	2
Bf109	2	—	2
Bf110	9	2	11
	22	5	27

The attack on the German forces in and near Montherme was continued during the night by AASF Battles, even though many of the 20 crews selected were untrained for nocturnal operations and others questioned the use of the Battle in a night bombing role. However, all aircraft returned safely, although the results of their attack on supposed fuel and ammunition dumps hidden in woods south of Bouillon were not observed. Bomber Command was also active in the area and operated over the battle front at Dinant, Aachen, Turnhout and Breda, losing one aircraft.

The night also saw the first Bomber Command attack on German industrial targets in the Ruhr. Of the 96 Wellingtons, Hampdens and Whitleys dispatched, 16 failed to attack any target at all, although all aircraft returned safely. Many fires were started and a number of violent explosions seen 'and the whole series of operations, if not productive of great results, provided valuable experience'.

Individual Claims—AASF and Air Component Hurricanes, 15 May

AM-	Sqn Ldr J.R. Kayll	615 Sqn	2 Bf110
	Flg Off H.N. Fowler	615 Sqn	Bf109 probable
	Flg Off W.H.R. Whitty	607 Sqn	Bf109
	Plt Off R.D. Grassick	607 Sqn	Bf109
0800-	Flt Lt P.R. Walker	1 Sqn	Bf110
	Flg Off P.H.M. Richey	1 Sqn	Bf110, Bf110 probable
	Flg Off J.I. Kilmartin	1 Sqn	Bf110
	Sgt F.J. Soper	1 Sqn	Bf110
	Sgt A.V. Clowes	1 Sqn	Bf110
0815-	Flt Lt C.D. Griffiths		
	Plt Off P.R. Hairs	501 Sqn	Do17
	Sgt P.F. Morfill		
AM-	Flt Lt J.S. Owen	504 Sqn	Ju88 damaged, Bf109 damaged
	Plt Off P.T. Parsons	504 Sqn	Bf109 damaged
AM-	Flg Off A.B. Angus	85 Sqn	2 He111
	Flt Lt R.H.A. Lee	85 Sqn	He111
	Sgt G. Allard	85 Sqn	He111
	Sgt C.E. Hampshire	85 Sqn	He111 damaged
1000-	Plt Off J.R. Hardacre	504 Sqn	Ju87
	Plt Off B. Van Mentz	504 Sqn	Ju87, Hs126 damaged
	Flt Lt W.B. Royce	504 Sqn	Bf109 probable
	Sgt G.H. Spencer	504 Sqn	Bf109 probable
1100-	Flt Lt M.M. Carter	3 Sqn	Do17
	Plt Off P.M. Gardner	3 Sqn	Do17
PM-	Plt Off J.R. Hardacre	504 Sqn	Ju88
1320-	Flg Off E.J. Kain	73 Sqn	Bf110 probable
	Flg Off N. Orton	73 Sqn	2 Bf110
	Plt Off D.S. Scott	73 Sqn	Bf110
1500-	Flt Lt L.T.W. Thornley		
	Plt Off T.C. Jackson	615 Sqn	Hs126
	Plt Off D.J. Looker		
1500-	Flg Off P. Collard	615 Sqn	Hs126 damaged, Bf109 damaged
1530-	Flg Off H.E. Horne	615 Sqn	Hs126
1620-	Flt Lt W.M. Churchill	3 Sqn	Bf109, Bf109 probable
	Flg Off D.A.E. Jones	3 Sqn	Bf109
	Plt Off J. Rose		
1630-	Plt Off H.P. Dixon	607 Sqn	2 He111
	Flg Off I.B.M. Russell		
1820-	Flg Off J.R. Cridland	501 Sqn	Do17
	Sgt J.E. Proctor	501 Sqn	Bf110
1820-	Sqn Ldr J.W.C. More	73 Sqn	He111
	Flt Lt J.E. Scoular		
	Sgt L.S. Pilkington	73 Sqn	Do17 damaged
1845-	Flt Lt R. Voase Jeff	87 Sqn	Do17
	Plt Off R.P. Beamont	87 Sqn	Do17
	Flg Off R.M.S. Rayner	87 Sqn	Bf110
	Plt Off K.W. Tait	87 Sqn	Bf110
	Flg Off R.F. Watson	87 Sqn	Bf110 probable

In addition, two unidentified pilots, flying Gladiators, may have accounted for two He111s.

Losses—AASF and Air Component Hurricanes, 15 May

Dawn-	L1610	3 Sqn	Sqn Ldr P. Gifford: force-landed near Wevelgem, accident; pilot unhurt, returned.
AM-	P2622	615 Sqn	Flg Off H.N. Fowler: shot down near Dinant by Bf109 of III/JG53; pilot baled out, PoW.
AM-	P2870	607 Sqn	Sqn Ldr L.E. Smith: shot down near Dinant, probably by Bf109 of III/JG53; pilot killed.
0800-	L1681	1 Sqn	Flt Lt P.R. Walker: shot down near Vouziers by Bf110C of III/ZG26; pilot unhurt, returned.
	L1943	1 Sqn	Flg Off P.H.M. Richey: shot down near Vouziers by Bf110C of III/ZG26; pilot baled out unhurt, returned.
0815-		501 Sqn	Hurricane damaged by return fire from Do17Z of II/KG3 and force-landed Bétheniville; pilot unhurt.
		501 Sqn	Hurricane damaged by return fire from Do17Z of II/KG3 and force-landed Bétheniville; pilot unhurt.
mid-AM-	N2546	3 Sqn	Plt Off M.M. Stephens: force-landed when returning from patrol; accident, pilot unhurt, returned.
1100-	L1846	3 Sqn	Flg Off C.A.C. Stone: aircraft damaged by return fire from Do17Z of 8/KG76 and force-landed at Vitry; pilot unhurt.
	L1645	3 Sqn	Sgt J.L.C. Williams: shot down near Overijse by Bf109 of III/JG26; pilot killed.
	N2534	3 Sqn	Flt Lt M.M. Carter: shot down north of Maubeuge by Bf110C of II/ZG76; pilot killed.
	N2422	3 Sqn	Plt Off N.D. Hallifax: shot down north of Maubeuge by Bf110C of II/ZG76; pilot PoW.
1320-	P2579	73 Sqn	Flg Off N. Orton: shot down west of Vouziers by Bf110C of I/ZG2; pilot baled out, wounded.
	L1693	73 Sqn	Sgt L.J. Humphries: shot down west of Vouziers by Bf110C of I/ZG2; pilot baled out, wounded.
		73 Sqn	Sgt L.Y. Friend: aircraft damaged west of Vouziers by Bf110C of I/ZG2 and force-landed; pilot unhurt, returned.
1500-	P2554	615 Sqn	Plt Off D.J. Looker: shot down by ground fire; baled out, wounded.
1630-	P2619	607 Sqn	Flg Off I.B.N. Russell: shot down by return fire from He111 of 9/KG51 and crash-landed; pilot wounded.
1845-	P2828	85 Sqn	Flg Off D.H. Allen: shot down south of Ath by Bf110C of 5/ZG26; pilot baled out, returned.
	L1775	85 Sqn	Plt Off J.H. Ashton: shot down south of Ath by Bf110C of 5/ZG26; pilot baled out, returned.
	L1964	85 Sqn	Flg Off T.G. Pace: shot down south of Ath by Bf110C of 5/ZG26 and crash-landed; pilot wounded and burned.
1845-	P2538	87 Sqn	Plt Off T.J. Edwards: shot down south of Lille by Bf110C of II/ZG76; pilot killed.

CHAPTER VIII

THURSDAY 16 MAY
MORE REINFORCEMENTS

'The 109s came in on our bottom squadron. I could see their guns firing. Two Hurricanes steamed smoke and a third went out of formation and turned away.'

Plt Off Roland Beamont, 87 Squadron.

The Situation in Holland and Belgium

Following the effective surrender of Dutch forces, troops of the French 7th Armée were compelled to leave their positions in South Beveland due to persistent strafing attacks by low-flying Bf109s and Bf110s. It was feared by the local Allied commanders that the collapse of the Zeeland front was imminent unless more fighter aircraft could be sent to oppose the Luftwaffe assault.

The Belgian Army was making preparations to withdraw through Antwerp, with the intention of holding the lowest reaches of the Scheldt and a line continuing south along the Willebroek Canal to Brussels. The BEF was also ordered to start withdrawing towards the line of the River Escaut, while the French 1st Armée was forced back by the German thrust towards the Charleroi-Brussels Canal.

'South of the 1st Armée the Germans were making their fastest progress. Already in the morning Hirson was reported as occupied by the enemy, who was soon pushing his advanced troops forward to La Capelle and Vervins, while beyond Montcornet he reached towards Marle and Laon. In general it was clear that the Germans were finding little to oppose them in their westward progress in this area.'

Having evacuated Grimbergen emergency airfield at dawn, the remaining six CR42s of the Aeronautique Militaire Belge flew to Aalter, from where one pilot reported shooting down a Messerschmitt while escorting a Fox on a reconnaissance sortie. That evening the CR42s departed for the French airfield at Norrent-Fontès, there joining a few ancient Fairey Fireflies which the Belgians had recovered from storage. These, and a few equally obsolescent Foxes, were all that remained of the Aeronautique Militaire Belge. At least one Fox was shot down by Flak during the day and its wounded pilot taken prisoner, although he escaped later.

The Situation in Northern France

During the morning renewed requests for more Hurricanes flowed in from France, including one impassioned plea from Air Marshal Barratt, AOC RAF France. However, the SASO (Air Vice-Marshal D.C.S. Evill DSC AFC) emphasised that the remaining RAF bases in France could not take more than five fresh squadrons. Further pressure came from Lord Gort, GOC BEF, who stressed the intensity of the air fighting and the need for Hurricane replacements.

The War Cabinet met at 1130 and agreed that four fighter squadrons should be sent forthwith and that preparations be made for the dispatch of two more:

'In consequence of the Cabinet decision to send the equivalent of four fighter squadrons immediately, Fighter Command was ordered by midday by Air Ministry to detail eight separate flights from Hurricane squadrons for reinforcement to the RAF Component. Six of these flights left during the afternoon and two the following morning, proceeding to Lille/Marcq (two), Lille/Seclin (two), Merville (one), Vitry-en-Artois (two) and Abbeville (one). The intention was that fuel and ammunition facilities for initial operations should be ready in France, but that the flights should be supported by their own personnel and equipment, to be moved across in transport aircraft. In addition to these reinforcing flights, arrangements were also made for 20 experienced Hurricane pilots to proceed to France, in exchange for 20 tired (or wounded) pilots from the RAF Component.'

Although the War Cabinet had agreed to these proposals, the decision was not welcomed by Air Chief Marshal Dowding, AOC Fighter Command, who immediately composed a letter to the Air Ministry outlining the inherent dangers of this action:

'I have the honour to refer to the very serious calls which have recently been made upon the Home Defence fighter units in an attempt to stem the German invasion of the Continent. I hope and

believe that our armies may yet be victorious in France and
Belgium, but we have to face the possibility that they may be
defeated. In this case I presume there is no one who will deny that
England should fight on, even though the remainder of the Continent of Europe is dominated by the Germans. For this purpose it is
necessary to retain some minimum fighter strength in this country
and I must request that the Air Council will inform me what they
consider this minimum strength to be, in order that I may make my
dispositions accordingly. I would remind the Air Council that the
last estimate which they made as to the force necessary to defend
this country was 52 squadrons, and my strength has now been
reduced to the equivalent of 36 squadrons.

Once a decision has been reached as to the limit on which the Air
Council and the Cabinet are prepared to stake the existence of the
country, it should be made clear to the Allied commanders on the
Continent that not a single aeroplane from Fighter Command
beyond the limit will be sent across the Channel, no matter how
desperate the situation may become. It will, of course, be remembered that the estimate of 52 squadrons was based on the assumption that the attack would come from the eastwards except in so far
as the defences might be outflanked in flight. We now have to face
the possibility that attacks may come from Spain, or even from the
north coast of France. The result is that our line is very much
extended at the same time as our resources are reduced.

I must point out that within the last few days the equivalent of ten
squadrons have been sent to France, that Hurricane squadrons
remaining in this country are seriously depleted, and that the more
squadrons which are sent to France the higher will be the wastage
and the more insistent the demand for reinforcements. I must
therefore request that as a matter of paramount urgency the Air
Ministry will consider and decide what level of strength is to be left
to Fighter Command for the defence of this country, and will assure
me that when this level has been reached, not one fighter will be
sent across the Channel however urgent and insistent the appeals
for help may be.

I believe that, if an adequate fighter force is kept in the country,
if the fleet remains in being, and if Home forces are suitably
organised to resist invasion, we should be able to carry on the war
single-handed for some time, if not indefinitely. But, if the Home
Defence Force is drained away in desperate attempts to remedy the
situation in France, defeat in France will involve the final, complete
and irremediable defeat of this country.'

Dowding instructed Wg Cdr The Duke of Hamilton, his personal emissary, to depart for France to report directly on the situation. Next day, the Duke flew to France in a Magister and commenced a tour of various airfields. He would return three days later and his subsequent report stressed that no further Hurricanes should be sent to France.

Air Operations over Belgium and Northern France

Reconnaissance flights were continued by Air Component Blenheims and Lysanders during which one of the latter was shot down. The Blenheims also suffered losses and two failed to return to base, while a third was shot down by a Hurricane as it returned to Glisy (see later). During the afternoon, a Blenheim of 18 Squadron brought back news that German guns and transport were travelling along the Jauchelette-Gembloux road and, as a result, all available Blenheims of 57 and 59 Squadrons, together with the Lysanders of 26 Squadron, were ordered to stand by for bombing operations. However, they were not called upon until the next day and there were few operations undertaken by AASF Blenheims before then.

During an operation in the Brussels-Wavre area, a He111P of 9/ KG27 experienced severe icing caused by a navigational problem and wandered into Swiss airspace. On emerging from cloud, the Heinkel was intercepted by two Swiss Air Force Bf109s. Two of the crew were wounded and baled out before the bomber overflew Zurich, where it was again attacked. With its port engine pouring smoke, the stricken aircraft (1G+HT) was belly-landed near Kemleten and the two remaining crew members were arrested and interned.

67 Wing, AASF

There was not much aerial activity within 67 Wing's sector, the three squadrons being engaged mainly in moving bases. Nevertheless, patrols were carried out and Flt Lt John Scoular of 73 Squadron (Hurricane H) engaged and damaged a He111 near Châlons-sur-Marne before the Squadron moved to Villeneuve, leaving behind five damaged Hurricanes (including N2404 and P2810), which were set on fire before departure. That evening, 501 Squadron moved from Bétheniville to the small airfield at Anglure, via Villeneuve, leaving behind seven unserviceable Hurricanes, although four of these were made flyable later and were collected by 103 Squadron pilots, who flew them to Rheges; another had been retained for use by the Squadron:

> 'When some Hurricanes were ferried in for 501 Squadron and then flown off again, one had been left behind. When the 103 Squadron boys had a look at it they realised the pilot had not put it in the correct pitch for take-off. The pilots [of 103 Squadron] flew it on

raids for a few days as their own personal escort, until 501 Squadron unhappily got to know about it and quickly claimed it back.'

Also on the move was 1 Squadron, ordered to evacuate to the airfield at Conde/Vraux, between Reims and Paris, where 114 Squadron was based. Before leaving, two of the unit's unserviceable Hurricanes were pushed into a bomb crater in the middle of the aerodrome and burnt. The Squadron welcomed the return of one of its pilots when Plt Off Roland Dibnah, a Canadian, arrived from England aboard Flamingo G-AFVF in company with several others.

60 Wing, Air Component

87 Squadron received some reinforcement pilots, as revealed by the unit's diarist, who wrote in retrospect:

> 'Six aircraft and pilots arrived early one morning from Amiens. No spare pilots available so the ferry pilots, who had no definite orders, elected to stay. Some were squadron pilots, some straight from FTS and some with no previous experience on Hurricanes (although this was not known at the time). Names not recorded, but only two returned to the UK. They went into action almost immediately and joined the mass patrols carried out by 87 and 504 Squadrons. It is safe to say they achieved some success before they themselves went missing.'

The six were, it would seem, Flg Off D.H. Ward, Flg Off J.H.L. Allen (both New Zealanders), Flt Sgt I.J. Badger and Sgt A.N. Trice from 151 Squadron, Plt Off P.W. Comely from 145 Squadron and Flg Off J.M. Strickland from 213 Squadron. All were, despite the note to the contrary in 87 Squadron's ORB, squadron pilots with some experience on Hurricanes. Indeed, Flg Off Derek Ward had been with 151 Squadron for almost two years. As the latter prepared to climb out of his aircraft on arrival at Lille/Marcq, ground personnel were somewhat surprised to see a little black Scottie terrier pop its head over the side of the cockpit! This was two-year-old 'Whisky', who invariably accompanied his master on non-operational flights. Ward commented later:

> 'He was a real doggie airman. Nothing gave him greater pleasure than to sit on my knee in the Hurricane. With his ears cocked up, he'd stare before him as we often did 300 mph. He'd been on the Squadron since he was six weeks old.'

Several 87 Squadron pilots were flown to Glisy later during the morning in a 24 Squadron Rapide to collect replacement Hurricanes, but only one aircraft was immediately available and this was flown back to Lille by Flg Off Watson. The other pilots remained at Glisy to await the arrival of further Hurricanes, due imminently from England.

Earlier that morning six Hurricanes—three each from 87 and 504 Squadrons—had been dispatched to patrol east of Seclin. The two sections had became separated and the 87 Squadron trio sighted bombers across the Belgian border, as recalled by Sgt Gareth Nowell:

> 'Our first action was to attack aircraft raiding a nearby Belgian town. There was low cloud and Dennis David went below it and was fired on by anti-aircraft guns.'

Nine twin-engined aircraft identified as Do17s were then encountered in the Mons-St Ghislain area and were engaged:

> 'David and myself attacked. David broke off the attack but I pressed on and shot down the left-hand aircraft of the enemy formation. I was unable to see where David had gone, so I attacked on my own, using a variety of attacks against the remaining eight enemy aircraft. I dived through the formation, attacked from port side, head-on and from the rear.'

Nowell believed he had possibly accounted for four more of the 'Dorniers' before his propeller was shot off by return fire, which obliged him to force-land L1614 in a field near Goeferdinge, about ten miles north-west of Ninove (his third force-landing in six days), narrowly missing a road crowded with refugees. Having failed to ignite the Hurricane's fuel tanks, Nowell was approached by a Belgian officer who escorted him to the nearby village, from where he was taken by car to the nearest railway station, but was arrested by a gendarme who suspected him of being a fifth columnist. However, Nowell was able to escape by hitching a ride with a British Army convoy and eventually reached his unit at Seclin early next morning.

Meanwhile, the 504 Squadron section led by Flt Lt John Owen encountered a Ju88, at which Plt Off Trevor Parsons fired four bursts as he followed it in and out of cloud; he believed that he had probably damaged it. Owen then engaged a He111 which he claimed 'almost certainly' shot down, since smoke belched from both engines and his Hurricane was covered in oil from the stricken bomber. Plt Off Bob Renison also engaged a Heinkel, which he saw go down in flames following his attack. A Bf109 attempted to get onto the tail of his Hurricane, but this he evaded then dogfought without result. The bombers engaged by 504 Squadron were Ju88s of I/KG30, two of which were shot down:

Ju88A of 2/KG30 flown by the Staffelkapitän, Hptm Karl Hielscher, was damaged by AA fire near Ninove then shot down by fighters north of Wavre and crash-landed: one killed and three wounded.

Ju88A of 3/KG30 flown by Lt Rudolf Bürner shot down west of Brussels: crew baled out and PoW of the British.

An early afternoon patrol by a section of 85 Squadron Hurricanes encountered a twin-engined bomber approaching Glisy aerodrome and this was pursued by Sgt Len Crozier. On the ground at Glisy, watching the action, were the 87 Squadron pilots awaiting the arrival of replacement Hurricanes, one of whom was Plt Off Darwin, who noted in his diary:

'Sgt Crozier of 85 Squadron came across the aerodrome chasing a Blenheim. He fired a burst over the drome and the Blenheim's starboard engine went "phut". It did a right-hand circuit and just as it eased the throttle to land it blew up. A terrible sight.'

Apparently the Blenheim—L4852 of 53 Squadron returning from a reconnaissance sortie—had fired the correct colours of the day, but Crozier had mistaken the flares for return fire. Flt Lt Daly—whose aircraft had been similarly attacked by a Hurricane the previous day—and his crew (Sgt W.B.B. Currie, observer, and air gunner AC P.J. Blandford) all suffered serious burns in the crash.

The luckless Sgt Crozier and his companions had only just returned to Lille/Seclin when the airfield was targeted by a formation of He111Hs from III/LG1, escorted by Bf109s from II/JG2 and I/JG27. Both 85 and 87 Squadrons scrambled all available Hurricanes, as Sgt Cyril Hampshire recalled:

'I was leader of a section. We sat in our kites awaiting the scramble and I saw Allgood [Sgt Harold Allgood, a replacement pilot]—in a u/s Hurricane [L1898] and flying to Merville—shot down by a 109. He crash-landed, wounded. We were then ordered to scramble and we went off from the south of the airfield—B Flight went from the east side and we all met in the middle. Miraculously there were no collisions. Sgt Crozier [N2389] climbed to about 600 feet and was then shot down on fire—he baled out and his hands were so badly burned he could not knock his parachute off and was dragged. I shot down a He111.'

Records indicate that Sgts Allgood and Crozier were shot down by Oblt

Helmut Bolz and Uffz Hans-Joachim Hartwig of 5/JG2. In addition to the claim made by Sgt Hampshire, it seems that Flt Lt Dickie Lee also claimed a Heinkel, as did Sgt Sammy Allard, although only one such aircraft was lost, all three having probably attacked the same machine. In fact, III/LG1 did not suffer the loss of any of its bombers, but a reconnaissance Heinkel of 1(F)/121 was shot down near Tirlemont, from which Lt Günter Fischer and his crew baled out. Meanwhile, Sgt Albert Deacon engaged and shot down one of the Messerschmitts near the airfield, as noted by Sgt Hampshire:

> 'During this incident a 109 pilot was shot down [by Sgt Deacon] and brought to our Flight office—he was very arrogant, claiming he would soon be free again. I think he was disappointed. But it sticks in my mind how our ground crews reacted to him. Without protection they could have lynched him.'

Flg Off Roddy Rayner and Plt Off Dennis David (L1630) of 87 Squadron also engaged the Messerschmitts and shared one, but newcomer Sgt Alan Trice (L2000) was shot down and killed west of Mons. Two Hurricanes were claimed by Lt Wilhelm von Schetelig and Lt Hans-Jürgen Hepe of 5/JG2 about five minutes after the initial strike, and may have been responsible for the loss of Trice. However, I/JG27 lost two of its Messerschmitts, both from 1 Staffel. The pilot of one baled out and the other crash-landed at Jeneffe following a combat with a Hurricane south of Brussels. Two of 85 Squadron's Hurricanes also failed to return and it was learned later that Flg Off Allan Angus (L1641), one of the unit's leading pilots, had been shot down and killed about six miles south of the airfield. The other missing pilot, Plt Off Michael Rawlinson (P2535), was also killed when his aircraft crashed near Quievrain, 15 miles south-west of Mons. They were probably the victims of Lt Rudolf Krafftschick and Lt Igor Zirkenbach of 1/JG27.

Fatigue and exhaustion were evident amongst both air and ground crew and many of the pilots had been in constant action for seven days. According to one war correspondent, Sgt Sammy Allard of 85 Squadron was found to be asleep in the cockpit of his aircraft following its landing; he wrote:

> 'One sergeant pilot [Allard] went to sleep after landing his machine, and they decided to let him sleep on till the dawn patrol next day. But at dawn they could not wake him, so they put him in an ambulance and sent him off to hospital. It took about 30 hours before he reached the hospital, and he slept all the time.'

Another pilot admitted:

'I had about an hour and a half's sleep that night, and did four patrols the following day. Bombs were bursting on the aerodrome as I took off on my second patrol. On my third patrol I fell asleep three times over German-occupied territory.'

At 1730, 60 Wing ordered 85, 87 and 504 Squadrons each to put up a dozen Hurricanes, as Plt Off Roland Beamont of 87 Squadron recalled:

'We flew a three squadron formation to patrol along the Luxembourg border. Suddenly I saw four aeroplanes appear over the back of the formation and another four behind them. The 109s came in on our bottom squadron. I could see their guns firing. Two Hurricanes steamed smoke and a third went out of formation and turned away. Before anyone could do anything about it, the 109s pulled sharply up straight into cloud, totally out of reach.'

The Messerschmitts were from 3/JG76 and the victorious pilots were Oblt Franz Eckerle and Lt Werner Raithel. The unit which came under attack was 85 Squadron and both Flg Off Count Manfred Czernin* (L1630) and Plt Off Hugh Clark (P2824) force-landed, the latter having been wounded. It was three days before Czernin was able to return to Lille/Seclin where, in the meantime, he had been posted as missing. Only Plt Off Brian Van Mentz of 504 Squadron was able to make an interception and engaged a Bf109, which disappeared after his attack 'emitting clouds of smoke'.

Hurricanes from Lille/Seclin later engaged five Bf110Cs of 1/ZG1 over Brussels and one was claimed by an 85 Squadron pilot; two others were claimed by Flg Off Roddy Rayner and Plt Off Chris Darwin of 87 Squadron and one of these was believed to have crashed into the Fôret-de-Soignies. 1/ZG1 suffered no losses although Lt Wolfgang Schenck was wounded, while Lt Gerhard Schmidt claimed a 'Spitfire' shot down in return.

85 Squadron had suffered severe losses during the day: six Hurricanes shot down with the deaths of two experienced pilots; three others had sustained wounds or burns and one was missing. Thus, the Canadian pilots of 242 Squadron recently attached to the Squadron became replacements rather than reinforcements as originally intended.

---

* Flg Off Count Czernin, born in Berlin of an Austrian father and an English mother, daughter of the 2nd Baron Grimthorpe, had joined the RAF in 1935 and served initially as a bomber pilot, but transferred to the Reserve in 1937. Recalled at the outbreak of war, he retrained as a fighter pilot and served briefly with both 504 and 213 Squadrons before joining 85 Squadron in France on the eve of the German invasion.

61 Wing, Air Component

It was all quiet on the Vitry front until the afternoon, when Flg Off Bob Weatherill (P2574 AF-F) and Plt Off Gordon Stewart (P2571 AF-G) of 607 Squadron, having returned from an uneventful local patrol at 1410, were immediately ordered off again, this time accompanied by Plt Off Peter Dixon (P2536 AF-R), Plt Off Peter Parrott (P2874 AF-B) and Flg Off Bob Pumphrey (P3448 AF-H). They came upon five Do17Zs flying in close formation, as Plt Off Parrott recalled:

> 'So close were they that we could only attack from astern one at a time. We each carried out an attack with apparently hardly any effect, although I could see some strikes, except for one aircraft which dropped out of formation, but then rejoined its position and flew on. Although their rear gunners could have given a five-gun concentrated fire against us, they did not appear to be doing it. I was expecting to go in for a second attack, but I believe our leader had used all his ammunition in his first, and only, pass and we broke away.'

A similar result followed an encounter between three other Hurricanes of 607 Squadron, led by Flt Lt George Plinston (P2574 AF-F), and ten Do17Zs at about 1700, when only Plt Off Tony Dini (P2874 AF-B) was able to engage. He attacked one, but could claim only a 'doubtful' before it and the others escaped in cloud. Meanwhile, Plt Off Dick Demetriadi (P2571 AF-G) had become separated and returned on his own 30 minutes after the other pair had landed.

Following the death of Sqn Ldr Smith, the Squadron received a new Commanding Officer in the guise of Sqn Ldr George Fidler; at the same time a replacement pilot, Sgt Leslie Ralls, arrived from 501 Squadron on attachment. Of this period, Flg Off Bill Whitty recalled:

> 'Even when we didn't meet 109s there was much AA, even at 13/ 14,000 feet where I was hit; the ground crews worked wonders in getting the aircraft back into service. Also the armourers and GDHs made up the .303 belts from scratch as it was several days before the UK shipped us belted ammo.'

Plt Off Peter Parrott added:

> 'There was a shortage of spares for the Hurricanes. I remember two aircraft which would normally have been grounded; on one the Air Speed Indicator was unserviceable due to a bullet having cut the pipe between the pitot head and the ASI. The cut was in the wing. The other aircraft had unserviceable flaps which meant a faster

approach and landing. Fortunately, Vitry was a large airfield with clear approaches.'

With the Luftwaffe roaming the skies and penetrating further into French airspace by the day, 24 Squadron was instructed to transfer its communications aircraft based at Vitry to Le Bourget, DH89s G-ADNH and G-ADBV together with Vega Gull P1750 departing during the course of the day.

Also on the move was 615 Squadron, which headed northwards across the Belgian border to Moorsele, a small civilian airfield east of Courtrai. Shortly after take-off for the new base, newly-attached Plt Off Bob Grassick (KW-X) sighted what he believed to be a Ju88, engaged and claimed it shot down. This was, in fact, a returning Flak-damaged reconnaissance Blenheim (N6168 TR-A) of 59 Squadron, which was hit in the fuel and oil tanks during Grassick's attack. Despite this additional damage, Flt Lt G.V. Smither was able to belly-land the Blenheim at Vitry without injury to his crew, although the gunner, Aircraftman D.J. Pitcher, had been slightly wounded during Grassick's attack.

At Moorsele, the pilots from Vitry were joined by the remainder of the Squadron from Abbeville. Flg Off Peter Collard flew the unit's Master (N7577) to Vitry to ascertain if any more Hurricanes had been made serviceable, only to find they had all been burnt. Shortly after taking off for the return flight to Moorsele the Master was attacked by a Messerschmitt, but only one bullet hit the aircraft and, although it pierced the canopy, Collard was unhurt and he was able to evade and reached the airfield safely.

Patrols were immediately flown by 615 Squadron from the new base, during one of which Flg Off Tony Eyre (N2337) pursued, but could not catch, a Do17. Earlier in the patrol he had seen some biplanes, identifying these as Belgian Fairey Foxes, which were presumably withdrawing to bases across the frontier.

At 1500, Flt Lt Leslie Thornley led nine Hurricanes of 615 Squadron on another patrol, as escort to a 4 Squadron Lysander. Near Tirlemont the formation was bounced by Bf109s of II/JG26 and Thornley (N2335) was shot down and killed almost immediately, probably by Uffz Hugo Dahmer of 4 Staffel. Plt Off Tom Jackson (N2338) was also on the receiving end of the initial attack by the Messerschmitts, and recalled:

'I opened the cockpit as I could not see much to rear. About a minute later, while flying with the sun behind, we were bounced. The first I knew of it was when I was hit. An aircraft went past beneath me and I gave chase, but my engine cut. A second 109 came by and I had a go at him—believe bits of his tail came off. Fired at it again from behind. Saw aircraft all over the place.'

Another Bf109 slipped in behind Jackson's Hurricane and opened fire from close range:

> 'My aircraft was hit heavily and there was a huge explosion. I had my gloves and flying boots on, but not my flying helmet. I did not unplug oxygen lead etc, just leapt out after releasing side panel. Opened the parachute and thought: "God, it's quiet".'

As he floated down, he realised the lenses of his goggles and the glass on his watch had been blown out, while his trousers had been practically burned away. He had suffered several splinter wounds and had burns round his face and legs. At about 1,500 feet he saw eight men on horses below and, as he landed, they dismounted and pointed rifles at him—German cavalry. Of his capture, he recalled:

> 'One soldier produced a big knife and cut open my collar, and another produced a hypodermic syringe and injected me. A vehicle arrived and I was told to get in; an oberleutnant sat in the back and covered me with a pistol. My own pistol had six rounds of locally bought .38 ammunition, as I had used that issued potting cans in a river. These appeared to be blunt-nosed and I thought the German might think they were dumdum, but he could not open my pistol so fired off rounds into the ground—I was greatly relieved. I was taken to a field hospital at Tirlemont and spent two days in a room with eight or nine German officers; one badly wounded with a stomach injury made lots of noise. I was moved to a large building with a stone floor, amongst some hundreds of British troops, and then transferred after a week to Maastricht.'

Plt Off Brian Young, a South African from Natal, was also shot down. His Hurricane (P2577) burst into flames and crashed near Essene, but not before he had managed to bale out with burns to his upper body and face. As he floated down, British soldiers fired at him and he was wounded by three machine-gun bullets then, as he landed, by shrapnel from a hand grenade thrown in his direction. It was only when the soldiers reached the barely-conscious pilot that they realised he was not German. Young was taken to a hospital outside Dieppe, from where he was evacuated by hospital train and ambulance to St Nazaire. However, as the ambulance arrived at the harbour it was hit by gunfire which killed all the occupants apart from Young, who eventually reached the UK aboard a hospital ship. It seems probable that Plt Offs Jackson and Young were shot down by Hptm Herwig Knüppel and Lt Otto-Heinrich Hillecke of Stab II/JG26.

In return, only 615 Squadron's attached Canadian Plt Off Bob

Grassick (KW-X) managed to make a definite claim, reporting that he had shot down one of the attackers. The German pilot, Fw Erwin Stolz of 5 Staffel, baled out and was taken prisoner. The Lysander (L4814) was also shot down, falling to Fw Karlheinz Bothfeld of 1/JG27 near La Capelle. A second Lysander from this unit was intercepted by six Bf110Cs of 1/ZG1 but managed to escape, although it was claimed shot down by Hptm Wolfgang Falck and Uffz Fritz Dünsing; the Lysander's gunner claimed one of the attackers in return.

63 Wing, Air Component
From Merville at 1730, Sqn Ldr Pat Gifford of 3 Squadron led a patrol over the Wavre-Louvain area, when a German aircraft was sighted, as Sgt Basil Friendship (L1609) recalled:

> 'Patsie Gifford sighted a Messerschmitt and chased it. Wilkie [Sgt Wilkinson] and I followed as it dived down to low level over—as it turned out—the German front lines. Terrific light AA fire encountered. Wilkie broke to the right and I broke to the left, then circled a pom-pom type gun which was firing at me. I zig-zagged, climbed and dived until I was out of range. Sqn Ldr Gifford did not return but I didn't see him hit the ground.'

Sgt Roy Wilkinson (L1899) added:

> 'We gained some height to have a better look around when from out of nowhere came a Messerschmitt 110, which shot down Sqn Ldr Gifford. I managed to shoot down the 110. I moved into position to get a full deflection shot that sent the enemy plane into a long curving dive with one engine pouring smoke. I turned my Hurricane on its wing as I realised I had more 110s on my tail. As a Hurricane could out-turn a 110, I thought I had outsmarted the Huns. Glancing ahead, I saw a Messerschmitt 109 approaching head-on, with flashes indicating shell-fire emerging from his nose. There was no time for any sort of logical thought. I held my line, as did the other pilot, then opened fire at about 200 yards. The enemy aircraft screamed over my head and I never knew if I killed the pilot or not. When I returned to Merville, Walter Churchill had received confirmation from the front line that the CO had been shot down and that I had got the 110.'

The Bf110C (2N+HH of 1/ZG1) crashed near Walem, one mile north of Mechelen, with the deaths of Lt Heinrich Brucksch and his gunner, Gfr Heinz-Werner Roth. However, Hptm Adolf Galland of Stab/JG27 reported downing a Hurricane one mile south of Lille at 1830, but since

Sgt Wilkinson reported that he had seen the Bf110 shoot down Sqn Ldr Gifford's Hurricane, it would seem that the latter had fallen to the Bf110 crew and that Galland had attacked Wilkinson's Hurricane.

With the death of Sqn Ldr Gifford, Flt Lt Walter Churchill assumed command of the Squadron. One of his first duties was to promote Sgt Wilkinson to command A Flight, although he remained an NCO, in place of Flg Off Walter Bowyer, who was about to return to the UK for a rest.

An evening patrol by 79 Squadron sighted a Do215 and three of the Luftwaffe's new twin-boom FW189As (attached to 9(H)/LG2 for operational assessment) in the Wavre area. The Hurricanes attacked and claimed all three of the reconnaissance machines shot down, one each by Plt Off Tom Parker, Sgt Harry Cartwright and Plt Off Douglas Clift. The latter later expressed doubts about the identity of his victim, believing that it might have been a Dutch Fokker G-1, an aircraft of similar shape. Despite his misgivings, records show that two FW189s were indeed shot down. One crashed near Ramillies-Offus, about eight miles south-west of Hannut, with the loss of Uffz Heinz Schmitz and his crew; the other crash-landed near Orbais-Ernage, north-west of Gembloux, with Oblt Gerhard Wöbbeking and his two crew members wounded.

During the action, Sgt Cartwright's aircraft (N2483) was damaged by return fire and was then intercepted by a Bf109 flown by Oblt Karl-Wolfgang Redlich, Staffelkapitän of 1/JG27; the damaged Hurricane force-landed at Braine-le-Comte. Meanwhile, two other Hurricanes were hit by ground fire, including that flown by Plt Off Lionel Dorrien-Smith, which returned with a damaged tail unit.

Prime Minister Churchill flew to Paris aboard a Flamingo during the afternoon, escorted by a flight of Hurricanes, and arrived at Le Bourget shortly after 1600, from where he and his staff were driven to Quai d'Orsay. There he was greeted by Prime Minister Reynaud, Minister of National Defence Edouard Daladier and Général Maurice Gamelin (GOC French Army). The hopelessness of the situation soon became apparent, the French having already accepted defeat as inevitable. Of the meeting, Churchill wrote:

> 'I asked Général Gamelin when and where he proposed to attack the flanks of the Bulge [referring to the area of the German break-through]. His reply was: "Inferiority of numbers, inferiority of equipment, inferiority of method"—then a hopeless shrug of the shoulders.'

Gamelin repeated the request for more aircraft, particularly fighters. Churchill added:

'In the course of his appeal Général Gamelin said that fighters were needed not only to give air cover to the French Army, but also to stop the German tanks. At this I said: "No. It is the business of the artillery to stop the tanks. The business of the fighters is to cleanse the skies over the battle." It was vital that our metropolitan fighter air force should not be drawn out of Britain on any account.'

Notwithstanding, Churchill sent a coded telegram to the War Cabinet at 2100 following his meeting with the French leaders, part of which read:

'The question we must face is whether we can give further aid in fighters above four squadrons, for which the French are very grateful... I personally feel that we should send squadrons of fighters demanded (ie six more) tomorrow, and, concentrating all available French and British aviation, dominate the air above the Bulge for the next two or three days.'

The War Cabinet responded favourably shortly before midnight and Churchill immediately advised his French counterpart, but added the warning that unless the French made a supreme effort, all would be lost. In fact, Général Gamelin had already expressed his belief that the battle was lost and that he could guarantee the safety of Paris for only two more days. Churchill had also been advised that the French had only about a quarter of their fighter aircraft left. His commitment to send further Hurricanes to France obligated him to cable US President Roosevelt for help:

'Our most vital need is the delivery at the earliest date of the largest possible number of Curtiss P-40 fighters, now in the course of delivery to your army.'

Due to the lack of suitable airfields and facilities, it was agreed that three of the additional six Hurricane squadrons (17, 32 and 151 Squadrons, together with specially formed composite units 56/213, 111/253 and 145/601 Squadrons) would fly to France each morning and operate from French bases until midday, then return to England while the other three squadrons replaced them. The decision to send half-squadrons to France was based on the theory that if a squadron was lost, the remaining half could be used to rebuild it but, despite instructions to the contrary, four of the flights amalgamated into these composite squadrons were from units which had already supplied flights to the Air Component. Every Hurricane squadron in Fighter Command (with the exception of 46 Squadron which had been sent to Norway) was now involved to some degree in supplying pilots or aircraft to aid the French cause.

The Reinforcing Flights

At about 1830, five Hurricanes of B Flight of 56 Squadron arrived at Vitry from RAF Martlesham Heath, having been led by a Blenheim; the remaining machine (N2553 US-C) flown by Plt Off Fraser 'Barry' Sutton had been delayed due to engine problems, and Sutton followed on his own. East of Calais he was intercepted by a Hurricane of 3 Squadron, flown by Sgt Peter Hillwood (a former member of 56 Squadron), who guided him to Merville. There he refuelled, then headed for Vitry where he rejoined B Flight. Also arriving at Vitry were six Hurricanes of B Flight of 229 Squadron under the command of Flt Lt Fred Rosier, six of B Flight of 253 Squadron and six of A Flight of 245 Squadron under Flt Lt John Thomson; the latter were attached to 615 Squadron at Moorsele for operations. As Rosier's Hurricane taxied in, he was greeted by an officer who told him to stand by to scramble as a 40 plus raid was approaching. After some time Rosier sent one of his pilots to find out what was going on. The pilot returned to say that the airfield appeared practically deserted and that the officer who had given the order to stand by had apparently forgotten they had arrived! A forceful character, Rosier did not hesitate to brandish his service revolver to obtain billets for his men for the night. The new arrivals were left to fend for themselves, being ignored by the other units in residence who, after seven days of unrelenting combat, were in no fit state to look after untrained newcomers.

Six Hurricanes of A Flight of 601 Squadron were to be attached to 3 Squadron at Merville, and six more from A Flight of 242 Squadron arrived at Lille/Seclin under Flt Lt Don Miller and were attached to 85 Squadron for operations; a number of the Squadron's ground crew arrived at Arras aboard a SABENA Ju52 (OO-AGW). Shortly after their arrival, there was an air raid as German raiders attempted to catch the miscellany of transports and communications aircraft on the ground. At Coulommiers airfield two Vega Gulls (P1751 and P1764) were destroyed, as was DH89 W6423. Another DH89 (W6424), which had been damaged previously, was set on fire at Amiens, while DH84 G-ACIU was set on fire at Mourmelon.

Personnel of the Reinforcing Flights

B Flight, 56 Squadron	B Flight, 229 Squadron
Flt Lt I.S. Soden	Flt Lt F.E. Rosier
Flg Off F.C. Rose	Plt Off G.M. Simpson
Plt Off P.D.McL. Down	Plt Off A.M. Dillon
Plt Off F.B. Sutton	Plt Off M.A. Bussey
Flt Sgt F.W. Higginson	Plt Off D.DeC.C. Gower
Sgt C. Whitehead	Sgt G.B. Johns

A Flight, 242 Squadron
Flt Lt D.R. Miller
Flg Off L.E. Chambers
Plt Off M.K. Brown
Plt Off A.H. Deacon
Plt Off R.H. Wiens
Plt Off D.G. MacQueen

A Flight, 601 Squadron
Flt Lt Sir A.P. Hope*
Flg Off W.P. Clyde
Flg Off G.R. Branch
Flg Off G.N.S. Cleaver
Flg Off R.M.B. Rowley
Flg Off P.B. Robinson

B Flight, 253 Squadron
Flt Lt H.T. Anderson
Plt Off P.L. Dawbarn
Plt Off J.K.G. Clifton
Plt Off J.D.B. Greenwood
Plt Off D.N.O. Jenkins
Sgt G. Mackenzie

A Flight, 245 Squadron
Flt Lt J.A. Thomson
Plt Off D.S. Yapp
Plt Off T.R. Kitson
Plt Off D.A. Pennington
Plt Off J.S. Southwell
Sgt R.W.E. Jarrett

Although there was no shortage of Hurricanes at the RAF's main depot at Glisy, where stocks were kept topped up by a stream of new aircraft delivered from the UK, 253/B Flight arrived with old fabric-winged Hurricanes still fitted with two-blade wooden propellers and obsolete TR9D radio sets (which were virtually useless since they had a range of about two miles), and were without armour protection for the pilot.

Flt Lt Guy Harris of A Flight of 253 Squadron and Flt Lt Humphrey Russell (who was in charge of the RAF Biggin Hill Operations Room) were just two of the pilots who ferried new Hurricanes to Glisy, where they spent the night in a hangar and returned to RAF Northolt aboard a Harrow transport next day. Flg Off M.H. Constable-Maxwell and Plt Off R.P. Fisher of 56 Squadron also ferried Hurricanes to Glisy and returned to RAF North Weald aboard an Anson.

Among the reinforcing pilots arriving separately from their units were a trio from 145 Squadron, Plt Off R.A. Sanders, Sgt E.D. Baker and Sgt A. Bailey. The unit(s) to which they were attached is not known, although it is believed that Dickie Sanders was attached to 81 Squadron, the communications unit, with which he was killed a few days later. 615 Squadron received two new pilots from the UK, Plt Offs Denis Crowley-Milling and Roy Bush, the latter a New Zealander from Wellington. Both were destined to fly Gladiators on airfield defence duties at Abbeville. 504 Squadron also received a number of replacement pilots including Plt Offs W. Barnes, A.W. Clarke and Lord Allerton, and Sgt H.D.B. Jones, while Sqn Ldr John Hill arrived from Air HQ to take command following the death of Sqn Ldr Parnall; Hill

---

* Flt Lt Sir Archie Hope was the 17th Baron of Craighill, having succeeded his father to the title in 1924.

had commanded 85 Squadron immediately prior to the outbreak of the war. The latter unit also received three replacement pilots in the guise of Plt Off J.E. Marshall and Sgts F.R. Walker-Smith and Butler, while Plt Off A.V. Gowers returned to flying duties following a spell in hospital.

Summary

A much quieter day in the air for the Hurricanes resulted in only 14 'confirmed' claims for the loss of 13 Hurricanes, the majority of which fell to Bf109s; five Hurricane pilots were killed, one taken prisoner and four wounded. In the previous three days, since the appearance of Bf109s and Bf110s in large numbers over the battle areas, AASF and Air Component Hurricane squadrons had suffered the loss of at least 52 Hurricanes, with 25 pilots killed, three taken prisoner and a further 11 wounded, losses which began seriously to worry Dowding and his commanders.

Claims by AASF and Air Component Hurricanes, 16 May

Type	Confirmed	Probable	Damaged	Total
He111	3	1	1	5
Do17	1	—.	6	7
Ju88	—	—	1	1
FW189	3	—	—	3
Bf109	3	—	1	4
Bf110	4	—	—	4
	14	1	9	24

Luftwaffe Losses Attributed to AASF and Air Component Hurricanes, 16 May

Type	60% to 100%	Under 60%	Total
Ju88	2	—	2
FW189	2	—	2
Bf109	2	1	3
Bf110	1	1	2
	7	2	9

With the coming of darkness, Bomber Command dispatched nine Whitleys to attack communications in and near Maastricht, Aachen and München-Gladbach and all aircraft returned safely. However, one of six Hampdens sent to attack German industrial targets crashed near Cherbourg on the return flight, although all six Wellingtons that raided oil plants at Bottrop and Gelsenkirchen returned safely.

Individual Claims—AASF and Air Component Hurricanes, 16 May

| AM- | Flt Lt J.E. Scoular | 73 Sqn | He111 damaged |

AM-	Sgt G.L. Nowell	87 Sqn	Do17, 4 Do17 possible
	Plt P.T. Parsons	504 Sqn	Ju88 damaged
	Flt Lt J.S. Owen	504 Sqn	He111 probable
	Plt Off R.J. Renison	504 Sqn	He111
1430-	Flg Off R.F. Weatherill		
	Plt Off G. McK. Stewart		
	Plt Off H.P. Dixon	607 Sqn	Do17 possible
	Plt Off P.L. Parrott		
	Flg Off R.E.W. Pumphrey		
1500-	Plt Off R.D. Grassick	615 Sqn	Bf109
1630-	Flt Lt R.H.A. Lee	85 Sqn	He111
	Sgt G. Allard	85 Sqn	He111
	Sgt A.H. Deacon	85 Sqn	Bf109
1630-	Flg Off R.M.S. Rayner	87 Sqn	Bf109
	Plt Off W.D. David		
1700-	Plt Off A.S. Dini	607 Sqn	Do17 doubtful
1730-	Sgt R.C. Wilkinson	3 Sqn	Bf110
1730-	Plt Off B. Van Mentz	504 Sqn	Bf109 damaged
	Flg Off R.M.S. Rayner	87 Sqn	Bf110
	Plt Off C.W.W. Darwin	87 Sqn	Bf110
	Unknown pilot	85 Sqn	Bf110
PM-	Plt Off T.C. Parker	79 Sqn	FW189
	Plt Off D.G. Clift	79 Sqn	FW189
	Sgt H. Cartwright	79 Sqn	FW189

Losses—AASF and Air Component Hurricanes, 16 May

AM-	L1614	87 Sqn	Sgt G.L. Nowell: aircraft hit by return fire from Do17 and crash-landed near Goeferdinge; pilot unhurt.
1500-	N2335	615 Sqn	Flt Lt L.T.W. Thornley: shot down by Bf109 (possibly of 4/JG26) near Tirlemont; pilot killed.
	N2338	615 Sqn	Plt Off T.C. Jackson: shot down by Bf109 (possibly of Stab II/JG26) near Tirlemont; pilot baled out, PoW.
	P2577	615 Sqn	Plt Off B.P. Young: shot down by Bf109 (possibly of Stab II/JG26) south of Brussels; pilot baled out, severely burned.
1630-	L1898	85 Sqn	Sgt H.H. Allgood: shot down by Bf109 of 5/JG2 and crash-landed north-west of Lille; pilot wounded.
	N2389	85 Sqn	Sgt L.A. Crozier: shot down by Bf109 of 5/JG2 near Lille; pilot baled out, burned.
	L1641	85 Sqn	Flg Off A.B. Angus: shot down by Bf109 of 1/JG27 near Fretin, south-west of Lille; pilot killed.
	P2535	85 Sqn	Plt Off M.G.H. Rawlinson: shot down by Bf109 of 1/JG27 near Quievrain, south-west of Lille; pilot killed.
	L2000	87 Sqn	Sgt A.N. Trice: shot down by Bf109 (possibly of 5/JG2) west of Mons; pilot killed.
1730-	P2825	3 Sqn	Sqn Ldr P. Gifford DFC: shot down by Bf110C of 1/ZG1 near Wavre; pilot killed.
1730-	L1640	85 Sqn	Flg Off Count M.B. Czernin: shot down by Bf109 of 3/JG76 and crash-landed; pilot unhurt, returned.
	P2824	85 Sqn	Plt Off H.D. Clark: shot down by Bf109 of 3/JG76 and crash-landed; pilot wounded.

PM-	N2483	79 Sqn	Sgt H. Cartwright: aircraft damaged by return fire from FW189 of 9(H)/LG2 then shot down by Bf109 of 1/JG27 and crash-landed near Braine-le-Comte; pilot unhurt, returned.

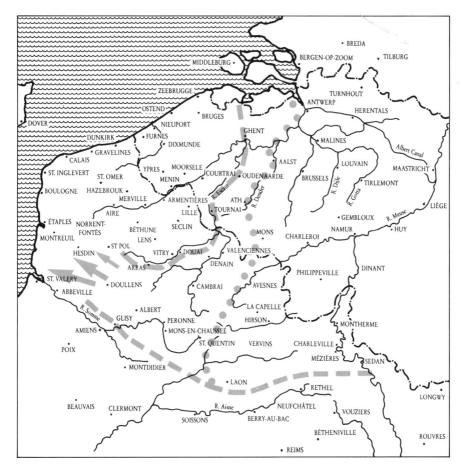

See synopsis of events (overleaf).
● German advance   — Allied line

Synopsis of Events 17-21 May

17 May   The Germans poured through the gap between the Allied Northern and Southern Armies. 601/A Flight arrived at Merville, where it was attached to 3 Squadron, as was a further reinforcement of six Hurricanes from 213/B Flight. Hurricanes from 32 and 151 Squadrons, plus 111/B Flight, 213/A Flight and 601/B Flight arrived at Abbeville; these units were to operate by day and return to UK that evening.

18 May   The main German thrust reached the line Cambrai–St Quentin. 1 Squadron moved to Anglure, 73 Squadron to Gaye, 79 Squadron to Merville (where the composite 145/601 Squadron arrived to operate for the day) and 253/B Flight to Lille/Marcq, where 111/A Flight, 213/A Flight and 17 Squadron arrived, while 56/A Flight went to Lille/Seclin; 253/A Flight and 111/B Flight arrived at Vitry in the morning, followed by 151 Squadron in the afternoon, but following the evening raid Vitry was evacuated and surviving Hurricanes returned to the UK, except 607 Squadron and 56/B Flight which went to Norrent-Fontès.

19 May   The Germans reached Peronne. There were no Allied forces between them and the sea. Lille airfields were now evacuated and 85 and 87 Squadrons arrived at Merville, as did 17 and 32 Squadrons from UK; composite 111/253 also operating from UK. 504 Squadron moved to Norrent-Fontès, where 607 Squadron retained a Flight, although 56/B Flight returned to the UK.

20 May   The corridor between Arras and the Somme was opened and advanced units of the Panzers reached the coast. Merville evacuated and all units back to the UK; Moorsele evacuated and 615 Squadron moved to Norrent-Fontès, but that base also evacuated that evening—all flyable Hurricanes back to the UK. Only the three AASF units—1, 73 and 501 Squadrons—remained in France.

21 May   A British counter attack at Arras caused a brief panic, but after initial success, failed. From then on the fate of the Northern Armies was sealed.

CHAPTER IX

FRIDAY 17 MAY
11 GROUP LENDS A HAND

'The Dornier dived and began hedge-hopping in an effort to get away, but Ian followed him, firing all the time. We watched them disappear behind some trees.'

Plt Off Barry Sutton, B Flight 56 Squadron.

The Situation in Holland and Belgium

Although the French 7th Armée was forced to evacuate South Beveland and the island of Walcheren, it still retained three divisions south of the Scheldt Estuary. But the call there, as elsewhere, was for more RAF fighters.

The outlook was just as bleak in Belgium, where the army began to withdraw from the Antwerp fortifications and to fall back to the line of the west bank of the Scheldt. Although Brussels and Mechelen were occupied by the Germans during the evening, there remained a certain misplaced optimism:

'Belgian morale was reported to be exceptionally high—a fact ascribed to the British fighter activities and the small losses thus so far incurred by the Belgians during their extensive movements.'

Elements of the BEF also began pulling back to the Dender. The German breakthrough to the south of the French 1st Armée caused a hasty regrouping of British forces to meet the threat to the right flank. The French 1st Armée meanwhile was falling back to hold a line south from Ath through Lens to Mons, where the remains of the French 9th Armée was located, but the only forces opposing the Germans between Maubeuge and Attigny were, in the main, hastily assembled reserves.

Air Operations over Belgium and Northern France

Lysanders of 4 Squadron, operating from the advanced landing ground at Aspelare, continued to carry out tactical reconnaissances over the Louvain area, while those from 16 Squadron were ordered to reconnoitre the area to the right of the BEF, where one was lost to Bf109s. Lysanders from both 2 and 26 Squadrons were also operative in the battle areas during the day.

Bomber Command's 82 Squadron had been ordered to send a dozen Blenheims to attack concentrations of vehicles near Gembloux, and were to receive protection over the target area by Hurricanes from 87 Squadron. The Blenheims departed RAF Watton at 0445 but as they approached Nivelles, one was shot down by Flak. An estimated 15 Bf109s of 1/JG3 (although in fact there were only six) then attacked and shot down no fewer than ten of the bombers and seriously damaged the other two, one of which force-landed. The sole surviving Blenheim, badly damaged, returned to RAF Watton at 0820. The Hurricanes had arrived over the target area at the appointed time, but the Blenheims had been intercepted before reaching Gembloux. Of the 33 crew members aboard the missing aircraft, 20 were killed, three taken prisoner and others wounded.

Later that morning, Air Component Blenheims and Lysanders were ordered to attack mechanised units on the Landrecies to Le Cateau road. The order was rescinded by HQ when information was received that the convoy was in fact French, but it was too late to recall all units. Blenheims of 18 and 57 Squadrons, together with bomb-carrying Lysanders of 16 Squadron, carried out a series of attacks on the Le Cateau-Cambrai road, where two of the Blenheims were intercepted by Bf110s and shot down. A similar fate befell Lysander L4796, although this was the victim of a Bf109 of 6/JG26. There remained much confusion:

'By now there was no doubt that the column was French; but a further report was brought into RAF Component Headquarters at 1315 by a Staff officer who had made a special reconnaissance in a Moth. This was to the effect that 15 to 20 definitely German tanks were on the road Landrecies to Le Cateau.'

During the course of a reconnaissance flight, a 2 Squadron Lysander crew saw three Bf109s take off from an airfield near the west bank of the Scheldt. As the Lysander (L4815 KO-N) dropped down to 5,000 feet, the trio of Messerschmitts (from II/JG2) was again sighted 10,000 feet above and they commenced line astern diving attacks. The Lysander's gunner claimed one of the attackers shot down in flames and a second badly damaged, but the reconnaissance machine was holed in a petrol tank and force-landed at Douai, where the gunner set fire to it to prevent it falling into enemy hands.

Blenheims were again sent out and duly bombed the road between St Quentin and Peronne:

> 'Whether this was in fact another French column is not clear, but none of the intelligence summaries of the day report the enemy as being west of St Quentin at this time. It is difficult to resist the conclusion that RAF Component was not in possession of a sufficient picture of the battle to order an operation of this sort with safety.'

Meanwhile, Air Component squadrons in the north had begun withdrawing southwards. Ten French units had already withdrawn from the Reims-Mézières-Laon triangle, and were soon followed by a further four groupes of fighters and one of bombers. Général d'Astier de la Vigerie (GOC Northern Zone and Air Commander of the French 1st Armée), who had moved his HQ from Chauny to Chantilly, apparently advised each fighter groupe that it was to send its own pilots to the rear to ferry back replacement aircraft, thereby depleting its own operational capacity; but even this was no easy task, since:

> 'Even at the peak of the battle, the depots closed down on Sundays and after hours!'

67 Wing, AASF

During the night a column of French tanks passed through the village of Conde-sur-Marne and its commander informed 1 Squadron's Sqn Ldr Halahan at Conde/Vraux airfield that Reims had fallen. Unable to contact 67 Wing HQ, Halahan ordered his ground party to evacuate to the airfield at Anglure, some 30 miles to the south-west. At 0300, Halahan departed by road with the spare pilots, leaving Flt Lt Johnny Walker in charge of the Hurricanes, which were to follow at dawn:

> 'The Hurricanes of 67 Wing reached the 71 Wing aerodromes early in the day, not a little confusion being caused when 73 and 501 Squadrons landed at Villeneuve, apparently without the existing occupants [105 Squadron] having received any warning of their arrival. Since the Wing Headquarters had certainly been warned by AASF, the failure seems to have occurred between Wing and squadron.'

Due to the shortage of combat-worthy aircraft, five pilots of 501 Squadron pilots had earlier been sent by road to Villeneuve to collect new Hurricanes. However, the roads were jammed with refugees and they were forced to drive throughout the night, reaching Villeneuve at dawn. Having collected the new Hurricanes, the five tired pilots (including Plt Off Kenneth Lee, Sgt Ginger Lacey, Sgt Don McKay and Sgt Paul Farnes) set off for the return journey to Bétheniville where, on arrival, they discovered that the Squadron had evacuated. Nobody amongst those left behind seemed to know where the Squadron had gone so, having refuelled, they flew to a French base just outside Troyes, where it was realised that French petrol was not suitable for the Hurricanes' engines, so the aircraft were covered by camouflage netting while the pilots made enquiries as to the whereabouts of their unit. Next morning, having telephoned RAF HQ, the French Commandant was able to advise the five pilots that 501 Squadron was at Anglure, to where they flew without further ado.

At 0900, A Flight of 1 Squadron, still at Conde/Vraux, took off to investigate a report that dive-bombers were attacking retreating Allied troops near Sedan; Flt Lt Johnny Walker reported:

> 'Detailed for offensive patrol against dive-bombers east and west of Sedan. On reaching Vouziers at a height of 8,000 feet (base of cloud), in a break a strong force of enemy fighters [Bf110Cs of V(Z)/LG1] was seen above. As the cloud was decreasing towards the east, it would have been impossible to fulfil a mission against the dive-bombers with the enemy fighters in such strength above. I climbed to attack this fighter formation, which turned south-west into the sun. I obtained a satisfactory position at 18,000 feet and attacked. As the fight developed, more and more 110s entered the combat, up to a total of about 25.'

As a result of the combat, both Walker and Flg Off Hilly Brown were credited with single victories, while Flg Off Iggy Kilmartin claimed one and a probable and Sgt Frank Soper two. Flg Off Pussy Palmer was seen probably to shoot down another before his own aircraft (P2820) was hit and fell away emitting black smoke. However, he was able to bale out of his burning aircraft and was fired at by two French soldiers as he floated down, but was not hit and returned later. Brown reported that he had shot down the Messerschmitt responsible for shooting down Palmer and then engaged a He111, which he also claimed. Walker's aircraft suffered damage in the action, a cannon shell having penetrated the wing and aileron. He landed at a French airfield where a temporary repair was made with a hammer and chisel. Soper's aircraft (Hurricane L1905/H) also sustained damage from 'numerous perforations' and although he returned safely to Conde/Vraux, the Hurricane was considered to be beyond unit repair. Paul Richey wrote:

'We walked round it [Soper's aircraft] counting the holes. There were three cannon-shell holes and about 30 bullet holes; one bullet had entered the fuselage from behind, gone through the harness slit in the armour plating behind Soper's back and stopped on hitting the harness cable just short of his neck. There were plenty of dents in the armour plating, too; thank God we had the stuff—it had already saved many lives.'

The Messerschmitts of V(Z)/LG1, which had been escorting He111Hs of KG53 when engaged by the Hurricanes, reported the loss of three aircraft:

Bf110C of 14/LG1 shot down west of Reims: Oblt Werner Methfessel (victor of at least eight combats) and Uffz Heinz Resener killed.

Bf110C of 14/LG1 shot down west of Reims: Uffz Friedrich Schmitt and Obgfr Heinz Schmidt killed.

Bf110C of 14/LG1 shot down west of Reims: Lt Kurt Schalkhauser and Uffz Joachim Jäckel baled out, PoW of the French.

73 Squadron experienced a relatively quiet day. Although it had patrols up during the morning and early afternoon, it was not until 1925 that two sections led by Flg Off Cobber Kain (P2559/D) encountered a formation of what he believed to have been 15 Bf110s 'stacked up in fives', but were almost certainly Do17Zs of II/KG3. Kain attacked the top flight and 'seriously damaged one'. A second twin-engined aircraft was claimed probably destroyed by Plt Off Don Scott, although he correctly identified his victim as a Do17. Kain then attempted to engage a Ju88, as Charles Gardner reported:

'Kain was just about to attack a lone recce Ju88 when ten Messerschmitts [of I/JG76] dived out of the sun, but he got away after shooting one down.'

The Bf109 crash-landed near Nives and the pilot was unhurt, while one of the Dorniers was seriously damaged and also force-landed.

501 Squadron continued to carry out patrols from its new base at Anglure. During an afternoon patrol, a section of Hurricanes saw a column of German tanks rumbling along the Landrecies to Le Cateau road and strafed these, as Sgt Ginger Lacey recalled:

'It was like shooting at elephants with a pea-shooter. The tank commanders didn't even pay us the compliment of closing their turrets: they just ducked their heads as we came over and stuck them out again as soon as we'd gone past. The tanks rolled on completely undamaged.'

60 Wing, Air Component

During the morning 85 Squadron saw the departure of Flt Lt Dickie Lee, Flg Off Ken Blair, Plt Off John Ashton, Plt Off Paddy Hemingway and Sgt Sammy Allard, all of whom were flown to RAF Hendon aboard an ATA Ensign for three days' leave. At the same time Flt Lt Bob Boothby and Plt Off John Lecky drove to Le Touquet on 48 hours' leave. Among the new pilots arriving were Flg Off Jerrard Jeffries and Plt Off Geoffrey Pittman of 17 Squadron, both of whom were posted to 85 Squadron.

It was a quieter day in the air for 85 Squadron, although during the course of one patrol two sections of Hurricanes were engaged just before 1600 by seven Bf109s from Stab and I/JG3, the German pilots reporting their opponents as '30 Spitfires'. Two of the Messerschmitts were claimed shot down by Plt Off Pat Woods-Scawen, another by Plt Off Russell Wiens of the attached 242/A Flight, and a probable by Sgt Cyril Hampshire. 1 Staffel reported the loss of Lt Karl Haberland, who baled out and was taken prisoner by the French, and Lt Helmut Reumschüssel, who apparently shot down Woods-Scawen's aircraft (N2319) before being attacked by another—presumably that flown by Wiens. Reumschüssel also baled out but evaded capture and returned to his unit two days later. One of the 242/A Flight pilots, Plt Off Don MacQueen (P2655), was forced down with a damaged engine and, although he landed safely, had a difficult time trying to convince a mob of angry peasants that he was not German. Wood-Scawens' descent meanwhile was witnessed by Plt Off Roland Beamont of 87 Squadron:

'Suddenly sounds of a dogfight came from the direction of Lille and a Hurricane with a trail of smoke behind it did a complete loop, at the top of which a puff of white showed that the pilot had baled out, and it went straight in from some 12,000 feet at incredible speed.'

Woods-Scawen was slightly wounded but was soon back with the Squadron.

504 Squadron had only two Hurricanes serviceable and four pilots were sent to Glisy in a Rapide to collect replacement aircraft. Meanwhile, Plt Offs Trevor Parsons and Ken Wendel were at readiness in the two Hurricanes when they were ordered off at 0430 to fly to Charleroi, there to meet more Hurricanes arriving from England. The pair then patrolled Gembloux-Charleroi where they experienced light ground fire, before Parsons sighted a 6th Armee Hs126 of 2(H)/41 and attacked

from the port quarter, closing to 50 yards. The Henschel dived for the ground but then straightened out and was lost from sight. Parsons believed he had 'done considerable damage' and, in fact, the aircraft crashed near Jumet, north of Charleroi. Both Fw Hans-Hein Broderson and his observer, Lt Hermann Lenne, were killed.

The Wing's other unit, 87 Squadron, saw no action during the day, although its pilots provided escort for two Blenheim reconnaissance sorties, one to Louvain and the other to Tournai. Flt Lt Robert Voase Jeff was one of those granted leave in England and he departed during the morning aboard one of the transports. However, the unit received a new A Flight Commander during the day—Flt Lt Ian Gleed—who had been serving with 266 Squadron on Spitfires and had just recovered from a flying accident. He had been ordered to report to 87 Squadron following the death of Flg Off Jack Campbell on 12 May; however, although his movement to France was one of priority, he was not allocated a Hurricane, but instead was placed in charge of 300 airmen destined for France and travelled by troopship and French railway to Lille/Seclin, the journey taking four days!

61 Wing, Air Component
From Vitry, at 0425, a section of three Hurricanes of 607 Squadron, led by Flg Off Francis Blackadder in P2574 AF-F, set out to escort a Blenheim of 53 Squadron on a reconnaissance flight. Although no enemy aircraft were seen by the Hurricane pilots, the Blenheim failed to return from its task and was assumed to have been shot down by ground fire. At 0550 six Hurricanes of the newly arrived 56/229 Squadron carried out the unit's first patrol over Brussels; nothing untoward was sighted except AA fire and all returned safely.

Plt Off Peter Parrott of 607 Squadron received a pleasant surprise when he was awakened by his friend, Plt Off Peter Dixon:

> 'After six days (and 14 operational sorties) I was given the day off. However, at 0730 I was still in bed when Peter started throwing pebbles at my window. When I poked my head out of the window he told me that we were going on leave to the UK and that there was an ATA Ensign on the ground, but the pilot was not going to wait long in a very hostile environment. I thought he was pulling my leg and said something like: "Don't be daft, the real war has started now, we can't be going on leave." However, he convinced me as, being the last two arrivals on the Squadron, we were the only two who had not had UK leave.
>
> I packed an overnight bag and was off to the airfield. The Ensign was stripped completely bare of seats and carpets, down to the bare fuselage and bulkheads. There were about eight of us from various

squadrons (including Flg Offs Humpherson and Forster of 607 Squadron, and Sgt Gareth Nowell of 87 Squadron) sitting on the floor and bracing ourselves against bulkheads as we took off. Arriving at Hendon, nobody knew anything about us. The Station Adjutant eventually telephoned the Air Ministry for instructions and was told to send us all away on ten days leave.'

He added:

'On the following Sunday morning I received a telegram at home ordering me to report immediately to 145 Squadron at Tangmere. Peter Dixon was also posted to 145 Squadron and was lost over Dunkirk.'

At 0930, four Hurricanes of 56/229 Squadron scrambled in pursuit of raiders which had dropped bombs on Vitry and the oil refinery just outside Douai. Plt Off Barry Sutton of 56/B Flight wrote:

'A Dornier appeared over the airfield, flying high and out of the sun. This was the first enemy aircraft I had seen either from the ground or from the air, and I was so engrossed in looking at it that I had to be thrown into a small trench. A second later there came the scream of a falling bomb. Ian [Soden], Higginson and someone from 229 Squadron roared off. The Dornier had now overshot the airfield and turned as if to make a second run. He also lost height and was at about 800 feet. Spellbound we watched him turn away suddenly as he apparently saw Ian [flying N2437] climbing hard after him. Then followed the most thrilling spectacle I have ever seen. Ian, by now well on his tail, started firing. We heard the noise of his Brownings above that of the engines of both machines. The Dornier dived and began hedge-hopping in an effort to get away, but Ian followed him, firing all the time. We watched them disappear behind some trees.'

The Dornier crashed into a field near the airfield and Soden landed beside the wreckage to collect a souvenir (an ammunition pan); he reported that there were no survivors. This was almost certainly Lt Otto Grüter's aircraft of 6/KG76. A second bomber appeared from the east but was soon chased by the other two Hurricanes. The bomber released one bomb on Douai before it fled, pursued by Flt Sgt Higginson (N2440 US-H), who claimed it shot down.

At the same time as the 56/229 Squadron section had scrambled, Flg Off Bob Pumphrey (P2571 AF-G) of 607 Squadron took off on his own, followed 10 minutes later by Plt Off Tony Dini (P2874 AF-B) and later still by a section from B Flight, following the sighting of the Do17Zs of 6/KG76 north-east of Cambrai. Both Pumphrey and Dini claimed Dorniers shot down, as did Plt Off John Humphreys when his section arrived. Flg Off Francis Blackadder followed with another section of Hurricanes, but these failed to locate the bombers. 6/KG76 reported losing two Dorniers and were probably the same aircraft as attacked by 56 Squadron:

> Do17Z of 6/KG76 flown by Lt Otto Grüter shot down near Cambrai: crew killed.

> Do17Z of 6/KG76 flown by Fw Erwin Hauser shot down near Cambrai: crew baled but pilot killed; others PoW of the French.

The alarm was sounded again at 1030 at Vitry and Flt Lt Fred Rosier and some of his 229/B Flight hurriedly took off, but returned half an hour later having not sighted any raiders. It was the turn of a 56/B Flight section to patrol at 1210, when heavy AA was experienced and Sgt Cliff Whitehead's aircraft (N2523 US-S) suffered splinter damage to one wing and its tail.

Owing to the vulnerability of the Blenheims for reconnaissance flights in the increasingly hostile sky, 607 Squadron was instructed to dispatch Hurricanes to carry out low-level tactical sorties for the army. One of the first of these was undertaken by Flg Off Blackadder (P2574 AF-F) at 1125, who reconnoitred the Cambrai area—and was back within 25 minutes. He was off again at 1230, this time accompanied by Flg Off Bob Pumphrey (P2571 AF-G) and Plt Off Gordon Stewart (P3448 AF-H); all three returned safely within half an hour.

At 1430 five Hurricanes of 56/B Flight set off on patrol and, ten miles east of Cambrai, they engaged seven unescorted He111Ps of I/KG54 and immediately attacked from dead astern. Flt Lt Ian Soden (N2437), Flg Off Frank 'Tommy' Rose (N2439), Flt Sgt Taffy Higginson (N2440 US-H) and Sgt Cliff Whitehead (N2523 US-S) each claimed one, and Plt Off Peter Down (L1992) was credited with a probable and a second as damaged; Flg Off Rose (whose brother, Jack, was serving with 3 Squadron at Merville) and Sgt Whitehead jointly probably destroyed another. Five Hurricanes from 607 Squadron were also in the area and both Plt Off Tony Dini (P2536 AF-R) and Plt Off Gordon Stewart (P2874 AF-B) engaged the He111s near Binche, two of which they claimed shot down. However, Stewart's aircraft suffered damage from return fire and he force-landed at Amiens, from where he returned later to Vitry, landing at 1945. I/KG54 reported the loss of three He111s:

> He111P of 2/KG54 flown by Uffz Oskar Schümann shot down near

Valenciennes: two killed, one PoW of the British, one PoW of the French.

He111P of 3/KG54 flown by Fw Paul Lenz shot down and crash-landed 12 miles north-east of Valenciennes: one killed, three PoW of the French.

He111P of 3/KG54 flown by Fw Adolf Lau shot down north-east of Valenciennes: three killed, pilot baled out and PoW of the French.

Operating from the advanced airfield at Moorsele, the Wing's 615 Squadron was also busy early in the morning. Three sections—each of three aircraft (including Plt Offs Vic Verity, Malcolm Ravenhill and John Collins, the replacement pilots from 229 Squadron)—departed at 0530 and were soon in action. Plt Off Ravenhill (P2907) reported:

'I was flying a zig-zag course for Brussels. My section leader attacked a Henschel. Heavy AA forced me to break to the right (No 3 followed me and we lost contact with the leader as we had a different R/T frequency). A few minutes later I sighted (at 0625) a single e/a which was patrolling a line north to south from the Meuse. The aircraft was camouflaged brown and green above and pale green underneath. I attacked from astern and took the e/a by surprise. The e/a dived to the ground with black smoke pouring from the engine. Near the ground he flattened his dive. No fire was observed from the rear cockpit of the Henschel.'

The Henschel, a 6th Armee machine of 1(H)/41, crash-landed and the pilot, Lt Peter Wirtz, and his observer, Oblt Wolfgang Steudel, survived. Plt Off Ravenhill continued:

'Whilst investigating, I sighted another similar aircraft and pro-ceeded to take an attacking position. At 200 yards the rear gunner opened fire and I watched the tracer bullets going above me. I closed to 100 yards and gave him a long burst, breaking away about ten yards astern of the enemy. The Henschel immediately spun down and crashed.'

It would seem that Ravenhill was mistaken in his belief that the Henschel had crashed, as this aircraft—from 1(H)/23 (also a 6th Armee unit)—was only slightly damaged and was able to return to its base, although the pilot, Uffz Heinz Bauer, had been wounded during the attack. Meanwhile, Ravenhill had become disorientated following the actions:

'I discovered I was alone. I proceeded to patrol west of Brussels. I eventually landed at Coulpiègne where I was informed by French personnel that I was approximately 30 miles south of Lille.'

He departed from Coulpiègne with the intention of flying to Vitry but, while over a heavily wooded area en route, ran out of fuel and was obliged to 'pancake the aircraft on top of the trees and crash through'. He was unhurt and made his way to Poix airfield, from where he was flown to Abbeville.

At about 0930, another section from 615 Squadron encountered a Ju88—L1+AR of 7/LG1 flown by Oblt Ernst Schwarz—between Charleroi and Wavre, which was shot down by Flt Lt Jim Sanders. There were no survivors from the bomber which crashed near Fines-lès-Raches, about six miles north-east of Douai. It seems probable that Sanders' Hurricane may have been hit by return fire, as he force-landed near Lille. During the day Flg Offs Tony Eyre and Dick Pexton flew the Squadron's Master (N7577) from Vitry to Glisy, from where they collected two new Hurricanes and returned with them to Moorsele.

Three consecutive patrols by 615 Squadron Hurricanes failed to meet enemy aircraft but, at 1900, the Squadron's C Flight (in fact, A Flight of 245 Squadron) encountered an estimated ten Bf109s (8/JG26) between Ath and Brussels. In the ensuing combat Plt Off John Southwell (Red 3 in N2501) claimed a Messerschmitt but was shot down himself:

'We were attacked by ten or more Messerschmitt 109s. After ten minutes I re-formed with Red 1 and was attacked by five 109s. One overshot me and I was able to get a burst of five seconds. E/a went down vertically and hit the ground. I had puncture in glycol tank and crashed near Pottignies [Petit-Enghien].'

Forty minutes later, another patrol met Bf109s of 2/JG76 near Cambrai, as reported by Plt Off Willie McKnight (KW-D):

'While patrolling over Cambrai the enemy (seven in number) attacked from below, followed by eight more. After warning rest of Squadron by R/T, I did a steep climbing left turn, followed enemy behind and fired. Smoke issued from enemy machine and I fired until he struck the ground.'

Lt Joachim Schypek was wounded by McKnight's attack but was able to bale out near Origny, where he was found by troops of 6 Panzer Division.

Although a dusk patrol by six Hurricanes of the attached A/245 Flight failed to locate any hostile aircraft, Sgt Raymond Jarrett became separated and lost and was obliged to force-land his Hurricane (N2702) near Dieppe, where the damaged aircraft had to be abandoned; Jarrett eventually reached Amiens, from where he was flown back to England in a returning Lysander.

63 Wing, Air Component

3 Squadron welcomed the arrival of the reinforcement Flight from 601 Squadron during the morning, the Hurricanes escorting an Ensign and a Bombay to Merville, the transports conveying 28 ground personnel. 79 Squadron also received an attachment when six Hurricanes from 213 Squadron's B Flight arrived at Merville about the same time. The Flight Commander, Flt Lt Derek 'Widge' Wight (flying RE-J of 229 Squadron), noted:

> 'Escort Blenheim left early and Green Section (self, Sgt Butterfield, P2824 AK-S and Sgt Lishman, AK-H) could not start.'

Wight followed with his section as soon as all were ready and arrived safely at Merville. Although 3 Squadron carried out a patrol during the morning in conjunction with the section from 213/B Flight, it was not until shortly after midday that a section led by Sgt Roy Wilkinson encountered a He111 near Charleroi. The bomber was attacked by Sgt Basil Friendship (L1609) and Plt Off Joe Hobbs (N2535), and was seen to crash on a road. Friendship recalled:

> 'I think there were two or three of us shooting at a He111. I claimed part of it.'

Two other sections—the Hurricanes flown by the attached 601 Squadron pilots—patrolled the same area, but failed to locate any hostile aircraft.

At 1430, Green Section of 213/B Flight was sent to patrol Landrecies-Avesnes-La Capelle-Wasigny, with top cover provided by nine Hurricanes of 3 Squadron, although no hostile aircraft were sighted. The other section of 213/B Flight took off for the Le Cateau area with five Hurricanes of 79 Squadron's B Flight, led by Sgt Alf Whitby. One of the 213/B Flight section, Sgt Valentine, who had become separated and lost, eventually force-landed P2677 AK-O and broke his arm in the process; he was taken to the hospital at Le Touquet for treatment before being evacuated back to England. Meanwhile, his colleagues sighted seven He111s, some Ju88s, a Dornier and at least a dozen Bf109s, the latter aircraft 6/JG52. Sgt Whitby (N2384) reported:

> 'I was leading a patrol of five aircraft over Le Cateau when 109s

sighted. E/a engaged and bursts fired as five enemy climbed into cloud. Reassembled two of formation and encountered Do215. Fired remainder of ammunition at very long range.'

Plt Off Douglas Clift (Green 1) added:

'Chased one [Bf109] which climbed into cloud bank. I climbed above cloud and sighted one Do215 flying east. E/a made use of cloud. I followed in and out until Ath district, where the e/a dived steeply. I carried out astern attack. Enemy fire silenced after second burst. Continued attack until ammunition used. E/a continued to dive. Did not see result as had to break away to avoid hitting ground.'

Although claimed as a Do215, the aircraft attacked by Whitby and Clift was a Do17Z of 4/KG76 which suffered some damage and two of its crew wounded, but was able to return to its base. Plt Off Lionel Dorrien-Smith (Green 2), however, was more successful:

'Got on to tail of one [Bf109]. Closed, climbing towards cloud— opened fire at 400 yards approximately. Fired two bursts. E/a stalled over and went down in vertical dive with a great deal of smoke and some flames coming from it. Did not follow down.'

One Hurricane (L2140) failed to return. Flg Off Bob Herrick, Acting Flight Commander of B Flight, was shot down by Fw Paul Boche of 6/JG52 and baled out over German lines, where he was taken prisoner.

Another Do215 reconnaissance aircraft was reported over Merville at 1530, which Flt Lt Widge Wight (P2824 AK-S) of 213/B Flight was ordered to pursue:

'Took off from Merville to chase Do215 over drome, but it turned in cloud at 20,000 feet and went south-east while I was searching north-east.'

A further patrol departed from Merville at 1730, Yellow Section of 3 Squadron led by Flg Off Denys Jones and Red Section by Flg Off Billy Clyde of 601/A Flight. Just after 1800 a formation of Do17Zs of II/KG76 was sighted near Merville and attacked by Yellow Section. The 5 Staffel Dornier flown by Oblt Helmut Weikert was seriously damaged and the crew baled out near La Capelle. The Hurricanes came under intense crossfire as they closed in, which caused damage to the aircraft of both Jones (L1609) and Sgt Peter Hillwood (L1899). As they broke away, they were attacked by Bf109s of 1/JG3 flown by Lt Gerhard Sprenger and Lt Heinz Schnabel. Jones baled out near Merville, but Hillwood stayed with his aircraft until he was forced to crash-land near Vitry, where the Hurricane burst into flames, and he suffered burns to his face and hands.

3 Squadron was asked to put up six aircraft for an evening patrol, which included three of the attached Flight from 601 Squadron. They joined forces with six more Hurricanes from 79 Squadron, including a section from the attached 213/B Flight. The dozen Hurricanes then patrolled the Vilvoorde-Braine-le-Comte area and, although no hostile aircraft were seen, heavy Flak was experienced near the Fôret-de-Nivelles. Flt Lt Widge Wight (P2824 AK-S), in charge of the 213/B Flight section, noted:

'Patrol Brussels. Leading 12 composite aircraft 213/79/3/601 Squadrons. Clouds at 3,000 feet. Got shot up by AA (five holes) and by tracer pom-pom. Lost one of 601 over Fôret-de-Nivelles.'

The missing pilot was Flg Off Guy Branch, a recipient of the Empire Gallantry Medal*, who had become separated from his colleagues in the twilight. Low on fuel and lost, he force-landed his aircraft (L1987) near Aire, and returned later to Merville 'drunk and inarticulate with an affluent Frenchman who had rescued him and then opened the wine cellar'.

11 Group, Fighter Command

At this stage, with pressure from above, Air Chief Marshal Dowding gave instructions for 11 Group to dispatch squadrons or flights of Hurricanes to France, there to assist the battered and fatigued AASF and Air Component units, the new squadrons to operate temporarily from French bases before they returned to the UK with the onset of dusk. Thus, at 0830, nine Hurricanes of 151 Squadron arrived at Abbeville from RAF Manston, followed later by eleven more from 32 Squadron, four from 601 Squadron's B Flight and six each from 111 Squadron's B Flight and 213 Squadron's A Flight, the latter having escorted a Bombay transport of 271 Squadron delivering stores from England.

The 151 Squadron Hurricanes were ordered to patrol the Lille-Valenciennes area at 1000. While flying at 12,000 feet, two aircraft were sighted at considerable distance to the south-east. Sqn Ldr Teddy Donaldson ordered Yellow and Blue Sections to remain above while he

---

* Flg Off Guy Branch had been awarded the Empire Gallantry Medal (later changed to George Cross) for the rescue of his pilot following the crash of their Hawker Demon biplane on 11 February 1937.

led Red Section down to investigate and identify. Once it was ascertained the aircraft were Ju87s (from III/StG51), Donaldson ordered No 1 Attack and called Yellow and Blue Sections to join him when a further 20 Ju87s were seen. In the ensuing series of combats, six of the dive-bombers were claimed shot down and four others were believed to have been severely damaged and therefore probably destroyed. Sqn Ldr Donaldson (P3316) was credited with two Ju87s, plus another unconfirmed, while a single victory was claimed by Flt Lt Freddy Ives (P3319), who also shared a probable with Sgt George Atkinson (P3315). The latter reported:

'I followed Flt Lt Ives down and approximately 200 yards behind him. His first target crashed and burst immediately into flames. He broke away and commenced attack on second aircraft. His attack was short and I followed up immediately he broke away. I opened fire at 150 yards. The second burst was delivered at approximately 80 yards. The e/a did not employ evasive tactics.'

Of his combat, Flg Off Dickie Milne (P3321) wrote:

'I closed on one which immediately commenced evasive tactics, doing vertical left turn and stall turn. The rear gunner commenced firing before me, his tracer bullets passing across and then beneath me. The gunner ceased firing when I was approximately 100 yards away. I clearly saw fabric and other pieces ripping away. I overtook, breaking to starboard, and on turning observed e/a fall in a straight line. It fell in the middle of a large field and was completely destroyed.'

Plt Off Les Wright (P3320) claimed another:

'I followed him and as he levelled up, I gave him a burst of three seconds from 50 yards. The e/a dived into ground and burst into flames.'

Yet another of the luckless dive-bombers fell to Plt Off John Bushell (P3223):

'I got on the tail of a Ju87. E/a dived from 500 feet to ground level and flew almost straight. Its rear gunner opened fire at approximately 400 yards with tracer, but it all passed to the port of me. I closed to 200 yards and opened fire, closing rapidly to 50 yards. E/a caught fire under port wing root. I had to pull up smartly to avoid ramming e/a. It was observed to crash by Plt Off Wright.'

Despite firing all his ammunition at one of the dive-bombers, Sgt Donald Aslin (P3313) could claim only a probable:

> 'An e/a went past me on port quarter and I engaged it. I saw no reply from the rear gunner after my first burst. I gave six bursts of between two and three seconds. I saw streams of white smoke.'

A probable was also granted to Plt Off Jack Hamar (P3312):

> 'As the leader attacked the first e/a, who were turning and diving in line astern, I saw smoke start pouring from this aircraft. As I was in a good position, I also gave it a short burst and as I turned away, saw it crash. By this time we were nearly at ground level and the next e/a was dead ahead. He went into a steep left-hand turn and I could only get a deflection shot. I saw my burst enter nose of this e/a and white vapour started coming out. As I broke away I received a fair burst from the rear gunner.'

An inspection of Hamar's aircraft on his return to Abbeville revealed ten bullet holes, while Flt Lt Harry Ironside's Hurricane (P3273) had suffered two strikes, one of which had also passed through the right sleeve of his tunic and flying jacket:

> 'I engaged a Ju87 from astern at about 200 yards. After two short bursts the rear gunner ceased firing and slumped down in the cockpit. Noticed considerable damage to the e/a. I also attacked another e/a, finishing my ammunition, with no noticeable result.'

Two other Hurricanes suffered minor damage from return fire.

Records show that III/StG51 lost seven aircraft shot down, all 14 crew members being listed initially as missing, including the Gruppenkommandeur, although four returned later:

> Ju87B of Stab III/StG51 shot down north of Landrecies: Maj Heinrich von Klitzing, Gruppenkommandeur, and Uffz Fritz Zander killed.

> Ju87B of 7/StG51 shot down north-west of Landrecies: Oblt Walter Klemme, Staffelkapitän, and Uffz August Jasper PoW of the French.

> Ju87B of 7/StG51 shot down and crash-landed north-west of Landrecies: Lt Helmut Glöckner and Uffz Hermann Pfauth PoW of the French.

Ju87B of 8/StG51 shot down north of Landrecies: Lt Gerhard Wanke and Uffz Siegfried Miehl killed.

Ju87B of 8/StG51 shot down near Boussois, four miles north-west of Landrecies: Uffz Günter Feist and Uffz Klaus Thismar killed.

Ju87B of 8/StG51 shot down near Aulnoye-Aymeries: Lt Max Rentsch and gunner baled out and rescued by troops of 5 Pz Division.

Ju87B of 9/StG51 shot down and crashed near Liniers: Lt Wilhelm Schwarze and gunner rescued by troops of 7 Pz Division.

On this occasion, seeing Hurricanes amongst the Ju87s must have been a welcome sight to the retreating troops. Air Commodore Goddard, SASO Air Component, described graphically the soldiers' lot:

'Our forward troops were perpetually the prey beneath the wheeling Stuka bombers. As in quick succession, they peeled off their circling to go screaming down with their one bomb to be released at point-blank at their target. The soldier who had the nerve to look up into that crescendo of diving fury would actually see with his own eyes each bomb come loose and fall from the Stuka's belly and make its plunge. Then as that flying bomb approached, enlarging as it neared, he would see its Stuka-flinger bank over and soar away. On would come that bomb into its crashing of intolerable violence and the prone soldier would feel, first, the shattering blast, then the scorching heat-wave and the earth convulsion, and maybe, too, a mighty thwack into his body of metal or clod; then finally a hard shower of fragmented earth and stones. All that he would endure, if he remained alive.'

Eleven Hurricanes of 17 Squadron arrived at Merville during mid-afternoon. At 1630 the Squadron patrolled north of Brussels where they too met a large formation of Ju87s—two dozen dive-bombers of IV(St)/LG1. Sqn Ldr George Tomlinson—recently returned from his adventures in Holland—'picked off one which fell burning to the ground'. Another immediately manoeuvred on to his tail and in trying to out-turn this, he stalled and force-landed P3277 about 15 miles south-east of Brussels, suffering slight facial injuries. Flg Off Dickie Meredith reported shooting down one and claimed a second as probably damaged:

'Opened fire at approximately 300 yards and closed to within 100 yards. E/a burst into smoke and went downwards in a sort of waffle.

I then engaged a second of the section who was trying to climb away.
I finished my ammunition at a range of 200 yards and I am sure I was
hitting him. I had one bullet hole in my port wing.'

Plt Off Ken Manger shot down one which crashed and burst into flames,
then chased a second, silencing the rear gunner:

'I did an astern attack on one, opening fire at 250 yards. I fired for
five seconds closing in all the time. The Ju87 started to give out
smoke from port side and dived into the side of a house, bursting
into flames. I then got on to the tail of another Ju87 and repeated my
attack until my ammunition was spent. I immediately broke away
and did not see any result.'

Plt Off Richard Whittaker reported that his victim also crashed in
flames:

'I did an astern attack on one e/a which broke away. Rear gunner
fired tracer which soon stopped. I got my sights on e/a and closed
right in and as I flashed past him saw him burst into flames and hit
ground.'

A second Hurricane failed to return from the engagement and Flg Off
Arthur Lines was posted missing. The Squadron claimed a total of five
Stukas shot down in the engagement, together with two probables.
Records show that IV(St)/LG1 lost three aircraft totally destroyed:

Ju87B of 10(St)/LG1 5% damaged in combat: the gunner, Gfr Ernst
Heller, was severely wounded and died on 3 June.

Ju87B of 11(St)/LG1 damaged in combat and crashed near Vaal,
west of Aachen: Gfr Ernst Gienger and Uffz Johann Donderer
killed.

Ju87B of 12(St)/LG1 shot down (reportedly by ground fire) four
miles north of Edingen: Oblt Wendelin Hartmann and Fw Alfred
Fleisch killed.

Ju87B of 12(St)/LG1 shot down three miles north-west of Halle:
Uffz Stefan Hofmann and Uffz Heinz Schmidt killed.

The remaining Hurricanes, having refuelled and rearmed at Merville,
returned to RAF Hawkinge later that evening. By 1930, 151 Squadron
had also arrived back in the UK, landing at RAF Manston, from where
Hamar's damaged aircraft (P3312) was flown to RAF North Weald for

repair. The Hurricanes of 32 Squadron, together with those of 111/B Flight, 213/A Flight and 601/B Flight, similarly returned to their respective UK bases that evening without having encountered enemy aircraft during the course of their patrols.

Meanwhile, in Belgium, the unlucky Commander of 17 Squadron, Sqn Ldr Tomlinson, having successfully set fire to his damaged aircraft, made his way towards Allied lines and eventually reached Norrent-Fontès. He was back in England within 30 hours, his second escape from the Continent in a week. The other missing pilot, Flg Off Lines, also succeeded in returning to England. On his return he reported:

> 'Each pilot of my Flight picked out a Ju87 which immediately broke formation and dived. I opened fire from astern at about 250 yards and after a burst of about three seconds saw it burst into flames and crash into a field. I was then separated from my Flight, but had already seen Sqn Ldr Tomlinson send down in flames another Ju87. I was returning to Merville alone when I was attacked by 18 Messerschmitt 109s out of the sun. One or two attacked me from directly ahead. I fired at these, using up all my ammunition. I did not observe any enemy casualties. My machine was then hit from behind by machine-gun fire and four cannon shells. The last cannon shell hit my port tank and set the Hurricane on fire. I used my parachute and made a delayed drop from 6,000 feet to about 1,500 feet. When my parachute opened I was fired on by French troops with rifles. Four holes were made in the parachute canopy.'

The Messerschmitts were from 8/JG26. A total of three Hurricanes were claimed by the German pilots—one each being credited to Lt Heinz Ebeling, Lt Hermann Ripke and Lt Gustav Sprick; one of these claims related to an aircraft of 615 Squadron shot down later during the patrol.

Summary

In contrast to recent days, not one AASF or Air Component Hurricane pilot was killed during the day's actions, although one was taken prisoner when he was shot down. However, at least 16 Hurricanes were lost, of which three were not due to enemy action.

Claims by AASF, Air Component and 11 Group Hurricanes, 17 May				
Type	Confirmed	Probable	Damaged	Total
He111	8	2	1	11
Do17	4	2	—	6
Do215	—	—	1	1
Ju88	1	—	—	1

Ju87	11	5	—	16
Hs126	3	—	—	3
Bf109	7	1	1	9
Bf110	5	3	—	8
	39	13	3	55

Luftwaffe Losses Attributed to AASF, Air Component and 11 Group Hurricanes, 17 May

Type	60% to 100%	Under 60%	Total
He111	3	—	3
Do17	3	1	4
Ju88	1	—	1
Ju87	10	1	11
Hs126	3	—	3
Bf109	3	—	3
Bf110	3	—	3
	26	2	28

That night (17/18 May) a force of Bomber Command Wellingtons set out to raid Namur (20 aircraft) and targets on the Meuse (27 aircraft), while six Hampdens targeted Gembloux. However, once in the air, the two Wellington squadrons tasked to attack Namur were ordered to bomb Gembloux instead, but only one squadron received the revised instructions. In addition, two dozen Whitleys were dispatched to bomb the oil refineries at Bremen, and 48 Hampdens were sent to attack three refineries at Hamburg. All aircraft returned and all but nine crews reported to have completed their mission successfully.

Individual Claims—AASF and Air Component Hurricanes, 17 May

0500-	Plt Off P.T. Parsons	504 Sqn	Hs126
0530-	Plt Off M. Ravenhill	615 Sqn	2 Hs126
0900-	Flt Lt P.R. Walker	1 Sqn	Bf110
	Flg Off M.H. Brown	1 Sqn	Bf110
	Flg Off J.I. Kilmartin	1 Sqn	Bf110, Bf110 probable
	Sgt F.J. Soper	1 Sqn	2 Bf110
	Flg Off C.D. Palmer	1 Sqn	Bf110 probable
0930-	Flt Lt I.S. Soden	56/B Flt	Do17
	Flt Sgt F.W. Higginson	56/B Flt	Do17
0930-	Flg Off R.E.W. Pumphrey	607 Sqn	Do17
	Plt Off A.S. Dini	607 Sqn	Do17
	Plt Off J.S. Humphreys	607 Sqn	Do17
0930-	Flt Lt J.G. Sanders	615 Sqn	Ju88
1200-	Sgt A.H.B. Friendship Plt Off J.B. Hobbs }	3 Sqn	He111
1430-	Flt Lt I.S. Soden	56/B Flt	He111
	Flg Off F.C. Rose	56/B Flt	He111
	Flt Sgt F.W. Higginson	56/B Flt	He111
	Sgt C. Whitehead	56/B Flt	He111

	Plt Off P.D.McL. Down	56/B Flt	He111 probable, He111 damaged
	Flg Off F.C. Rose	56/B Flt	He111 probable
	Sgt C. Whitehead		
1430-	Plt Off A.S. Dini	607 Sqn	2 He111
	Plt Off G.McK. Stewart		
1430-	Sgt A.W. Whitby	79 Sqn	Bf109 inconclusive
	Plt Off D.G. Clift	79 Sqn	Do215 damaged
	Plt Off L.R. Dorrien-Smith	79 Sqn	Bf109
1600-	Plt Off P.P. Woods-Scawen	85 Sqn	2 Bf109
	Plt Off R.H. Wiens	242/A Flt	Bf109
	Sgt C.E. Hampshire	85 Sqn	Bf109 probable
1730-	Flg Off D.A.E. Jones	3 Sqn	Do17 probable
	Sgt P. Hillwood		
1900-	Plt Off J.S. Southwell	245/A Flt	Bf109
1925-	Flg Off E.J. Kain	73 Sqn	Bf109, Bf110 probable
	Plt Off D.S. Scott	73 Sqn	Do17 probable
1940-	Plt Off W.L. McKnight	615 Sqn	Bf109

Individual Claims—11 Group Hurricanes, 17 May

1000-	Sqn Ldr E.M. Donaldson	151 Sqn	2 Ju87, Ju87 probable
	Flt Lt F.A. Ives	151 Sqn	Ju87
	Flg Off R.M. Milne	151 Sqn	Ju87
	Plt Off L. Wright	151 Sqn	Ju87
	Plt Off J.M. Bushell	151 Sqn	Ju87
	Plt Off J.R. Hamar	151 Sqn	Ju87 probable
	Sgt D.R. Aslin	151 Sqn	Ju87 probable
	Flt Lt F.A. Ives	151 Sqn	Ju87 probable
	Sgt D.R. Aslin		
1630-	Sqn Ldr G.C. Tomlinson	17 Sqn	Ju87
	Flg Off R.V. Meredith	17 Sqn	Ju87, Ju87 probable
	Plt Off K. Manger	17 Sqn	Ju87, Ju87 damaged
	Plt Off R.C. Whittaker	17 Sqn	Ju87
	Flg Off A.P. Lines	17 Sqn	Ju87

Losses—AASF and Air Component Hurricanes, 17 May

0530-	P2907	615 Sqn	Plt Off M. Ravenhill: force-landed out of fuel following combat with Hs126s; pilot unhurt, returned.
0900-	P2820	1 Sqn	Flg Off C.D. Palmer: shot down near Reims by Bf110C of V(Z)/LG1; pilot baled out, unhurt.
	L1905	1 Sqn	Sgt F.J. Soper: aircraft damaged in combat near Reims by Bf110C of V(Z)/LG1 and force-landed at Conde/Vraux; pilot unhurt.
		1 Sqn	Flt Lt P.R. Walker: aircraft damaged in combat with Bf110C of V(Z)/LG1; pilot unhurt.
0930-		615 Sqn	Flt Lt J.G. Sanders: aircraft believed damaged by return fire from Ju88 of 7/LG1 and force-landed near Lille; pilot unhurt.
1430-	P2874	607 Sqn	Plt Off G.McK. Stewart: aircraft damaged by return fire from He111P of I/KG54 and force-landed near Amiens; pilot unhurt.

1430-	P2677	213/B Flt	Sgt A.F.C. Valentine: became lost on patrol and force-landed; pilot broke arm.
	L2140	79 Sqn	Flg Off R. Herrick: shot down near Valenciennes by Bf109 of 6/JG52; pilot baled out and PoW.
1600-	N2319	85 Sqn	Plt Off P.P. Woods-Scawen: shot down east of Lille by Bf109 of 1/JG3; pilot baled out, slightly wounded.
	P2655	242/A Flt	Plt Off D.G. MacQueen: aircraft damaged east of Lille by Bf109 of 3/JG3 and force-landed; pilot unhurt, returned.
1730-	L1609	3 Sqn	Flg Off D.A.E. Jones: aircraft damaged by return fire from Do17Z of 5/KG76, then shot down near Merville by Bf109 of 1/JG3; pilot baled out, unhurt.
	L1899	3 Sqn	Sgt P. Hillwood: aircraft damaged by return fire from Do17Z of 5/KG76, then damaged near Cambrai by Bf109 of 1/JG3 and crash-landed near Vitry; pilot burned.
1900-	N2501	245/A Flt	Plt Off J.S. Southwell: shot down south of Brussels by Bf109 of 8/JG26 and crash-landed near Petit-Enghien; pilot unhurt, returned.
1925-	L1987	601/A Flt	Flg Off G.R. Branch: aircraft possibly damaged by Flak over Fôret-de-Nivelles and force-landed near Aire out of fuel; pilot unhurt, returned.
?	N2702	245/A Flt	Sgt R.W.E. Jarrett: became lost on patrol and force-landed near Dieppe; pilot unhurt.

Losses—11 Group Hurricanes, 17 May

1000-	P3312	151 Sqn	Plt Off J.R. Hamar: aircraft damaged by return fire from Ju87 of IV(St)/LG1; pilot unhurt.
1630-	P3277	17 Sqn	Sqn Ldr G.C. Tomlinson: stalled and force-landed south of Brussels in combat with Ju87 of IV(St)/LG1; pilot slightly injured, returned.
	P2822	17 Sqn	Flg Off A.P. Lines: shot down south of Brussels by Bf109s of 8/JG26; pilot unhurt, returned.

CHAPTER X

SATURDAY 18 MAY
VITRY THE TARGET

'We saw this formation of bombers... and noticed their bomb doors were open in a very unfriendly manner and the air gunners blasting off at us...and decided the best thing to do would be to dive for the nearest ditch.'

LAC Bill Bowman, 607 Squadron.

The Situation in Belgium and Northern France

In the north the main French and Belgian forces, together with the BEF, were by now falling back towards the Escaut, where a new line was to be established. Thus, the Franco-Belgian frontier positions were held east to Maubeuge, and from there the Sambre and Oise rivers were intended to constitute a defensive line southwards. But events soon forced a further withdrawal when German forces crossed the Oise in several places and the Sambre defences were breached at Landrecies.

Lysanders of 2, 4, 16 and 26 Squadrons were kept busy carrying out tactical reconnaissance sorties in the Cambrai area. Late in the day German tanks were reported at St Quentin and just south of Peronne. However, these flights were not without loss and two Lysanders failed to return, while two more were written off after landing. One crew from 16 Squadron reported an engagement near St Quentin with a Hs126 of 1(H)/14Pz, which the gunner claimed shot down. With the Lysanders fully occupied, a Gladiator was sent to reconnoitre the evacuated Rosières airfield, where the pilot reported seeing armoured vehicles on the St Quentin-Ham road. Air Component reconnaissance Blenheims were also out during the day and one of these, from 59 Squadron, failed to return and was reported later to have crashed near Tournai.

The progress of the German advance units in the direction of Cambrai and Peronne caused further moves by Air Component units during the day. There remained much confusion:

'It was now becoming very difficult indeed to obtain reports of our own air activity. Units were moving to other stations as their own became liable to the risk of air attack. These moves and the attendant delay in re-establishing communications entailed great delay or even prevented the obtaining of information.'

67 Wing, AASF

At 0600, the Hurricanes of 1 Squadron still at Conde/Vraux departed for Anglure minus Sgt Frank Soper's aircraft (L1905/H), 'which strongly resembled a Swiss cheese and was accordingly cremated with full honours'. En route to Anglure, Plt Off Charles Stavert (N2353) engaged and shot down a Do17P of 3(F)/31, although Fw Kernbüchler and his crew survived the crash. 1 Squadron's diarist recorded:

'After shooting down the Dornier he pushed off at a rate of knots in what he fondly imagined was a homeward direction; seeing an aerodrome beneath him, bethinking of well-filled tankards, he approached to land. After putting his flaps down he suddenly realised it was German and seeing a He111 landing ahead, shot it down and pushed off with all speed, his petrol lasting him until over friendly territory.'

Stavert force-landed his aircraft (N2353) in a ploughed field a few miles from Conde/Vraux and arrived back at the airfield as the rear party was about to leave, so he travelled to Anglure with them.

Eight Hurricanes of 1 Squadron took off at 1430 from Anglure as part of an escort for six Blenheims of 18 Squadron from Goyencourt, which were to bomb German columns near Cambrai. Flg Off Hilly Brown, leading the Hurricanes, reported:

'I took off as leader of a Flight of eight aircraft, destination Merville. At 1520, on approaching St Quentin, we were assaulted by very heavy AA fire. Thinking we had been mistaken for e/a, I slowly turned through 180° waggling my wings, but the fire continued. My Flight was now widely separated, and as I came south a Hs126 passed across under me. I delivered two attacks, and on each occasion the e/a turned through 180° and came toward me. After my second attack, which I pressed home, the e/a was not to be seen. I experienced no fire from him. This was about five to ten miles south-east of St Quentin.'

The Hurricane (L1856) flown by Sgt Rennie Albonico was seen suddenly to go into a dive, apparently to investigate troops on the ground near St Quentin, and was promptly shot down by ground fire, although he survived to be taken prisoner. Meanwhile, Brown led his Flight to Plivot, where the Hurricanes were refuelled by ground crews of 139 Squadron; they returned to Anglure at dusk.

Five pilots of 501 Squadron were flown aboard a DH89 (G-ADBV) of 24 Squadron to Glisy, from where they were to collect new Hurricanes as the unit was down to six serviceable aircraft; of the flight back to Anglure, Sgt Paul Farnes (flying P2714) recalled:

> 'Led by Gus Holden, the five of us force-landed after dusk in a field at Nozay; it was pretty well dark when we landed, but we all got down safely. We walked to a nearby farm and were entertained with food and drink by a local farmer, after which we spent the night on hay in the stables with the cattle—but after several bottles of wine this was of little consequence! We returned next morning to the field where we had landed and found that high-tension cables ran along one side—we must have gone either over or under them when landing!'

73 Squadron meantime was busily engaged in moving to Gaye, near Sézanne, and, as such, its pilots were not involved in any operational sorties. On arrival at Gaye it was discovered that there were no stocks of petrol or oil for the Hurricanes, although supplies were on their way. To add to the increasing daily catalogue of confusion, French machine-gunners opened fire on 24 Squadron's Vega Gull (P1750) as it approached to land at Reims to collect mail. The pilot, who was wounded, was taken to Villeneuve for treatment, but the damaged Vega Gull was abandoned.

60 Wing, Air Component

At 0700 six Hurricanes of 85 Squadron from Lille/Seclin, which included a section from 242/A Flight, together with three more of 87 Squadron (led by newly arrived Flt Lt Ian Gleed) from Lille/Marcq, set off to patrol over the Le Cateau quadrant, where they encountered a formation of Bf110Cs from I/ZG26. All three Canadians of 242/A Flight were shot down, as were two of 85 Squadron, and only Sgt Cyril Hampshire of the latter unit returned to base; he recalled:

> 'I was leading a section with two Canadian officers, each being replacements with about 10 to 12 hours in Hurricanes. There was another section from B Flight and a section from 87 Squadron, led by a Flight Lieutenant [Gleed]. We were patrolling when we encountered a squadron of Messerschmitt 110s. The Squadron turned right, putting 85/B Flight in the lead and 87's section second and my section last. When we got there it was a general mêlée. I

dived on to a 110 and fired and all my tracer went into the cockpit area. It was found later crashed. From this sortie I was the only pilot to return—all B Flight's chaps were missing as were my two wing-men. I don't know about 87's lot.'

Flg Off Derek Allen (P2701) was shot down for the second time in three days, but this time was killed, while Flg Off Bill Lepine (N2425) baled out slightly wounded and was taken prisoner. Of the three missing Canadians, Plt Off Russell Wiens (L1665) wrote later:

'I was shot down by a Messerschmitt 110, or rather by about four of them. We were out on patrol and we ran into about twelve of them and did we have a scrap! We saw them first and went right in on their tail. I got one with my first burst and then followed a general mêlée. I was trying to manoeuvre for another one when a 110 nearly collided with me. The rear gunner and I had an argument. I gave him about 500 rounds and could see him fold up. I don't know whether the plane crashed or not, but if it did I have three. My engine cracked up owing to bullets in the cooling and oil system. I did not parachute because it is not safe any more owing to parachute troops. The French pot them on the way down. I crashed in a valley on top of some trees. I immediately wrote off the plane, but got away with a bit of concussion and a stiff leg and a cut face. I was out for an hour or so and it is lucky she did not burn. The French found me first and thought I was German. Three of them pulled guns on me and I thought I was done, but I passed out again and woke up in British hands.'

Wiens' colleague, Plt Off Marvin Brown, was wounded in the right leg but managed to bale out of N2320. He was taken to a first aid station, where he met Wiens. After treatment both pilots were put into an ambulance heading for Cambrai, but when the driver was informed that the town had fallen, he headed instead for the coast, from where the two wounded pilots were evacuated to England. Shortly after their departure for Cambrai, the third downed Canadian, Flg Off Lorne Chambers, was taken to the same first aid post. He had managed to bale out just before his burning aircraft (L1922) exploded and suffered burns to his face, hands, right leg and both feet. He too was put aboard an ambulance on its way to Cambrai, which was however diverted to a nearby hospital, where he was deposited, there to be captured next day when the area was overrun by German troops.

Meanwhile, the 87 Squadron section had fared better; Flt Lt Gleed (P2798 LK-A) wrote:

'I waggle my wings; nine of us against five of them. This looks easy.

What the hell are the leading section doing? Still in vic formation, they sail on. The enemy are flying in rather a wide vic formation. I decide on the right-hand plane.'

Gleed shouted orders over the R/T for his two companions—Flg Off Rafael Watson (P2829 LK-G) and Plt Off Chris Darwin—to attack; he continued:

'Blast it! I am going too fast: they are past me. As they pass, their rear gunners fire at me; their tracer goes over my head. As I turn, the sky seems full of black crosses. To my right a Hurricane goes down in flames; by it there's a white puff as a parachute opens. At last I get my sights on—a full deflection on the inside of the turn. I thumb the firing button: a tearing noise as my guns fire. My bullets hit his petrol tanks, a stream of white vapour pours from his wing tanks—his wing's on fire. He turns on his back, trailing fire and smoke behind, and plunges into a wood below.'

As Gleed pulled away, he was attacked by three more Bf110s, but one of these overshot his Hurricane:

'Only 25 yards range. God! I can't miss. My windscreen is covered with muck. I've hit his oil and glycol tank. I turn as tight as I can. A flash from below—that last one has just hit the deck; no parachutes.'

Out of ammunition, Gleed dropped down to tree-top level and sped away from the action, completely disorientated. He then observed another Hurricane:

'Just as I am drawing up to format on this Hurricane, he dips; I catch a fleeting glimpse of flying brick, and seemingly quite slowly, a Hurricane's tail, with the red, white and blue stripes, flies up past my cockpit. I glance behind and see a cloud of dust slowly rising. He must have had some bullets in him to have hit that house. Wonder who it was?'

It seems probable that the Hurricane seen to crash was that flown by Flg Off Allen of 85 Squadron, who was killed. Without a map to help him, Gleed became hopelessly lost, but after flying north for some time he sighted an aerodrome near the coast which turned out to be Berck-sur-Mer near Le Touquet, a French Naval aerodrome. There he was given a map and directions while his Hurricane was refuelled. He then flew back to Seclin, where he was relieved to find his two section

companions, Flg Off Watson and Plt Off Darwin; the former claimed a
Bf110 destroyed and the latter a probable. Darwin noted:

> 'I opened fire at 180-100 yards deflection shot . . . and think I must
> have killed the pilot as it dived down vertically to the wood. I did not
> see it crash as there were a number of 110s on my tail.'

Two Bf110s of I/ZG26 were shot down during the engagement and a
third damaged:

> Bf110C of 2/ZG26 shot down near Le Cateau and crashed about 20
> miles south-west of Maubeuge: Lt Horst Hessel and Gfr Friedel
> König killed.

> Bf110C of 3/ZG26 seriously damaged and crash-landed at
> Vogelsang airfield: crew unhurt.

> Bf110C of 3/ZG26 15% damaged in combat: Lt Walter Manhart
> unhurt, but his gunner, Uffz Otto Bräutigam, was wounded.

When the survivors of the 85/87 Squadron formation returned they
found six more Hurricanes had arrived at Lille/Marcq; these were from
A Flight of 111 Squadron: Flt Lt R.P.R. Powell, Flg Off H.M. Ferriss,
Plt Off D.S.H. Bury, Plt Off I.C. Moorwood, Sgt W.L. Dymond and
Sgt J.T. Craig. Contrary to instructions, both Flights of 111 Squadron
were now operating from French bases.

More Hurricanes arrived at Lille/Seclin during the afternoon, Sqn
Ldr E.V. Knowles at the head of six aircraft of A Flight, 56 Squadron:
the pilots were Flt Lt J.D. Joslin, Flg Off J.H. Coghlan, Plt Off B.J.
Wicks, Plt Off R.P. Fisher (a New Zealander) and Sgt J.W. Elliott.
Also arriving from England, under the temporary control of 60 Wing,
was A Flight of 213 Squadron—Flg Off E.G. Winning, Flg Off W.N.
Gray, Flg Off R.A. Kellow, Plt Off L.G.B. Stone, Sgt P.P. Norris and
Sgt M.E. Croskell; on the way over from England they had escorted a
Bombay transport to Abbeville. Yet more Hurricanes landed at Lille/
Marcq during the afternoon, to refuel, these from 17 Squadron from
RAF Hawkinge, the nine aircraft led by Flt Lt Bill Toyne.

87 Squadron was in action again at 1330 when, led by Sqn Ldr Dewar,
the Hurricanes encountered over a wood east of Brussels an estimated
80 Ju87s, protected by Bf109s. One section only was able to attack
Stuka stragglers, one of which Plt Off John Cock (P3889) claimed shot
down in flames; he also damaged another, as did Plt Off Ken Tait. The
Messerschmitts kept the other Hurricanes occupied, although there
were no losses.

Bomber Command launched a raid against German forces in the Le

Cateau area during the afternoon when 20 Blenheims from 15, 21 and 40 Squadrons were dispatched from RAF Wyton. The French had promised fighter cover over France but, when this did not materialize, the 21 Squadron formation wisely turned back. However, the other two Flights pressed on and the six Blenheims of 15 Squadron were attacked by Bf109s of 3/JG2. Four of the bombers were shot down and the other two damaged.

Both 111/A Flight and 253/B Flight (which had arrived at Lille/Marcq from Vitry earlier in the day) were sent off at 1525, ostensibly to escort the Blenheim raid. However, the formation leader—Flt Lt Harry Anderson of 253 Squadron—became lost and it was left to Flt Lt Peter Powell (111/A Flight Commander) to take control of the situation. Followed by the others, Powell dropped down to determine their exact whereabouts, then flew back to Douai before heading in the direction of Valenciennes. En route they encountered nine Bf110Cs of ZG26, whose I Gruppe was escorting Heinkels of I and II/KG54, while II Gruppe provided escort for two Staffeln of Do17Zs of II/KG76. Flt Lt Powell (N2340) led the Hurricanes into the attack against the unsuspecting Zerstörer and personally delivered a port section attack 'on e/a which broke formation and dived down out of control', then carried out a further attack from close range, passing about 15 feet under the Messerschmitt.

Yellow 1, Flg Off Michael Ferriss (L1822), attacked a Bf110 head-on with a three second burst and reported:

> 'Front of e/a collapsed and it dived out of control. A further three second burst was given in a beam quarter attack and pieces fell out of port engine. Aircraft spun down out of control. Crew baled out but as they were over enemy territory, I shot them both.'

Ferriss then attacked a second Messerschmitt from astern at 300 yards, closing to 200 yards:

> 'Pieces fell out of port engine and e/a dived out of control with smoke pouring from port engine.'

A third Bf110 was engaged with a burst of six seconds and again he reported that he saw pieces of one engine break away before it issued volumes of black smoke and the aircraft dived into cloud. Not yet finished, Ferriss went after another of the Messerschmitts, firing his remaining ammunition and seeing strikes. On the way back to Lille he was intercepted by two more Bf110s, but they left him alone when he carried out feint attacks.

Plt Off David Bury (Red 2, flying L1973) also claimed a Bf110, causing its starboard engine to explode before it turned over on to its back and crashed, while Plt Off Iain Moorwood (L2001) engaged two more, but then lost them in cloud:

'Four bursts of about three seconds each, closing to 200 yards, then second attack [firing] a long burst at his fuselage, but unable to see results as I was being fired at from starboard.'

A further Messerschmitt was claimed by Sgt John Craig before his own aircraft (L1607) was damaged by another:

'I saw one Messerschmitt 110 coming towards me at about the same height. As it turned away I put a long burst at 100 yards' range into his belly. It fell away quickly to starboard and dropped out of control. Immediately afterwards I was attacked from the rear by a 110. After taking avoiding action, I turned to see it shot down by a Hurricane. During the attack I heard something strike the under-side of the engine, but continued the fight. I attacked another 110 and gave him two short bursts but no effect was noticed. I then heard the Flight Commander calling us to rejoin formation but I saw a 110 in the clouds below, so proceeded to get into an attacking position. Whilst doing this the engine of my aircraft started to vibrate very badly and the cockpit quickly filled with smoke and fumes.'

Craig was able to crash-land the damaged aircraft in a field about a mile north of Vimy and was uninjured:

'In the next field was a crashed Heinkel. All its crew were dead. Two had been killed in the air, one seriously wounded and had since died, and the fourth came out of the crash unhurt but had been shot by French soldiers.'

253/B Flight had by now joined the action and claimed two of the Dorniers shot down plus four probables. Flt Lt Harry Anderson (a Canadian from Winnipeg), leading the attack, reported:

'Two bursts of three seconds then I flew into cloud. Inconclusive.'

Plt Off John Greenwood claimed one probable:

'I got on to an aircraft and pressed the button. I found my guns still on "safe" so had to turn them on. I was by then right in the middle of a mass of German aircraft but I got behind one and gave it a great burst—a Dornier which I believe was shot down.'

Plt Off John Clifton's target fell in flames:

> 'With 15 other Hurricanes, B Flight intercepted two Do215s, but
> when we attacked, six more Dorniers and six 110s materialized. I
> attacked a bomber and gave it two longish bursts and the starboard
> engine burst into flames. The aircraft spun down.'

Plt Off David Jenkins claimed one bomber shot down and a second
probably so before engaging the escort:

> 'While attacking a 110, a bullet from his rear gun pierced my engine.
> I broke away and flew to the first aerodrome I could find and this
> was Glisy. I carried out a successful force-landing and the aircraft
> was undamaged except the engine was practically seized as I had
> been flying nearly half an hour with no oil.'

Sgt Gilbert Mackenzie also claimed a probable:

> 'I put three bursts into a Dornier—the starboard engine emitted
> clouds of black smoke. It dived and I followed it down to 3,000 feet,
> then I spotted another Dornier at which I fired a burst.'

As he was returning to Lille, Sgt Bill Dymond (L1522) of 111/A Flight
sighted one of the Do17s at 16,000 feet, which he attacked:

> 'One burst from astern below and two at 250 yards from dead
> astern. Aircraft burst into flames and dived vertically from 5,000
> and hit the ground with a terrific explosion.'

Only one Dornier was totally destroyed, although two others suffered
damage, while ZG26 lost one Bf110C with two others seriously damaged:

> Do17Z of 4/KG76 shot down and crashed near Wavre: crew baled
> out, one wounded.

> Do17Z of 4/KG76 5% damaged in combat: one crew member
> wounded.

> Do17Z of 4/KG76 10% damaged in combat: one crew member
> wounded.

> Bf110C of 1/ZG26 severely damaged in combat south of Vitry and
> crash-landed at Köln-Ostheim: crew unhurt.

> Bf110C of 2/ZG26 severely damaged south of Vitry and crash-
> landed near Düren: crew unhurt.

Bf110C of 4/ZG26 shot down south of Vitry and crashed near Bugnicourt, eight miles south-east of Douai: Uffz Emil Landgraf PoW of the French, Uffz Fritz Mathis killed.

At 1635, 17 Squadron was ordered off from Lille to patrol Seclin, where it was reported that aircraft were machine-gunning civilians, and encountered an aircraft identified as a Do215 (which was in fact a Do17P from 4(F)/14) escorted by two Bf110Cs of 5/ZG26. Flt Lt Bill Toyne ordered his Blue Section to attack the reconnaissance-bomber and the other two sections to engage the escort; he reported:

'I climbed towards the Dornier and surprised him from behind and below, giving him a three second burst at 300 yards with half deflection. He then dived steeply to the ground and I momentarily lost sight of him. I next saw him with Blue 2 [Plt Off Bird-Wilson] on his tail. Blue 2 broke away and I attacked from astern at 250-100 yards with two five second bursts. The e/a's starboard engine stopped, his rear gunner was out of action, and he pancaked into a field five to eight miles south-east of Seclin.'

Lt Georg Losse and his crew survived the crash. As Plt Off Harold Bird-Wilson (YB-K), Blue 2, climbed towards the sun he had noticed AA fire on his port side:

'At once saw two e/a (a Messerschmitt 110 and a Do215). On approaching the e/a from astern, the Messerschmitt saw us and dove like mad. The Do215 was left on its own and turned, dived and did everything possible to get away. He came into my sights. I was about 300 yards away when I first opened fire and the e/a's rear gunner had two short bursts at me, then stopped firing altogether. I gave him another longish burst and he went into a gradual turn to the port. My rounds were finished but Blue 1 went into the attack and finished the e/a off.'

Blue 3, Flg Off Capel Adye, also fired at the Dornier before engaging a Messerschmitt:

'Leader engaged and attacked [the Dornier] from approximately the rear as aircraft was using evasive tactics. I opened fire from ahead, using three-quarter deflection. Aircraft half-rolled and dived vertically followed by Blue leader and three other Hurricanes. I looked behind me and into sun and noticed a Messerschmitt 110 followed by one Hurricane. I anticipated it using diving evasive tactics, which it did, followed by Hurricane. I used three-quarter deflection shot from starboard side and other Hurricane from astern. Held fire for six seconds. White smoke from starboard engine. Pulled emergency boost and came in from astern as other Hurricane had pulled away. Opened fire at approximately 250 yards with ten seconds burst. Black smoke was now pouring from port engine, but e/a was rapidly drawing away. Speed reached at pull out was 382 mph. E/a by this time was well out of range, black smoke still pouring from starboard engine.'

Meanwhile, the other Messerschmitt had succeeded in getting on to the tail of Plt Off Ken Manger's Hurricane, but was itself followed by Flg Off Bill Harper, who closed to 50 yards:

'I fired at him. In following him down, e/a observed damaged and turned left gently and disappeared. One engine of e/a damaged.'

The presence of the pursuing Hurricane enabled Manger to perform a steep right-hand turn and get on to the Messerschmitt's tail:

'I continued firing until I had closed to less than 100 yards and my ammunition was finished. Oil and petrol was issuing from his port engine so much that I could not see, as it was enveloping my machine. I broke away and watched other Hurricanes attacking.'

Sgt Wynn attacked the same aircraft:

'E/a dived to ground level and I closed to 200 yards and fired long bursts. His port engine burst into blue smoke and e/a disappeared around the corner of a wood.'

The wildly manoeuvring Zerstörer was also attacked by Sgt Bill Etherington:

'The 110 I attacked dived to ground level already with a disabled engine, having been fired at by Sgt Wynn and Plt Off Manger, and the rear gunner had been killed. E/a was lost sight of and was not seen again.'

Flt Lt Joslin of 56/A Flight led three Hurricanes on patrol at 1825, together with a section from 213/A Flight. About eight Bf109s from 2/JG3 were seen near Maubeuge and engaged by Flg Off John Coghlan (N2400), who claimed one shot down, and by Flt Lt Joslin (N2431), who could only report a probable. However, 2/JG3 reported the loss of Uffz Hans Ehlers and Uffz Heinz Göringer; the former crash-landed south of

Valenciennes and was taken prisoner by French troops, while the latter baled out south of Maubeuge and was rescued by German troops. Joslin then engaged a 12th Armee Hs126 of 3(H)/41 flown by Oblt Walter Erxleben, which he shot down south-west of Maubeuge; both pilot and observer (Fw Fridolin Hösl) were killed. Next during this successful patrol a He111H of Stabsstaffel KG1 was encountered and engaged by Flt Lt Coghlan and Sgt Jimmy Elliott (N2432) and claimed probably destroyed. In fact the Heinkel crash-landed near Graux, about 15 miles south-west of Namur, although the crew survived. The Hurricanes returned safely to Lille/Seclin, except that flown by Coghlan, who landed at Boulogne, from where he returned to RAF Biggin Hill after refuelling, where he was joined later that evening by the remainder of 56/A Flight.

85, 87 and 504 Squadrons were ordered off at 2100 to provide escort for Blenheims of 18 Squadron which were to bomb German columns near Cambrai. The Hurricanes of 87 Squadron, with Sqn Ldr Dewar at their head, were followed by those of 504 Squadron. Having just passed Mons, six Bf109s (aircraft of 1(J)/LG2) approached at 3,000 feet above 504 Squadron and were sighted by Plt Off Frisby, who gave the alarm over the R/T. Plt Off Trevor Parsons heard the warning but apparently Flt Lt John Owen and Plt Off Bob Renison did not. Owen was shot down in flames and was seen to bale out, but a Bf109 allegedly opened fire at Owen as he floated down and he was found to be dead on reaching the ground. Plt Off Brian Van Mentz attacked the Messerschmitt he believed to be responsible and claimed it damaged. Meanwhile, Renison's aircraft was seen by Parsons to also go down; although the Canadian managed to bale out safely, only to be taken prisoner. 87 Squadron's Flt Lt Gleed had witnessed Renison's fate:

> 'I saw a black dot, then a puff of white as the pilot's parachute opened. Poor devil! He would land in Jerry territory.'

1(J)/LG2 claimed two Hurricanes, one by Staffelkapitän Oblt Adolf Bühl, and the other by Fw Heinz Pöhland, who was also shot down (presumably Van Mentz's victim), although he was able to return later to his unit.

As if the depleted 85 Squadron had not suffered sufficiently during the morning's action, the Squadron learned that while returning from 48 hours' leave Plt Off John Lecky had been killed when the car in which he was travelling crashed; the accident also inflicted injury on his companion, Flt Lt Bob Boothby, who was as a result in hospital. The day saw the arrival from England of a new Squadron Commander, Sqn Ldr Michael Peacock DFC, who relieved the fatigued Sqn Ldr Oliver, although the latter was posted to 60 Wing as its temporary commander, vice Wg Cdr Boret having suffered a nervous breakdown.

61 Wing, Air Component

At about 0615, Vitry saw the arrival of six Hurricanes from A Flight of 253 Squadron under Flt Lt Guy Harris (with Plt Off F.W. Ratford, Plt Off D.B. Bell-Salter, Plt Off J.D. Ford, Plt Off J.T. Strang, a New Zealander, and Sgt R.A. Brackley) and six more from B Flight of 111 Squadron under Sqn Ldr John Thompson (with Flt Lt C.S. Darwood, Flg Off S.D.P. Connors, Flg Off D.C. Bruce, Plt Off J.A. Walker and Sgt R. Brown). The two Flights were to form a composite squadron. On arrival, the pilots were informed they were to escort Blenheims on a raid but this order was later rescinded.

Flt Lt Ian Soden (N2437) and Flt Sgt Taffy Higginson (N2440 US-H) of 56/B Flight carried out a dawn patrol over and around the airfield, during which Soden engaged and shot down Uffz Horst Liebe's Do17P of 3(F)/10 about six miles south-east of Vitry. Having landed, refuelled and rearmed, he was off again at 0720, again accompanied by Flt Sgt Higginson and joined by Plt Off Barry Sutton (N2553 US-C), to undertake a patrol between Brussels and Ghent. Another reconnaissance Do17P was sighted, this a machine of 4(F)/14 flown by Lt Alexander Schreiner. Sutton wrote later:

> 'We peeled off and dived on him, all three of us firing. He must have had either very good armour plating or else our shooting was bad, for he continued to keep his height and course for some seconds, though we swarmed all around him like wasps. I was flying number three position, so followed the other two in our first dive. Higginson, who was number two, "crowded" me off the target, so that after a very short burst I had to pull out of the dive to avoid hitting Higginson.'

Sutton's aircraft was hit by return fire and suffered minor damage to its port mainplane. Nonetheless, he followed Soden for a repeat attack:

> 'We both got in a burst of about five seconds this time and watched the Dornier stick his nose down and hare for the ground. I followed him right down to a few feet from the ground. One of us had obviously crippled the machine and put the rear gunner out of action, because there was no return fire. Flames leapt out of his port engine and the Dornier skidded across one field and through a hedge into another on its belly before finally pulling up in a cloud of dust. By the time we had climbed again and regained formation, the Dornier was blazing furiously.'

At 0740, two Hurricanes of 607 Squadron flown by Flg Off Francis Blackadder (P2571 AF-G) and Plt Off Gordon Stewart (P3448 AF-H) departed on patrol, meeting a lone Do17 (probably an aircraft of II/ KG76) near Denain. As the Hurricanes closed in on the Dornier's tail, both were hit by return fire. Blackadder, who reported the attack on the bomber as 'inconclusive', force-landed at Vitry, badly damaging his aircraft; Stewart also force-landed, although he was able to fly back to Vitry later.

607 Squadron lost one of its stalwarts during the morning when Flg Off Bob Weatherill (P2536 AF-R) failed to return from a tactical reconnaissance flight for the Army in the Cambrai area; his aircraft was intercepted and shot down near Cambrai by Hptm Georg Mayer of 2/ JG51 and he was reported later to have been killed. Two more pilots were dispatched on reconnaissance sorties at 1015. Flg Off Bob Pumphrey (P2874 AF-B) returned an hour later with his report, followed closely by Plt Off Tony Dini (AF-E), who had encountered a formation of Do17s:

'Saw 12 e/a approaching Cambrai from north. Attacked, broke up enemy formation. All e/a returned fire with front guns. I put an engine of two e/a out of action, using some deflection shots.'

Pumphrey was instructed to fly to RAF Manston with his report, departing in P3535 AF-C within half an hour of his return.

The composite 111/253 Squadron was ordered to patrol the Cambrai-Le Cateau area and, over Cambrai at 1030, a section of 111/B Flight met a Hs126 of 3(H)/41. This was promptly shot down by Sqn Ldr John Thompson (N2459), Flt Lt Charles Darwood (L2051) and Flg Off David Bruce (L1718). Both Uffz Emanuel Müller and his observer, Ofw Oswald Steeger, suffered wounds but survived to be taken prisoner by French troops. Shortly after, another Henschel of 3(H)/41 was sighted by Flt Lt Harris (N2545) of A/253 Flight:

'We were flying at about 10,000 feet when a Henschel 126 passed beneath us. Immediately a couple of Hurricanes dived in pursuit of it, so I joined in with them. It at once went down to ground level with two of us chasing it around trees and haystacks. To my surprise I was the only one left firing at it . . . eventually it nose-dived into a field and burst into flames.'

Before the Henschel crashed, both pilot and observer had managed to bale out of the doomed aircraft and succeeded in reaching safety. A complete Staffel of Armee Co-operation aircraft—Fi156s of the 12th Armee's 3(H)/21, at least eight machines—was then seen flying in formation, two of which were reportedly pursued by Plt Off Freddie Ratford (L1701) and Plt Off David Bell-Salter (L1655) of A/253 Flight, and each claimed one shot down. As only one Fi156 was lost, with the death of its pilot, Uffz Franz Holzapfel, it seems probable that Ratford and Bell-Salter attacked the same aircraft.

At 1045, three Hurricanes of 56/B Flight, led by Flt Lt Ian Soden (N2437), plus three of 229/B Flight under Flt Lt Freddie Rosier (L2141), departed Vitry to patrol between Brussels and Antwerp. Fifteen minutes into the flight they sighted at about 8,000 feet an estimated 60 Bf109s—aircraft of II/JG2. Flt Lt Rosier reported:

> 'Saw two flights of 109s (30 in each) milling around as if in a dogfight. The six Hurricanes attacked them. I singled out e/a and attacked and saw it go down conclusively. I then fired my remaining ammunition into another e/a but did not see it go down. I then broke off the engagement and returned to Vitry.'

The other two 229/B Flight Hurricanes were shot down by Lt Hans-Jürgen Hepe of 5 Staffel and Uffz Karl-Heinz Harbauer of 4 Staffel; Plt Off Desmond Gower baled out of P2676 and returned safely to Vitry on foot, but Plt Off Michael Bussey was taken prisoner when his aircraft (P2729) crashed between Brussels and Antwerp. They had been 'last seen in the middle of the 109s who were circling around them', reported Rosier later. 56/B Flight's leader, Flt Lt Soden, also claimed a Bf109 shot down, although this may have been the same aircraft as that attacked by Rosier as only one Bf109 was reported lost in this action, a machine of 6 Staffel, in which Uffz Wilhelm Muhs was killed when it crashed near Louvain.

Yet more Hurricanes arrived at Vitry at 1500, when nine aircraft of 151 Squadron landed. But time was running short for Vitry. It was inevitable that German reconnaissance aircraft would soon spot the assemblage of Hurricanes on the airfield, as not only was 607 Squadron operating from there but also 56/229 and 111/253 Squadrons—and now 151 Squadron.

Just after 1545, Flt Lt Ian Soden and Sgt Cliff Whitehead of 56/B Flight were ordered off, together with Blue and Yellow Sections of 151 Squadron, to engage a trio of He111Ps of III/KG54 observed passing over the aerodrome. Sgt George Atkinson of Blue Section (P3315) reported:

> 'Leader [Flt Lt Ives] went in and attacked. Plt Off Wright pulled to starboard and made a No 2 Attack. I followed up and gave one burst of two seconds at about 250 yards and broke away to port. I met three more He111s flying east on my starboard side. I attacked the port aircraft. I saw him go down in a dive, flames coming from the port engine. I lost the other two aircraft as they went in cloud.'

Flt Lt Soden pursued and engaged another (or the same) Heinkel, which was seen to crash-land about six miles north of Arras. Whitehead however was unable to carry out an interception. Only one bomber was lost during this action, that flown by Uffz Otto Ellinghaus of 9 Staffel. Following his combat with the bombers, Sgt Atkinson had become separated from the other members of Blue Section:

'I then met Yellow Section and formed up with them. I heard leader order line astern attack on about 12 Messerschmitt 110s, one of which I saw explode in the air. I attacked another 110 from port quarter, three-quarter deflection shot. I opened fire from 250 yards and gave burst of eight seconds without known result. I flew north-west looking for aerodrome. I hit the coast at Le Touquet and landed.'

Meanwhile, Flt Lt Harry Ironside (P3273) reported that he shot the tail unit completely off one Messerschmitt:

'I fired a short burst at one e/a with little result—another 110 flew across my sights and I gave him a three second burst. I saw the fuselage foremost of the tail unit crumple and the tail unit began to break off. One member of the crew jumped by parachute and was shot by French AA while descending.'

Flg Off Dickie Milne's aircraft (P3321) suffered some damage from another Messerschmitt, but he was able to land safely. A second Bf110 was shot down by Plt Off John Bushell (P3223), which caught fire and was also seen to crash:

'I saw one of the Messerschmitt 110s dive away in a southerly direction. As he appeared to be under control and unfollowed, I gave chase and after pulling the boost plug and giving full throttle I gradually overhauled him. At 600 yards the rear gunner opened fire with tracer—apparently two guns. I opened fire at 300 yards and closed to 100 yards, when e/a caught fire under port engine. I was smothered in oil and smoke and broke off the engagement. The fire died down and e/a commenced to climb slowly. I attacked again at 150 yards when something, which looked like a wheel, fell away from port engine nacelle and fire burst out again. As I broke away the engine appeared to blow up with showers of sparks and e/a dived into a field and blew up. I observed one parachute descending.'

A third Bf110 was reported shot down by Sgt Don Aslin (P3313):

'I climbed to approximately 6,000 feet and saw a Messerschmitt 110 in engagement with another Hurricane about five miles on port beam. I turned towards it and dived with full throttle and got quarter attack developing into full astern. The e/a dived and pulled up into climbing left-hand turn. I got in full deflection shot at about 50/60 yards. Continuous tracer from rear gunner of e/a, but inaccurate owing to violent manoeuvres of e/a. The port engine of e/a on fire, but flickered out again. The e/a levelled out and I started gentle dive. I got another burst in from dead astern from about 100 yards and port engine caught fire again. The crew jumped (two first, then one) and the machine crashed. I feel sure that three crew jumped.'

Other sections of Hurricanes from 253/111 Squadron had been sent off when news of the action reached Vitry and they also encountered the Bf110Cs of II/ZG26, which were escorting a formation of He111Hs of II/KG1. Flt Lt Guy Harris (N2545), the 253/A Flight leader, claimed a Heinkel probably destroyed before he was engaged by one of the Bf110s in a twisting dogfight, during which he was unable to gain the advantage. Another of the bombers was claimed by Plt Off Freddie Ratford (L1701) and other pilots reported seeing Plt Off John Ford (L1600) shoot down another, although the latter failed to return. However, having baled out safely, Ford turned up at Vitry a day or so later. Plt Off John Strang's Hurricane (P2761) was also hit and crash-landed, although the pilot was unhurt. The 111/B Flight section was more successful and Sqn Ldr Thompson (N2549) claimed one Bf110 shot down and possibly a second:

'I climbed above cumulus cloud and saw a Messerschmitt 110 being chased by a Hurricane at a distance of about 400 yards. The e/a turned straight across my beam from port to starboard and I carried out an attack from this position, closing to about 100 yards. I broke away to port and saw the other Hurricane close in to attack. The 110 turned with smoke pouring from both engines. I attacked again, closing to about 50 yards with a five second burst and saw e/a diving to almost ground level. I was attacked from behind by another 110. I did a sharp climbing turn to port. The e/a passed underneath me in a port climbing turn. I lowered nose of aircraft and opened fire from about 200 yards. E/a disappeared into cloud with flames pouring from both engines.'

One member of Thompson's section, Plt Off Jas Walker (L1589), a Canadian from Alberta, engaged the Heinkels:

'They immediately broke formation and attempted to escape, but one was intercepted over Douai and forced to land with both engines u/s. I circled aircraft and two of the crew who had descended from the aircraft were killed by French peasants who had arrived on the scene.'

56/B Flight had also scrambled its other section and they, too, encountered the Bf110Cs a few miles south of Vitry. In a series of fierce dogfights Sgt Cliff Whitehead (N2523 US-S) claimed two shot down and Flt Sgt Taffy Higginson (N2440 US-H) and Flg Off Leonid Ereminsky (L1992) one apiece. Hurricanes of 32 and 615 Squadrons from Moorsele had meanwhile apparently encountered the same He111/Bf110 formation, one of the bombers being claimed damaged by 32 Squadron's Plt Off John Flinders (N2460). However, in the confusion, Plt Off Douglas Grice (N2463)—also of 32 Squadron—had become separated near Le Cateau:

'I eventually joined with a squadron whose markings were SW [253/ A Flight from Vitry]. I had been with this squadron about ten seconds when below six to ten Messerschmitt 110s appeared and a general dogfight ensued. I fired two short bursts at one 110 and the last I saw of it, it was diving straight for the ground. I noticed bits flying off the e/a, but I was unable to follow it down below 1,500 feet as I had another 110 on my tail following me down. The scrap lasted two or three minutes until one by one the enemy disappeared.'

The Messerschmitt unit, 5/ZG26, lost four aircraft shot down and a further two seriously damaged for claims of three Hurricanes shot down in return:

Bf110C of 5/ZG26 (3U+AN) shot down and crash-landed between Douai and Cambrai: Staffelkapitän Hptm Eberhard Trützschler d'Elsa (wounded) and Uffz Hermann Rössler PoW of the French.

Bf110C of 5/ZG26 shot down south-west of Cambrai: Lt Lothar Heckert and Uffz Ernst Berger PoW of the British.

Bf110C of 5/ZG26 shot down near Cambrai: Fw Hermann Schönthier baled out and PoW of the French, but Uffz Aloys Kommans was killed.

Bf110C of 5/ZG26 shot down east of Cambrai: Fw Walter Hammacher wounded but baled out, as did his gunner.

Bf110C of 5/ZG26 45% damaged in combat near Cambrai and force-landed at As airfield: Oblt Artur Niebuhr and Uffz Klaus Theissen unhurt.

Bf110C of 5/ZG26 35% damaged in combat near Cambrai and force-landed at As airfield: Ofw Kurt Rochel and Uffz Willi Schöffler unhurt.

Bf110C of 5/ZG26 5% damaged in combat near Cambrai: Uffz Mathias Nicolay (gunner) wounded.

Hptm Theo Rossiwall of 6 Staffel wrote later:

'At first everything was fine. Hptm d'Elsa led his formation off at medium height amidst scattered cloud. As nothing was going on he decided to see what was happening below the clouds. The Staffel went down through the clouds . . . and found itself in the middle of some 40 Spitfires [sic]. Immediately a dogfight took place as everybody let loose and three English aircraft fell away burning. At As airfield the pilots of the other Staffeln were standing around waiting. They had also had a fight above the clouds but had landed a long time ago. The 5th Staffel should have been back by now and there were some worries that something could have happened to them. The Kommandeur paced up and down afraid of the fate of his men. Then at last a machine with a red painted nose appeared. On its side it wore the Pik-As, the badge of the 5th Staffel. It was Ofw Kurt Rochel; his aircraft had received a few hits but he and his wireless operator were unhurt and he reported what had happened, excited still by the combat. He said it was the heaviest fighting which he had been through.

After some time Oblt Artur Niebuhr also landed with damage to one of his engines and several other places. Slowly the others came in one after the other and by nightfall only three [four, in fact] crews were still missing—among them the Staffelkapitän himself. But the men didn't give up hope—the aircraft could have landed at another airfield; they could still come home. When it started to get dark and no telephone call had come in, it slowly dawned upon us that the Staffel had made its first sacrifices. Hptm d'Elsa had led the unit for a long time and had trained it; his loss hit the men very hard.'

II/KG1 lost three Heinkels to the Hurricanes of 253, 111 and 32 Squadrons:

He111H of II/KG1 shot down south of Vitry and crash-landed east of Valenciennes: Oblt Kohlbrock and his crew survived and were rescued by troops of 5 Pz Division.

He111H of 6/KG1 shot down south of Vitry and crash-landed east of Le Cateau: crew survived and rescued by troops of 7 Pz Division.

He111H of 6/KG1 shot down south-west of Vitry and crash-landed eight miles south-west of Avesnes: crew survived and rescued by troops of 32 Inf Division.

Heinkels of I/KG54 simultaneously raided Amiens/Glisy aerodrome—the RAF's main airfield for receiving replacement Hurricanes and Blenheims—where bombs destroyed Anson R3411 of 3 (Continental) Ferry Flight in which Plt Off F.W. Hillman had intended to evacuate Hurricane ferry pilots, although the aircraft was not occupied at the time of the raid and no casualties occurred amongst crew or passengers. Two Hurricane pilots of 4(C) Ferry Flight had just arrived from England and immediately took off to intercept the raiders. Both were successful. One of these, Plt Off R. Bicknell, claimed two of the Heinkels damaged:

'The e/a appeared while I was on the ground at Glisy. I jumped into a Hurricane which was running and took off. At about 1600 I made my first attack from the starboard quarter and 2,000 feet above the enemy, who were at 10,000 feet. My reflector sight failed to operate so I made the attack with no sights. I singled out the centre flight leader as my target and passed through the formation in my attack. My second attack was badly judged and I broke away without pressing home the attack. I carried out a stern chase for the last attack on a stray e/a. Two e/a were definitely running on one motor when I left off the attacks due to lack of ammunition.'

His companion, Plt Off Charles Bird*, added:

'Took off in P2726 which I had just ferried from England and, having climbed to 500 feet, gave chase after e/a which were heading in north-easterly direction. After 30 minutes' climbing I was able to reach the enemy's height and had overtaken them. One was lagging about 1,000 yards behind the rest and I carried out an astern attack on it, but had not enough speed to make a good attack. I then climbed until I was about 1,000 feet above it and dived down, coming up under its belly. I fired three short bursts. At the second burst his port engine started to burn and on third it caught fire. The last I saw of the machine it was descending at an angle of about 30° with its port engine well ablaze. It disappeared in clouds just afterwards and I lost sight of him. I then attacked the other six machines

---

* On 25 July 1940, during the Battle of Britain, Plt Off Charles Bird shot down a Ju88 of 5/KG51 near Cirencester but, on breaking away, his Hurricane spun in and crashed; Bird was killed.

and I received three bullets through my starboard wing. I then broke off the fight as I was almost out of petrol and as the Heinkels had reached 22,000 feet and I had no oxygen. I estimate that the e/a must have come down 80 miles north-east of Amiens. I then returned to Glisy.'

The Heinkel was possibly an aircraft of 3/KG54 flown by Fw Willi Kümmel which crash-landed about 18 miles south-east of Arras. The crew were taken prisoner by French troops.

All available Hurricanes were ordered off from Vitry on the approach of raiders, but as the last section of three (Flg Off Tommy Rose and Plt Off Barry Sutton of 56/B Flight together with Plt Off Tony Dillon of 229/B Flight) were becoming airborne, Bf110Cs of I/ZG26 and Bf109s of II/JG26 suddenly appeared and began strafing. Barry Sutton wrote:

'We had just taken off and had barely got our wheels up when things began to happen. Bullets began blasting and rattling all over the machine [N2553 US-C]—one must have hit the glycol pipe in the cockpit, for steam began to shoot everywhere. Although we were at only about 300 feet, I whipped over in the beginning of a half-roll— better to go straight into the deck than stop any more of the stream of lead from behind. It was the most unlovely of manoeuvres, but it worked . . . I managed to scrape into Vitry. No signs of Tommy and Dillon or the rest of the Squadron or of what had attacked us.'

Both Flg Off Rose* and 18-year-old Plt Off Dillon were pursued by the Messerschmitts and were eventually shot down and killed; the former's Hurricane (N2439) came down at Brebières and the latter's (L1802) at Castillon Hill, near Mons. Pilots of I/ZG26 claimed two Hurricanes shot down. Meanwhile, other Hurricanes had been engaged by the Bf109s of II/JG26 as they climbed for height; Flt Lt Rosier of 229/B Flight reported:

'Just as we were taking off the 109s dived on us and, of course, we were at a disadvantage. The sky was immediately full of dogfights. I got on the tail of one but just then I was hit by another. My Hurricane [L2142] caught fire. I found I couldn't open the cockpit. I couldn't get out. The aircraft must have blown up for the next thing I remember was falling through the air. After pulling the parachute release, I saw that my trousers were on fire. I attempted to extinguish the flames with my hands.'

---

* Flg Off Tommy Rose was the other pilot shot down in error by Spitfires of 74 Squadron on 6 September 1939 (see footnote, p. 60).

Two 253 Squadron Hurricanes were similarly shot down attempting to gain height, although both Plt Off David Bell-Salter (N2545) and Sgt Bob Brackley (L1655) survived the subsequent crash-landings uninjured. The Hurricanes of 111/B Flight were also engaged by an estimated 14 Bf109s and Flt Lt Charles Darwood (L2051) was shot down and killed. His aircraft was seen by Flg Off David Bruce to pull up suddenly after it was attacked and, whilst in a climb, he saw the pilot slump forward. It was assumed that Darwood had been seriously wounded, if not killed, and the Hurricane crashed near the airfield. Only Flg Off Dudley Connors (L2482) was able to respond and claimed a Bf109 shot down. Connors then saw 17 Ju88s (aircraft of III/LG1), which he pursued, shooting down a 9 Staffel machine in flames near Amiens. The bomber crash-landed and was totally destroyed although the crew survived and were rescued by troops of 7 Pz Division. Another of Rosier's Flight, Plt Off Geoff Simpson, a New Zealander from Christchurch, reported sighting five or six Bf110s at 20,000 feet:

'I took off from Vitry and saw e/a in front of me heading south-east. It was attacked by two Hurricanes (possibly Rose and Dillon) who broke off the engagement. E/a carried on under perfect control. Its starboard engine started to pour out white smoke but this stopped. I opened fire at 200 yards and e/a appeared to go out of control, but straightened out again. I closed to about 30 yards, giving a good long burst. E/a did a stall turn to the left and appeared as if it would dive into the ground. I broke away to the right. E/a recovered itself and flew eastwards at about 20 feet. I attacked again from the starboard beam, using up the last of my ammunition in a full deflection shot. E/a hit ground near Montecourt, south-east of Douai, and broke up but did not catch fire. No person got out of the wreckage.'

607 Squadron's Hurricanes were attacked by the Bf109s as they climbed from the airfield. Flg Off Blackadder managed to evade, but Plt Off Dini's Hurricane suffered some damage, which forced him to return to Vitry. Meanwhile, Plt Off Barry Sutton of 56/B Flight, who had suffered a bullet wound to his heel, took off immediately in another Hurricane (a machine belonging to another squadron), but had to land again as its wheels would not retract and it lacked engine power:

'As I came in a second time, a Hurricane shot clean past me, careered across the aerodrome and finished up on its nose on the far side in a cloud of dust. Some poor devil trying to get back in a hurry. Looked as though he might have been badly shot up.'

A witness to the raid was Plt Off Allan Simpson, a Canadian pilot of 13 Squadron, a unit which was in the process of moving from Douai to Abbeville:

> 'As we passed Vitry we noticed the sky full of aircraft. It was the greatest number we had seen all at once. About 40 Messerschmitt 109s and 110s had attacked Vitry during refuelling. It cured our fighters of refuelling all their aircraft at once. Three Dorniers came in formation quite low over the tail-end of our convoy, machine-gunning it.'

The elated Messerschmitt pilots of II/JG26, on returning to their base, reported having met Moranes (sic) and Hurricanes near Vitry and claimed ten of the former and one of the latter, although it is believed that all the claims were in fact made against the Hurricanes from Vitry: Hptm Herwig Knüppel and Lt Otto-Heinrich Hillecke of Stabsstaffel each claimed one, while pilots of 4 Staffel claimed four more—one apiece by Fw Hermann Hoffmann, Oblt Ludwig Roos, Hptm Karl Ebbinghausen (the Staffelkapitän) and Fw Willi Roth. Two more were credited to Lt Eckart Roch and Fw Hermann Meyer of 5 Staffel, and a further three to Oblt Alfred Pomaska, Lt Wolfgang Kosse and Lt Peter Blohm of 6 Staffel.

The devastating challenge to Vitry's Hurricanes by the Bf109s and Bf110s was quickly followed by an assault on the airfield by three Staffeln of Do17s from III/KG76, the first attacking at 1830, as LAC Bill Bowman, an engine fitter with 607 Squadron, recalled:

> 'We saw this formation of bombers somewhere over Douai and— with the uncanny aircraft recognition of RAF ground crew—we said "Blenheims" and continued with our work. I looked up a little later and saw this formation coming over the cement works on the edge of the drome and noticed their bomb doors were open in a very unfriendly manner and the air gunners blasting off at us . . . and decided the best thing to do would be to dive for the nearest ditch. We all did this except LAC Stan Johnson, who manned our Lewis gun and blasted off a full pan at these raiders.'

Sqn Ldr Teddy Donaldson of 151 Squadron was keen to get his remaining Hurricanes airborne, but permission to take off was not forthcoming:

> 'We observed seven Do215s [sic] passing the aerodrome about five miles to the south. I requested permission to be allowed to take off as they appeared to be turning the whole time in the Vitry direction.

My request was refused. The Dorniers bombed the aerodrome with incendiary and burnt out about 14 [sic] Hurricanes and one Blenheim.'

Flt Lt Guy Harris (who was waiting for his aircraft to be refuelled) added:

'There was a mad rush away from our machines and we dived into a shallow ditch at the edge of the field. From there we fired our revolvers at the Dorniers as they swept down our line of Hurricanes, releasing showers of small bombs; some exploded on impact, while others lay around on the ground. Six Hurricanes had direct hits and burst into flames, mine included.'

Following further attacks by the Dorniers at 1900 and 1930, all available Hurricanes were scrambled from Vitry. Bf110Cs of II/ZG76 were sighted at 1950, as Sqn Ldr Donaldson noted:

'I immediately asked permission to take off again. This time it was granted and I yelled "Scramble whole squadron". I pulled the plug and climbed after two Messerschmitt 110s which were the remains of six of the escort. When I had climbed to 6,000 feet, the Messer-schmitts attacked. They passed vertically down behind me and I was able to flick-roll in behind one of them, which dived to ground level into the smoke of the burning Hurricanes. I followed, pulled the plug but although I was doing well over 400 mph I could not gain on him. At 800-600 yards he fired at me with what appeared to be cannon. At 600 yards I opened fire and fired off all my rounds without a break. About half-way through my ammunition, the e/a's port engine caught fire and he slipped to the right. I finished the rest of my ammunition. I noticed that the smoke from the e/a's port engine got less and less. He did not crash.'

Donaldson added:

'Whilst I was firing at this Messerschmitt 110, a stream of bullets passed on my port side over me. I thought it was the other 110, but on looking round I saw it was another Hurricane (one of my squadron). His shots were not near the 110 and I have told him (the offending pilot) not to do that sort of thing again as it was most disconcerting and without accuracy.'

607 Squadron had scrambled its B Flight and these engaged both Bf109s and Bf110s near the airfield. Plt Off Jim Humphreys (P2693) claimed a

Bf109 damaged and Flg Off Bob Pumphrey (P2571 AF-G) a Bf110 probably destroyed. Flt Lt Ian Soden (N2437) of 56/B Flight had also taken off to intercept the Bf110Cs of II/ZG76, but was shot down almost immediately and crashed just outside the aerodrome perimeter; in the few days he had led his Flight into action, he had proved himself to be a gallant, inspiring and successful leader; his body was recovered later and buried at nearby Biache-St Vaast.

When news of the attack on Vitry reached Merville, a section of Hurricanes from 79 Squadron and two of 213/B Flight were sent to help; Plt Off Don Stones (P3451) of the former unit recalled:

'I was sent off as Vitry had just been bombed. I saw six or seven Hurricanes burning on the airfield and then saw what I took to be the rest of this squadron patrolling above. Flying up to join them I was stupid enough to find they were 110s. I managed to get two of them but one rear gunner put a shot through my oil tank and I had to put down in a field and hitch-hike back to Norrent-Fontès.'

Another 79 Squadron pilot—Flg Off Fred Duus—reported shooting down a Do17 (probably a Bf110), while Plt Off Harry Atkinson of 213/B Flight claimed a Bf110 about 15 miles north-west of Lille. His leader, Flt Lt Widge Wight, flying 79 Squadron's NV-L, had a different story to tell when he arrived on the scene:

'Took off alone to investigate aircraft reported to south. Saw AA bursts over Arras at 5,000 feet so went there. Saw eight or nine Messerschmitt 110s at 6,000 feet. Attacked rear one and found guns not loaded. Was then spotted and opened fire on, but got away OK. Very exciting 30 minutes!'

II/ZG76 lost three aircraft to the Hurricanes from Vitry and Merville:

Bf110C M8+XA of Stab/ZG76 shot down six miles north-west of Douai: Maj Walter Grabmann, the Geschwaderkommodore and a six victory Spanish Civil War ace, baled out and PoW of the French, but his gunner, Fw Richard Krone, was killed.

Bf110C of 4/ZG76 shot down near Douai: Lt Jürgen Uhlhorn and Gfr Horst Neumann killed.

Bf110C of 5/ZG76 shot down and crashed south of Denain: Uffz Helmut Jörke killed, Uffz Gerhard Schablowski baled out.

At least seven Hurricanes, together with four of 615 Squadron's redundant Gladiators (N2303, N2304, N2306 and N5899) and a

Blenheim (an aircraft of 53 Squadron which had just arrived on completion of a reconnaissance sortie) had been destroyed on the ground at Vitry; although there were no serious casualties, petrol tankers and fuel dumps had been hit. 111 Squadron suffered the loss of two aircraft totally destroyed (L1718 and L1589) and 253 Squadron four (including L1660 and L1669), while 56/B Flight lost US-L (a replacement aircraft) and the unserviceable US-C (N2553) further damaged, while another replacement aircraft, US-P (P3055), suffered damage. In addition, 607 Squadron's Magister (P6343) was also destroyed.

Meantime, the wounded Plt Off Sutton of 56/B Flight had been driven to a field dressing station, where he met the badly burned Flt Lt Rosier of 229 Squadron; both were later evacuated by ambulance to Frévent, then to a hospital at Le Tréport and from there to Dieppe by ambulance, by train to Cherbourg, and finally by boat to Southampton. 56/B Flight now took a former member under its wing, when 3 Squadron's burned and injured Sgt Peter Hillwood arrived at Vitry.

As soon as the air had cleared, 151 Squadron departed for RAF Manston and were joined there by three undamaged Hurricanes of 111/ 253 Squadron, flown by Sqn Ldr Thompson, Flt Sgt Ron Brown (111/B Flight) and Flt Lt Harris (253/A Flight). The remaining pilots of 111/253 Squadron were told to make their own way back, so they headed for Arras, from where they were flown back to England aboard a DH89 of 24 Squadron.

Earlier in the afternoon, shortly before the raid on Vitry got under way, the new commander of 60 Wing, Wg Cdr Harry Broadhurst DFC AFC, had arrived at the airfield. His first impressions were not good*:

> 'I found that my predecessor had been invalided home with a nervous breakdown and that the three squadrons on the station were without serviceable squadron commanders. To say that chaos reigned would be an understatement, and I was soon under orders to retreat with the remains of the Wing to Merville.'

Thus, that evening, 607 Squadron and 56/B Flight were ordered to withdraw to Norrent-Fontès, to where 607 Squadron's airworthy Hurricanes were flown—including P3535 AF-C (Flg Off Blackadder), P3448 AF-H (Flg Off Pumphrey), P2874 AF-B (Plt Off Dini), P2671 AF-G (Sgt Ralls), P2693 (Plt Off Humphreys) and N2586 SD-B (Plt Off

---

* Wg Cdr Harry Broadhurst joined the RAF in 1926 and served on the North-West Frontier before returning to the UK in 1931. By the outbreak of the Second World War he was commanding 111 Squadron and with this unit shot down a He111 of Stab KG26 on 29 November 1939, for which he was awarded a DFC. Prior to his posting to France he commanded RAF Coltishall.

Demetriadi). Surviving Hurricanes of B Flight were also flown out, as noted by Flg Off Bill Whitty:

'That night we moved out and many pilots slept in their planes at Norrent-Fontès.'

Flg Off Ereminsky, Plt Off Down and Flt Sgt Higginson evacuated 56/B Flight's three remaining Hurricanes (including N2440 US-H and N2523 US-S), while Sgt Whitehead accompanied the ground personnel.

Apart from the brief skirmish with the KG1 Heinkels, 32 and 615 Squadrons at Moorsele had experienced a relatively quiet day in the air, although for the pilots from 32 Squadron who had arrived there from RAF Biggin Hill at first light, it was a long day; Flt Lt Peter Brothers recalled:

'It was a very tiring business, because we were getting up at three o'clock in the morning, having breakfast, getting airborne in the dark, flying inland across the French coast and arriving at [Moorsele] first light. The chaps there, 615 Squadron, were rather jumpy because refugees were streaming down that road, and that morning one of their sergeants had been found with a knife in his chest.'

The only other patrol of note undertaken by 615 Squadron during the day was when two Hurricanes of the attached 245/A Flight became separated and lost, Plt Offs Denis Pennington and Derek Yapp landing near Dunkirk; they returned to Moorsele next day.

63 Wing, Air Component
Five Hurricanes—a section from 3 Squadron and a pair from the attached 601/A Flight—were in action early, having taken off from Merville at 0620. At 2,000 feet five miles south of Douai, they encountered nine Do17Zs of 2/KG76 and engaged. Plt Off Mike Stephens (N2546 QO-S), leading the Flight, attacked first and shot down the nearest bomber, closely followed by Plt Off Peter Gardner (N2464), who reported:

'I was No 2 of Blue Section and we went into the vic. I took No 2 enemy aircraft and gave him a long burst of ten seconds. I saw the bullets going in and then I was hit in the radiator and oil tank. I was covered in fumes so put it down on the ground and then burned it as I was near enemy territory. The e/a which got me was shot down by the aircraft which attacked after me [Plt Off Bisgood].'

Gardner force-landed ten miles south of Douai and was unhurt, as was Bisgood, who was also obliged to force-land his Hurricane (L1940). Another Dornier was claimed jointly by Flt Lt Sir Archie Hope (N2605) and Flg Off Gordon Cleaver (L1690), but Hope's aircraft was hit by return fire and he too force-landed, badly damaging the Hurricane when belly-landing in a field at Grevillers; he was unhurt and soon returned to Merville on a borrowed army motorcycle. Two of the Dorniers were lost:

> Do17Z of 2/KG76 flown by Ofw Rudolf Richter shot down crash-landed near St Ghislain: crew PoW of the French.

> Do17Z of 2/KG76 flown by Fw Nikolaus Koch severely damaged and crashed at Köln-Ostheim: crew survived.

At 0740, Sgt Roy Wilkinson (N2435) and Sgt Basil Friendship (L1846 QO-B) of 3 Squadron scrambled, in great haste, in an attempt to intercept a Do17Z of 5/KG76 seen over the aerodrome, part of the same formation of seven Dorniers engaged by sections from 79 Squadron and 213/B Flight. However, the 3 Squadron duo were unable to make contact, although the other sections were successful; one Dornier was claimed shot down by Flg Off Jimmy Davies of 79 Squadron, and another damaged by Plt Off Tom Parker, who reported:

> 'I attacked the port aircraft who were behind the others. Enemy closed up, returned fire and dived. I think I hit both aircraft and received one shot in the oil tank and one in my main spar.'

The third member of the 79 Squadron section, Plt Off Lionel Dorrien-Smith, noted:

> 'Sighted seven e/a proceeding west—order given to attack. E/a turned and headed east, closing to two tight vics astern. Attack delivered from above and behind. Fired two bursts and broke away owing to bullets entering cockpit.'

The trio from 213/B Flight, flying as Green Section, also engaged, catching the Dorniers ten miles north-east of Arras. Plt Off Harry Atkinson reported:

> 'Ordered to attack. Green Section attacked last. Smoke seen issuing from No 2 of rear section. One e/a dropped six bombs at random. Introduced attack on No 3 of rear section. Rear gunner fired for short time. Two hits on own aircraft. E/a dropped rapidly

after attack. One of our aircraft broke away and was seen trailing some white vapour.'

Sgt John Lishman noted:

'I was Green 3 and carried out an attack on the e/a on the right-hand side of the formation. I held a burst for 13 seconds and saw large volume of black smoke coming from e/a's starboard engine. I broke away to port.'

One Dornier crash-landed near Avesnes. The crew survived and were rescued by German troops.

Sgts Roy Wilkinson (N2435) and Basil Friendship (N2434) of 3 Squadron were off again at 1055, joined on this occasion by Plt Off Joe Hobbs (L1646) and Sgt Ralph Ware (L1670), the pilots briefed to patrol Cambrai, where 20 Ju87s were encountered. Only Friendship was able to engage however, and subsequently reported that he had shot down one of the dive-bombers seen straggling at the rear of the formation.

Later, at about 1530, Red Section of 3 Squadron, led by Flg Off Billy Clyde (N2435), patrolled Douai at 18,000 feet and met a lone Bf110C of ZG26 (a straggler from either I or II Gruppe, part of the force raiding Vitry). This was pursued and claimed shot down by Plt Off Jack Rose (L1990).

A dozen more Hurricanes arrived at Merville during the early afternoon: B Flight of 601 Squadron led by Sqn Ldr Loel Guinness MP (a member of the Irish brewery family), with Flg Off The Hon J.W.M. Aitken (son of Lord Beaverbrook, the newspaper magnate and newly appointed Minister for Aircraft Production), Flg Off W.H. Rhodes-Moorhouse (whose father had won the first aerial VC in 1915), Flg Off T.E. Hubbard, Flg Off C.J.H. Riddle and Flg Off C. Lee-Steere; and A Flight of 145 Squadron (Flt Lt R.G. Dutton, Plt Off E.J.C. Wakeham, Plt Off R.D. Yule, Plt Off K.R. Lucas, Plt Off M.A. Newling and Plt Off A. Elson). The Hurricanes had been led to the airfield by Plt Off Lionel Dorrien-Smith of 79 Squadron, who had flown to RAF Manston specifically for the task.

At 1525, Hurricanes of 79 Squadron and 213/B Flight took off from Merville as part of the escort to the Blenheims of 18 Squadron from Goyencourt; Flt Lt Widge Wight of the latter unit (flying 229 Squadron's RE-N) noted:

'Rendezvous over Douai at 18,000 feet. About 36 other Hurricanes at various heights. [Blenheims] bombed objective near Avesnes. Nothing seen, of course.'

At about the same time, the composite 145/601 Squadron was dispatched to patrol over Belgium and, near Brussels at 1625, met a dozen unescorted He111Ps of I and II/KG4. Three of the bombers were claimed by A/145 Flight, two and a probable by Flt Lt Roy Dutton (N2495)—one of which he shared with Plt off Bob Yule (N2496), a New Zealander—and one by Plt Off Ernest Wakeham (N2771), while probables were credited to Plt Off Kenneth Lucas (N2598) and Plt Off Mike Newling. Dutton reported:

'I was Red Leader. I and my section arrived over Brussels at 1625 at 10,000 feet. It was reported on the R/T that e/a were flying east-north-east to starboard and below at 7,000 feet. I saw two e/a and attacked in formation with No 3 of section. E/a disappeared in cloud before attack could be pushed home. I then saw one He111 which I attacked from 250 yards giving about two to three seconds' burst—was hit and went down with smoke issuing from both engines. I then saw another He111 which I attacked, and broke off engagement when flames were coming from port engine. My No 2 [Plt Off Yule] went in to attack the aircraft and reported putting it out of action completely. I then saw another He111, which I attacked, and continued until all my ammunition expended and return fire too hot. I turned round and saw it was being attacked by at least two Hurricanes, one of which went down trailing blue black smoke [Plt Off Newling's aircraft]. I watched it and did not see the pilot bale out.'

Plt Off Wakeham, who was flying in Yellow Section, also claimed a Heinkel and damaged a second:

'Followed two Heinkels down to ground level in a steep dive. E/a drew out of dive abreast so I was too near. I broke away to starboard and turned completely round, then carried out a No 1 Attack from dead astern. I gave bursts of three to four seconds from 200-250 yards and broke away as I was closing too quickly. As I was positioning for second attack, e/a changed position and I fired three to four seconds' burst. I immediately noticed the undercarriage drop and smoke poured from both engines. I did not notice any return fire. As I broke away, e/a appeared to go straight into ground. I returned to attack another e/a and gave two to three seconds' bursts, finishing up all my ammunition and left it with port engine smoking badly.'

During his attack on one of the Heinkels, Plt Off Newling's aircraft was hit by return fire and the Hurricane (N2600) crashed in flames; however, he baled out safely over Pamel, a village south-west of Brussels, near the River Dender. On landing, he was helped by some villagers, including a 13-year-old boy, who escorted him along German lines until they reached the Dender. Newling had a flute in his pocket, which he blew to attract the attention of British troops on the other side of the river. Having made contact, he waded across and was met by an Army vehicle which took him to Merville; from there he was flown back to England two days later.

601/B Flight had also managed to get amongst the Heinkels, as Sqn Ldr Guinness' subsequent report revealed:

> 'I observed a formation of He111s followed by a further formation of two. These formations were rapidly approaching cloud and I ordered the Squadron to attack from astern. Owing to cloud it was not possible to make pre-arranged attacks. I approached the right-hand aircraft of the stern formation of two and opened fire at 300 yards, possibly less. The enemy tried to get into cloud but I caught him. When both his engines were obviously shot up and he appeared to be going down, I attacked his leader. I managed to get a long burst into this aircraft and I could see the bullets striking him all the way up. I was subjected to extremely heavy fire and when my ammunition was gone I broke off the attack.'

Two more Heinkels were claimed by Flg Off The Hon Max Aitken (N2568) and Flg Off Willie Rhodes-Moorhouse (L2088); Aitken reported:

> 'I attacked one from astern, which broke away. I followed it down into a cloud firing one burst before entering. On emerging I fired another burst and hit his port motor. He tried to climb back to the clouds, but could not make it, so he dived. I followed and hit the starboard motor, which caught fire. His rear gunner continued firing. He [the pilot] retained control of the plane though losing height rapidly. We were now over German lines and I was out of ammunition, so I broke away. I did not see him crash, but one side of the plane was blazing and the other belching smoke. I landed back at Merville. My machine was hit in the spinner and tailplane.'

Flg Off Christopher Riddle (L1819) was credited with a probable:

> 'I turned on to the tail of left-hand machine of second pair, opening fire at 400 yards as enemy was making for cloud. One engine was on fire before entering cloud. On emerging out of cloud, enemy was losing height—I was overtaking too fast and just avoided colliding, having fired all my ammunition. Did not see aircraft crash as on

pulling out I went straight into cloud. My aircraft was hit by one bullet.'

Sqn Ldr Guinness' aircraft (L2034) was badly damaged in this engagement:

'My aircraft sustained the following damage: a bullet through the windscreen expended itself on the armour plating behind my head and went out through the hood; my hydraulics were shot away; the rudder badly holed; the fuselage struts shot through; the propeller boss shot through; and there were various other bullets in the wings. The aircraft had to be left at Merville, as the engineering officer did not consider it fit to fly.'

Having landed and refuelled at Merville, the remaining Hurricanes returned to RAF Tangmere. Three Heinkels of I and II/KG4 failed to return and one other suffered damage:

He111P of 2/KG4 (5J+IK) flown by Lt Helmut Zeiss shot down by four Hurricanes west of Brussels and crashed six miles north-west of Louvain: pilot survived, crew killed.

He111P of 5/KG4 flown by Staffelkapitän Hptm Kurt Leythaüser shot down south-west of Brussels and crash-landed six miles west of Louvain: crew survived, two wounded.

He111P of 5/KG4 flown by Lt Hoepel shot down near Brussels and crash-landed near Beauvechain, six miles south-west of Tirlemont: one killed, one wounded.

He111P of 5/KG4 5% damaged in combat near Brussels: one crew member killed.

So ended another day of heavy combat. The Hurricane pilots were fighting a losing battle.

Summary

During the day, at least 33 Hurricanes were shot down or crash-landed as the result of combat, the majority of which fell to the Messerschmitts. Seven Hurricane pilots were killed, a further five were taken prisoner and four wounded. Half of the claims made by the Hurricane pilots were against bombers, many of which were without any obvious escort, while the Bf110s were again subjected to a severe mauling although the sections and flights of Hurricanes were often overwhelmed by sheer numbers.

Claims by AASF and Air Component Hurricanes, 18 May

Type	Confirmed	Probable	Damaged	Total
He111	11	7	6	24
Do17	12	4	7	23
Ju88	1	—	—	1
Ju87	2	—	1	3
Hs126	6	—	—	6
Bf109	4	1	3	8
Bf110	21	8	3	32
	57	20	20	97

Luftwaffe Losses Attributed to AASF and Air Component Hurricanes, 18 May

Type	60% to 100%	Under 60%	Total
He111	9	1	10
Do17	8	2	10
Ju88	1	—	1
Hs126	4	—	4
Fi156	1	—	1
Bf109	4	—	4
Bf110	12	4	16
	39	7	46

Part of Bomber Command's effort on the night of 18/19 May was again directed against the Meuse crossings, although on a smaller scale than on the previous night, when a dozen Wellingtons and a similar number of Hampdens bombed targets at Namur, Dinant, Yvoir-Anhée, Givet and Gembloux. All aircraft returned safely. In addition, a dozen Wellingtons bombed the marshalling yards at Köln-Eifeltor, Wedau and Vohwinkel, while 24 Whitleys attacked the oil refinery at Hannover. Two of the latter failed to return, including one shot down into the sea on the outward leg by a Bf110, which was also claimed destroyed by the Whitley's gunners.

Individual Claims—AASF and Air Component Hurricanes, 18 May

Dawn-	Flt Lt I.S. Soden	56/B Flt	Do17
0620-	Plt Off M.M. Stephens	3 Sqn	Do17
	Plt Off P.M. Gardner Plt Off D.L. Bisgood	} 3 Sqn	Do17
	Flt Lt Sir A.P. Hope Flg Off G.N.S. Cleaver	} 601/A Flt	Do17
0630-	Plt Off C.M. Stavert	1 Sqn	Do17, He111
0720-	Flt Lt I.S. Soden Plt Off F.B. Sutton Flt Sgt F.W. Higginson	} 56/B Flt	Do17
0740-	Flg Off J.W.E. Davies	79 Sqn	Do17
	Plt Off T.C. Parker	79 Sqn	2 Do17 damaged
	Plt Off L.R. Dorrien-Smith	79 Sqn	Do17 damaged
	Plt Off H.D. Atkinson	213/B Flt	Do17 damaged

	Sgt J.A. Lishman	213/B Flt	Do17 damaged
1015-	Plt Off A.S. Dini	607 Sqn	2 Do17 damaged
1030-	Sqn Ldr J.M. Thompson		
	Flt Lt C.S. Darwood	111/B Flt	Hs126
	Flg Off D.C. Bruce		
	Flt Lt G. Harris	253/A Flt	Hs126
	Plt Off D.B. Bell-Salter	253/A Flt	Hs126
	Plt Off F.W. Ratford	253/A Flt	Hs126
1045-	Flt Lt F.E. Rosier	229/B Flt	Bf109, Bf109 damaged
	Flt Lt I.S. Soden	56/B Flt	Bf109
1055-	Sgt A.H.B. Friendship	3 Sqn	Ju87
AM-	Sgt C.E. Hampshire	85 Sqn	Bf110
	Plt Off R.H. Wiens	242/A Flt	Bf110, Bf110 probable
	Flt Lt I.R. Gleed	87 Sqn	Bf110, Bf110 probable
	Flg Off R.F. Watson	87 Sqn	Bf110
	Plt Off C.W.W. Darwin	87 Sqn	Bf110 probable
1330-	Plt Off J.R. Cock	87 Sqn	Ju87
	Plt Off K.W. Tait	87 Sqn	Ju87 damaged
1520-	Flg Off M.H. Brown	1 Sqn	Hs126
1530-	Plt Off G.M. Simpson	229/B Flt	Bf110
	Plt Off J. Rose	3 Sqn	Bf110
	Flt Lt R.P.R. Powell	111/A Flt	Bf110 probable
	Flg Off H.M. Ferriss	111/A Flt	2 Bf110, 2 Bf110 damaged
	Plt D.S.H. Bury	111/A Flt	Bf110
	Sgt J.T. Craig	111/A Flt	Bf110
	Sgt W.L. Dymond	111/A Flt	Do17
	Flt Lt H.T. Anderson	253/B Flt	Do17 probable
	Plt Off J.P.B. Greenwood	253/B Flt	Do17 probable
	Plt Off J.K.G. Clifton	253/B Flt	Do17
	Plt Off D.N.O. Jenkins	253/B Flt	Do17, Do17 probable
	Sgt G. Mackenzie	253/B Flt	Do17 probable
	Flg Off S.D.P. Connors	111/B Flt	Bf109
1550-	Flt Lt I.S. Soden	56/B Flt	He111
	Flt Lt F.A. Ives		
	Plt Off L. Wright	151 Sqn	He111 damaged
	Sgt G. Atkinson		
	Sgt G. Atkinson	151 Sqn	He111 probable
1600-	Plt Off R. Bicknell	4(C) Ferry Flt	2 He111 damaged
	Plt Off C.A. Bird	4(C) Ferry Flt	He111
1600-	Flt Lt G. Harris	253/A Flt	He111 probable
	Plt Off F.W. Ratford	253/A Flt	He111
	Plt Off J.D. Ford	253/A Flt	He111
	Plt Off D.H. Grice	32 Sqn	Bf110 probable
	Plt Off J.L. Flinders	32 Sqn	He111 damaged
	Sqn Ldr J.M. Thompson	111/B Flt	Bf110, Bf110 probable
	Plt Off J.A. Walker	111/B Flt	He111
	Flg Off S.D.P. Connors	111/B Flt	Ju88
	Sgt C. Whitehead	56/B Flt	2 Bf110
	Flt Sgt F.W. Higginson	56/B Flt	Bf110
	Flg Off L. Ereminsky	56/B Flt	Bf110
1630-	Sqn Ldr E.M. Donaldson	151 Sqn	Bf110 damaged

	Flt Lt H.H.A. Ironside	151 Sqn	Bf110
	Plt Off J.M. Bushell	151 Sqn	Bf110
	Sgt D.R. Aslin	151 Sqn	Bf110
1630-	Plt Off J.S. Humphreys	607 Sqn	Bf109 damaged
	Flg Off R.E.W. Pumphrey	607 Sqn	Bf110 probable
1630-	Flt Lt R.G. Dutton	145/A Flt	He111, He111 probable
	Plt Off E.J.C. Wakeham	145/A Flt	He111, He111 damaged
	Flt Lt R.G. Dutton ⎫ Plt Off R.D. Yule ⎭	145/A Flt	He111
	Plt Off K.R. Lucas	145/A Flt	He111 probable
	Plt Off M.A. Newling	145/A Flt	He111 probable
	Flg Off The Hon J.W.M. Aitken	601/B Flt	He111
	Flg Off W.H. Rhodes-Moorhouse	601/B Flt	He111
	Flg Off C.J.H. Riddle	601/B Flt	He111 probable
	Sqn Ldr T.L.E.B. Guinness	601/B Flt	2 He111 damaged
1635-	Plt Off H.A.C. Bird-Wilson ⎫ Flt Lt W.A. Toyne ⎭	17 Sqn	Do17
	Flg Off C.F.G. Adye	17 Sqn	Bf110 probable
	Plt Off W.J. Harper ⎫ Plt Off K. Manger ⎪ Sgt N.R. Wynn ⎬ Sgt W.J. Etherington ⎭	17 Sqn	Bf110 probable
1825-	Flt Lt J.D. Joslin	56/A Flt	Hs126, Bf109 probable
	Flg Off J.H. Coghlan	56/A Flt	Bf109
	Flg Off J.H. Coghlan ⎫ Sgt J.W. Elliott ⎭	56/A Flt	He111 probable
1830-	Plt Off D.W.A. Stones	79 Sqn	2 Bf110
	Flg Off F.J.L. Duus	79 Sqn	Do17
	Plt Off H.D. Atkinson	213/B Flt	Bf110
2100-	Plt Off B. Van Mentz	504 Sqn	Bf109 damaged

Losses—AASF and Air Component Hurricanes, 18 May

0620-	N2464	3 Sqn	Plt Off P.M. Gardner: aircraft damaged by return fire from Do17Z of 2/KG76 and force-landed ten miles south of Douai; pilot unhurt, returned.
	L1940	3 Sqn	Plt Off D.L. Bisgood: aircraft damaged by return fire from Do17Z of 2/KG76 and force-landed south of Douai; pilot unhurt, returned.
	N2605	601/A Flt	Flt Lt Sir A.P. Hope: aircraft damaged by return fire from Do17Z of 2/KG76 and force-landed near Grevillers; pilot unhurt, returned.
0630-	N2353	1 Sqn	Plt Off C.M. Stavert: force-landed near Conde/ Vraux following combat, out of fuel; pilot unhurt.
0700-	P2701	85 Sqn	Flg Off D.H. Allen: shot down between Le Cateau-Cambrai by Bf110C of I/ZG26; pilot killed.
	N2425	85 Sqn	Flg Off W.N. Lepine: shot down between Le Cateau-Cambrai by Bf110C of I/ZG26; pilot baled out, wounded, PoW.
	L1665	242/A Flt	Plt Off R.H. Wiens: shot down between Le Cateau-Cambrai by Bf110C of I/ZG26 and crash-landed; pilot injured.
	L1922	242/A Flt	Flg Off L.E. Chambers: shot down near Cambrai by Bf110C of I/ZG26; pilot baled out, wounded, PoW.

	N2320	242/A Flt	Plt Off M.K. Brown: shot down west of Cambrai by Bf110C of I/ZG26; pilot wounded.
0740-	P2873	607 Sqn	Flg Off W.F. Blackadder: aircraft damaged by return fire from Do17Z of II/KG76 and force-landed at Vitry; pilot unhurt.
0740-		79 Sqn	Plt Off T.C. Parker: aircraft damaged by return fire from Do17Z of 5/KG76; pilot unhurt.
1000-	P2536	607 Sqn	Flg Off R.F. Weatherill: shot down near Cambrai by Bf109 of 2/JG51; pilot killed.
1045-	P2676	229/B Flt	Plt Off D. DeC.C. Gower: shot down between Brussels and Antwerp by Bf109 of II/JG2; pilot baled out, returned.
	P2729	229/B Flt	Plt Off M.A. Bussey: shot down between Brussels and Antwerp by Bf109 of II/JG2; pilot baled out, PoW.
1520-	L1856	1 Sqn	Sgt R.A. Albonico: aircraft damaged by ground fire and crash-landed near St Quentin; pilot PoW.
1525-	L1607	111/A Flt	Sgt J.T. Craig: shot down near Vitry by Bf110C of I/ZG26 and crash-landed near Vimy; pilot unhurt, returned.
		253/B Flt	Plt Off D.N.O. Jenkins: aircraft damaged by Bf110C of I/ZG26 and force-landed at Glisy; pilot unhurt.
1530-	N2439	56/B Flt	Flg Off F.C. Rose: shot down by Bf109 of II/JG26 or Bf110C of I/ZG26 and crashed near Brebières; pilot killed.
	N2553	56/B Flt	Plt Off F.B. Sutton: aircraft damaged near Vitry by Bf109 of II/JG26 or Bf110C of I/ZG26 and crash-landed at Vitry; pilot slightly wounded.
	L1802	229/B Flt	Plt Off A.M. Dillon: shot down by Bf109 of II/JG26 or Bf110C of I/ZG26 and crashed near Castillon Hill, Mons; pilot killed.
	P2757	229/B Flt	Flt Lt F.E. Rosier: shot down near Vitry by Bf109 of II/JG26; pilot baled out, burned.
	L2051	111/B Flt	Flt Lt C.S. Darwood: shot down near Vitry by Bf109 of II/JG26; pilot killed.
	P2797	607 Sqn	Plt Off A.S. Dini: aircraft damaged by Bf109 of II/JG26 and crash-landed at Vitry; pilot unhurt.
	N2545	253/A Flt	Plt Off D.B. Bell-Salter: aircraft damaged by Bf109 of II/JG26 and force-landed Vitry; pilot unhurt.
	L1655	253/A Flt	Sgt R.A. Brackley: aircraft damaged by Bf109 of II/JG26 and force-landed Vitry; pilot unhurt.
1550-	L1755	151 Sqn	Flg Off R.M. Milne: aircraft damaged by Bf110C II/ZG76 and force-landed Vitry; pilot unhurt.
	L1850	151 Sqn	Sgt G. Atkinson: aircraft damaged by Bf110 of II/ZG76 and force-landed near Vitry; pilot unhurt.
1600-	L1611	253/A Flt	Plt Off J.D. Ford: aircraft damaged near Vitry by He111 of II/KG1 or Bf110C of II/ZG26 and force-landed; pilot unhurt.
	P2761	253/A Flt	Plt Off J.T. Strang: aircraft damaged near Vitry by Bf110C of II/ZG26 and force-landed; pilot unhurt.
1625-	N2600	145/A Flt	Plt Off M.A. Newling: shot down west of Brussels by return fire from He111P of KG4; pilot baled out, returned.

	L2034	601/B Flt	Sqn Ldr T.L.E.B. Guinness: aircraft damaged by return fire from He111P of KG4 and force-landed Merville; pilot unhurt.
1800-	N2437	56/B Flt	Flt Lt I.S. Soden: shot down near Vitry by Bf110C of II/ZG76; pilot killed.
1830-	P3451	79 Sqn	Plt Off D.W.A. Stones: aircraft damaged by Bf110C of II/ZG76 and force-landed near Norrent-Fontès; pilot unhurt.
2100-	L1912	504 Sqn	Flt Lt J.S. Owen: shot down north-east of Mons by Bf109 of I(J)/LG2; pilot killed.
	L1944	504 Sqn	Plt Off R.J. Renison: shot down north-east of Mons by Bf109 of I(J)/LG2; pilot baled out, PoW.
PM-	Plt Off J.W. Lecky		85 Sqn killed (motor accident)
	Flt Lt J.R.M. Boothby		85 Sqn injured (motor accident)

CHAPTER XI

SUNDAY 19 MAY
AIR BATTLES OVER LILLE

'I was escorted in by the mechanics grabbing the wingtips and giving me the thumbs-up sign. I was able to indicate three fingers. They flung their caps in the air, grinning like Cheshire Cats.'

Plt Off Lew Lewis, 85 Squadron.

Prime Minister Churchill chose this day to broadcast to the nation:

'A tremendous battle is raging in France and Flanders. The Germans, by a remarkable combination of air bombing and heavily armoured tanks, have broken through the French defence north of the Maginot Line, and strong columns of their armoured vehicles are ravaging the open country. In the air, often at serious odds, even at odds hitherto thought overwhelming, we have been clawing down three or four to one of our enemies, and the relative balance of the British and German air forces is now considerably more favourable to us than at the beginning of the battle. In cutting down the German bombers we are fighting our own battle, as well as that of France. My confidence in our ability to fight it out to the finish with the German Air Force has been strengthened by the fierce encounters which have taken place and are taking place.'

The Situation on the Northern Front

An official report noted that 'the enemy continued to keep in touch with the Allied withdrawal' although there was no great pressure on the retreating troops. The report continued:

'The position was thus that the right flank of the retreating armies of the north was being continuously bent round to form, in conjunction with scratch elements from the rear, a defensive front to the south.'

However, the greater threat came from the German breakthrough:

> 'It is now estimated that some 20 enemy divisions, of which eight or nine were armoured and four motorised, were advancing through the gap in the Allied line.'

The report added ominously:

> 'The enemy threw his full strength into the advance north-west through the gap to the Channel coast.'

And concluded:

> 'The reorganized 7th Armée had no chance of standing successfully in the path of the advancing enemy and it began detraining at Peronne, in order to strengthen the front on the south at the German penetration. Its role was to stand along the Somme and Ailette between Peronne and Coucy-le-Château, and thus straddle the Oise.'

Disturbed by the rapidity of events, Air HQ of the AASF sent a signal to Air Ministry at midday, complaining that:

> 'There were no organized forces opposing the main thrust to the west between La Fère and Le Cateau, only small elements of the French 9th Armée with the British 23rd Division and the French 7th Armée re-forming at Douai in reserve.'

Early morning reconnaissance of the area immediately north of the Rethel-Blanzy stretch of the Aisne revealed two mechanized columns advancing towards the Neufchâtel-Montcornet road. Air Marshal Barratt ordered an immediate air strike by all available Battles drawn from the Air Component's decimated squadrons. A total of 33 aircraft were to participate and were to receive the protection of 26 Hurricanes from 67 Wing's 1, 73 and 501 Squadrons.

67 Wing, AASF
Both Flg Off Cobber Kain and Flg Off Ginger Paul of 73 Squadron were up on dawn patrol when, at 0525, they sighted a pair of aircraft identified as Do215s (but were in fact Do17Zs of II/KG3), which were pursued. Kain caught his opponent east of Metz and Paul shot down the other machine east of the airfield. Although damaged, both bombers were able to reach safety, one landing at Trier with 20% damage although the other crash-landed at Wiesbaden-Erbenheim, 40% damaged.

At 1000, a dozen Hurricanes of 1 Squadron—the Flights led by Flt Lts Johnny Walker and Prosser Hanks—departed from Anglure to cover the bomber operation. The Squadron's official report of the operation detailed subsequent events (A Flight is referred to in the report as Red Flight and B Flight as Blue Flight):

'Take-off 1015. Detailed for Blenheim [there is no record of any Blenheims taking part in this operation] cover patrol in Rethel-St Quentin [area] from 1040 to 1055. Several formations of enemy bombers, accompanied by fighters, seen when on the way to patrol line. Carried on to carry out patrol. At 1100, when north-east of Rethel, a formation of four sections of three e/a in line astern, and a section of three e/a flying to one side of the main formation, was sighted flying west. Some difficulty was experienced in recognising them. They were thought at first to be Blenheims returning from the raid which we had been covering. They turned out to be He111s.'

The Heinkels were part of a III/KG27 formation detailed to attack targets in the Soissons-Compiègne-Noyon sector.

'Red Flight delivered an echelon starboard attack. This was not pressed home as it might have been, owing to an R/T message to "Look out behind!". Red 2 [Flg Off Hilly Brown] did not hear the message, so pressed home his attack. The aircraft [he attacked] left the formation with both engines smoking and both wheels down. From then on individual attacks were delivered. Red 1 [Flt Lt Walker] delivered several attacks and later attacked one with its wheels down. This e/a, after a good burst, emitted smoke from both engines and glided down towards the ground. Ammunition being exhausted, Red 1 landed at a French aerodrome, then returned to base.

Red 2 [Brown] again attacked e/a which had broken away from formation on his first attack and then left him to go after serviceable formation. Later he attacked the outside man, who broke away. Since he thought his ammunition was getting low, he followed e/a to ground and saw it land in a ploughed field 12 miles west of Château-Thierry. Three prisoners were seen taken by French soldiers. Red 3 [Flg Off Paul Richey] did not return. We understand he has a neck wound. Red 4 [Flg Off Bill Stratton], who was flying line astern on leader, did not get the order to "form echelon right". He delivered several individual attacks. On one of these the e/a emitted black smoke and broke formation. However, it seemed to recover and rejoin.

Red 5 [Flg Off Iggy Kilmartin] attacked an isolated e/a on the first attack. He got in a good burst, the warning "Look out behind!" coming as he was firing. The e/a dropped out of formation, white smoke coming from its engines. Attacked a lone He111 going north-east at 1,500 feet and saw no rear gunfire. On the first burst e/a jettisoned bombs and on second attack he went down into a valley with undercarriage down. Considering object obtained, Red 5 returned to base. Red 6 [Sgt Frank Soper] was keeping lookout during first attack. Saw starboard e/a emit smoke from port engine. Attacked No 2 of rearmost formation of three and both engines poured smoke. Made a second attack on leader and saw port engine smoking but was forced to break away owing to damage to port petrol tank and engine. Force-landed near Château-Thierry.'

Brown was credited with shooting down one Heinkel and probably a second, while Walker was also credited with a probable. Stratton, Kilmartin and Soper were each awarded a 'damaged'; the engine of the latter's aircraft (L1925), when hit by return fire, belched flames, so it was dived vertically until the fire receded. With his cockpit full of glycol fumes, Soper was forced to carry out a 'blind', wheels-up landing, and subsequently struck his head on the gunsight. On regaining conscious-ness, he thumbed a lift to Château-de-Pricory. The Squadron report continued:

'While Red Flight were attacking, Blue Flight kept 2-3,000 feet above and behind to ward off any enemy fighters. Seeing that there were none, Blue Flight awaited for a favourable opportunity to attack. No 1 [Flt Lt Hanks, P2682] attacked a straggler which was already losing height, but after two short bursts found that only two guns were firing and broke away and just followed and watched. No 2 [Plt Off George Goodman] had already returned home through lack of oxygen. No 3 [Flg Off Boy Mould] attacked starboard e/a of a formation of three with no apparent result, went in again and attacked a straggler and smoke emitted from starboard engine. On his third attack he developed engine trouble and returned to base.

No 4 [Flg Off Pussy Palmer] attacked another straggler after another Hurricane had broken away and saw it go down in flames. He attacked another which broke formation, sinking slightly, by which time he had run out of ammunition. No 5 [Plt Off Richard Lewis] attacked an e/a at which two Hurricanes had already fired and which was smoking slightly, but did not see it hit the ground. He then attacked another e/a and after two short bursts saw it diving away with starboard engine on fire. No 6 [Plt Off Charles Stavert] fired at a straggler and saw one engine giving out black smoke and the other give out white smoke, but then his guns seized up.'

Palmer was credited with a Heinkel shared (apparently having attacked the same aircraft as Mould), Lewis with a probable and Mould and Stavert each with one damaged. Flg Off Paul Richey, who failed to return from this operation, wrote later:

> 'I went in astern of the extreme right-hand aircraft of a rear sub-formation of three. I fired several bursts and was converging fast when I got in the Hun's slipstream. I was nearly on top of him and, judging by the way he suddenly slowed down, I think I must have damaged his engines.'

Richey carried out a second attack on the same bomber, after which it was seen to go down in a vertical spiral. Despite some shrapnel damage to one wing, he pursued another Heinkel:

> 'I had him in range and opened fire. Between bursts I noticed I was getting a hell of a lot of crossfire from the formation . . . there was a bang and what appeared to have been a cannon-shell opened a big hole in my port wing. Suddenly smoke poured from both my Heinkel's engines, his wheels dropped and he went down in a shallow diving turn.'

A third Heinkel was then pursued by Richey, one which was lagging behind the formation:

> 'I had him beautifully steady in my sights and poured short savage bursts as I closed . . . suddenly grey smoke steamed from both his engines, then from his wing roots and fuselage, and in a second he was completely enveloped in it.'

As Richey rolled his Hurricane over to the left of the formation, his aircraft was hit and he was wounded, pieces of an armour-piercing bullet having lodged itself against the front of his spine, at the base of the neck:

> 'Almost at once there was a shower of blood down my right side . . .
> I saw my right arm, drenched in blood, bent up in front of me. There was no feeling in it.'

He tried to bale out, but was unable to open the hood and, after an exhausting struggle, found himself gliding into a field with a dead engine. The Hurricane (P2805) remained in one piece during the crash-landing, although Richey was still not able to open the hood. However, with his remaining strength, he gave another heave and the hood opened sufficiently for him to climb out. After some time, two French soldiers appeared and took him to a hospital near Château-Thierry, from where he was transported to Paris for further treatment.

III/KG27 lost five He111Ps totally destroyed in this action:

He111P of 8/KG27 shot down: crew baled out, survived.

He111P of 8/KG27 flown by Oblt Kurt Bormann shot down and crash-landed about 15 miles north of Château-Thierry: two crew killed, three PoW of the French.

He111P of 8/KG27 flown by Fw Fritz Bürger shot down and crash-landed about seven miles north-east of Château-Thierry: crew PoW of the French.

He111P of 9/KG27 flown by Fw Engelbert Heiner shot down and crash-landed south-west of Soissons: crew PoW of the French.

He111P of 9/KG27 flown by Fw Karl-Ernst Pöhlmann shot down and crash-landed south of Soissons: two killed, three PoW of the French.

73 Squadron was also heavily engaged, as noted by Charles Gardner:

'12 Hurricanes [in fact there were 13, 73 Squadron having been joined by a stray Hurricane from 501 Squadron] saw two formations of Heinkels—together with five Ju88s—all escorted by three layers of Messerschmitt 110s, higher up. The Hurricanes attacked and managed to cut the Heinkels into two groups of unequal size. Not until too late did the Messerschmitt 110s see what was happening. As soon as they opened fire, one Heinkel was seen to go down in a spin, completely out of control (attacked by three Hurricanes, one after the other). The leader [Flt Lt John Scoular, Hurricane S] saw the first Heinkel he attacked dive with the tail falling to pieces. He also saw black objects, tied together, strung out astern. The Heinkel crashed near Berry-au-Bac. Later Scoular got in three good bursts at another Heinkel—which went down out of control near Reims. One more Heinkel crashed after three Hurricanes had attacked and put the engines out of action.'

It seems probable that the bombers attacked by 73 Squadron were Ju88s of I and II/KG51, escorted by Bf110Cs of V(Z)/LG1, although some pilots may have encountered stray Heinkels from the formation attacked by 1 Squadron. Gardner's account continued:

'The other Hurricane Flight, led by Flg Off Cobber Kain [P2535/K], was in the thick of a scrap and Kain got a Ju88 head-on, in one burst.

A Messerschmitt 110 made a belated appearance and had an engine set on fire for its pains. It was then seen to go down out of control. Suddenly the air cleared and Kain and one other Hurricane [Plt Off Don Scott] provided escort for a lone Blenheim.'

Two Heinkels were credited to Scoular, one of which he shared with Sgt Alf Marshall; Kain was credited with a Ju88 and a Bf110, while Flg Off Ginger Paul claimed a Heinkel and Sgt Lionel Pilkington (P2539) recorded a He111 probably destroyed:

'Think I got a He111 but one of the rear gunners gets my oil tank and I fly back. See three He111s doing dive-bombing 200 yards away; also run into 15 Messerschmitt 110s. Fly back in cloud and land at French bomber drome. Given a fine lunch. Ken calls in a Maggie for me in the afternoon.'

Two other Hurricanes failed to return, although both Plt Off John Thompson (N2385) and Plt Off Neville Langham-Hobart (P2543) force-landed safely; the latter had suffered nothing worse than swollen knees from a collision with the dashboard, while Thompson reported later:

'Took off on defensive patrol (Green 3), section leader Flg Off Paul. About 11 o'clock two Dorniers were sighted and the section leader led the Squadron to attack them. I fired a long burst into one, no results were observed. I climbed up to 10,000 feet and was unable to locate the remainder of the Squadron even after a ten-minute search. I flew south-west on compass and saw two Dorniers and attacked from behind. Smoke came from the starboard engine and she dived away and was not seen again. I continued south-west and was attacked from the rear by two Messerschmitt 110s. I dived down to 1,000 feet to escape and they followed for about five minutes. One put a cannon hole in my port wing. After flying for some while I observed a large town and descended to make a precautionary landing in a large field. Nearing the finish of the run I hit a concealed ditch and struck my head against the reflector sight and became unconscious. When I came to, the aircraft was facing the opposite direction; the prop and the undercarriage were smashed and the starboard wing damaged. The landing was made at Montarois [Montereau], about 50 miles south-east of Paris. French soldiers came and took me to a large military camp.'

Thompson was driven to Paris where he reported to the Air Attaché's office. He received instructions to return to the Squadron by rail, which he succeeded in doing two days later.

I and II/KG51 reported the loss of three Ju88s and another damaged:

> Ju88A of 3/KG51 flown by Oblt Werner Schallenberg shot down near Soissons: two killed, two baled out and PoW of the French.

> Ju88A of 4/KG51 severely damaged in combat north of Reims and crash-landed: crew survived, unhurt.

> Ju88A of 5/KG51 flown by Lt Franz Thelen shot down about 18 miles south-west of Reims by 'six Hurricanes': two killed, two baled out and PoW of the French.

> Ju88A of 6/KG51 5% damaged in combat south of Reims: one killed.

501 Squadron pilots also sighted many German aircraft but, although ordered to engage, were unable to make any interceptions.

It had been another costly operation. Six Battles failed to return from the operation, including two of 12 Squadron shot down by Bf109s of 1/JG51; all three dispatched by 142 Squadron were lost as was one from 150 Squadron; of the 18 missing crew members, four were killed or died of their wounds and eight were taken prisoner, while the remaining six were able to return to their units. The Hurricanes had also been tasked to escort 20 L'Aeronautique Navale Loire-Nieuport 401s and 411s of AB2 and AB4 to attack the bridge at Origny-Sainte-Benoite, but had been unable to rendezvous. During their attack one of the French machines was shot down by Flak and two others damaged.

Lysanders of 26 Squadron were also pressed into action as bombers during the day; one pilot* attacked tanks under heavy ground fire and survived to report the situation, but two others—L4773 RM-B and N1202—failed to return. Another Lysander crew (from 2 Squadron) reported meeting 20 Ju87s bombing the bridge at Oudenaarde, one of which was claimed shot down.

60 Wing, Air Component, Lille
87 Squadron at Lille/Marcq dispatched an early morning patrol (comprising two Australians and two New Zealanders) to the Le Cateau-Cambrai area, led by Flg Off Dick Glyde, who reported:

> 'I was leading a patrol of four Hurricanes at 7,000 feet. Sighted

---

* The Lysander pilot was Plt Off George Leslie Sinclair, a Canadian, who was awarded a DFC for his performance in France. He later flew Spitfires and became a wing commander. In 1948—as 'Lee' Sinclair—he volunteered to fly for the Israelis in the the War of Independence (see *Spitfires over Israel* by Brian Cull and Shlomo Aloni with David Nicolle, published by Grub Street 1993).

Henschel flying west along Le Cateau-Cambrai road. Attacked Henschel in turn, firing short bursts. Henschel took vigorous evasive action and finally crashed in flames, exploding on hitting the ground. Each member of the patrol had an equal share in shooting it down.'

Plt Off John Cock (P3889) noted:

'All opened fire in converging attack, but e/a eluded fire by stalling. Aircraft set on fire after third burst. Eventually aircraft exploded and tail flew off and crashed in field near Le Cateau-St Amand.'

Flg Off Derek Ward added:

'The leader dived to one side of the enemy. No 1 and No 2 carried out a stern attack with apparently no damage. I then attacked. The rear gunner ceased firing and smoke began to pour out of the e/a. Nos 4 and 1 followed through with short bursts. The e/a was still under control and was carrying out effective evasive tactics. I then went in and closed to within 50 yards when the aircraft blew up.'

The other Hurricane, piloted by Flg Off 'Buzz' Allen—a New Zealander from Auckland—was hit by return fire and the pilot wounded in the left arm by a piece of shrapnel, but he was able to reach Lille/Marcq safely. The crew (Obgfr Karl-Heinz Kramer and Oblt Hermann Grether) of the Henschel, an aircraft of 1(H)/11Pz which had been spotting for 10 Pz Division, were killed.

Meanwhile, from neighbouring Lille/Seclin, Flg Off Count Manfred Czernin of 85 Squadron was sent off at 0600 to carry out an aerodrome patrol:

'I was doing aerodrome patrol at 10,000 feet when I saw air condensation fairly high above me, going south-east. I climbed up after them and saw it was seven Do17s. I caught them up at Valenciennes. They were keeping in a tight vic formation. I attacked the last one on the starboard side from out of the sun and immediately he broke away with his port engine on fire. He did not come out of the resulting dive and crashed in flames in a wood by a railway station east of Valenciennes. I attacked the formation again, opening fire from beam and saw one more Do17 break away and dive down with smoke pouring from both engines. At about 10,000 feet he burst into flames and seemed to break up. I attacked again but with no further success.'

The Dorniers were from 9/KG76 but only one was lost, that flown by Oblt Rudolf Strasser, which crashed with the loss of the crew. The escorting Bf109s of I/JG3 failed to sight Czernin's lone Hurricane while Czernin did not report seeing any Messerschmitts in the vicinity.

85 Squadron sent up another section just before 1000 to patrol the aerodrome, as reports of raiders in the vicinity had been received. A formation of Bf109s—from 2(J)/LG2 and II/JG26—was sighted approaching the airfield, but too late to warn the crews of two Lysanders of 4 Squadron practising landings at Lille/Marcq. Both were speedily shot down by the Messerschmitts with the loss of both crews, one of which fell to Oblt Friedrich von Wangerov and the other to Lt Werner Tismar, both of 2(J)/LG2. Watching the one-sided action from the ground was 87 Squadron's Plt Off Roland Beamont, who wrote later:

'Over beyond the aerodrome one of the Lysanders was dropping earthwards with a 109 hammering away on its tail. Suddenly wondering where the other Lysander was, I saw it just cruising overhead at 1,000 feet, and even as I looked at it, another 109 broke away from the formation and dropped down in a diving turn on to the Lysander's tail. It opened fire at about 200 yards . . . I could see the cannon bursting on the sides of the Lysander's fuselage, which nosed over sharply and dived into the ground.'

Meanwhile, Plt Off Lew Lewis of the 85 Squadron patrol (flying a 213 Squadron aircraft, AK-A, on this occasion) engaged the Messerschmitts and claimed two shot down. His companion, newly attached Flg Off Jerrard Jeffries, claimed a probable.

All available Hurricanes were scrambled from Lille/Marcq, including A Flight of 504 Squadron. Other pilots on the ground subsequently witnessed Hurricanes shoot down four of the raiders before six more Messerschmitts arrived and were engaged by the 504 Squadron Hurricanes; Flg Off Michael Royce claimed one shot down and Plt Off John Hardacre probably a second, before the latter was hit by another and baled out of P3555. The new Commanding Officer, Sqn Ldr John Hill (P3551), who was flying his first sortie with the Squadron, was also shot down and baled out at 18,000 feet. As he neared the ground, he was fired at by French shotgun-wielding peasants and pellets peppered his right leg.

Sqn Ldr Hill was quickly surrounded by the peasants, who believed he was German although he managed to convince them otherwise; a French military car then arrived but, as he was about to be driven away, a British Army vehicle was encountered and Hill was apprehended as a fifth columnist! As he reached into his pocket to produce his identity card, the British soldiers opened fire, forcing Hill to dive into a nearby ditch to avoid the bullets. This new development obviously put doubt in the minds of the onlookers, since they proceeded to drag him out of the ditch and beat him into unconsciousness. He escaped further injury only by the timely intervention of a French Air Force officer who was attracted to the scene and who recognised Hill as an old friend! The battered Squadron Leader was taken back to Lille, the car full of pots of honey and jam, eggs and bunches of flowers pressed on him by his former assailants and their families.

Meanwhile, other Hurricanes were involved in the mêlée above and around Lille, as revealed in the subsequent report filed by Plt Off Pat Woods-Scawen of 85 Squadron:

'At approximately 1000, I was on the aerodrome when I saw three Hurricanes engaged in combat with several e/a. I took off and shot down one e/a in flames, five miles east of Seclin, after burst of two seconds; the puff of smoke when the e/a crashed was seen from the aerodrome. I climbed to 5,000 feet and engaged a second Messerschmitt 109 which dived, emitting black smoke, to the ground after several bursts of three seconds from 100 yards. I was unable to see where this e/a crashed because I was attacked from the rear by two e/a. My ammunition was exhausted so I broke off the engagement.'

Flt Lt Ian Gleed (P2798 LK-A) of 87 Squadron scrambled from Lille/Marcq with his section and met five Bf109s at 12,000 feet near Aalst:

'Took off on sight with two other Hurricanes—attacked five 109s which had shot down two Lysanders. After a long chase caught up and fired all my rounds at one, at 200-100 yards. E/a last seen with smoke pouring out but still under control, flying at approximately 150 mph. E/a dived down to ground level.'

One of Gleed's section, Flg Off Derek Ward, reported:

'We [85 and 87 Squadrons] took off in a panic from Lille. AA fire directed us. We were attacked from above by 109s. A free for all developed. I was in a steep right-hand turn when I saw an e/a attacking a Hurricane 400 feet below. I dived and attacked the e/a who broke away and carried out evasive tactics. His coolant began to pour out. I broke off the engagement as I mistook a Hurricane coming up behind for a 109. Two Hurricanes continued to fire at this e/a. I followed with a final burst and when I last saw e/a it was at ground level, flying at about 140 mph.'

The third member of the section, Flg Off Roddy Rayner, reported shooting down one of the Bf109s in flames. Three Hurricanes of 87 Squadron's B Flight also managed to get airborne—Flg Off Dick Glyde, Plt Off Jimmy Dunn and Flt Sgt Ivor Badger—closely followed by two more flown by Plt Off Roland Beamont and Flg Off Jimmy Strickland. Survivors of the Messerschmitt formation were intercepted and engaged. Beamont:

> 'I found a small dogfight in progress which turned out to be Jimmy Dunn knocking hell out of a 109 which eventually crashed in flames.'

Flg Off Glyde attacked the same aircraft as that engaged by Gleed and Ward:

> 'I was at 8,000 feet and saw a 109 at a lower level being attacked by two other Hurricanes. He was evading them very well and I decided to join in. I took several deflection shots at him and eventually got on his tail. He continued to take vigorous action but after another burst vapour began to stream from his engine, which then lost power considerably. He was still taking very determined evasive action and I could not get in a conclusive burst. Suddenly he banked over the vertical at 500 feet and disappeared below me. I thought he had gone in and flew round looking for the wreckage but he must have got away, though I don't think his engine could have taken him far. We were near Tournai at the time.'

Flt Sgt Badger claimed two more, one of which was credited as a probable, but Flg Off Strickland (who was born in the Philippines of British parents) was shot down (in P2687) and baled out with an 'armful of splinters'. He then suffered a leg wound from a bullet fired by a French soldier as he floated down. Both Dunn and Glyde returned with their Hurricanes 'a mass of bullet holes' but neither was hurt. It transpired that during the confused action Glyde had fired at Badger's aircraft in error.

Six Hurricanes were claimed shot down by 2(J)/LG2, Fw Günter Schmitz being credited with two and Lt Helmut Mertens, Lt Werner Tismar, Ofw Hermann Staege and Ofw Georg Schott one apiece. In return, the pilots of 85, 87 and 504 Squadrons claimed a total of eight Bf109s and six probables. Four of the Messerschmitts were in fact shot down, II/JG26 losing three aircraft, including that flown by the Gruppenkommandeur, who was killed:

> Bf109E of 2(J)/LG2 flown by Oblt Friedrich von Wangerov shot down and crashed north-west of Lille: pilot killed.

Bf109E of II/JG26 flown by Gruppenkommandeur Hptm Herwig
Knüppel shot down south of Lille: pilot killed.

Bf109E of 4/JG26 flown by Staffelkapitän Hptm Karl Ebbinghausen shot down east of Lille and crash-landed: pilot wounded,
returned.

Bf109E of 4/JG26 damaged in combat near Lille and crash-landed
near Brussels: pilot unhurt, returned.

Flt Lt Harry Anderson led five of 253/B Flight off at the first oppor-
tunity. The Hurricanes climbed to engage, but came under attack from
Bf109s of I/JG3 which had arrived on the scene and both Anderson
(L1674) and Sgt Gilbert Mackenzie (L1667) were shot down and killed;
Anderson's aircraft crashed near Lille and Mackenzie's fell near
Cysoing, about seven miles south-east of the town. Three Hurricanes
were claimed by the Messerschmitt pilots, one apiece being credited to
Hptm Günther Lützow, Lt Helmut Tiedmann and Uffz Hans Heise.
Other pilots of B Flight were more successful and Plt Off John Clifton
reported:

'About 15 fighters took off from the aerodrome, but I went to meet
the 109s with about five of 253 Squadron. The 109s split up and I
followed one and opened fire on it—it went into a dive and I lost
sight of it. I then returned to the aerodrome for more ammunition.'

Plt Off John Greenwood added:

'I took off with three other pilots from B Flight to attack about ten
109s which had just shot down a Lysander. At 1045 we had climbed
to 10,000 feet and I attacked one of the enemy from astern. The e/a
dived and turned away but I got in three bursts of about six seconds
each. The e/a was then diving steeply and smoke was pouring from
the engine. I pulled out of my dive and looked around for another
enemy but saw nothing so returned to Lille to refuel. Two missing.'

At about midday, a section from 85 Squadron patrolled in the vicinity of
Lille/Seclin, as recalled by Plt Off Lew Lewis (again flying AK-A):

'Our instructions were to carry out an offensive patrol and land at
Merville. I was flying in a section of three, led by Flg Off
Stephenson, when the left-hand gun panel came loose and made
formation flying difficult. On reporting to section leader, was
ordered to break off and land at Lille. It was probably due to lack of
sleep over a period of days that I was unaware of three 109s, which

had become interested in me as I headed for Lille/Seclin. The first inkling was tracer over the wings, much too close for comfort. A tight turn gave me a look at the attackers, the leader coming head-on and opening up with his cannon. Within what seemed yards, he flicked over on to his back and presented his belly as he broke away in a steep dive. I remember my head hitting the top of the cockpit cover as I rammed the stick forward and gave him all I had at point-blank range. Fuel streamed out as he dived into the deck and blew up. The other two—possibly less experienced pilots—made a half hearted pass at me, formed up and headed for the Belgian border. At first my inclination was to leave well alone, but there they were, just above and a little ahead. Out came the booster and the Hurricane surged forward, placing me in an ideal position to squirt at one and, as the fuel streamed out, the remainder of the bursts into the other. Neither made any attempt at evasion, giving me the idea that they had been on a training flight, and once their leader was accounted for, they headed for home. All three crashed within a fairly close distance of each other.'

It seems that Lewis may have shot down Oblt Lothar Krutein of 4/JG2, who was wounded and baled out near Tournai, where he was captured by British troops (although he was released a few days later when German troops overran the area where he was being held); another of his victims may have been Uffz Hans-Joachim Hartwig of 5 Staffel, who crash-landed near Courtrai and was also taken prisoner. The Messer-schmitts of II/JG2 were providing cover for He111s of III/KG28 operating in the Douai area. Lewis continued:

'Landing at Lille, I was escorted in by the mechanics grabbing the wingtips and giving me the thumbs-up sign. I was able to indicate three fingers. They flung their caps in the air, grinning like Cheshire Cats. Sqn Ldr Oliver came over to see why I had not landed at Merville, as agreed. The mechanics were quick to inform him that three planes had been bagged by me. The CO said that he had had a grandstand view. Needless to say he was delighted and I was told I would be recommended for the DFC.'

Hurricanes of 85 and 87 Squadrons were hastily scrambled from the Lille airfields as the bombers approached and, near Orchies, the Heinkels and their escort were encountered. Flt Lt Gleed wrote:

'After a panic take-off encountered approximately 20 e/a. I had my eye on a He111 which had separated itself and was some way behind the protecting Jerry fighters. I was soon up to him, aimed carefully and gave him a short burst; a stream of smoke from his port engine. I was closing rapidly now, sights on again; this time I gave him a long burst.'

Oil streamed from the crippled bomber, covering Gleed's windscreen and he only narrowly avoided colliding with his victim. As he flashed by he saw a puff of white as a parachute opened. The Heinkel spiralled down and 'hit the ground in the centre of a large wood and blew up with a terrific flash', while the parachutist was seen to land in a field, where he 'soon disappeared under a crowd of people'.

Flg Off Rayner had attacked the same aircraft:

'Flt Lt Gleed and myself, after a panic take-off, encountered one He111 over Orchies. I attacked from starboard quarter and Flt Lt Gleed from astern simultaneously. Aircraft dived into ground and blew up. One of the crew escaped by parachute.'

Gleed added:

'Another Hurricane [obviously referring to Rayner] attacked from the quarter but only fired 20 rounds from each gun. I fired all my rounds.'

One 87 Squadron aircraft failed to return and it was learned that Plt Off Jimmy Dunn's aircraft (L1620) had been shot down in flames by the Messerschmitts. Although he suffered burns, Dunn had been able to bale out and, when visited in hospital, reported that he had shot down a Bf109 before being hit by another. Flg Off Rafael Watson landed P2829 LK-G with difficulty, its control wires having been shot away. Four Hurricanes were claimed by pilots of II/JG2, one each being credited to Oblt Hans Hahn, Lt Julius Meimberg, Lt Fritz Müller and Fw Siegfried Schnell. III/KG28 lost one Heinkel as a result of the raid, with a second damaged:

He111P of 9/KG28 severely damaged in combat and crash-landed near the Belgian-German border: two crew killed and one wounded.

He111P of 9/KG28 10% damaged in combat: crew unhurt.

The attack on Lille/Seclin by KG28 was followed by another by Heinkels of KG54. Hurricanes scrambled to intercept and, as he climbed for altitude, Plt Off Art Deacon of 242/A Flight noticed two of the bombers fall in flames. These were possibly the victims of Sgt John Little of 85 Squadron, who was seen to shoot down two before his aircraft (P2562) was shot down in flames by a Messerschmitt; Little was killed. Deacon attacked another bomber and saw the pilot bale out, before another Hurricane closed in and followed it down. Yet another Heinkel was attacked by Sgt Len Jowitt of 85 Squadron's B Flight:

> 'Took off to intercept bombers which bombed base. One broke away from the formation and I attacked from the rear at a range of 100-150 yards. It started smoking and throwing out oil. I fired again and it burst into flames. I followed it down and saw it crash and explode half a mile south of Templeuve, in the fork of the railway junction.'

Flt Lt Don Miller of 242/A Flight returned with his Hurricane (P2808) damaged, as a result of a combat with a Bf109 from I/JG2, and force-landed. Two pilots of 504 Squadron—Plt Off Brian Van Mentz and Sgt Maurice Mapletoft—found themselves at a disadvantage when, from out of the sun, they were attacked by four Bf109s. Mapletoft was seen by Van Mentz going into attack, but his aircraft (N2355) was hit and he was wounded, although he was able to bale out. Meanwhile, Van Mentz engaged one of the Messerschmitts but saw no results.

The Hurricanes had only just returned to Lille/Seclin when they were scrambled again, as a dozen Do17Zs of I/KG77 were seen approaching at 12,000 feet. One of the 15 Hurricanes was flown by Flt Lt Gleed, who reported:

> 'I saw a mass of Jerries over Lille, which they were bombing heavily; the usual fighter escort was weaving above them. I glanced back at the crowd of Hurricanes behind me. The bombers sailed through the sky, their metalwork glinting. High above, the protecting fighters darted here and there. Black anti-aircraft bursts appeared unpleasantly close to us, as usual behind and below the bombers; the bursts were just about landing in the middle of the pursuing Hurricanes.'

Gleed selected a Dornier at the rear of the formation and opened fire:

> 'Attacked from dead astern, closing to 25 yards. Got him! The starboard engine is blazing furiously. The Dornier sailed on, still in close formation, his whole wing burning. Then suddenly it toppled on to its side and just dropped from the sky. Out of the corner of my eye I saw the massive formation splitting, with several bombers spiralling down.'

Weaving their way through cumulus over Cambrai, 11 Hurricanes of 32 Squadron from Merville (to where they had flown that morning) encountered a lone Do17 (a straggler from the I/KG77 formation), escorted by a Staffel of Bf109s from I/JG2. Sgt John White (N2582), leading Green Section, was nearest to the Dornier at which he fired a long burst:

'No rearguard action from e/a, which had presumably just bombed Cambrai or town below on fire. Tail unit of e/a came off and it went down in smoking spiral.'

One Dornier, a machine of the Stabsstaffel, was severely damaged and crash-landed at Sandweiler airfield in Luxembourg; the crew survived but the aircraft was totally destroyed. A second Dornier suffered damage and one crew member wounded, although it was able to return safely to base. Sgt White continued:

'Several Messerschmitts noticed diving from above so took refuge in cloud as my ammunition was expended.'

On seeing White's plight, Flt Lt Peter Brothers (N2588) attempted to go to his aid, but three more fighters were then sighted above:

'I turned sharp left as they dived on my tail. They turned away and as I was turning a 109 flew across my sights. I gave him a short burst and he slowly turned on his back and dived, inverted, at about 45°. I followed him down but he gained speed and remained inverted. I looked round and saw another 109 on my tail. I turned steeply to the left and he opened fire with tracer. His shooting was hopeless and I saw his tracer pass behind me. I turned on to his tail but as I was firing he dived into a cloud and I lost him. I circled round but all aircraft appeared to have gone home.'

Another Bf109 was attacked by Flt Lt Michael Crossley (N2461), who reported:

'Fired a full deflection shot as Messerschmitt 109 flew across my bows from right to left. I followed him round and saw him turn slowly on his back and dive to earth. I then found another wheeling round on my left, trying to get behind me. I continued to turn steeply left and easily turned inside him after one-and-a-half circuits. When he saw this he straightened out and climbed hard. I followed up to 20,000 feet very slowly catching up but lost him in the bright sky.'

Plt Off Dudley Grice (N2459) reported shooting down a Bf109 near Le Cateau, then damaged a second from which streams of white vapour were seen as it spun down:

'I fired two bursts of about two seconds at the first 109, using full to three-quarters deflection. The machine burst into flames. The second Messerschmitt I attacked from dead astern in a steep climb at about 300 yards. On opening fire streams of white vapour appeared from the e/a—petrol possibly. At the end of the burst (six seconds) the 109 flick-rolled upwards and then started spinning. I watched it spinning for 5-6,000 feet but did not see it go in.'

Another Messerschmitt was claimed by Plt Off John Flinders (N2463):

'I saw 109 on my starboard side below me, also turning to starboard. I positioned myself on his tail and as he came out of the turn, opened fire. After about three seconds he turned slowly on his back and dived inverted. The aircraft gained speed very rapidly and although I dived after him to about 6,000 feet, I was left behind. The machine was still inverted and diving when I lost sight of him in the clouds. I saw one aircraft which I believe to be a Hurricane in flames and the pilot descending by parachute.'

It would seem that the Bf109 attacked by Flinders may have been the same aircraft as that engaged by Flt Lt Brothers. Meanwhile, Sgt Guy Turner (N2657) engaged yet another and reported:

'Dead astern attack after 109 had overshot. Black smoke trail and pieces flying off. No parachute seen.'

Plt Off Victor 'Jack' Daw (N2527), having chased a Bf109 into the clouds, found himself alone and decided to head back to RAF Biggin Hill. Emerging from cloud, he spotted three Bf110Cs of 5/ZG26 coming towards him and opened fire. The nearest aircraft 'just exploded into a shower of fragments'. This was Oblt Artur Niebuhr's aircraft from which he and his gunner, Uffz Klaus Theissen, baled out. On checking his compass, Daw realised he had been flying in the wrong direction, but reached Biggin Hill safely.

Plt Off Alan Eckford (N2409) claimed a Bf109 damaged, while Sgt Gerald North (N2583) believed his victim probably crashed:

'E/a observed at 12,000 feet and, after shooting down one Hurricane, it turned as if to shoot at the pilot who had taken to his parachute. The 109 approached from astern. I turned and attacked, firing three times. When last seen, e/a was travelling earthwards, absolutely vertically, at estimated speed of 400 mph and it did not apparently pull out.'

The downed Hurricane pilot was Flg Off John 'Millie' Milner (N2462). Flt Lt Crossley related later that he had seen Milner's Hurricane wheel over on its back, with a great sheet of smoke and flame streaming behind and saw a white parachute blossom out; several weeks later the Squadron received a postcard from Milner, sent from a German prison camp:

> 'Sorry I left you the other day. I wasn't thinking. Wonder if you are still at the Bump? [RAF Biggin Hill]. Do drop in and see me anytime you're around these parts—love to everyone and good luck. Millie.'

The Messerschmitt pilots of I/JG2 claimed six Hurricanes following the skirmishing with aircraft from 32, 85, 87 and 504 Squadrons and 242/A Flight. Oblt Otto Bertram (White 1) claimed two, but was also shot down and crash-landed, although he was unhurt and was able to return to his unit. Other Hurricanes were claimed by Oblt Karl-Heinz Krahl, Lt Hans-Joachim von Moller, Ofw Werner Machold and Uffz Hans Schmid.

Shortly before 1300, patrolling Bf109s of I/JG1 sighted a flight of six Lysanders of 16 Squadron on their way to Abbeville from Glisy and two of these were promptly shot down by Hptm Wilhelm Balthasar and Fw Hans Umbach; one of the Lysanders force-landed, but the other crashed with the loss of both crew members. One of the Messerschmitts failed to return and crash-landed between Charleville and Mézières, but whether shot down by a Lysander gunner or a patrolling Hurricane from Lille has not been ascertained.

At 1415 more raiders were reported approaching Lille/Seclin, as a result of which all available Hurricanes were scrambled and these met Do17Zs from III/KG76 near Tournai at 8,000 feet. Flt Lt Ian Gleed of 87 Squadron:

> 'After a panic take-off attacked about 24 Do17s near Tournai in company with about 20 Hurricanes. E/a was attacked from astern and slightly below. Port engine burst into flames and aircraft spiralled into ground. No evasive action taken by enemy.'

Gleed's target may have been a Dornier of 7 Staffel, in which two members of the crew were wounded. At that point a Bf109 from II/JG27, flying cover for the bombers, manoeuvred on to the tail of Gleed's aircraft, followed closely by another. Gleed entered into a tight turn and continued holding this line until one of the Messerschmitts broke away, rolled on to its back and dived vertically. He followed, opened fire and saw a large piece fly off the target aircraft, but the other attempted to get on his tail. Having evaded this, he returned to Lille/Marcq. Flg Off Roddy Rayner, having also claimed a Dornier, returned with about 20 bullet strikes in his aircraft (P2683) following an attack by Fw Adolf Borchers, one of four pilots of 1/JG77 operating in the area as cover for German troops.

Flg Off Dickie Glyde engaged only the Messerschmitts:

'I had climbed to 13,000 feet over Douai when I saw another Hurricane [presumably that flown by Gleed] being attacked by two 109s. I joined in with a slight advantage of height and engaged one of the e/a. He evaded me, dived steeply and we came at each other head-on, both firing but without any apparent effect. He passed a few feet below me. I then got on his tail and fought him down to about 1,000 feet, taking short bursts at him as he kept turning right. I finally got his engine with a full deflection shot and he jumped out and landed by parachute near a wood a few miles south-east of La Bassée.'

Glyde's victim was almost certainly the Staffelkapitän of 5/JG27, Oblt Hans-Christian Schäfer, who was wounded but able to bale out and was captured by French troops.

Three He111s (stragglers from KG54) were sighted over Lille/Marcq at 1530 and Plt Off John Clifton of 253/B Flight took off with one or two others in pursuit but, as the bombers were at a great height, the Hurricanes were forced to give up the chase. The composite 56/213 Squadron, which had returned to Lille/Seclin in the morning, was on patrol when it encountered 15 He111s (also KG54 machines) some 20 miles south of Lille. Flg Off John Coghlan (N2400) of 56/A Flight attacked one and silenced the rear gunner, but the bomber evaded his further attack near Maubeuge, and was last seen with both engines smoking. Covering Bf109s of II/JG27 were engaged by 213/A Flight, one of which was claimed shot down by Plt Off Laurence Stone (AK-K). This was probably Lt Helmut Strobl's 5 Staffel machine (Black 2) which crash-landed near Lille; the pilot survived, evaded capture and was rescued by German troops. However, Stone's aircraft (N2538) was then hit by French AA fire, which forced him also to crash-land. The remaining Hurricanes landed at Lille/Seclin, where they refuelled and then departed for RAF Biggin Hill.

A patrol from 85 Squadron encountered Bf109s of I/JG3 at 1550, as reported by Plt Off Pat Woods-Scawen:

'I was leading Blue Section of three aircraft on patrol between

Seclin and Lille/Marcq when I saw a single e/a travelling east. I
suspected a trap so I broke away the remainder of the section to
cover me and delivered a stern attack on the e/a from 100 yards,
giving one burst of two seconds. The e/a dived steeply, emitting
smoke, and made a crash-landing in a field five miles west of
Tournai. There was another crashed aircraft in the same field. This
engagement was observed by Plt Off Shrewsbury, who joined me
and continued with me on patrol.'

Woods-Scawen's victim was probably Lt Heinz Schnabel of 1 Staffel,
who was wounded but able to crash-land his damaged aircraft near
Philippeville. Some 20 minutes later, Woods-Scawen was again in
action:

'I was patrolling Lille to Seclin at 8,000 feet when I saw a Do17
travelling slowly east at the same height. I suspected a trap and
climbed into the sun behind it. From this position I was able to see
seven 109s [from Stab I and 2/JG77] at my own height (approximately 10,000 feet). They were quite near so I attacked them head-
on, firing continuously from 600 yards till they passed under me. I
saw the leading aircraft pouring smoke as it dived away. I turned as
rapidly as possible and prepared to engage, but what appeared to be
a cannon-shell hit my engine, which burst into flames. I evacuated
my aircraft with all speed and landed safely by parachute two miles
south-west of Lille. I was shot at twice by French [soldiers] on the
way down.'

Woods-Scawen was apparently shot down by Ofw Walter Leyerer of 2
Staffel, who claimed a Hurricane in the area at this time.
     The next big raid occurred at 1630, when two dozen He111Ps of II/
KG4 were reported north-east of Seclin at 12,000 feet. 85 Squadron
engaged the aircraft of 6 Staffel and Sqn Ldr Peacock, leading the
Hurricanes, related later (with tongue firmly in cheek) how he flew up
the centre of the vic and shot down the leader 'so that all the others, who
had been too busy formating to look at their maps, would get lost!'.
However, Peacock's Hurricane came under intense crossfire from the
gunners in the other bombers and was shot down, although he was able
to bale out safely. Another bomber was claimed by Flg Off Count
Manfred Czernin:

'I was ordered up with the whole Flight to attack enemy approaching base. E/a split up immediately and I picked out one and stuck on
his tail. He took no avoiding action and after a longish burst went
down in flames. Attacked a second and saw smoke and oil pouring

from port engine and e/a started to descend but had to break off attack owing to lack of ammunition and was being attacked myself.'

It seems probable that both Peacock and Czernin engaged the same bomber, as only Uffz Johann Kettner's aircraft was shot down and this crash-landed about seven miles north-west of Lokeren; the observer was killed and the other crew members taken prisoner by British troops.

A photographic-reconnaissance Spitfire crashed about ten miles east of Lille during the day, having been intercepted by a Bf109 of 4/JG26 when returning from a sortie to Hamburg and Bremen; the pilot was killed. The Lille-based Hurricane squadrons remained on readiness but were not called into action during the remainder of the afternoon. Then, at 1800, the squadrons were ordered to evacuate to Merville, as 87 Squadron's Plt Off Chris Darwin noted:

'We were ordered to move to Merville—[Grp Capt] Fullard saw us all off. Arrived—no accommodation, no food as usual. Supper in a chicken farm.'

Meanwhile, the last two serviceable aircraft of 253/B Flight (flown by Plt Offs John Greenwood and John Clifton) were ordered to return to RAF Kenley. Unserviceable aircraft were destroyed and the unit's remaining pilots and ground personnel were ordered to make for the coast.

61 Wing, Air Component
Having evacuated Vitry, Norrent-Fontès was the temporary home of 607 Squadron and the survivors of the composite 56/229 Squadron. One of 607 Squadron's ground crew, LAC Bill Bowman, recalled:

'Some half dozen of us were dispatched in a lorry back to Vitry to collect the Officers' kit from their billets. So off we went in the opposite direction to everyone else, being repeatedly told by the French Army that we were going in the wrong direction and that the Germans would capture us. For our defence, between us we had one .45 revolver and three rounds of .38 ammunition. We didn't feel particularly happy but we did get to the village and collect the kit. It was very distressing as people were asking what they should do— should they stay there or join the refugees. We told them to stay; it seemed the only thing to do. On the way back we gave a lift to some refugees who were proceeding on foot, and the hopelessness of their situation was made clear when we asked where they wanted to go and their answer was "anywhere", as long as it was away from the advancing Germans.'

Flt Sgt Taffy Higginson and Sgt Cliff Whitehead of 56/B Flight were also instructed to return to Vitry, there to destroy damaged Hurricanes US-C and US-P and petrol stores and equipment. When they finally left Vitry, the Germans were only three to four miles away.

However, from the other direction came nine Hurricanes of 151 Squadron, led by Sqn Ldr Teddy Donaldson, operating from RAF Manston, which arrived at 1330 to patrol the Tournai-Oudenaarde and Courtrai-Roubaix areas. No hostile aircraft were sighted and the Hurricanes returned to Manston at the end of their patrol. Shortly before 1600, nine more Hurricanes—these from 17 Squadron, which had arrived at Norrent-Fontès earlier in the day—joined a section of 607 Squadron for a patrol between Cambrai and Valenciennes. A Do17P of 3(F)/11, escorted by Bf109s of I(J)/LG2, was encountered at 1620 south of Cambrai and was claimed shot down by Plt Off Richard Whittaker:

> 'I saw a Do17 or 215 flying west at about 6,000 feet. I broke away to attack from the sun and saw four Messerschmitt 109s about 2,000 feet on the port side. I did an astern attack on e/a [Dornier]. Rear gunner fired tracer before I opened fire. I opened fire at 200 yards and observed smoke coming from port engine of e/a, which went down in right-hand dive. I then saw the Messerschmitt 109s coming to attack me and dived to ground level.'

While Whittaker was attacking the Dornier, his colleagues engaged the escort. For the loss of two Hurricanes shot down—N2408 and N2525 flown by Plt Off Robert Harris and Sgt Charles Pavey respectively—three Bf109s were claimed, two by Flt Lt Bill Toyne:

> 'I came out of the sun on to his quarter, completely surprising the 109 and gave a three second burst from astern. The e/a burst into black smoke and flames and I broke to port, climbing for about 2,000 feet. I then saw another 109 below me, also flying east. I attacked him from astern, coming out of the sun and surprising him. After a three second burst he burst into flames and went into a steep dive. I broke away to look behind me and saw three 109s go into line astern and attack me. I executed a steep climbing turn to starboard, turning easily inside the e/a.'

The other Bf109 was credited to Sgt George Steward, who chased it for 40 miles before it crash-landed:

> 'Surprise attack burst [the Messerschmitt's] main petrol tank. White smoke emerged and he half-rolled, but pulled out at approximately 1,100 feet. I followed him and fired all my ammunition at

him and he gradually lost height and came to ground. Pancake landing.'

Sqn Ldr Humphrey Edwardes-Jones, the Squadron's new commander, reported black and white grey from the first Bf109 he attacked, and then engaged a second:

'Just opening fire when a cannon-shell hit my starboard mainplane from rear. I climbed in steep left-hand turn to avoid three e/a below me.'

Five Bf109s attacked Red Section from out of the sun and Flg Off Capel Adye followed them down, as they swept past in a steep dive:

'Caught up at approximately 1,200 feet and engaged right-hand e/a at 50 yards. E/a burst into black smoke, obliterating aircraft from view and dived vertically, but I did not see it strike the ground.'

Adye was then attacked by the other four, which were joined by four more, but was able to escape in cloud. On emerging, he circled and sighted an aircraft below:

'Noticed Do17 slowly circling below at about 300 feet. Both engines appeared to be stopped. [It] struck the ground with some violence.'

This was obviously Whittaker's victim, which crashed south of Cambrai with the loss of Lt Meyer and his crew. Another Bf109 was engaged by Plt Off Harold Bird-Wilson (YB-K), who was credited with its probable destruction:

'I engaged one aircraft. E/a dived away steeply to 5,000 feet. Astern attack on e/a—continued to dive but more steeply, then I gave him a second burst. He rolled over on his back and went into an upside down, very steep dive. I had to break off my attack because another e/a was on my tail.'

Of the two missing pilots, Sgt Pavey (N2525) baled out safely five miles east of Cambrai, but was later captured by the Germans and became a prisoner of war. The other, Plt Off Harris, was killed when his aircraft (N2408) crashed near Noyelles-sur-Selle. Meanwhile, 607 Squadron's new Commanding Officer, Sqn Ldr George Fidler, found himself being pursued by a Messerschmitt. One of his section, Sgt Leslie Ralls (N2586 AF-B) reported:

'E/a got me by surprise and I saw him turning in behind me. He opened fire on beam. I climbed and turned sharply. Straightening out, I saw 109 in front of me attacking another Hurricane [Fidler's P3535 AF-C]. On opening fire with slight deflection, e/a turned on its back and dived to ground.'

Fidler's aircraft was badly damaged and he was forced to bale out near Cambrai, where he was taken prisoner. Three Hurricanes were claimed by pilots of I(J)/LG2, two of which were credited to Ofw Hermann Guhl and the other to Fw Günter Schmitz. In return, two Messerschmitts were lost:

Bf109E of 2(J)/LG2 shot down south-west of Cambrai: Lt Friedrich Strakeljahn wounded, baled out and PoW of the French (released two days later by German troops).

Bf109E of 1(J)/LG2 severely damaged in combat south-west of Cambrai: pilot baled out over occupied territory and returned safely.

On another patrol, flown by B Flight of 607 Squadron, a number of Ju88s of III/LG1 were sighted, as recalled by Flg Off Bill Whitty:

'Bazin and myself ran into a Ju88 head-on. We got a burst in and chased him in and out of cloud banks without anything definite.'

Plt Off Jim Humphreys was more successful and shot down a Ju88 of 9/LG1, but whether this was the same machine is not known. The crew survived and were taken prisoner. The unit's final mission of the day involved Flg Off Francis Blackadder (P3448 AF-H), who was asked to fly a reconnaissance for the Army, which he successfully accomplished.
  Flg Off Whitty remembered:

'The six pilots of 607 Squadron operated with a Flight from 17 Squadron under Sqn Ldr Edwardes-Jones. I returned with them to Hawkinge in a Hurricane in which the two lower tubular struts to the tail assembly had been broken by Flak (clamps had been placed across the breaks) and was told "land with your tail up". Which I did and went on to Croydon next morning and gave the plane, plus many holes, to the civil repair depot. The rest of the Squadron arrived around noon and all but four original 607 Squadron pilots were posted away.'

Plt Off Down, Flg Off Ereminsky and Flt Sgt Higginson of 56/B Flight were ordered, at 1730, to fly the unit's three remaining Hurricanes back to RAF North Weald; Sgt Whitehead remained, as there was not an aircraft for him, and he was instructed to join the ground party, which had orders to head for Boulogne. There they boarded a departing vessel, having abandoned all their equipment, and reached Dover safely. Although some units were evacuating Norrent-Fontès, the remaining Hurricanes of 504 Squadron arrived there from Lille, followed by the ground personnel that night.

Still operating from Moorsele, 61 Wing's 615 Squadron carried out a number of mainly uneventful patrols during the day, although on one sortie Plt Off Willie McKnight's aircraft (KW-F) had its fuel tanks holed by small arms fire when over Douai. On another patrol, McKnight and others strafed troops on the Arras-Cambrai road, but it was not until 1940 that a section of four reported sighting hostile aircraft—an estimated 15 Bf109s, apparently aircraft from 9/JG26—at 10,000 feet, north-east of Tournai. Flg Off Tony Eyre (L1289 KW-V) reported:

'I was No 2 in formation of four when Blue 4 warned us over R/T of the approach of e/a. I turned 90° to starboard, then 180° when I attacked from the starboard quarter a 109 which was attacking one of our formation at about 400 feet below. I turned away and, searching for the rest, saw an aircraft, which I believe was the one I attacked, diving spirallingly [sic] with black smoke pouring from it. I then sighted another 109 below me which I dived on and attacked slightly below with a long burst. I immediately broke away since my ammunition was nearly exhausted.'

Although Eyre was credited only with two probables, it appears that he shot down Oblt Helmut Brucks, who baled out between Lille and Courtrai and was taken prisoner by British troops. However, Flg Off Dick Pexton failed to return after being seen to attack one of the Bf109s; his Hurricane (N2331) was apparently attacked by Oblt Gerhard Schöpfel and Uffz Bernard Eberz, each of whom claimed a Hurricane shot down. The Squadron learned later that Pexton had been wounded in both legs, but had been able to bale out and had come down in friendly territory.

During the day, the survivors of the 242 Squadron attachment—Plt Offs Willie McKnight, Bob Grassick and Stan Turner—flew back to RAF Kenley. Time was running short for the RAF in France, as Sqn Ldr Kayll recalled:

'On the evening of the 19th we were surprised to see a German motorcycle and sidecar driving round the aerodrome [Moorsele] and we could hear gunfire to the east. Then we were ordered to move to Merville at first light, only keeping enough ground staff to see the aircraft off. During the night (about 10 pm) a Belgian officer arrived and said that he had been ordered to blow up the aerodrome immediately. It took until about 1 am to persuade him not to do this, owing largely to the efforts of our adjutant and a few drinks. A compromise was reached in that he would dig holes and place the mines, leaving a straight take-off lane for us to use at dawn. One of the results of our frequent moves was that we had not had sufficient time to keep the starter batteries charged. Only one battery was serviceable and had to be used by all aircraft, mechanics being used to start the engines of the less experienced pilots.'

63 Wing, Air Component

At dawn two sections of 3 Squadron Hurricanes took off from Merville to patrol Lille at 20,000 feet. Sgt Ernie Ford (P2699) became separated, then sighted a Do17P of 4(F)/11 near Lille which he claimed shot down. The reconnaissance machine force-landed near Marquion, west of Cambrai, and the crew was rescued by Panzer troops. 79 Squadron was also in action early in the morning when Plt Off Don Stones (L1716) encountered a 6th Armee Hs126 of 1(H)/41, which crashed in a field near Tournai following his attack. One member of the crew was seen to emerge from the wreck and dash for cover. In fact, both pilot and observer survived and were rescued by troops of the German 18 Infantry Division. Flt Lt Widge Wight (flying RE-N of 229 Squadron) and his 213/B Flight were also up early:

'Offensive patrol Arras-Cambrai-Lille-Douai-St Quentin area. Saw nothing. Ground haze owing to smoke of burning towns to east, very thick. Got lost and came out over St Omer. All OK.'

All remained fairly quiet in 63 Wing's sector until 1530, when eight Hurricanes of 3 Squadron led by Sgt Roy Wilkinson (P3454 QO-A), together with a section of 213/B Flight, engaged 18 He111Ps of KG54 about five miles south of Lille. Five of the bombers were claimed shot down by Wilkinson (two), Sgt Basil Friendship (P3318 QO-K), Sgt Jimmy Sims (N2435) and Plt Off Joe Hobbs (P2351). Of the action, Friendship noted:

'Turned bombers back and possibly shot one down—smoke was issuing from starboard engine.'

Wilkinson reported that he opened fire with a long burst, which severed a wing of the first Heinkel he attacked; the aircraft then exploded, showering the pursuing Hurricanes with debris which caused damage to Flg Off Gordon Cleaver's 601/A Flight aircraft (L1690), who was obliged to carry out a crash-landing. Wilkinson's Hurricane was also hit by debris, as he recalled:

'I felt a great crash in the side of my aircraft, tossing me to one side.'

However, he recovered control and then spotted a straggler below, on which he carried out a diving attack, and closed to 200 yards. Having expended his ammunition, he reported the Heinkel to have crashed. Meanwhile, the 213/B Flight trio—Plt Off Harry Atkinson (P2795), Plt Off Max Sizer (P2834 AK-S) and Sgt Sam Butterfield (P2673)—pursued two Hs126s of the 6th Armee's 2(H)/41 at low level and jointly shot down Uffz Walter Ehemann's aircraft about eight miles south of Tournai; Ehemann and his observer, Lt Walter Bujalla, were killed.

The composite 111/253 Squadron took off from RAF Hawkinge at 1425 to patrol Cambrai-Le Cateau where, at 1515, a formation of Do17s was sighted at 10,000 feet. Plt Off Len Murch of 253/A Flight attacked three of the bombers and used all his ammunition, but no strikes were seen. Ten minutes later the Hurricanes encountered a large formation of up to 60 He111Ps of KG54 escorted by an estimated 30 Bf110Cs of II/ZG26, which both Flights attacked. Bf109s of I and III/JG3 were also present. Flt Lt Guy Harris (N2590) of 253/A Flight recorded:

'I opened fire [at a Heinkel] and saw white smoke coming from his starboard engine. However, at this moment someone delivered me a sharp blow in the back with a red-hot hammer. I found that my right leg did not work and that there was blood oozing through my jacket, by my right thigh.'

After flying for half an hour, he reached the coast and landed at Dieppe airfield, from where he was taken to a makeshift hospital in the casino on the seafront, where his wounds were treated. From there he was taken to St Nazaire, where he boarded a hospital ship and eventually reached Liverpool.

Meanwhile, Plt Off Freddie Ratford (L1660) was seen to shoot down a Heinkel but also failed to return; he was later reported to have been killed when his aircraft crashed near Riencourt-lès-Cagnicourt, about ten miles south-east of Arras. Two Hurricanes were claimed at this time by Lt Friedrich Freiherr von Cramon and Ofw Karl Wilfert of I/JG3 and it seems probable that they had attacked Harris and Ratford.

Sqn Ldr John Thompson, who led the seven Hurricanes of 111/A Flight, admitted later that they had not initially seen the escort when he attacked the Heinkels. On engaging one bomber—which was believed to have fallen—Thompson (L1773) was attacked from above by a Bf110C of II/ZG26 and his engine was hit, obliging him to force-land.

On his subsequent return to England, he reported:

> 'When on patrol east of Cambrai, I observed a large formation of e/a proceeding west at about 10,000 feet. I attacked one Heinkel from astern—a burst of about two seconds from about 100 yards to 50 yards. White smoke issued from both engines. At this moment my cockpit filled with white vapour and I realised my cooling system had been hit. I dived vertically to about 2,000 feet and flew west until my engine seized solid over Beauvais. I made a landing on an aerodrome under construction. My undercarriage collapsed on landing due to damage from combat. I attached myself to 70 Wing and returned to England on 20 May from Boulogne.'

Meanwhile, Plt Off David Bury (L1734) and Plt Off Iain Moorwood (L1720) were also shot down, although it seems they fell to Bf109s of III/JG3 flown by Lt Winfried Schmidt, Lt Franz Achleitner and Fw Anton Kuhn; both were killed. Bury's aircraft crashed near Gravelle, about eight miles north-east of Arras, while Moorwood crashed near Sains-lès-Marquion. Flg Off Dudley Connors (L1564) had followed the CO into the attack on the bombers and claimed three shot down, but his own aircraft suffered damage from return fire.

A Bf109 engaged Flt Lt Peter Powell (L1973) as he climbed above the bomber formation. Powell manoeuvred on to its tail and opened fire, later reporting that it had turned over on its back and dived. This may have been the aircraft of Uffz Hubert Stephan of 9/JG3, who was shot down during this engagement and baled out between Lille and Rouboix, where he was taken prisoner by British troops.

By this time Powell was down to the level of the Heinkels again and observed one with a damaged port engine—possibly one of Connors' victims—which he pursued and attacked, watching it crash as he pulled away. Although the engine of Flg Off Michael Ferriss' aircraft (L2001) was 'running rough', he became involved with a succession of Bf110s, which attacked him from ahead and port quarter. Before he managed to evade and escape, he saw his own fire hit one of the Messerschmitts. On landing, Sgt Bill Dymond reported that he had seen three aircraft falling in flames before he was engaged by six Bf109s, which he managed to evade. The survivors of the composite unit landed at Merville to refuel, from where the majority returned to England that evening.

Red Section (four Hurricanes) of 3 Squadron's A Flight, led by Flg Off Billy Clyde (including Flg Off Gray from 213/A Flight) took off at 1445, followed 15 minutes later by Blue Section, led by Flt Lt Sir Archie Hope; they were to carry out patrols in the Lille area. At 1615, the Hurricanes engaged a dozen He111Ps of KG54 at 9,000 feet near Renoix, ten miles south of Lille. Escort for the bomber Staffel was provided on this occasion by Bf109s of I/JG77. Flg Off Bill Gray (Red 2, flying R4099 AK-L) reported:

'I was ordered on patrol about 1445 with six aircraft from 3 Squadron. About 1520 our attention was attracted by AA bursts ahead of which I saw 12 enemy bombers. I attacked one of two stragglers and, after three short bursts, smoke was seen from his port engine and eventually flames. I then broke off the attack and made a second attack on another Heinkel. I fired the remainder of my ammunition and black smoke appeared. One of our aircraft took over the attack and sent it down in flames. Altogether, three Heinkels were seen to go down in flames. The Heinkels were flying in box formation except for the two stragglers. The Heinkels appeared to spray oil backwards when attacked, with a view to obscuring the attacker's windscreen.'

Plt Off Peter Gardner (Blue 2) added:

'On seeing 12 Heinkels returning from raid, we went into attack. Red Section went in first. No 2 of the enemy formation started to pour white smoke from the port engine. I went in when he had finished and port engine burst into flame. I then broke away.'

Plt Off Jack Rose (Red 3):

'I was positioned to attack the Heinkel on the port flank and closed very rapidly, firing for a few seconds up to very close range and, as I was about to break away, the Heinkel's port engine erupted oil which covered my windscreen. I throttled back, gained a little height and pulled back the cockpit hood . . . I couldn't reach far enough to wipe the front of the windscreen without releasing my seat harness . . . As I was doing a speed of somewhere between stalling and cruising, my seat harness undone, more or less standing on the rudder stirrups and half out of the aircraft, I suddenly saw tracer fly past and felt strikes on the Hurricane. I was being attacked by a 109.'

Rose's Hurricane (N2535) went into a spin and trailed glycol and petrol, although he was able to make a landing at Seclin. On inspection, it was discovered that the Hurricane's radiator had been hit by a cannon-shell and another had removed much of the starboard aileron, while the wings and fuselage were peppered by bullet strikes. Rose had been intercepted by the same I/JG77 formation that had 10 minutes earlier shot down Plt Off Woods-Scawen of 85 Squadron, and his aircraft was claimed by Oblt Karl-Gottfried Nordmann.

Shortly after 1500, Flt Lt Widge Wight (P2795) of 213/B Flight was ordered to patrol the aerodrome at 20,000 feet. He noted:

'Saw AA over Arras and went there in the sun. Saw six 109s at 15,000 feet and dived out of sun at nearest. Short burst of three to four seconds at close range and he half-rolled jerkily, dived vertically and then went into shallow dive to the south, white smoke coming out the whole time. Think I got him.'

The composite 145/601 Squadron was in action at 1510, meeting a formation of He111s—again aircraft from KG54—escorted by Bf110Cs of II/ZG26 and Bf109s of I/JG27 south-east of Cambrai. 601/B Flight claimed three of the bombers shot down, one by Flg Off The Hon Max Aitken (P3460):

'We were in the sun and dived down on them from starboard beam. We turned to carry out a stern attack. The enemy were flying in very close formation. They opened fire at about a range of 600 yards. The formation we attacked was in a vic of seven machines. The 110s attacked us but I did not see them. I attacked the left-hand machine and he immediately broke formation and flew in a shallow dive to the north. I fired one more burst and followed him down. He struck the ground and slid through a hedge. The crew of two got out and ran back into the hedge.'

Two Heinkels were claimed by Flg Off Tom Hubbard and Flg Off Hugh Riddle (whose younger brother, Christopher, was also on the Squadron); Hubbard reported:

'As No 2 of Green Section met formation of Heinkels in vic coming towards us as we were turning and approximately 4-5,000 feet below. Being the nearest to them I dived towards the nearest one, receiving a hit before opening fire, which I did at 350 yards and continued until Heinkel had smoke and flames coming from both engines. At this point my own cockpit filled with smoke, so I knew my aircraft was damaged and I made a force-landing with flaps and undercarriage down at Noyelles, south of Arras. On learning from a major of the Durham Light Infantry that facilities were not available for repair, I returned to my aircraft [P2684] and fired it.'

A Bf109 pilot of 1/JG27, Lt Igor Zirkenbach, claimed a Hurricane in this location and may have been responsible for the damage to Hubbard's aircraft. Flg Off Lee-Steere (L2057) was credited with a probable:

'Turned to starboard to carry out a stern attack on right-hand machine of a formation of three He111s which then broke away and dived in a right-hand turn at about 320 mph. It was apparently not badly damaged and I followed it down to 4,000 feet, giving further bursts of about five seconds which set the starboard engine alight. This e/a was seen going down over Hamel—I was then unable to see the e/a.'

Flg Off Willie Rhodes-Moorhouse (L2088) was frustrated in his attack on the bombers:

'When just within range I opened fire on the starboard side of the formation, when I saw four or five Messerschmitt 110s approaching from the right and ahead; so I turned towards them and I passed through their formation, firing all the time. When my reserve petrol tank was shot and the cockpit filled with petrol, I then dived vertically and landed.'

Two more bombers were claimed by Flt Lt Roy Dutton (N3314) and Plt Off Ernest Wakeham (N2711 SO-D) of 145/A Flight, while Sqn Ldr J.D. Miller (N2713) claimed a probable. Wakeham reported:

'When flying No 2 of Red Section I sighted sections of He111s and Do215s [sic] flying west. I was detailed to attack formation of He111s and did a No 1 Attack on outside Heinkel of section, but broke away on closing and being hit. On returning to attack again I noticed it was diving to ground level. I followed it to the ground, delivering two more attacks and saw it finally force-land in a field near Arras. On circling I saw the pilot get out and some soldiers approached.'

Wakeham's aircraft had been hit by return fire during the engagement and it was found that a bullet had penetrated the air pipeline, which had prevented his four port guns from firing. Plt Off Alan Elson (N2723) attacked the same Heinkel as Flt Lt Dutton, then saw another, trailing smoke, on his starboard side:

'Before I got to extreme close range, I was forced to break away owing to my windscreen being splintered by a bullet.'

Elson's Hurricane was also hit in the fuselage and one bullet pierced a propeller blade, although he was able to land safely. Immediately following the action with the bombers, Flg Off Aitken of 601/B Flight sighted a small formation of Ju87s from II/StG2, which he attacked:

'I saw a Ju87 flying east at 100 feet dodging over the fields and followed him. He did not seem to have a rear gunner and had not seen me. I closed right on his tail and used the rest of my ammunition. His tailplane and elevator fell off and he hit the ground. There was only little left of the plane. My aircraft was hit in the spinner.'

These successes were not achieved without loss, however; apart from Flg Off Tom Hubbard's aircraft, 601/B Flight lost a second when Flg Off Hugh Riddle crash-landed L2081 between Arras and Cambrai. In addition, 145/A Flight suffered the loss of Plt Off Kenneth Lucas, who was killed when his aircraft (N2598) crashed near Warloy-Baillon, about five miles west of Albert, and was almost certainly the victim of Oblt Gerhard Homuth of 3/JG27.

A section of 213/B Flight was ordered to patrol Oudenaarde at 1730, as reported by Flt Lt Widge Wight (P2795):

'E/a [Hs126] was sighted at 4,000 feet. On delivering attacks, the e/a dived steeply to ground level and I then returned to 2,000 feet to have a look around. I then returned to the attack and delivered two astern, one quarter and one beam attack and the e/a's engine stopped and the pilot at once began to land. One other aircraft dived and fired after this. The e/a crashed on landing.'

Wight's companions were Plt Off Max Sizer (P2673) and Plt Off Harry Atkinson, both of whom fired at the Henschel, another machine of 2(H)/41; Uffz Gerhard Meermann's 6th Armee aircraft crashed west of Aalst, where the pilot and his wounded observer, Fw Herbert Carl, were rescued by German troops.

Before darkness curtailed further operational flying from Merville, both Plt Off Charles Jeffries (L1670) and Sgt Basil Friendship (L1990) of 3 Squadron were instructed to deliver messages, the latter flying to Abbeville and back. From Abbeville during the day Plt Offs Denis Crowley-Milling and Roy Bush—newly arrived pilots attached to 615 Squadron's B Flight—had attempted to engage a formation of Do17s sighted near the airfield, but their Gladiators lacked the necessary performance to catch the bombers.

Following the previous day's attack by Heinkels on Amiens/Glisy aerodrome, the Station Commander instructed crews of 3 (Continental) Ferry Flight, who had ferried Blenheims from England, to help with the evacuation. As there no longer existed any means of communication with Glisy, a Lysander of 26 Squadron was dispatched at first light to reconnoitre the area, but this was shot down by a Bf109 of I/JG27 as it returned to the airfield. Keen on retribution, several of the Blenheim pilots requested permission to take off in Hurricanes, but were refused on the grounds that they were not operationally trained to fly fighter aircraft!

The Heinkels of all three Gruppen of KG54 had been heavily committed to the battle during the afternoon, and had suffered accordingly at the hands of pilots from the various Hurricane units:

He111P of Geschwader-Fuhrungskette/KG54 shot down and crashed north-east of Tournai: four members of crew killed, although Geschwaderkommodore Obst Karl Lackner and Geschwader Adjutant Oblt Heinrich Howe, who were on board as observers, baled out; both were wounded and PoW of the French and British respectively.

He111P of Stabsstaffel/KG54 flown by Uffz Hugo Senft shot down and crashed four miles north-east of Tournai: two killed, one PoW of the British, two PoW of the French including the Staffelkapitän, Maj Josef Segschneider.

He111P of Stabsstaffel/KG54 flown by Uffz Rudolf Wirthwein shot down and crashed near Tournai: one killed in the air, two killed in the crash and wounded pilot rescued by German troops.

He111P of 1/KG54 flown by Lt d.Res. Alfred Priebe shot down and crash-landed near Cambrai: one killed in the air, two PoW of the British, one PoW of the French.

He111P of 3/KG54 flown by Lt d.Res. Klaus Brückhändler shot down west of Lille and exploded in the air: crew killed.

He111P of 3/KG54 flown by Lt d.Res. Horst Frieke shot down and crash-landed south of Lille: one killed in the air, others PoW of the French (but soon released by German troops).

He111P of 3/KG54 flown by Staffelkapitän Hptm Hans Widmann 25% damaged in combat and force-landed on return: one mortally wounded.

He111P of 4/KG54 flown by Uffz Ernst Baum shot down and crashed near La Capelle: crew killed.

He111P of 4/KG54 flown by Uffz Wilhelm Czech shot down and crash-landed near Lille: one killed in the air, one killed on the ground, one PoW of the French, one rescued by troops of 6 Pz Division.

He111P of 4/KG54 flown by Uffz Kurt Westerhold shot down and crash-landed south of Lille: one killed in the air, two PoW of the British, one rescued by troops of 6 Pz Division.

He111P of 4/KG54 flown by Lt Franz Gottschling shot down and crashed south of Lille: two killed in the air, one PoW of the British, one PoW of the French.

He111P of 6/KG54 flown by Uffz Alfred Isselhorst shot down and crashed south of Lille: pilot baled out and PoW of the British, others killed.

He111P of 7/KG54 flown by Lt Fritz von Berlepsch shot down and crashed between Tournai and Lille: crew baled out and PoW of the French.

He111P of 8/KG54 flown by Lt Gottfried Mehlhorn shot down and crashed near Tirlemont: crew survived and returned.

The loss of of so many aircraft and their crews was a severe blow to KG54, but losses the all-powerful Luftwaffe could afford at this stage to achieve its aim.

Summary

Although AASF and Air Component Hurricane pilots claimed nearly 100 victories—74 'confirmed' (including 34 He111s and 21 Bf109s) plus 25 probables—during the day's fierce fighting no fewer than 22 Hurricanes were shot down and at least 13 more force-landed, with the loss of eight pilots killed, seven wounded and three taken prisoner. At least 24 of the 35 Hurricanes lost fell to Bf109s but, in return, Hurricane pilots accounted for 14 of their main adversaries—a better exchange rate than of late. 60 Wing's Hurricane pilots had engaged in almost constant defence of their airfields and Lille town during the day and claimed a total of 15 Bf109s shot down, with a further six probables, plus seven He111s, five Do17s and a Hs126.

Claims by AASF and Air Component Hurricanes, 19 May				
Type	Confirmed	Probable	Damaged	Total
He111	34	7	6	47
Do17	10	—	1	11
Ju88	2	—	—	2
Ju87	1	—	—	1
Hs126	4	—	1	5
Bf109	21	18	4	43
Bf110	2	—	1	3
	74	25	13	112

Luftwaffe Losses Attributed to AASF and Air Component Hurricanes, 19 May			
Type	60% to 100%	Under 60%	Total
He111	20	2	22
Do17	4	4	8

Ju88	4	1	5
Ju87	—	1	1
Hs126	4	—	4
Bf109	14	1	15
Bf110	1	—	1
	47	9	56

Two Blenheim IFs of 604 Squadron, using RAF Manston as an advance airfield, operated over France that night. One crew claimed damage to an unidentified aircraft as it was about to land at Merville. However, following a five second burst, the aircraft was lost from sight. The other Blenheim reported an attack on another aircraft which had its landing lights on, but this was also lost from sight after one burst of fire.

Bomber Command dispatched Wellingtons to attack targets in Northern France and Belgium: four operated against Givet and 11 dropped incendiaries on the forests around Fumay and Bouillon, with the object of firing fuel and ammunition dumps, although results were not observed. The crews of the latter aircraft were briefed to use their HE bombs against bridges over the Brussels-Charleroi Canal, which were also attacked by other Wellingtons. Finally four more aircraft attacked railways and roads near Gembloux. All Wellingtons returned. Meanwhile, a dozen Whitleys raided the synthetic oil plant at Gelsenkirchen and 36 Hampdens similarly visited the oil refinery at Salzbergen. Two of the former failed to return.

Individual Claims—AASF and Air Component Hurricanes, 19 May

0525-	Flg Off E.J. Kain	73 Sqn	Do17
	Flg Off H.G. Paul	73 Sqn	Do17
0530-	Sgt E.G. Ford	3 Sqn	Do17
0530-	Plt Off D.W.A. Stones	79 Sqn	Hs126
0530-	Flg Off R.L. Glyde		
	Plt Off J.R. Cock		
	Flg Off D.H. Ward	87 Sqn	Hs126
	Flg Off J.H.L. Allen		
0600-	Flg Off Count M.B. Czernin	85 Sqn	2 Do17
1000-	Plt Off A.G. Lewis	85 Sqn	2 Bf109
	Flg Off J. Jeffries	85 Sqn	Bf109 probable
	Plt Off P.P. Woods-Scawen	85 Sqn	2 Bf109
1000-	Flg Off M.E.A. Royce	504 Sqn	Bf109
	Plt Off J.R. Hardacre	504 Sqn	Bf109 probable
1000-	Flt Lt I.R. Gleed		
	Flg Off D.H. Ward	87 Sqn	Bf109 probable
	Flg Off R.L. Glyde		
	Flg Off R.M.S. Rayner	87 Sqn	Bf109
	Plt Off H.J.R. Dunn	87 Sqn	Bf109
	Flt Sgt I.J. Badger	87 Sqn	Bf109, Bf109 probable
1100-	Flg Off P.H.M. Richey	1 Sqn	3 He111
	Flg Off M.H. Brown	1 Sqn	He111, He111 probable

	Flg Off P.W.O. Mould	} 1 Sqn	He111
	Flg Off C.D. Palmer		
	Flt Lt P.R. Walker	1 Sqn	He111 probable
	Plt Off R.G. Lewis	1 Sqn	He111 probable
	Flg Off W.H. Stratton	1 Sqn	He111 damaged
	Flg Off J.I. Kilmartin	1 Sqn	He111 damaged
	Plt Off C.M. Stavert	1 Sqn	He111 damaged
	Sgt F.J. Soper	1 Sqn	He111 damaged
1100-	Flt Lt J.E. Scoular	73 Sqn	He111
	Flt Lt J.E. Scoular	} 73 Sqn	He111
	Sgt A.E. Marshall		
	Flg Off E.J. Kain	73 Sqn	Ju88, Bf110
	Flg Off H.G. Paul	73 Sqn	He111
	Sgt L.S. Pilkington	73 Sqn	He111 probable
	Plt Off J.E.P. Thompson	73 Sqn	Do17 damaged
1130-	Sgt R.C. Wilkinson	3 Sqn	2 He111
	Sgt A.H.B. Friendship	3 Sqn	He111
	Sgt J.A. Sims	3 Sqn	He111
	Plt Off J.B. Hobbs	3 Sqn	He111
1130-	Plt Off H.D. Atkinson		
	Plt Off W.M. Sizer	} 213/B Flt	Hs126,
	Sgt S.L. Butterfield		Hs126 damaged
1200-	Plt Off A.G. Lewis	85 Sqn	3 Bf109
	Sgt J.McG. Little	85 Sqn	2 He111
	Sgt L. Jowitt	85 Sqn	He111
	Plt Off A.H. Deacon	242/A Flt	He111
1200-	Flt Lt I.R. Gleed	} 87 Sqn	He111
	Flg Off R.M.S. Rayner		
	Plt Off H.J.R. Dunn	87 Sqn	Bf109
1200-	Sgt J.W. White	32 Sqn	Do17
	Flt Lt M.N. Crossley	32 Sqn	Bf109 probable
	Flt Lt P.M. Brothers	32 Sqn	Bf109 probable
	Plt Off D.H. Grice	32 Sqn	Bf109, Bf109 damaged
	Plt Off J.L. Flinders	32 Sqn	Bf109
	Sgt G. Turner	32 Sqn	Bf109 probable
	Sgt G. North	32 Sqn	Bf109 probable
	Plt Off A.F. Eckford	32 Sqn	Bf109 damaged
	Plt Off V.G. Daw	32 Sqn	Bf110
1230-	Flt Lt I.R. Gleed	87 Sqn	Do17
1500-	Flt Lt I.R. Gleed	87 Sqn	Do17, Bf109 damaged
	Flg Off R.M.S. Rayner	87 Sqn	Do17
	Flg Off R.L. Glyde	87 Sqn	Bf109
1500-	Flt Lt R.D.G. Wight	213/B Flt	Bf109 probable
1510-	Flt Lt R.G. Dutton	145/A Flt	He111
	Plt Off E.J.C. Wakeham	145/A Flt	He111
	Sqn Ldr J.D. Miller	145/A Flt	He111 probable
1510-	Flt Lt The Hon J.W.M. Aitken	601/B Flt	He111, Ju87
	Flg Off T.E. Hubbard	601/B Flt	He111
	Flg Off H.J. Riddle	601/B Flt	He111
	Flg Off C. Lee-Steere	601/B Flt	He111 probable
1515-	Flg Off S.D.P. Connors	111/A Flt	2 He111
	Flt Lt R.P.R. Powell	} 111/A Flt	He111
	Flg Off S.D.P. Connors		

	Sqn Ldr J.M. Thompson	111/A Flt	He111 probable
	Flt Lt R.P.R. Powell	111/A Flt	Bf109 probable
	Flg Off H.M. Ferriss	111/A Flt	Bf110 damaged
	Flt Lt G. Harris	253/A Flt	He111 damaged
	Plt Off F.W. Ratford	253/A Flt	He111
1530-	Plt Off L.G.B. Stone	213/A Flt	Bf109
1530-	Plt Off J.K.G. Clifton	253/B Flt	Bf109 damaged
	Plt Off J.P.D. Greenwood	253/B Flt	Bf109 probable
1550-	Plt Off P.P. Woods-Scawen	85 Sqn	Bf109
1610-	Plt Off P.P. Woods-Scawen	85 Sqn	Bf109 probable
1615-	Flg Off W.N. Gray	213/A Flt	He111
	Flg Off W.N. Gray	213/A Flt	He111
	Plt Off P.M. Gardner	3 Sqn	
	Flg Off W.P. Clyde	601/A Flt	He111
	Plt Off J. Rose	3 Sqn	He111
	Plt Off J.B. Hobbs	3 Sqn	He111
1620-	Plt Off R.C. Whittaker	17 Sqn	Do17
	Flt Lt W.A. Toyne	17 Sqn	2 Bf109
	Sgt G.A. Steward	17 Sqn	Bf109
	Sqn Ldr J.H. Edwardes-Jones	17 Sqn	Bf109 damaged
	Flg Off C.F.G. Adye	17 Sqn	Bf109 probable
	Plt Off H.A.C. Bird-Wilson	17 Sqn	Bf109 probable
1620-	Sgt L.J. Ralls	607 Sqn	Bf109
1630-	Sqn Ldr M.F. Peacock	85 Sqn	He111
	Flg Off M.B. Czernin	85 Sqn	He111, He111 damaged
1730-	Flt Lt R.D.G. Wight		
	Plt Off W.M. Sizer	213/B Flt	Hs126
	Plt Off H.D. Atkinson		
1940-	Flg Off A. Eyre	615 Sqn	2 Bf109 probables
PM	Plt Off J.S. Humphreys	607 Sqn	Ju88

Losses—AASF and Air Component Hurricanes, 19 May

1000-	P3555	504 Sqn	Plt Off J.R. Hardacre: shot down near Lille by Bf109 of 2(J)/LG2; pilot baled out.
	P3551	504 Sqn	Sqn Ldr J.H. Hill: shot down near Lille by Bf109 of 2(J)/LG2; pilot wounded, baled out.
1000-	P2687	87 Sqn	Flg Off J.M. Strickland: shot down near Lille by Bf109 of 2(J)/LG2; pilot wounded, baled out.
1030-	L1674	253/B Flt	Flt Lt H.T. Anderson: shot down near Lille by Bf109 of I/JG3; pilot killed.
	L1667	253/B Flt	Sgt G. Mackenzie: shot down near Lille by Bf109 of I/JG3; pilot killed.
1100-	P2805	1 Sqn	Flg Off P.H.M. Richey: shot down near Château-Thierry by return fire from He111P of III/KG27 and crash-landed; pilot wounded.
	L1925	1 Sqn	Sgt F.J. Soper: aircraft damaged by return fire from He111P of III/KG27 and force-landed near Château-de-Pricory; pilot slightly hurt.
1100-	N2385	73 Sqn	Plt Off J.E.P. Thompson: shot down by Bf110C of V(Z)/LG1 and crash-landed south-east of Paris; pilot unhurt.
	P2543	73 Sqn	Plt Off N.C. Langham-Hobart: shot down by Bf110C of V(Z)/LG1 and crash-landed; pilot unhurt.

	P2539	73 Sqn	Sgt L.S. Pilkington: aircraft damaged by return fire from 'He111' (probably Ju88 of KG51) and force-landed at base; pilot unhurt.
1130-	P2800	601/A Flt	Flg Off G.N.S. Cleaver: aircraft damaged by debris from He111P of KG54 and force-landed south of Lille; pilot unhurt.
1200-	L1620	87 Sqn	Plt Off H.J.L. Dunn: shot down near Orchies by Bf109 of II/JG2; pilot wounded, baled out.
	P2829	87 Sqn	Flg Off R.F. Watson: aircraft damaged by Bf109 of II/JG2 and force-landed; pilot unhurt.
1200-	P2562	85 Sqn	Sgt J.McG. Little: shot down near Lille by Bf109 of 1/JG2; pilot killed.
1200-	P2808	242/A Flt	Flt Lt D.R. Miller: aircraft damaged near Lille by Bf109 of 1/JG2 and force-landed at base; pilot unhurt.
1200-	N2355	504 Sqn	Sgt M.V. Mapletoft: shot down west of Lille by Bf109 of 1/JG2; pilot wounded, baled out.
1200-	N2462	32 Sqn	Flg Off J.C. Milner: shot down between Cambrai-Le Cateau by Bf109 of 1/JG2; pilot baled out, PoW.
1500-	P2683	87 Sqn	Flg Off R.M.S. Rayner: aircraft damaged near Tournai by Bf109 of 1/JG77 and force-landed at Lille/Marcq; pilot unhurt.
1510-	L2081	601/B Flt	Flg Off H.J. Riddle: shot down between Arras and Cambrai by Bf110C of II/ZG26 and crash-landed; pilot unhurt, returned.
	P2684	601/B Flt	Flg Off T.E. Hubbard: shot down between Arras and Cambrai by Bf109 of 1/JG27 and crash-landed at Noyelles; pilot unhurt, returned.
		601/B Flt	Flg Off W.H. Rhodes-Moorhouse: aircraft damaged between Arras and Cambrai by Bf110C of II/ZG26; pilot unhurt.
1510-	N2598	145/A Flt	Plt Off K.R. Lucas: shot down by Bf109 of 3/JG27 and crashed near Warloy-Baillon; pilot killed.
1515-	N2590	253/A Flt	Flt Lt G. Harris: aircraft damaged by Bf109 of I/JG3 and force-landed at Dieppe; pilot wounded.
	N2542	253/A Flt	Plt Off F.W. Ratford: shot down south of Arras by Bf109 of I/JG3; pilot killed.
1515-	L1774	111/A Flt	Plt Off D.S.H. Bury: shot down north-east of Arras by Bf109 of III/JG3; pilot killed.
	L1720	111/A Flt	Plt Off I.C. Moorwood shot down south-east of Arras by Bf109 of III/JG3; pilot killed.
	L1733	111/A Flt	Sqn Ldr J.M. Thompson: aircraft damaged by Bf110C of II/ZG26 and crash-landed near Doullens; pilot returned.
1530-	N2538	213/A Flt	Plt Off L.G.B. Stone: aircraft damaged by French AA fire and force-landed south of Lille; pilot unhurt.
1610-	P2547	85 Sqn	Plt Off P.P. Woods-Scawen: shot down near Lille by Bf109 of 2/JG77; pilot baled out, returned.
1615-	N2535	3 Sqn	Plt Off J. Rose: aircraft damaged by Bf109 of I/JG77 and force-landed at Seclin; pilot unhurt.
1620-	N2408	17 Sqn	Plt Off R.E. Harris: shot down near Le Cateau by Bf109 of I(J)/LG2; pilot killed.

	N2525	17 Sqn	Sgt C.W.J. Pavey: shot down near Le Cateau by Bf109 of I(J)/LG2; pilot baled out, PoW.
1620-	P3535	607 Sqn	Sqn Ldr G.M. Fidler: shot down south-west of Tournai by Bf109 of I(J)/LG2; pilot baled out, PoW.
1630-	P2551	85 Sqn	Sqn Ldr M.F. Peacock: shot down near Seclin by return fire from He111P of 6/KG4; pilot baled out, returned.
1940-	N2331	615 Sqn	Flg Off R.D. Pexton: shot down between Arras and Cambrai by Bf109s of 9/JG26; pilot wounded, baled out.

CHAPTER XII

MONDAY 20 MAY
THE WRITING ON THE WALL

'We found a large quantity of German transport on this perfectly straight road and were able to do some damage. Unfortunately we lost three aircraft.'

Sqn Ldr Joe Kayll, 615 Squadron.

The Situation on the Northern Front

The Military summary revealed the dire predicament now facing the Allies:

'The Allied forces north of the German penetration were, with the enemy advance towards the coast, becoming increasingly cut off from any contact with those in the south. The situation obviously demanded Allied action to "close the gap", either by the northern armies fighting their way south, or by the southern armies fighting their way north, or by both simultaneously.'

Cambrai had fallen and Amiens was about to follow.

With the departure for England of the remaining Blenheims and three of the Lysander squadrons, tactical reconnaissance sorties on the flank of the BEF were carried out in the morning by five Air Component Hurricanes:

'At 0830 they reported a continuous column of enemy mechanised transport on the Cambrai-Arras road, with the head halted at Marquion, where the Canal du Nord had to be crossed. Another column was approaching the Canal at Sains, a mile or two south of Marquion. Extensive fires were reported in Le Cateau, Cambrai, Douai and Arras.'

67 Wing, AASF

73 Squadron at Gaye was called upon to fly just one defensive patrol during the day, but the three bombers reported in the vicinity of the aerodrome were driven off by AA fire.

Similarly, 501 Squadron at Anglure was not called into action; neither was 1 Squadron. With most of his original pilots suffering fatigue and exhaustion, the latter unit's Sqn Ldr Halahan requested they be sent back to England forthwith. To his surprise, the Air Ministry agreed and, within hours, Flt Lts Walker and Hanks, Flg Offs Kilmartin, Stratton, Palmer and Mould, Plt Off Lewis and Sgt Soper were on their way home, while Halahan himself was advised of imminent replacement. Three new pilots arrived for the Squadron that very day, including Flt Lt F.E. Warcup and Flg Off D.S. Thom, the latter from 43 Squadron.

60/63 Wing, Air Component, Merville

With the arrival of 85 and 87 Squadrons at Merville, there were about 50 Hurricanes dispersed around the airfield—far too many for the ill-equipped and under-staffed Operations Room, under the command of Sqn Ldr Jack Satchell, to handle. Satchell had been CO of 234 Squadron on its formation in 1939, but had been badly injured in a car crash, and by the time he had recovered his command had gone to another. When he reported back for duty, he was just in time to draw the short straw for the job of fighter controller in France, based at Merville. The timing could not have been worse: the German attack had just commenced. Satchell himself admitted that he had very little idea of the duties involved and this lack of proper training for the job, plus the primitive equipment available at Merville, made ground control of the fighters virtually impossible.

The control centre was the former flying club hut; the half dozen or so telephones linking control to the forward observation posts all had exactly the same ring, which added a touch of farce to the proceedings as the airmen struggled to find the right telephone to answer! It is little wonder that attempts to control the Hurricane units were doomed to total failure, since any orders passed to the fighters were usually at least 30 minutes old. Added to this, both pilots and controller had only the most rudimentary local geographic knowledge. Thus, interceptions were in the main achieved through pure chance, and usually meant that the Hurricanes were at great tactical disadvantage.

All four squadrons at Merville put up dawn patrols. First off, at 0415, was a section of 3 Squadron, led by Sgt Roy Wilkinson (P3454), who recalled:

> 'We ran into a couple of stray He111s just over Lille. The battle was on. We attacked, approaching from different heights and out of the sun.'

During the ensuing battle with the bombers—aircraft of I/LG1—Plt Off Joe Hobbs (N2434), Sgt Jimmy Sims (P3318) and Sgt Basil Friendship (N2351) exhausted all their ammunition, by which time the German gunners had either used up all theirs or had been killed. Wilkinson rejoined the section after the mêlée, then carried out another attack on one of the damaged bombers:

> 'I had some ammunition left and closed to about 100 yards and let a burst go, killing the pilot; the aircraft half-rolled, then crashed. I then caught up with the other Heinkel that was not returning any fire but was still staggering about the sky. As I closed in I let go with a short burst. The engine on the port side caught fire, then the aircraft nosed forward. No one was seen to leave the aircraft. It hit the deck, exploding in a fireball on impact.'

Uffz Max Böge and a member of his crew managed to bale out before their 2 Staffel machine crashed, but the other two crew members were killed. As he was returning to Merville, Wilkinson sighted a low-flying Hs126 of 3(H)/14 near Renaix:

> 'Sighted Hs126 at 5,000 feet. He immediately dived to ground level and zig-zagged in and out of trees. Fired all rounds off at him. Silenced rear gunner but apparently e/a got away.'

The Henschel, which had been spotting for 7 Pz Division, was damaged but was able to return to its base safely.

Five Hurricanes of 213/B Flight joined forces with three of 79 Squadron to fly a river protection patrol in the Oudenaarde-Tournai area, leaving Merville at 0555. Flt Lt Widge Wight (P2795), who led the patrol, reported:

> 'AA bursts over Courtrai at 10,000 feet and saw Do17 at that height. Attacked and he flew up sun. Opened on his port engine—white smoke and oil at once, so fired at starboard engine: white smoke. Closed and finished with long burst at fuselage. Bits flying off. Atkinson (No 2) said riddled with holes when he closed. E/a was seen to crash by other pilots later, about 20 miles east. My aircraft covered in oil.'

Both Plt Off Harry Atkinson (P2673) and Plt Off Max Sizer (P2802) attacked the Dornier, as did Sgt Alf Whitby (P2698) of the 79 Squadron section, as his report suggested:

> 'Do215 observed slightly ahead of AA bursts. The leader attacked

and the e/a turned east. I went across the turn and fired a burst into the e/a, turning him north again. He again turned east and I expended the remainder of my ammunition into machine to head him off again.'

Sgt Whitby was correct in his identification on this occasion, as the aircraft attacked was a Do215B of 3(F)/ObdL, which crashed near Tournai; the pilot, Uffz Erich Luther, and one other were able to bale out before the Dornier crashed, but three others were killed. Two Hurricanes of 3 Squadron were sent off early to reconnoitre the German advance and both encountered Do17 reconnaissance aircraft; Flg Off Guy Branch (P2699/D), of the attached 601/A Flight, reported:

'Returning from recce north of Arras, saw Dornier flying east into the sun, direction of Douai. Climbed after him. Made one attack from port beam to avoid effect of sun but did not allow enough deflection; the sunshade was too dark due, perhaps, to oil on windscreen. Returned to No 1 Attack, opened fire at 300 yards, closed to 150 yards. Dornier's port motor gave out black smoke and he swung to the left, losing height. One bullet struck my windscreen and petrol and glycol entered cockpit (hood was open). I continued firing until blinded, then pulled away to port and climbed up with whitish vapour streaming back on either side from engine; smothered with petrol or glycol inside cockpit. After about ten seconds the engine gave up the ghost—I could not see any instruments so do not know precise cause. I then jumped and landed at Izel. Soldiers on the ground said the plane came down in flames but I saw none up to the time of jumping—only vapours and liquid. I think it quite possible the Dornier got away on one engine.'

The reconnaissance Do17P of 3(F)/10 was severely damaged and, when over occupied territory, the crew baled out. Meanwhile his colleague, Plt Off Mike Stephens (P3449) was equally successful in his engagement with another Dornier:

'I was detailed to make a recce of area Arras-Douai-Cambrai-Bapaume. [At 0505] when north of Cambrai, flying at 3,000 feet, I sighted a Do17 and pursued it. When I was at about 400 yards the e/a opened fire. At 200 yards I opened fire and the e/a dived steeply to the ground. I pursued him and observed him crash and burst into flames. The crash occurred about six miles south-east of Cambrai.'

Uffz Karl Beyer and his crew from 5(F)/122 perished in the crash.
Later, two further reconnaissance sorties were undertaken by Plt Off

Charles Jeffries and Plt Off Mike Stephens (his second of the morning) and their reports confirmed the German advance along the Arras road. At 0720, in response to these reports, 3 Squadron dispatched six Hurricanes to carry out strafing attacks on the convoy, then five miles south of Arras. Sgt Roy Wilkinson (P3454), leading the Flight, recalled:

'Sighted convoy moving towards Arras. Attacked and strafed rows of lorries and troops. When attack was broken off, four petrol lorries and two ammunition lorries were burning fiercely. Many other transport presumed damaged by machine-gun fire.'

Sgt Basil Friendship (N2351) added:

'Ground strafing advancing enemy mechanised column (two miles long) south of Arras.'

Plt Off Mike Stephens (P3449) had been delayed in getting away:

'I followed the remainder of the Squadron to Arras at about half hour interval. Over the Arras-Cambrai road I saw a Henschel 126 which I attacked with no certain result other than that the air gunner was put u/s.'

The Henschel from 3(H)/41 (operating on behalf of 8 Pz Division) was in fact severely damaged and the observer/gunner, Lt von Reden, killed, although the wounded pilot, Lt Boehm, reached German territory before he force-landed his aircraft. Stephens continued:

'I then saw a mechanized column proceeding towards Arras and attacked this from about 150 feet. The tracer showed that the column of lorries was definitely being hit but no explosions or fires were apparently caused.'

Flg Off Count Manfred Czernin of 85 Squadron gained a further success during an early morning patrol, as his report revealed:

'I was ordered to patrol a sector about 12 miles south-east of Arras with my Flight, but as my engine would not start, the Flight took off without me. When finally I got off I tried to catch up with my Flight, but I did not see them again. South of Arras I perceived a Henschel 126 at about 400 feet. I did a No 1 Attack which seemed to have no effect, but he dived down to about 20 feet. I followed him and got in a long beam attack, after which he crashed down in a field. The pilot and observer got out, seemingly unhurt and ran across the field. I turned and got in one burst on them and both went down.'

Despite Czernin's efforts to kill the crew of the Henschel of 3(H)/14, both survived and were able to return to their unit, part of 7 Pz Division. The early morning activity continued when Plt Off Peter Comely of A Flight 87 Squadron sighted several Ju88s between Douai and Arras. He attacked one which dived to the ground and was seen to crash in flames. Two hours later Comely enjoyed a second success, again shooting down a Ju88:

'Patrolling Lille-Courtrai saw AA firing at Ju88—dived from 10,000 feet to attack 88 which was at 6,000 feet approximately. Caught enemy at 2,000 feet and fired short burst at 300 yards. Closed in to 200 yards and fired a long burst at 50 feet—port engine set on fire and black smoke from starboard engine. Enemy crashed in field four miles south-east of Roubaix, breaking fuselage in half.'

Another Junkers was engaged by Flt Lt Ian Gleed and Plt Off Ken Tait, one of six bombers sighted flying at 12,000 feet near Arras; Gleed wrote:

'Attacked Ju88 in company with Plt Off Tait—carried out No 1 Attack. E/a dived away from us to ground level. We pulled emergency boost control and gradually caught up. We both fired all our ammunition in about four bursts. The aircraft crashed, appearing to hit high-tension cables, and blew up approximately ten miles south-east of Valenciennes.'

Plt Off Tait engaged two more of the bombers and fired his remaining ammunition, claiming hits on both. Meanwhile, Flg Off Roddy Rayner attacked two escorting Bf110Cs of I/ZG26 and claimed one shot down and the other damaged.

One of 85 Squadron's replacement pilots, Sgt Harry Howes, was to achieve even greater success when he attacked a formation of Do17Zs from I/KG3 (escorted by Bf110Cs of I/ZG2) approaching Abbeville:

'Took off from Merville at appoximately 0900 led by Flg Off Stephenson, forming a rear section of B Flight. At 0910 both sections were approaching Arras. At 0915 Flg Off Stephenson broke away from B Flight and headed approximately north-west after e/a [Do17s] heading for coast. We followed e/a for a short while until the wave turned south. Flg Off Stephenson went into attack. I was about to follow when a Messerschmitt 110 attacked me from the rear. I avoided the attack then observed more 110s above me. During this period, 11 of the e/a had broken away from wave and were heading towards Abbeville. I had extra height than e/a, so made a quarter rear attack on the port flank, sending one e/a down in flames. I made another attack from almost above the leader of the e/a on the port flank. He crashed into the ground and burst into flames.

The Messerschmitts were making things really hot for me by this time so I flew into close range (approximately 150 yards) of the rear e/a, firing into the whole wave as they came into my sights. My aircraft [P2555] was badly hit during this attack and commenced to dive. I gained control at 10,000 feet and saw three e/a going down, apparently very much out of control, thick smoke coming from two of them. The other e/a had turned away from Abbeville. I glided east and force-landed at Abbeville (aircraft definitely u/s).'

Only one Dornier, an aircraft of 3 Staffel, suffered damage during the attack and a crew member was wounded. However, a Messerschmitt of Stab I/ZG2 flown by the Staffelkapitän, Oblt Fritz Lüders, was shot down and crashed near Neufchâteau; both Lüders and his gunner, Uffz Leonhard Baron, were killed in the crash.

Green Section of 79 Squadron took off from Merville at 1015, meeting a 9 Pz Division Hs126 of 3(H)/12Pz near Arras. This was shot down, all three pilots sharing in its demise, as Plt Off Don Stones (P3462) recorded:

'I was leading Green Section when Green 3 called up and we attacked e/a at 3,000 feet. He dived to about 200 feet and several more Hurricanes arrived and attacked. I made six or seven attacks and saw e/a crash into a field.'

Sgt Len Pearce (Green 3) added:

'On sighting e/a on starboard beam, I told leader and turned right. Opened fire at 400 yards, full deflection and e/a dived to ground. I broke upwards to attack and saw leader and No 2 [Sgt Harry Cartwright] following e/a down to attack. Followed Green 1 and 2 in successive attacks until e/a force-landed in a field and one man was seen to run from it. Lost sight of Green 1 and 2. When at 12,000 feet saw four aircraft. Flew sunwards, identified them as 109s and dived. They were circling and I found one straggling behind. I had just pulled tracer on to target when guns ceased firing—ammunition expended.'

A second Henschel was shot down at 1020 by five pilots of 213/B Flight, led by Flt Lt Widge Wight (P2795), who noted:

'Patrol Arras at 10,000 feet. Saw Henschel 126 at 2,000 feet so dived. After scrap, forced him to land (near Neuville). Crew ran for haystack, which Sizer [Plt Off Max Sizer, P2673] shot up. We shot up aircraft. One bullet from ground through wing root.'

The other three pilots who participated in shooting down the Henschel —a machine from 2(H)/23Pz spotting for 1 Pz Division—were Plt Off Harry Atkinson (L1803), Sgt Sam Butterfield (P2834) and Flg Off Bill Gray (R4099 AK-L), the latter attached from A Flight.

Nine Hurricanes of 151 Squadron were joined by others from 17 and 56 Squadrons to escort Blenheims of 21 and 107 Squadrons from RAF Watton and RAF Wattisham respectively, which were to bomb Marquion on the Courtrai-Arras road at about 1030. No hostile aircraft were encountered, and although several Blenheims were damaged by AA fire all managed to return to their East Anglian bases. Merville-based Hurricanes were also ordered to strafe the Arras road at 1045, as Flg Off Billy Clyde (N2453) reported:

'I was on patrol, leading nine aircraft when Ops Merville ordered ground strafing of transports on Arras-Marquion road. This was successfully carried out. During attack, bombs from Blenheims were falling further up the road. Much AA encountered—two machines badly damaged [Flt Lt Sir Archie Hope's N2546 and Flg Off Peter Robinson's P3278] but both returned to Merville. Enemy tanks in fields along roads three miles east of Arras.'

Flg Off Clyde was instructed to make a second attack on the convoy:

'At 1300 I was ordered to take three aircraft to ground strafe enemy convoys between Marquion and Tournai. Attack successfully carried out—only small arms fire encountered. One machine shot about but serviceable. Damage to convoys and troops.'

At 1315 six He111s raided Merville, where seven bombs fell on the airfield, but caused little damage. Plt Off Peter Gardner (L1990) was among a trio of 3 Squadron pilots scrambled to intercept the raiders:

'I took off from Merville to chase six He111s which were bombing our aerodrome, but was unable to find them. I met a Do17 flying north and went into attack. I used all my ammunition and saw it disappear into cloud, going vertically with starboard engine burning. It tried to escape me by going in and out of clouds. Its rear gunner was killed quite early—no fire from rear gunner after first few seconds (I received one bullet in starboard wing). I was later chased by a Messerschmitt 110 and landed at Manston.'

The Do17P of 3(F)/10 crashed north of Arras but not before Uffz Walter Blaskowitz and his crew baled out; all were captured by British troops. Flt Lt Widge Wight (P2795) and Plt Off Max Sizer (L1803) of 213/B Flight also scrambled as the bombers approached, but were unable to engage. As the attack on Merville got under way, a section of 79 Squadron returned. Flg Off Freddie Duus reported:

'I was returning from patrol of Arras when I sighted one aircraft above cloud at 15,000 feet. I approached and on climbing through the clouds I saw 20 Messerschmitt 109s. I dived below cloud and my attention was drawn by AA fire near Merville aerodrome. I saw eight aircraft approaching the aerodrome—He111s—one was trailing behind. I attacked from astern at about 450 yards; got in long burst and the port engine began to smoke. I then believe flames appeared from the same engine, but at the same moment I saw the Messerschmitt formation diving out of the sun at me. I broke off my attack and dived steeply. Messerschmitts did not catch me up.'

As soon as Flg Off Clyde's section had returned to Merville, he was requested to carry out a repeat strafe of the convoys, as he recalled:

'Ops Merville ordered four machines to strafe same target. Attack successfully carried out. Result of previous ground strafing seen to have had effect—traffic diverted. All machines returned safely.'

Sqn Ldr Michael Peacock of 85 Squadron led a further strafing attack on a convoy on the Arras road at the same time, but with disastrous results. Flg Off Count Manfred Czernin was a member of the Flight:

'We delivered two attacks from 1,000 feet to 20 feet and were subjected to intense AA fire, which seemed to be extremely accurate, shaking my aircraft severely. On my second attack I perceived a field on the south side of the road filled with tankers (petrol) and armoured cars. For the third attack I went north of Arras and delivered my attack through the smoke into the field. After about three seconds the dump started to burn. I looked around; smoke and flames reached to about 150 feet. I am under the impression the two following machines were caught by the explosion as I saw no more of them.'

Indeed, both Sqn Ldr Peacock (L2141) and Plt Off Richard Shrewsbury (P3426) failed to return and were reported later to have been killed. A third pilot, Plt Off Roger Burton (P2427), was also killed. Although it was believed that they had fallen to debris or ground fire, it seems probable that they were engaged by Bf109s of II/JG3 as they broke away from their respective attacks, as two Hurricanes were claimed shot down by Hptm Erich von Selle, the Gruppenkommandeur, and Lt Franz von Werra* of the Stabsschwarm, and a third by Lt Rudolf Heymann of 4 Staffel. Following the loss of Peacock, a signal was sent to Flt Lt Peter Townsend DFC of 43 Squadron (then based in Scotland) to travel to France with all haste, there to take command of 85 Squadron; events however were to prevent this move, although Townsend did take command on the Squadron's return to England.

Five Hurricanes of 213/A Flight, together with six from 79 Squadron, were ordered to rendezvous with Blenheims due to arrive from England at 1350. Plt Off Don Stones of the latter unit wrote:

'We were sent off to escort Blenheims that were flying out from Marham. If they didn't turn up we were to look for enemy aircraft, but if there were none we were to go down and attack German tanks. We were praying for Blenheims or enemy aircraft, but neither arrived so we had to go for tanks. The section ahead of me was led by Tom Parker with Sgt Pearce and Plt Off Dorrien-Smith. They attacked the St Quentin road while we took the Cambrai road.'

Sgt Ron McQueen added:

'I was on patrol over Arras, Plt Off Don Stones leading a section of three. Acting on instructions, the section broke up and attacked enemy troops and convoys. I made three attacks on a convoy of motor lorries standing by the roadside. There was light machine-gun fire from a stationary tank. Impossible to see effect of attacks. Saw several bombs explode on the ground and climbed up to investigate—a Dornier bomber was seen going into the clouds at about 8,000 feet.'

Both Plt Off Tom Parker (P2634) and Plt Off Lionel Dorrien-Smith (L2145) were shot down by ground fire; the former walked back to Merville via Arras, but the latter was killed. At 1515, Sgt Len Pearce engaged a Dornier flying east:

'Pulled tit and fell in behind, closing range to 400 yards when I opened fire as the e/a was approaching cloud. Most of the long burst

---

* Lt Franz von Werra was shot down on 5 September 1940, during the Battle of Britain, and was taken prisoner; having been foiled in an attempt to escape, he was sent to a PoW camp in Canada, from where he did successfully escape and eventually returned to Germany, only to be killed in a flying accident in 1942.

went in port engine but no effect seen. After following e/a for ten minutes through small clouds, got very lost and broke away without coming in range again. On returning westwards saw Henschel 126 to south, flying east 2,000 feet above me. Made attack directly below and aircraft entered cloud. On emerging, opened fire from dead astern and for one second only. After passing through another cloud, fired remaining ammunition. At beginning of burst e/a dived steeply and I lost sight of it in a haze.'

The Dornier attacked by Pearce—in fact a Do17P of 4(F)/11—crashed north of Arras with the loss of Fw Paul Klafke and his crew.

Half an hour later, at 1545, Flt Lt Ian Gleed led his Flight of six Hurricanes of 87 Squadron to strafe vehicles on the Arras road. En route, at 12,000 feet, Gleed attacked a Bf110, at which he fired two short bursts before it evaded by diving into cloud. He and his Flight then strafed the convoy, as he recorded later:

'I half-rolled on my back and screamed down, thumbing the gun button as my sights came on the black dots, which rapidly turned into tanks. I roared along the line, pulling out just in time to miss the tall poplar trees. I glanced behind. A shower of pom-pom shells were bursting just behind my tail. There was a crack, and the plane shuddered; a large hole had appeared in the right wing, just outside the petrol tank.'

One of his pilots, Flg Off Roddy Rayner, reported:

'Having been ordered to do a ground strafe, the Flight broke off and climbed to 10,000 feet. During the attack on the convoy I got separated and was attacked by a 109, which was one of a large formation. Enemy overshot and I was able to open fire from astern and it crashed in flames. Remaining 109s dived to attack. I hid in cloud and eventually returned to base.'

Plt Off Ken Tait also reported shooting down a Bf109 and believed he had inflicted damage on two more, before escaping from the attention of others. The Bf109s may have been from II/JG3, the unit that had engaged with the Hurricanes of 85 Squadron, which reported the loss of Lt Peter Wisser of 4 Staffel, who was killed when his aircraft crashed during a low level combat. He may have been engaged by Rayner and Tait.

Flg Off Billy Clyde was off again at 1600 at the head of six Hurricanes of 3 Squadron:

'Ops Merville ordered me to take six machines to attack same target. Attack successfully carried out—petrol lorry put on fire. All machines returned safely.'

At about the same time, Wg Cdr Broadhurst set off at the head of a patrol of Hurricanes from 79 Squadron and three from 213/B Flight. An hour later, when at 15,000 feet, four or five twin-engined aircraft, believed to have been Bf110s, were sighted near Arras, with about 25 more at 18,000 feet. In fact the aircraft encountered were Do17Zs of KG77 with an escort of Bf110Cs of I/ZG26. Wg Cdr Broadhurst claimed one of the 'Messerschmitts' shot down, although it would seem that he actually engaged a Dornier of Stabsstaffel, aboard which two of the crew were wounded. Meanwhile, Flt Lt Widge Wight (P2795) engaged a Bf110 and reported:

'Tried to stalk them but 79 Squadron section went for the bait of four or five, so climbed and attacked top lot. After six minutes' dogfighting, got all rounds off at one on top of stall turn. He fell out of the sky in "dead" way. I then made for home. Bullet holes in starboard wing, one in ammo tank.'

Plt Off Harry Atkinson (P2673) also engaged a Messerschmitt, but was unable to confirm its destruction. The 79 Squadron section reported seeing 20 Do17s and Bf110s at 14,500 feet (obviously the same KG77/ZG26 formation), and all three pilots engaged. Sgt Alf Whitby (P2698) claimed one of the bombers shot down although he did not see it crash, while Sgt Harry Cartwright singled out another:

'Whilst on patrol over Arras with Green Section, I saw four Do215s [sic] flying on the opposite course to us (at 15,000 feet). I used R/T to tell the leader that they were turning on us and turned on the beam of one, which I gave a long burst. Return fire was observed from rear gunner using incendiary. Two machines were on my tail and I used violent evasive action (claim: one inconclusive).'

Sgt Ron McQueen engaged one of the escort:

'I was about 300 feet below Plt Off Clift, who was leading the section, when the remainder of the Flight went in to attack the 110s and 215s. I was immediately attacked by three 110s coming out of the sun, and by diving and turning steeply succeeded in getting on the tail of one. I fired several bursts and the machine continued in a steep dive, although no smoke or flame was visible. I was unable to continue the action owing to attacks by the remaining two, whom I subsequently avoided by diving through the cloud layer at 8,000 feet. I observed another flight of six 110s on the return journey.'

Two Hurricanes were claimed shot down by the Bf110 pilots, one being credited to Hptm Wilhelm Makrocki, the Staffelkapitän, and the other to Lt Walter Manhart.

With the end in sight, orders were given for the evacuation of Merville. All flyable Hurricanes were to return to England without delay, the three attached Canadians of 242 Squadron—Flt Lt Don Miller, Plt Offs Don MacQueen and Art Deacon—departing for RAF Church Fenton by way of RAF Manston. Although Miller's aircraft was hit by ground fire en route, which holed his oil tank, he was however able to reach Manston. Flt Lt Widge Wight led his 213/B Flight back to England, where the Hurricanes landed at RAF Northolt first before flying on to RAF Wittering; Wight noted:

'No neck-twisting and reached England. Wizard reception on arrival [at Wittering] and great interest shown in holes in my aircraft [P2795] from Messerschmitt 110 battle!'

A number of transport aircraft were due to arrive from England to evacuate those pilots without aircraft, together with other key personnel, and Wg Cdr Broadhurst was instructed to remain at the airfield (with his Hurricane) in order to provide cover for the transports while they were on the ground; then, to form part of their escort for the return flight to England. Plt Off Jack Rose of 3 Squadron was amongst those without an aircraft and he departed, together with about ten ground crew, aboard a French civilian DC-2; also airlifted were Sqn Ldr Oliver, Plt Off Pat Woods-Scawen and Sgt Albert Deacon of 85 Squadron, Plt Offs Roland Beamont, Dennis David, Jimmy Dunn (suffering from burns) and Flg Off Jimmy Strickland (wounded) of 87 Squadron. An operationally u/s Hurricane of 87 Squadron was sent back directly to England, while the remainder were to provide escort for the transports. Plt Off Chris Darwin of the latter unit wrote in his diary:

'Hear the Germans might have got as far as Arras. Was so tired that I went into an evacuated house and slept. We have been bombed five times already. The last time I was having lunch at the Hôtel des Angies—very frightening! Saw one of our NCOs who said that the entire Squadron was evacuating. Rushed to the aerodrome and got to our machines. Flew via Beachy Head and landed at Tangmere and had a good sleep.'

One of the airmen left behind, Aircraftman Jim Davies, had the forethought to chalk a message on the fuselage of a departing Hurricane, which read: 'Please tell people at 58 Llandennis Road, Roath Park, Cardiff, that 164 Davies is OK.' The airman's parents were duly contacted. Having seen the last transport aircraft depart safely at 1800, Wg Cdr Broadhurst took off to join the escort:

> 'En route I was caught by four Messerschmitt 110s, which damaged the Hurricane somewhat, but I managed to escape and got back to England and landed safely.'

On inspection of his Hurricane, Broadhurst found that its oil tank had been damaged, only then fully appreciating just how lucky he had been to have reached England without the engine having seized*.

Flg Off Derek Ward had been tasked to fly 87 Squadron's operationally unserviceable Hurricane to England, a flight which turned out to be full of adventure. Due to the condition of the Hurricane, which lacked a gunsight and had no functional instruments except the compass, oil and petrol gauges, Ward decided not to risk his pet dog's life on the long sea flight and, subsequently, asked those returning aboard one of the transport aircraft to look after him. Sadly, in the confusion, 'Whisky' disappeared and could not be found by the time of the aircraft's departure. Meanwhile, Ward had managed to get airborne:

> 'The engine was badly overheating. Seven guns were loaded but there was no incendiary tracer. I intended to land at Abbeville to collect some kit which I had left there on the way out. On approaching Abbeville I saw that the town was in flames and two Do215s [sic] were dive-bombing the town. I climbed and attacked one of the machines and got in two bursts at 300 yards, pointing my guns in the general direction of the e/a. The e/a dived into cloud and I followed and gave the e/a some more bursts in the cloud. I came out and circled for ten minutes and saw another Dornier between clouds and attacked again. My engine began to overheat badly and some 109s attacked me from behind. I dived into cloud and eventually landed at Abbeville.

---

* Wg Cdr Broadhurst's battered Hurricane was fitted later with an uprated Merlin engine, apparently without the knowledge or permission of the appropriate authorities, and Broadhurst flew this aircraft on unauthorized operational sorties thoughout the Battle of Britain period. When this indiscretion was finally discovered by a visiting staff officer, Broadhurst argued—or so the story goes—that since the Hurricane had been written off as abandoned in France, it could not be confiscated! However, ground staff were ordered by the unimpressed senior officer to remove the engine, which effectively put an end to the affair.

I found that my machine had a puncture in the starboard tank and the petrol was spraying out. The aerodrome was being evacuated— u/s machines were being burned, chiefly Lysanders. The aerodrome crews were about to be evacuated and wished to burn my machine rather than take the risk of starting it again owing to the petrol spraying out of the starboard tank. I stuck a bayonet several times into the starboard tank to empty it and managed to persuade two airmen to fill my port tank. I had to leave without being rearmed. I took off and two miles east of the aerodrome I encountered six Do17s and six 109s. I attacked the leader of the 109s, which were coming head-on towards me, and gave the leader a burst. He swerved left and I dived past him towards the ground. Fortunately the 109s continued to escort the bombers and did not give chase. I then flew the aircraft to North Weald and landed it.'

Not all the pilots were able to leave by air, as Sgt Cyril Hampshire of 85 Squadron recalled:

'When the Squadron was withdrawn to Debden we only had two or three Hurricanes, a Master and a Magister left, so those of us with no aircraft went out through Boulogne by truck to a transit camp, through numerous refugees. That night Boulogne was bombed without any of us in the camp being hurt, and next day we embarked for Folkestone.'

However, others were more enterprising. Plt Off Ken Tait of 87 Squadron allegedly flew back to England at the controls of an abandoned Dutch aircraft, while Plt Off Lew Lewis of 85 Squadron found himself a Hurricane:

'It was apparent that we were being kicked out of France and those of us who were not wounded were told we had to make our own way home to England. Bofors guns were being turned on practically new Hurricanes to destroy them and make them unfit for use by the enemy. We came under attack by 109s which strafed rows of aircraft standing out in the open. I eventually found one Hurricane which, apart from a few bullet holes, seemed OK. We started her up and I was soon heading out over the Channel towards England. Landed Gatwick and on to Northolt.'

At 1745, 32 Squadron took off from RAF Manston to rendezvous with two other Hurricane squadrons as escort to Blenheims (from 21 and 107 Squadrons) briefed to raid Arras. At 1830, a Hs126 was sighted three miles north of Arras, flying westwards at a height of 8,000 feet. Sqn Ldr

John Worrall (N2532) and his No 2, Sgt Gerald North (N2583), dived down to engage the low-flying spotter aircraft, at which Worrall managed to get a burst before it was lost from sight. Sgt North reported later:

'Green 1 [Sqn Ldr Worrall] dived to attack and I followed watching Green 1 engage. After a few moments Green 1 broke away and I engaged e/a at about 100 feet. I fired and the e/a adopted evasive tactics, climbing and turning, displaying exceptional manoeuvrability. I engaged the e/a again at 50 feet from 100 yards and got in a long burst. The rear gunner then appeared to have been silenced, but there was a loud explosion from the direction of my port tank. The aircraft caught fire. I put it down with the wheels up in a ploughed field approximately ten miles south-east of Arras. It is possible that the e/a was destroyed but I did not witness it crash.'

The Henschel of 3(H)/41 (8 Pz Division) did nevertheless crash, and with it died the pilot, Oblt Seppell. The observer however was able to bale out and was rescued by troops of 7 Pz Division. Meanwhile, Sgt North had survived his crash-landing and, having ensured that his aircraft would continue to burn, started walking towards Arras. French police encountered along the road advised him that Arras had already fallen, so he made for Vimy instead, where he found British soldiers in occupation. He spent the night there, then set off in borrowed army transport for Merville, only to find the airfield abandoned. After inspection of some of the many abandoned aircraft on the airfield— mainly Hurricanes of 79 and 601 Squadrons—he came across a DH86 which looked intact, but decided against trying to start this as he had no experience of the type. Instead he set out for St Omer, where he met Sgt John Craig of 111 Squadron who had been shot down three days earlier.

Sgts North and Craig arrived at St Omer in time to witness a raid on the airfield by Do17s and Bf110s, which destroyed a Lysander and two Potez 63s on the ground and shot down a Lysander which had just taken off. Continuing on their way towards the coast, the two NCOs reached Mézières where they met Plt Off John Southwell of 615 Squadron who had been shot down in Belgium three days earlier, and had made his way back on foot. At Mézières the three pilots were provided with transport and soon reached Calais, where they boarded a Royal Navy drifter, arriving at Dover the following day.

Plt Off Allan Simpson of 13 Squadron, who had just reached Abbeville, recalled the confusion:

'German bombers were active, bombing convoys and refugees along the roads. They used screaming bombs which induced a certain amount of panic. Many refugees left their vehicles, deciding that the ditches were safer. Abandoned vehicles obstructed the road and had to be removed, usually by pushing them into the ditch. They also bombed Abbeville town, the aerodrome road and other convoys. Sometimes they flew quite low and machine-gunned people. On a parallel road a few hundred yards away, a bomber dropped ten bombs (five pairs), missing the road by a few yards. He was attacking a military convoy. A dive-bomber hit the petrol refinery. Some Hurricanes shot it down. The pilot was about 18 years old. The French Army took him prisoner. Visitors kept dropping in and I invited them to the hospitality of our slit trench during the attacks. There was a squadron leader who arrived in a Tiger Moth. We filled his tank with high octane petrol and sent him on his way. I hope he didn't explode.'

Another arrival at Abbeville was Flg Off Tom Hubbard of 601 Squadron, who reached the airfield after having been shot down near Arras the previous day. Plt Off Simpson continued:

'I gave Hubbard a Magister that was sitting on the aerodrome. My largesse reached a high point that day.'

61 Wing, Air Component

615 Squadron was very active during the day following the arrival at Norrent-Fontès of its 13 Hurricanes and the Magister. Three hours later, at 0800, the Squadron mounted an offensive patrol over Lille, while a section maintained a defensive patrol of the airfield.

Sqn Ldr Joe Kayll of 615 Squadron was ordered to provide three aircraft as part of a composite formation which was to attack the German advance along the Cambrai-Arras road. He recalled:

'There was a request from the Army that we should try to delay the German advance towards Arras on the road from Cambrai. We managed to get 12 serviceable aircraft together (three from 615, three from 504 and six from 607), 615 leading. We found a large quantity of German transport on this perfectly straight road and were able to do some damage. Unfortunately we lost three aircraft, including Flg Off Bob Pumphrey [P3448 AF-H] of 607, who managed to jump out at low level and survived as a PoW. Our mistake was to attack in sections of three in line astern and the Germans had a concentration of cannon and machine-guns at either side of the road.'

One of the 504 Squadron section was shot down and Plt Off Michael

Jebb crash-landed his aircraft (P3586). Although wounded, he was able to reach safety and was admitted to hospital, eventually being evacuated on the last ship to depart from Dieppe. Plt Off Dick Demetriadi's P2671 AF-G was also damaged, obliging him to crash-land, although he was unhurt. In addition, Sqn Ldr Kayll's aircraft was hit in the wing, but he was able to return to base. One of the returning pilots reported that the pom-pom gun which hit Kayll's aircraft was put out of action by another 615 Squadron pilot and its crew killed.

Flg Off Lionel Gaunce of 615 Squadron was dispatched to fly a reconnaissance sortie over the convoy and, on his return, reported seven lorries in flames and considerable confusion. At the same time, the Squadron's C Flight met ten Bf110Cs (from I/ZG26) and ten Ju88s of III/LG1 near Norrent-Fontès at 10,000 feet. Plt Off Vic Verity reported:

'I was patrolling Norrent-Fontès at 15,000 feet when I observed AA fire and a large formation of e/a bombing Aire. I carried out deflection attack on No 2 of rear bombers. I broke into clouds and did not see result. On emerging from cloud made another deflection attack on other side of formation. On breaking away from Ju88 I saw two Messerschmitt 110s attacking me from the side. E/a registered two hits on wings with cannon. This did not put me out of action and I evaded them by going into cloud. I again came out of cloud and made attack on No 1 Ju88, using all my ammunition. I observed smoke pouring from port engine of e/a. I was again attacked by two 110s and received hits with cannon behind the armour plating and fuselage. I dived to the ground evading e/a. I found my engine temperature was now registering 145° and fumes were coming from my engine, so switched off to prevent being overcome. Made force-landing on aerodrome but overshot, causing undercarriage to collapse. Aircraft [L2060] was badly damaged.'

His companion, Plt Off Denis Pennington, added:

'Patrolling above aerodrome at 8,000 feet. Saw AA fire to the north. I followed up and saw a number of 110s. One 110 attacked Plt Off Verity and followed him down, so I attacked the e/a at about 100 yards with one burst of about three seconds. Smoke poured out of one engine and it dived towards the ground. I broke away as I was being followed from the port beam by another 110. I went back to the aerodrome and saw Plt Off Verity force-land.'

Three hours later, at 1600, a section from 615 Squadron patrolled Arras-Douai-Lens, meeting a dozen He111Hs at 16,000 feet. Two were claimed shot down by Sqn Ldr Joe Kayll and Plt Off Petrus Hugo, a South African. Kayll reported:

> 'Attacked tail of formation with beam attack which put rear gunner out of action. Then attacked from astern, closing to 200 yards. Port engine stopped and was smoking badly. E/a went into a spin and disappeared through low cloud.'

Orders were received that evening to evacuate Norrent-Fontès. Nine Hurricanes of 615 Squadron (including L1289 flown by Flg Off Tony Eyre) and four of 607 Squadron escorted a departing SABENA SM73P (which was being operated by 271 Squadron) to RAF Kenley; on board the 18-seater airliner were 23 evacuees, including Wg Cdr Boret and his staff. Three operationally unserviceable Hurricanes of 615 Squadron returned to Kenley independently, as did at least four of the Squadron's Gladiators. These are believed to have included N2304 KW-R and N2306; one was flown back by Plt Off Roy Bush, another by Plt Off Denis Crowley-Milling (KW-P), one by 229 Squadron's Plt Off Malcolm Ravenhill (KW-T), and the fourth by a Lysander pilot of 16 Squadron.

Three Blenheims were found abandoned at Merville and these were flown back to England, one piloted by 615 Squadron's Flt Lt James Sanders. Earlier, 504 Squadron had dispatched six Hurricanes to RAF Manston, with two non-operational machines flying to Croydon, while four of 607 Squadron's battle-fatigued machines, believed to have been L2072 DZ-Z, P2586, P2617 and P2874 AF-B, departed for Croydon together with P3454 QO-A, L1846 QO-B, N2669 QO-D, P3318 QO-K and N25446 QO-S of 3 Squadron.

Flg Off Ken Newton, Plt Offs Buck Courtney and Dave Blomeley were three of the 607 Squadron pilots sent back to Croydon, as the latter recalled:

> 'The four Hurricanes we flew back were immediately scrapped, as they counted 87 bullet holes in one of them, which only had three engine bearers left.'

Having survived safely the fighting in France, they decided to celebrate and let off some steam; Blomeley continued:

> 'We went on the town and lunchtime saw us in a bar till 1 pm. There was a traffic jam and a large, square Rolls barred our way. Respect-fully we went round its rear except for Ken Newton. He jumped up on one wing, across the bonnet to the other side! Courtney passed out about 9 pm, so we emptied his pockets, put him in a taxi and

gave the driver a fictitious address in the East End. Eventually, Court ended up at a police station, where the cops paid the irate cabby. The cops put him up for the night, lent him a razor and gave him a huge breakfast next morning, then gave him a lift back to Croydon with a clean shirt. We, of course, had lost everything in France and were in shirts, slacks and short flying boots. The three of us pressed on to the "Propeller" at Purley, being ejected at 3 am, and most unpopular on our return to Croydon. Next morning three haggard, unshaven scruffy types met a beautifully shaven and polished Courtney. Most unfair!'

Ground personnel of the evacuating squadrons were more or less left to make their own way back to England. Typical of their experiences were those related by LAC Bill Bowman of 607 Squadron, who recalled:

'We then started our journey back to England—we hoped! Maintenance Flight had packed all their personal tool kits and as many other spares as we could on a trailer, and this was hitched to a lorry. We proceeded to Le Havre but no ship was available so we intended to go to Rouen, but heard that the Germans were travelling towards there as well, so we set off for Cherbourg and eventually arrived on the 21st and at night on the 22nd boarded a tramp steamer. We arrived at Southampton and were ordered down to the docks to unload the ship as the dockers refused to work overtime. We didn't feel too good about this and we were proposing to throw the afore-mentioned dockers in the harbour, but were persuaded by the foreman that perhaps this wasn't a good thing. After unloading the ship we were amazed to see they were then going to load tanks to take over to France, which seemed to be a stupid thing to do.'

Summary

With the Germans consolidating their gains and the British withdrawing its air force, there was reduced aerial activity during the day over Northern France and the majority of Hurricane losses occurred during ground strafing operations. Of the dozen Hurricanes shot down, at least seven were victims of the ground defences; three Hurricane pilots were killed and one taken prisoner.

Claims by AASF and Air Component Hurricanes, 20 May				
Type	Confirmed	Probable	Damaged	Total
He111	4	1	—	5
Do17	7	3	2	12
Ju88	3	—	3	6
Hs126	3	—	3	6

Bf109	2	—	2	4
Bf110	4	1	2	7
	23	5	12	40

Luftwaffe Losses Attributed to AASF and Air Component Hurricanes, 20 May

Type	60% to 100%	Under 60%	Total
He111	2	—	2
Do17	5	1	6
Ju88	2	—	2
Hs126	4	2	6
Bf109	1	—	1
Bf110	1	—	1
	15	3	18

It had been agreed with the French that the main area of RAF attack on the night of 20/21 May should be roughly the area bounded by Cambrai-Hirson-Vervins-St Quentin. Thus 20 Whitleys and 18 Hampdens were directed against the bridges over the Oise and Sambre. In addition, 32 Wellingtons attacked other targets within that area, while 18 Blenheims targeted columns of the Grammont-Oudenaarde road and 38 Battles attacked German lines of communication across the Meuse. From these operations, two Wellingtons, two Whitleys and one Battle failed to return.

Individual Claims—AASF and Air Component Hurricanes, 20 May

0500-	Sgt R.C. Wilkinson Sgt A.H.B. Friendship Plt Off J.B. Hobbs Sgt J.A. Sims	3 Sqn	2 He111s
	Sgt R.C. Wilkinson	3 Sqn	Hs126 damaged
0600-	Flt Lt R.D.G. Wight	213/B Flt	
	Plt Off H.D. Atkinson	213/B Flt	Do17
	Plt Off W.M. Sizer	213/B Flt	
	Sgt A.W. Whitby	79 Sqn	
0600-	Flg Off G.R. Branch	601/A Flt	Do17
	Plt Off M.M. Stephens	3 Sqn	Do17
0700-	Flg Off M.B. Czernin	85 Sqn	Hs126
0730-	Plt Off M.M. Stephens	3 Sqn	Hs126 damaged
0730-	Plt Off P.W. Comely	87 Sqn	Ju88
0915-	Sgt H.N. Howes	85 Sqn	2 Do17, 3 Do17 possible
0930-	Plt Off P.W. Comely	87 Sqn	Ju88
	Flt Lt I.R. Gleed Plt Off K.W. Tait	87 Sqn	Ju88
	Plt Off K.W. Tait	87 Sqn	2 Ju88 damaged
	Flg Off R.M.S. Rayner	87 Sqn	Bf110, Bf110 damaged
1015-	Plt Off D.W.A. Stones Sgt L.H.B. Pearce Sgt H. Cartwright	79 Sqn	Hs126

1020-	Flt Lt R.D.G. Wight	213/B Flt	
	Plt Off W.M. Sizer	213/B Flt	
	Plt Off H.D. Atkinson	213/B Flt	Hs126
	Sgt S.L. Butterfield	213/B Flt	
	Flg Off W.N. Gray	213/A Flt	
1300-	Plt Off V.B.S. Verity	615 Sqn	Ju88 damaged
	Plt Off D.A. Pennington	615 Sqn	Bf110
1315-	Plt Off P.M. Gardner	3 Sqn	Do17
1315-	Flg Off F.J.L. Duus	79 Sqn	He111 probable
1515-	Sgt L.H.B. Pearce	79 Sqn	Do17 damaged
1545-	Flg Off R.M.S. Rayner	87 Sqn	Bf109
	Plt Off K.W. Tait	87 Sqn	Bf109, 2 Bf109 damaged
1600-	Wg Cdr H. Broadhurst	60 Wing	Bf110
	Flt Lt R.D.G. Wight	213/B Flt	Bf110
	Plt Off H.D. Atkinson	213/B Flt	Bf110 probable
	Sgt A.W. Whitby	79 Sqn	Do17
	Sgt H. Cartwright	79 Sqn	Do17 damaged
	Sgt R.R. McQueen	79 Sqn	Bf110 damaged
1600-	Sqn Ldr J.R. Kayll	615 Sqn	He111
	Plt Off P.H. Hugo	615 Sqn	He111
1830-	Sqn Ldr J. Worrall	32 Sqn	Hs126 damaged
	Sgt G. North		

Losses—AASF and Air Component Hurricanes, 20 May

0600-	P2699	601/A Flt	Flg Off G.R. Branch: shot down by return fire from Do17P of 3(F)/10 and crashed near Izel-lès-Equerchin, six miles west of Douai; pilot baled out, returned.
0930-	P2555	85 Sqn	Sgt H.N. Howes: shot down by Bf110C of I/ZG26 and crash-landed near Abbeville; pilot unhurt, returned.
1030-	N2546	601/A Flt	Flt Lt Sir A.P. Hope: aircraft damaged by Flak and force-landed at Merville; pilot unhurt.
	P3278	601/A Flt	Flg Off P.B. Robinson: aircraft damaged by Flak and force-landed at Merville; pilot unhurt.
1040-	P3448	607 Sqn	Flg Off R.E.W. Pumphrey: shot down by Flak between Cambrai-Arras; pilot baled out, PoW.
	P3586	504 Sqn	Plt Off M. Jebb: shot down by Flak and crash-landed between Cambrai-Arras; pilot wounded.
1300-	L2060	615 Sqn	Plt Off V.B.S. Verity: aircraft damaged by Bf110C of I/ZG26 and crash-landed at Norrent-Fontès; pilot unhurt.
1400-	L2141	85 Sqn	Sqn Ldr M.F. Peacock: shot down ten miles east of Arras by Bf109 of II/JG3; pilot killed.
	P3426	85 Sqn	Plt Off R.W. Shrewsbury: shot down ten miles east of Arras by Bf109 of II/JG3; pilot killed.
	P2427	85 Sqn	Plt Off R.W. Burton: shot down by Bf109 of II/JG3 and crashed six miles north-east of Amiens; pilot killed.
1400-	P2634	79 Sqn	Plt Off T.C. Parker: shot down by Flak and crash-landed near Arras; pilot unhurt, returned.
	L2145	79 Sqn	Plt Off L.R. Dorrien-Smith: shot down by Flak near Arras; pilot killed.
1830-	N2583	32 Sqn	Sgt G. North: aircraft damaged by return fire from Hs126 of 3(H)/41 and crash-landed ten miles south-east of Arras; pilot unhurt, returned.

CHAPTER XIII

TUESDAY 21 MAY
PRELUDE TO DUNKIRK

'Over the brow of the meadow they went, no higher than their own height, two fliers, one entity, in instant harmony—Blount and his Moth.'

Air Commodore Victor Goddard, SASO Air Component.

The Situation in Belgium and Northern France

The German advance through the 'gap' finally achieved its main objective and reached the Channel coast: Amiens fell; Abbeville was threatened, as was Montreuil and Boulogne. There was severe pressure on the southern flank of the Allies about Arras, from where a counter-attack was launched by British and French armoured units.

Of the Air Component reconnaissance units, only 4 Squadron Lysanders and a Flight of 13 Squadron remained in France. During the day sorties were flown from Lille/Ronchin and St Omer and five Lysanders failed to return; three of these fell victim to Messerschmitts of I/JG1, 4/JG2 and I/ZG26. Lysanders of 16 Squadron also operated from RAF Hawkinge during the day, reconnoitring in the St Pol-Doullens-Amiens-Abbeville area; one of these also failed to return. In addition, four Blenheims from UK bases carried out reconnaissance flights over the Arras-Cambrai-Albert-Amiens area, one of these also being shot down, as were two of 18 Squadron.

At this stage of ultimate crisis, the French Government sacked its Commander-in-Chief, Général Gamelin, and installed in his place Général Maxime Weygand, fresh from the Levant. During the morning Weygand decided to visit his northern armies and flew from Paris, bound for Ypres, but en route his aircraft was attacked and forced to land at Calais. No one on board the aircraft was hurt but Weygand and his staff were forced to complete their journey by road.

67 Wing, AASF

Seven new pilots arrived at Metz for 73 Squadron, having been led there by Sgt Cyril Hampshire of 85 Squadron, who had been briefed for the task. Duty completed, Hampshire was instructed to leave his Hurricane and returned as a passenger in an 81 Squadron Dragon Rapide. The new pilots made their own way to Gaye, where 73 Squadron was then based.

11 Group, RAF Fighter Command

Nine Hurricanes of 151 Squadron set off from RAF Manston at 0900 to patrol over France, although no hostile aircraft were sighted. At about the same time, eight Hurricanes of 17 Squadron, together with others from 32 Squadron, were tasked to escort Blenheims to France, but the rendezvous was not achieved and instead the Hurricanes carried out a patrol over Arras, Abbeville and Amiens. At 1045, a Hs126 was sighted by Green and Blue Sections of 17 Squadron at 8,000 feet two miles north-east of Amiens. Plt Off Bird-Wilson (Blue 2 in YB-K) recalled:

> 'We had fun finding a Henschel 126 which we took on. The German was a very determined sort of chap and an excellent pilot. He was orbiting round the German forward positions and under the pro-tection of a fair amount of ack-ack. Nevertheless we did shoot him down and he went hard into the ground.'

Sgt Wynn (Green 1) added:

> 'On being attacked e/a turned head-on and dived down during which time he was attacked by other Hurricanes. At approximately 100 feet e/a levelled out and as one Hurricane broke away, I went in and fired at 200 yards range—two second burst—and broke away. Green 2 saw e/a crash after I broke away.'

The Henschel—5D+DK of 2(H)/31Pz, spotting for 5 Pz Division—turned over on to its back in a field, killing the observer, Oblt Adolf Köcher, but the injured pilot, Fw Adolf Herzig, was seen to emerge and run for cover. Apart from Bird-Wilson and Wynn, four other pilots were credited jointly with its destruction: Flt Lt Bill Toyne (Blue leader), Sgt George Steward (Blue 3), Flg Off Capel Adye (Green 3) and Flt Sgt Bill Jones (Green 2). Two of the Hurricanes landed at Le Havre and Le Touquet respectively to refuel before making the flight back to England.

151 Squadron mounted a second operation at 1720, when nine Hurricanes, together with others from 56 Squadron, set off to escort Blenheims tasked to bomb a railway junction ten miles south-east of Boulogne. The Blenheim formation—six from 82 Squadron and three

from 18 Squadron—on nearing the rendezvous point off the French coast, came under attack from a flight of Spitfires from 610 Squadron! Although the Spitfire leader opened fire, inflicting damage on one of 18 Squadron's aircraft, the following pilots realised the error in identification and pulled away from the attack, leaving the damaged Blenheim to carry out a successful belly landing at Wimereux; the uninjured crew set fire to the aircraft before they made their way to Boulogne, where they gained passage back to England.

Meanwhile, the 151 Squadron Hurricanes sighted a suspicious aircraft and Blue Section was ordered to investigate. On closer inspection, the aircraft was identified as a Hs126 which Sgt George Atkinson (P3315) engaged. He fired a four second burst at close range, following which the Henschel—a machine of 1(H)/14Pz from 2 Pz Division—blew up and crashed, its demise witnessed by Sqn Ldr Teddy Donaldson and Flt Lt Freddie Ives. No other hostile aircraft were encountered and all the Hurricanes returned safely.

At 1800, five Hurricanes of 253 Squadron and four from 229 Squadron departed RAF Hawkinge, in company with 145/601 Squadron, to carry out a sweep of the Arras-Béthune-Lens area, where dive-bombers were reported to be harassing British forces. Plt Off Geoff Simpson was leading Green Section of 229 Squadron and, on crossing the French coast, he sighted an aircraft below which he could not identify. He and his No 2, Plt Off Desmond Gower, dropped down to investigate and found it to be a French aircraft. Simpson then climbed back through the clouds to rejoin the formation, but lost contact with Gower, and on emerging saw a large formation of aircraft:

> 'I recognized them as 20 He111s [aircraft from III/KG1] escorted by an equal number of 110s [of II/ZG76] heading, as I thought, towards England. I turned north-west to follow them, but when off Cap Gris Nez I looked back and saw them circling over Calais. I turned back and coming from the sun attacked one of the Heinkels. I carried the attack home to within a few yards and saw him shudder violently. When I broke away the starboard engine was emitting thick clouds of black smoke. No fire was encountered from this aircraft. I then attacked a second Heinkel from below and silenced the gunner who started firing at me. The e/a's undercarriage dropped and smoke poured from the port engine. By this time my ammunition was practically exhausted and I saw tracers streaming on both sides from a 110. I dived into the clouds and returned to Kenley, where I landed at 2030.'

One Heinkel of 9 Staffel was shot down near Boulogne, from which Oblt Botho Stagge and his crew baled out; all survived and three were captured by British troops, the other by French forces. Plt Off Gower did not return and it was assumed that he had fallen foul of the Messerschmitts; his aircraft (P3546) crashed near Étaples, some 17 miles south of Boulogne, where his body was recovered later and buried nearby. 253 Squadron's CO, Sqn Ldr Elliott (P3552), also failed to return and was reported later to have been taken prisoner. Since no German aircraft had been sighted by the other pilots of 253 Squadron, it was assumed that his aircraft had been hit by AA fire. However, it seems probable that both Elliott and Gower were shot down by the Bf110Cs of II/ZG76.

B Flight of 601 Squadron also lost an aircraft during the patrol. When flying near Abbeville, Flg Off Christopher Riddle (L2088) was seen to leave the formation and was lost from sight. However, he turned up in England three days later, having force-landed, and was reunited with his brother, Hugh, who had also returned safely from France, having reached Paris from where he was flown back to England aboard a departing Flamingo.

Spitfires were active off the French coast throughout the day. A pilot of 54 Squadron claimed a He111 probable at 0820 and another pilot from the same unit similarly reported the probable destruction of a Ju88 between Calais and Dunkirk during the early afternoon. Spitfires of 74 Squadron engaged a number of bombers during the early evening between Calais and Dunkirk; two Ju88s were claimed shot down, plus a probable, together with two He111 probables, for the loss of one Spitfire.

Claims by AASF and Air Component Hurricanes, 21 May				
Type	Confirmed	Probable	Damaged	Total
He111	2	—	—	2
Hs126	2	—	—	2
	4	—	—	4

Luftwaffe Losses Attributed to AASF and Air Component Hurricanes, 21 May		
Type	60% to 100%	Under 60%	Total
He111	1	—	1
Hs126	2	—	2
	3	—	3

Although 41 Battles were tasked to attack communications in the Upper Meuse area that night, the operation was cancelled after about a dozen had taken off—in favour of a possible daylight attack against tanks in the Amiens-Arras-Abbeville area. Twenty-nine Wellingtons from the UK also attacked communications in the Upper Meuse area, while railways in western Germany were the main targets for 18

Wellingtons, 24 Hampdens and 54 Whitleys; six of the bombers sent to Germany failed to return.

Individual Claims—AASF and 11 Group Hurricanes, 21 May

1045-	Flt Lt W.A. Toyne		
	Flg Off C.F.G. Adye		
	Plt Off H.A.C. Bird-Wilson	17 Sqn	Hs126
	Sgt G.A. Steward		
	Sgt N.R. Wynn		
	Flt Sgt W.J. Jones		
1800-	Sgt G. Atkinson	151 Sqn	Hs126
1800-	Plt Off G.M. Simpson	229 Sqn	2 He111

Losses—AASF and 11 Group Hurricanes, 21 May

1800-	P3552	253 Sqn	Sqn Ldr E.D. Elliott: shot down while on patrol over Arras-Béthune-Lens, probably by Bf110C of II/ZG76; pilot PoW.
	P3546	229 Sqn	Plt Off D.DeC.C. Gower: shot down, probably by Bf110C of II/ZG76, and crashed near Étaples; pilot killed.
	L2088	601 Sqn	Flg Off C.J.H. Riddle: engine problem while on patrol and force-landed near Abbeville; pilot unhurt, returned.

Merville

Although Merville had effectively been evacuated by all flyable aircraft, throughout the morning a miscellany of aircraft—including Bombays, Ensigns, DH89s and various SABENA machines flown by crews from 24 and 271 Squadrons and the ATA—arrived from England with food and supplies, the same aircraft being required to evacuate as many redundant ground personnel as possible and to salvage abandoned stores and equipment, desperately needed at home.

The air evacuation did not proceed without loss however. Two requisitioned DH89s of 24 Squadron were damaged by enemy action and were subsequently abandoned—G-AEXP at St Omer and G-AFAH at Merville—while an Ensign and a SABENA SM73P were set on fire at the latter airfield. In addition, 271 Squadron lost one of its recently-acquired Belgian SM73Ps (OO-AGX) when it was shot down shortly after take-off from Merville with the loss of its RAF pilot and French crew; and a SABENA DC-3 (OO-AUI) was shot down near Arques, while 81 Squadron lost a communications aircraft over the Channel.

Not everybody had left Merville at this stage. Air Vice-Marshal Blount, AOC Air Component, and his SASO, Air Commodore Goddard, remained. But clearly the time to leave France had arrived—there was nothing left of their command. In the early morning darkness of 22 May, aware that all was lost, they carried out an inspection of the airfield, where the wrecks of about 20 RAF aircraft were strewn around —at least six Gladiators, eight or nine Lysanders, two Hurricanes, a Blenheim, a Dominie and three Tiger Moths were discerned, some of which carried battle damage while others had been partly dismantled for spares and some had been deliberately made unflyable; Goddard recalled:

> 'It suddenly struck me that he [Blount] must go, he had to continue to fight. It was common sense. Selecting a Lysander first, we found (as we had feared) that the fugitives had watered all the tanks still able to hold fluid. It was the same with a slightly damaged Gladiator. The Dominie had one of its propellers broken. We inspected each of the little biplanes [the Tiger Moths] in turn; the very last one [K3472] seemed, miraculously, to have nothing wrong with it. That Gypsy engine started like a bird!'

The Air Vice-Marshal climbed aboard the aircraft, familiarized himself with the controls and, following an enquiry as to which direction he should head, took off. Goddard looked at his watch. It was 0605:

> 'Soon the cowering grass showed separation from the Tiger Moth's wheels; they were off! Over the brow of the meadow they went, no higher than their own height, two fliers, one entity, in instant harmony—Blount and his Moth.'

Blount* reached England safely, as did Goddard a few days later in a battle-scarred Ensign.

A DH89 of 24 Squadron which arrived at Merville at 1030 the following morning carried a party of ten RAF fitters, armourers and W/T mechanics, under the command of Plt Off (formerly Lt Colonel, RFC) Louis Strange DSO MC DFC, a Great War fighter pilot. Strange had been sent to Merville to act as Ground Control Officer for the incoming transport aircraft, where he was also to investigate the possibility of rendering any of the abandoned Hurricanes serviceable. Following a close inspection of these—a total of 16 Hurricanes having been located—Strange considered that three were repairable and his party commenced work, as he recalled:

> '[We] got busy servicing the Hurricanes we had come to rescue. The

---

* On his return to England, Air Vice-Marshal Blount was given command of 22 (Army Co-operation) Group. On 27 October 1940 the aircraft in which he was a passenger crashed on take-off at Hendon, en route for Northern Ireland; he was amongst those killed.

first was soon away, with a good many bullet holes in it, the variable
pitch airscrew control tied into fine pitch with a bit of copper wire,
and a piece of telephone cable back to the cockpit to enable the pilot
to change pitch by breaking the copper wire with a good tug.'

The unidentified Hurricane pilot who flew this particular aircraft back
to England had earlier been shot down east of Merville; he had been
making his way to the coast by foot and, on reaching Merville, was
delighted to be offered the Hurricane and was soon on his way across
the Channel and back to his unit. Just before midday a second
Hurricane had been made airworthy and awaited a pilot. One was soon
to arrive. A dogfight between Hurricanes of 229 Squadron and Bf109s,
near the airfield, resulted in Plt Off Tony Linney being obliged to bale
out, although he reported later that he had shot down a Messerschmitt
first. He landed, quite by chance, within the periphery of Merville
aerodrome and was immediately offered the repaired Hurricane.
Within a short space of time he was on his way back to his home station,
much to the joy of his surprised Squadron colleagues. By late that
afternoon a third Hurricane was ready; again a pilot was awaited, but
this time it was Strange who was in for a surprise:

'I was surprised to see one of our own aircraft leave a busy dogfight
and streak down to drop one of the familiar little red and blue
message bags, telling me to bring the next serviceable Hurricane
back to England before nightfall.'

Although he had not flown a Hurricane previously—and there was no
one available at Merville to give him instruction—the 49-year-old
Strange felt confident of his ability to get the aircraft back to England.
He made arrangements for his men, then departed from Merville at
1940 and set course for home, being followed by ground fire as he pulled
away. At 8,000 feet he was suddenly bounced by six Bf109s and bullets
ripped into one wing before he was able to evade by side-slipping and
then dived to tree-top level:

'I pulled the throttle right back, put the nose down a bit, and slipped
in towards No 2 as he came. Nos 3, 4, 5 and 6 all overshot me. I had
to get down among the tree-tops as quickly as I could. Those
Messerschmitts chased me up the village street, down the château
drive and almost through the château front door.'

Strange was pursued all the way to the coast, where Royal Navy gunners
opened fire at the Messerschmitts and drove them away, enabling him
to fly back to England and land safely at RAF Manston. For his performance this day he was awarded a Bar to his 1918 DFC.

Also on the retreat from Merville was Sqn Ldr Jack Satchell and his Operations Room staff. On this date and without warning, German troops were seen on the road approaching Merville, obliging Satchell and his staff to climb through the toilet window at the rear of the Operations Room building and escape across fields. Hiding during the day and travelling by night, Satchell and his party eventually reached Boulogne, where they boarded a ship bound for England. The undignified view pursuing German troops had of RAF officers and airmen fleeing for their lives across the fields from Merville effectively signalled the end of the RAF's presence in Northern France.

An official report summed up the chaotic situation:

'The evacuation of the RAF Component entailed the loss of a vast quantity of equipment. Transport was directed towards Cherbourg, but that which left Boulogne later than the early hours of 20 May got no further than Abbeville. From what fragmentary accounts survive, one learns not so much of equipment destroyed as of equipment abandoned, either at stations or at the ports. From the operational viewpoint this was a serious loss, but from the historical viewpoint what mattered more was the destruction of practically all records of the formation. Many unit records were burnt before moving. Others, including those of Headquarters, were stacked ready for loading on the leave quay at Boulogne, but were then dumped into the harbour, presumably from an absence of shipping, time or forethought.'

CHAPTER XIV

SUMMARY, COMMENT,
CONCLUSIONS AND AFTERMATH

'The battle in France is full of danger to both sides. Although we
have taken heavy toll of the enemy in the air and are clawing down
two or three to one of their planes, they have still a formidable
numerical superiority.'

Prime Minister Winston Churchill.

Of the 452 Hurricanes sent to France, only 66 returned to England at
the time of the withdrawal of the Air Component; of the 386 lost, 178
had been abandoned as unflyable, most having been rendered irrepar-
able by the retreating forces; of these, Air Component reported the loss
of 203 Hurricanes between 10 and 20 May, of which approximately half
were the result of combat. For example, 504 Squadron recorded that
16 Hurricanes had been taken to France and seven replacements
received. Of these, three were handed over to 73 Squadron at Reims,
eight returned to England and a dozen lost.

As far as can be ascertained, at least 499 victories and 123 probables
(for a total of 622) were claimed by the Hurricane pilots between 10 and
21 May, against assessed Luftwaffe losses of 299 aircraft destroyed and
at least 65 relatively seriously damaged (a total of 364), while suffering
the losses as indicated:

	Claims		Losses		
				Pilots	
	Confirmed	Probable	Hurricanes	Killed	PoW	Wnd
AASF						
1 Squadron:	63	11	21	2	1	4
73 Squadron:	33	7	15	3	0	4
501 Squadron:	32	1	6	2	0	0

Air Component

3 Squadron:	67	5	23(1)	6(2)	2	2
79 Squadron:	23¼	3	10	2	1	2
85 Squadron:	64½	21	25	7(3)	1	5(4)
87 Squadron:	55½	12	16	6	0	4
504 Squadron:	8	5	11	4	1	4
607 Squadron:	41	16	17	5	3	4
615 Squadron:	14	3	12	3	2	3

11 Group Reinforcements

17 Squadron:	16	6	9	3	3	0
32 Squadron:	4	5	2	0	1	0
56 Squadron:	16	4	3	2	0	1
111 Squadron:	13	4	5	3	0	0
145 Squadron:	5	4	2	1	0	0
151 Squadron:	10	5	1	0	0	0
213 Squadron:	6¾	2	2(5)	0	0	1(6)
229 Squadron:	4	0	5	2	1	1
242 Squadron:	3	1	5	1	1	0
245 Squadron:	1	0	2(7)	0	0	0
253 Squadron:	8	6	10	3	1	1
601 Squadron:	9	2	11	0	0	0
60 Wing:	1	0	0	0	0	0
4(C) Ferry Flt:	1	0	2(8)	1(9)	0	0
	499	123	215	56	18	36

(1 & 2) Including three aircraft and two pilots lost in accidents; (3 & 4) in addition, one pilot was killed and another injured in a road accident; (5 & 6) including one aircraft lost and its pilot injured in an accident; (7) including one aircraft lost in an accident; (8 & 9) both aircraft and one pilot lost in accidents.

According to the Luftwaffe Quarter-Master General's Returns, total losses sustained by Luftflotte 2 and 3 to all operational causes for the period 10 to 21 May amounted to 690 aircraft, of which 169 were Ju52s and 22 were Fi156s, few of which were the result of air combat; the remainder comprised:

Bombers/Reconnaissance		Ground Attack		Fighters	
He111	177	Ju87	59	Bf109	76
Do17	78			Bf110	38
Ju88	48				
Do215	3				
Hs126	20				

It is known that two FW189s and three Hs123s were also lost, plus one further Fi156, although these had not been recorded in the Luftwaffe Quarter-Master General's Returns by 21 May 1940. Of the above, it seems probable that at least 299 fell to the guns of the Hurricanes:

	60%-100%	Under 60%	
He111H/P	92	22	
Do17M/Z	28	19	
Ju88A	10	2	= 130 twin-engined bombers lost and 43 damaged
He111H	2	—	
Do17P	16	—	
Do215B	1	—	
Ju88A	4	—	
FW189	2	—	= 25 long-range reconnaissance lost destroyed
Ju87B	37	7	
Hs123A	3	1	= 40 ground attack aircraft lost and eight damaged
Hs126B	29	2	
Fi156C	1	—	= 30 short-range spotter and reconnaissance aircraft lost and two damaged
Bf109E	38	4	
Bf110C	36	8	= 76 fighters lost and 12 damaged

Churchill, Dowding and The Hurricane Tap

Virtually every account written about the Battle of France and the ensuing Battle of Britain makes great play of the fateful meeting of the War Cabinet on 15 May, when Dowding, with a carefully worded memorandum, was able to persuade Churchill to curtail the reinforcement of the fighter forces in France. In fact two days earlier Churchill himself had made the following statement to the War Cabinet:

> 'Whatever course the war in France took, we could not afford to use up fighters day by day until the defences of this island were impaired. It was true that our fighters would find it difficult to deal with the German attacks by night, but on the other hand the Germans would be unable to bomb our vital points with any accuracy. If however our fighter strength was seriously weakened, we would lay ourselves open to the greater accuracy of daylight attack. Such reinforcement that could be spared would be sent to the Army, but it must not be thought in any circumstances that it would be possible to send large numbers of fighters to France.'

This clearly refutes the popular myth that Churchill was prepared to squander the RAF fighter force in France, a decision taken before the French started asking for more fighters.

In the event, it can be seen that the controversy about who did or did not decide to turn off the Hurricane tap is irrelevant, since from 13 May onwards—and in ever increasing numbers—Hurricanes in flights and squadrons were flown across to France, some of which operated just for the day, while others were attached to squadrons already based in France. By the end of the first week, almost every Hurricane squadron in Fighter Command was represented in France in one way or another; even individual pilots who had ferried Hurricanes to front-line squadrons remained to fly with these units in some instances. To illustrate the point, on 17 May the following Hurricane units were represented in France: 1, 3, 17, 32, 56, 73, 79, 85, 87, 111, 145, 151, 213, 229, 242, 245, 253, 501, 504, 601, 607 and 615 Squadrons. In fact only 43, 46 and 605 Squadrons were not directly involved, but even two of these (43 and 605 Squadrons) had supplied pilots for service in France, while 46 Squadron was already in action in Norway. In addition, many of Dowding's Spitfire squadrons had supplied pilots to units in France.

All in all, the picture was one of total confusion. Despite decisions taken at the highest level, a policy of attrition had begun to take what appears to be, in hindsight, involuntary control. It can be argued that the real reason the Hurricane tap was turned off was the fact that after 20 May there were no airfields left in Northern France to where more Hurricanes could be sent.

The whole sorry story of the RAF in France, and in particular that of the Hurricane squadrons, was one of how not to wage an air war. The fighters had been frittered away with sections of three or flights of six Hurricanes having to face vastly superior formations of the enemy, a point that had been made at the height of the battle by Flg Off Paul Richey of 1 Squadron to a visiting senior officer from AASF HQ:

> 'We're operating in penny packets and are always hopelessly inferior in numbers to the formations we meet. My humble opinion is that we should not operate in formations less than two squadrons strong on bomber cover.'

The tactical training for fighter combat was inherently flawed, with tight formation flying being given priority over gunnery and tactics. As a consequence, Hurricane pilots often did not see the enemy fighters that bounced them. The lessons learned during the Phoney War were not generally acted upon and, while individually several pilots did very well, as a whole the Hurricanes in France suffered unnecessarily heavy losses due to lack of proper training and proper control, and—in several cases—from blatantly incompetent command: few squadron commanders led their squadrons in the air. In addition, the airfields from which the Hurricanes operated were just that—grass fields—without proper control towers or runways and mostly without any form of defence from attack by land or air.

Shortly before the Blitzkrieg started, a Bf109E-3 which had been captured and evaluated by the French was flown by Flg Off Hilly Brown of 1 Squadron to the Royal Aircraft Establishment at Boscombe Down, escorted by three Blenheims and a Hudson*. Before leaving France, Brown had flown the Messerschmitt in mock combat with a Hurricane piloted by Flt Lt Prosser Hanks, when it was found that the Hurricane was far more manoeuvrable and was slightly faster at ground level. However, at any altitude above this the German fighter had the advantage in speed. At Boscombe Down the Bf109 was allocated the serial AE479 and put through its paces; the subsequent report confirmed the findings of the 1 Squadron pilots:

'The Hurricane, even when fitted with the Rotol three-blade constant-speed airscrew, was inferior to the German fighter in all aspects with the exception of low-altitude manoeuvrability and turning circle at all altitudes.'

When matched against a Spitfire, the two aircraft were found to be more evenly matched, although the Messerschmitt could outclimb the Spitfire up to 20,000 feet and could always elude it in a dive, but the Spitfire possessed a definite superiority in manoeuvrability at all altitudes. The A&AEE report added:

'The general consensus of opinion among RAF pilots who had an opportunity to evaluate the Bf109E-3 in flight was that it provided a formidable opponent to be treated with respect.'

Strangely enough, the Hurricanes in France seldom came to grips with the Luftwaffe's Bf109s in any large-scale battles. Most of the Hurricanes' combats were against bombers, reconnaissance aircraft or the Bf110 formations. At this period, the Bf110 was held to be the Luftwaffe's premier fighter and most of the Hurricanes' larger scale combats—and losses—were against this type. However, the Hurricane proved that it was able to out-manoeuvre the Bf110 and was more than a match in single combat, but usually Hurricane sections and flights

---

* The Bf109E (WkNr1304) White 1 of 1/JG51 had landed by mistake on the French airfield at Strasbourg-Neuhof, following an engagement with MS406s of GCIII/7 on 22 November 1939, its pilot (Ofw Herfried Kloimüller) having become disorientated. From there the Messerschmitt was transferred to Orleans-Bricy, where it was flown in mock combat against two of France's latest fighters, the D520 and Bloch 152. The outcome of the evaluation was that the German machine had a superior performance to both French aircraft, although it did not have complete superiority in aerial combat. Following its evaluation by the A&AEE and the RAF, the aircraft was later (in 1942) sent to the United States for appraisal by the USAAF.

were overwhelmed by sheer weight of numbers. Moreover, the Hurricane had dispelled the myth that modern bombers did not require fighter escort, as testified by the losses inflicted on formations of unescorted He111s and Do17s.

Analysis of Hurricane vs Bf109 combats indicates that had these occurred more often, Hurricane losses would have been much heavier, although there was seldom an occasion when the German single-seaters engaged in dogfighting, their main tactic being one of hit-and-run, usually from out of the sun. A notable exception, when Hurricanes of 1 Squadron met Bf109s of I/JG53 on more or less equal terms in a series of dogfights on 14 May over Sedan, resulted in a 5:0 ratio in favour of the Hurricanes. A reversal of fortunes had, however, been suffered earlier by 17 Squadron, when five out of a dozen Hurricanes were shot down by I/JG51 near Rotterdam on 11 May. There were many other occasions when tight-flying formations of Hurricanes were bounced by two or three Bf109s, invariably with disastrous results for the RAF pilots.

Any advantage the British and French may have anticipated from their use—albeit limited—of the mobile RDF units, was lost in the chaos that followed the invasion. The support infrastructure and expertise left much to be desired and, as early as 10 May, Air Marshal Barratt wrote to the Air Ministry viewing with concern:

> '. . . the poor results being given by the stations already erected, and the slow progress being made in extending the chain beyond its present very limited area.'

A word of praise must be recorded for the RAF ground crews, working under the most terrible conditions on virtually undefended airfields; not fighting men, but tradesmen. It is a tribute to their courage and devotion to duty that they continued to function. When the order came to withdraw, many were left to make their own ways to the coast.

Throughout the twelve days and afterwards, UK-based squadrons supported the units in France along the Belgian and Dutch coasts. Aircraft of RAF Fighter Command—flying so far from home and invariably over the sea—suffered heavily in these exchanges. Paradoxically, 32 Squadron flew over to France almost daily from RAF Biggin Hill to operate and saw virtually nothing until 19 May. Obviously, the squadrons operating from the United Kingdom were initially at a disadvantage due to their lack of range, and their fuel capacity allowed them only a brief period of time available to perform their allotted tasks. Additionally, the fact that fighters flying from England over the Continent were beyond the capability of RAF Ground Control meant that no really effective operations could be mounted. When specific operations were planned, the rapidly changing ground situation often resulted in them being pointless and ineffective by the time they were executed. This resulted in most of the RAF effort being reduced to patrol, a wasteful use of resources.

The decision to send to France units which would operate from a French base during the day and return to their home UK base each evening was also wasteful, since most of the airfields lacked capacity and capability. In fact, the end result of this particular policy was merely to add to the already hectic state of confusion on the poorly equipped bases.

The small and generally inferior air forces of Holland and Belgium were virtually wiped out on the ground on the first day of the Blitzkrieg by the overwhelming onslaught of the Luftwaffe. The few aircraft which did survive the initial attacks put up a gallant defence which, while inflicting losses on the Luftwaffe, could only delay the inevitable outcome. Within four or five days the Dutch and Belgian air arms effectively ceased to exist.

The French Air Force—the Armée de l'Air—had been caught thoroughly unprepared for the war and had only just started to re-equip with more modern aircraft when the Germans attacked. Sixteen of the 28 French fighter Groupes de Chasse were equipped with the obsolescent Morane MS406, and eight of these were actually in the process of re-equipping with the excellent new Dewotine D520. Four of the remaining 12 Groupes had the Hawk-75, which gave a very good account of itself, while the other eight Groupes had the Bloch 151 and 152, both of which suffered considerable problems due to being rushed into service, but subsequently performed with distinction. To reduce further the effective number of French fighters available in the first two weeks of the campaign, five Groupes were in North Africa and Syria and did not take part in the Battle for France. Furthermore, at least five more Groupes were stationed in the south-east as part of Zones d'Operations Aèriènnes des Alpes (ZOAA), watching the Italians and thus far removed from the action.

Therefore, during the days immediately following the German attack, only eleven Groupes of French fighters were available in the critical Northern Sector (Zones d'Operations Aèriènnes des Nord or ZOAN) and the peculiar chain of command further divided the efforts of these Groupes. Four of these Groupes were under the command of the four individual army commanders, three for the defence of Paris and two for the defence of the bay of the Seine. The remaining two were for Naval co-operation. It is hardly surprising that in the vital opening days of the invasion the French fighter force was unable to impose any degree of co-ordinated effort against the Luftwaffe. It was basically due to the re-equipping of units during the initial stages of the battle that the Armée de l'Air fighter arm emerged stronger at the end of the Battle of

France than at the beginning. It is also worth mentioning that the age of many French fighter pilots was higher than in the Luftwaffe and RAF, and that a considerable number of French pilots had flown in fighter combat during the Great War.

One British historian was particularly scathing of the French effort when he wrote:

'The French Air Force, according to the French Air Minister from 1938 to 1940, had 3,289 modern aircraft available. Of these 2,122 were fighters. So where were the aircraft? Général d'Astier de la Vigerie, Air Commander of the First French Armée Group, said he had only 432 fighters, and 72 of those were RAF planes. Général Gamelin asked: "Why, out of 2,000 modern aircraft on hand at the beginning of May 1940, were fewer than 500 used on the north-east front?" So what really happened to all those missing aircraft? The German attacks upon the French airfields had unexpected results. Undamaged aircraft were hastily flown out of the immediate danger zone and parked at training fields, civil airports and rear echelon strips. Deliveries from the factories were diverted from front-line units and also parked in safe places. Eyewitnesses counted 200 aircraft parked at Tours airfield, 150 of them fighters.' *

It can be no real surprise, therefore, that a single-minded, professional, experienced, superbly equipped Luftwaffe, acting completely in concert with its army, was able to defeat and overrun a disorganized, poorly equipped, inexperienced Armée de l'Air, which had no idea how to support its own troops or indeed support itself in combat. It soon became apparent that the French were not ready to fight, and the RAF presence in France was really only a political gesture.

For the Germans the battle had been a resounding success. To overcome and defeat the Western Allies within such a short period of time was a triumph of planning and execution. From the initial strikes on 10 May, the Luftwaffe was the decisive factor and, by gaining control of the air and never relinquishing it, the Germans were able to dominate the battlefield. Only on that first day was the Luftwaffe used strategically, hitting airfields, road junctions and rail centres. Afterwards, the Luftwaffe reverted mainly to the tactical duties for which it was trained and equipped. Operating closely with the Wehrmacht as spotters, the many units with Hs126s pinpointed Allied troop concentrations or other targets, calling up the Ju87s or other bombers to wreak death and destruction. German fighter pilots had proved themselves to be

---

* See *Blitzkrieg* by Len Deighton. It should also be noted that after the Armistice, 2,648 modern French aircraft, including 700 fighters, were located on North African soil.

supreme: their aircraft, particularly the Bf109, were superior; their training and tactics were superior; and they had numerical strength. A German historian summed up the brief campaign accurately and adequately, thus:

'The first few days of the campaign in the West served to show that fortifications of traditional type could no longer stand up to combined air and ground attack. After "softening up" by the Luftwaffe, they were taken by armour and infantry. Even the strongly defended line of the Meuse was forced more swiftly than anticipated. Bold enterprises—such as the landing of airborne sappers on the strategic fortress of Eben-Emael and the Albert Canal bridges —achieved a temporary paralysis of the enemy, but required a swift advance by the Army as reinforcement. The lightly armed airborne units were themselves too weak to follow up their initial success. The same applied to the paratroop drops and airborne landings in Holland, where full surprise was not achieved owing to the existence of this force having been revealed by its use in Norway. The defence was able to prepare against this new method of assault, and this led to the failure of the landings round The Hague. The loss of several hundred transport machines, drawn largely from the Luftwaffe's training schools, had a damaging effect on the future flow of trained personnel. In France the Luftwaffe not only prepared the way for the rapid advance of the armoured corps, but safeguarded its long, exposed flanks. Though inexperienced in combating tanks, close-support and dive-bombing formations succeeded several times in thwarting armoured attacks against these flanks.'

Aftermath

But that was not the end of the story. The Hurricane squadrons with the AASF had retreated westward with the French main body, and would continue to operate in France until mid-June with no significant success, but merely as a political sop.

By dawn on 22 May the Germans had regained their momentum after the fright of the British counter-attack at Arras. A gap of 30 miles now separated the northern armies from the main forces in the south, and any ideas the Allies had entertained of closing it had now disappeared. With the exception of Calais and Boulogne, the Germans held the Channel coast from Gravelines in the north to the mouth of the Somme. The remnants of the Belgian Army, the French 1st Armée and the BEF were completely encircled and apparently facing total disaster.

The withdrawal of the Air Component meant that all air cover would have to come from bases in southern England, although the AASF squadrons that had withdrawn from their bases near Reims were operating from Rouen-Boos. This situation was to increase further the load on the desperately tired RAF pilots, since virtually every Hurricane unit had been drawn into the battle; even squadrons not directly engaged had been tapped to supply pilots. In addition, Dowding's precious Spitfire squadrons were being drawn into the fray as they commenced to patrol the Channel coast.

The three Hurricane squadrons of the AASF—1, 73 and 501—were the only RAF fighter units which remained in France and, having seen considerable action and suffered the inevitable losses such actions occasioned, were about to see the replacement of many of their battle-weary pilots. Those of 1 Squadron were replaced almost en masse, while those of 73 Squadron were advised of their immediate replacement. Although 501 Squadron had been just as heavily engaged, as it had only been in France since 10 May, it was, accordingly, not adjudged to be in need of respite.

Wednesday 22 May

The earliest action of the day saw nine Hurricanes of 151 Squadron patrolling the coast; at 0600 they encountered a Ju88 which was shot down between Calais and Boulogne. At around the same time, a patrol of Spitfires from 74 Squadron claimed the destruction of another Ju88. Both aircraft were probably from 8/LG1. No further actions occurred until mid-afternoon when a section of Spitfires from 65 Squadron claimed the probable destruction of another Ju88 over Dunkirk, this probably a machine from 9/LG1 or I/KG30.

At about noon, a patrol of Hurricanes from 605 Squadron was engaged by six Bf109s near Arras, losing two, before the survivors encountered a trio of He111s—possibly from III/KG27—south of Arras and claimed all three shot down, but two Hurricanes were hit by return fire; one pilot was killed, the other crash-landed his damaged aircraft. Action intensified around 1600 when a patrol of Hurricanes comprising Flights from 56, 213 and 242 Squadrons engaged a number of Hs126s between Arras and Cambrai, and a total of seven were claimed shot down with another probably destroyed. It appears that none of the spotter machines was destroyed, although some may have force-landed in the nearest open space when attacked.

The final combats of the day involved 32, 145, 151 and 601 Squadrons. Patrolling over the front lines near Arras, 32 Squadron became involved in a series of dogfights with Bf109s (possibly from I/JG1) and claimed four shot down and two probables for the loss of one Hurricane. The other three units were involved in actions near Merville, still being used by the RAF to ferry in supplies and evacuate personnel. A force of Ju87s were seen and at once attacked. Four were claimed shot down and a further two probably by 151 Squadron, while minutes later 145 Squadron bounced more Ju87s over St Omer and claimed six destroyed and three probables, plus a Bf109 probable. The German units involved were probably II/StG77, which lost four aircraft, and I(St)/TrGr186, which lost two. At about the same time 601 Squadron, whilst patrolling over Arras, claimed two Bf109s for no loss, possibly an action with I/JG27.

Thursday 23 May
During the day the RAF mounted several patrols over the French coast and encountered formations of German fighters—both Bf109s and Bf110s. For the first time the Luftwaffe fighter pilots had the decidedly uncomfortable experience of meeting in combat an opponent which was vastly superior to any previously encountered—the Spitfire—and in these initial clashes it was the British fighter which emerged the victor. In a frantic series of dogfights with 54 and 92 Squadrons over Calais, I/JG27 lost five aircraft in exchange for one Spitfire shot down; later in the day 92 Squadron fought the Bf110s of ZG26 and ZG76 over the same area, with each side losing two aircraft. The Hurricanes of 32, 56, 145, 229, 242, 253 and 601 Squadrons all engaged Luftwaffe fighter formations over Northern France—mainly I/JG1, I/JG3 and I/JG51—losing ten while claiming six, a rate of attrition the tired Hurricane units could hardly afford.

On the ground the Wehrmacht tightened its hold on the ports of Calais and Boulogne, both of which could not sustain a long defence. The main Allied Northern Army group began to pull back to a perimeter centred on the port of Dunkirk, but as yet the possibility of evacuation was not a serious consideration.

Friday 24 May
Again the RAF Hornchurch-based Spitfire squadrons enjoyed a fruitful day at the expense of the fighter pilots of JG27. In a series of combats over the coastal area, 54 Squadron claimed 13 Bf109s, 74 Squadron claimed five bombers, 92 Squadron seven bombers and 65 Squadron a Hs126. Against the bombers the claims were reasonably accurate, but claims against the Bf109s were over-optimistic with only four being lost, plus two damaged. The Hurricanes had a generally quiet day with only two claims, one by 111 Squadron and the other by the AASF's 73 Squadron, operating from Gaye airfield, east of Paris; the latter unit however lost two aircraft although both pilots survived, one having been badly burned.

Meanwhile, after a gallant but futile defence by a hopelessly inadequate garrison, Boulogne was taken and the defenders escaped literally under the guns of the Panzers as their rescuing destroyers engaged the German tanks in an artillery duel.

Saturday 25 May

The RAF continued with the policy of patrolling the French coast and the inland region. 17 Squadron intercepted a group of Ju87s of I/StG2 over Calais and claimed three plus a Do17 and a stray Hs126, while 54 Squadron—escorting FAA Swordfish on a bombing attack on German troops near Calais—clashed with Bf110s and Bf109s, claiming three of the former and one of the latter. Hurricanes of 605 Squadron also claimed four Ju87s of II/StG77 and a Hs126 over Calais at midday.

In these combats, 54 Squadron lost one pilot killed and two shot down—both of whom returned later—and 605 Squadron one pilot killed. 151 Squadron also engaged and lost two pilots without making any claims. French-based 73 Squadron claimed a Do17 during the day (another victory for Flg Off Cobber Kain), but also lost a pilot who became a PoW.

Sunday 26 May—Saturday 1 June: The Evacuation at Dunkirk

From 26 May, when the decision was taken to evacuate the BEF via Dunkirk, RAF Fighter Command was drawn into the difficult task of providing air cover for the operation, which was carried out with a degree of success that exceeded wildest expectations in what has become known as 'The Miracle of Dunkirk', when 338,226 Allied troops were brought safely across the Channel aboard a vast miscellany of vessels.

The story of the RAF's involvement in the success of the Dunkirk evacuation is outside the scope of this account*; however, during the six-day operation RAF Fighter Command reported that its pilots had accounted for 390 Luftwaffe aircraft destroyed (later amended to 258 destroyed and 119 probables, while actual losses were nearer to 130), while losing up to 100 Hurricanes and Spitfires. Pilot fatalities amongst those shot down exceeded 50%, including a number who had figured in the fighting in France and Belgium between 10 and 21 May:

26 May:	Flg Off Capel Adye	17 Squadron
	Flt Sgt Bill Jones	17 Squadron
27 May:	Flg Off Charles Lee-Steere	601 Squadron
28 May:	Flg Off Tim Winning	213 Squadron
	Plt Off Laurence Stone	213 Squadron
	Sgt Jimmy Elliott	56 Squadron
31 May:	Flg Off Bill Gray	213 Squadron
	Plt Off Gordon Stewart	242 Squadron
	Plt Off Peter Dixon	145 Squadron
	Plt Off John Collins	229 Squadron
1 June:	Flg Off Ian Russell	609 Squadron
3 June:	Flg Off Dickie Meredith	17 Squadron

* For detailed coverage of RAF operations over Dunkirk the authors recommend *The Air Battle of Dunkirk* by Norman Franks, published by William Kimber, 1983.

In addition, Plt Off Art Deacon of 242 Squadron was shot down and taken prisoner. Others were shot down and were either rescued from the sea or returned via Dunkirk, including Flg Off Ken Newton and Plt Off Buck Courtney of 151 Squadron, Sgt John Lishman of 213 Squadron, Plt Off Tony Linney of 229 Squadron (for a second time) and Flt Lt Dickie Lee (then flying with 56 Squadron); another was Flt Lt Freddie Ives of 151 Squadron, but he was tragically drowned when the vessel returning him to England was torpedoed. Others who had featured prominently in the fighting in France were killed or incapacitated in flying accidents, including Plt Off Tony Dini of 607 Squadron who was killed in a crash. The majority of those who survived the fighting in France and over Dunkirk were soon again to face the might of the Luftwaffe in defence of Britain, when many paid the supreme price.

The fighting continued in France however, although on a less intensive scale as the Germans consolidated their positions and strengthened their forces. In the air, in the Southern Sector of the front, the squadrons of the AASF soldiered on, reinforced in June by 17 and 242 Squadrons. These and the original units—1, 73 and 501 Squadrons—continued to fight an ever more pointless battle. Retreating from airfield to airfield, the squadrons (supported magnificently by the ground echelons) fought to the bitter end, covering a succession of mini-Dunkirks from Le Havre, Cherbourg, Brest and La Rochelle, finally leaving France via the Channel Islands to return to home shores in time to join their colleagues in the imminent onslaught of the Battle of Britain.

One bitter point of contention with the RAF was that the French authorities would not hand over captured Luftwaffe airmen to the British, despite promises from the former French Premier, M. Reynaud. Hence, when France finally capitulated, all German prisoners of war in French hands were released, including 400 pilots. For example, 21 Bf110 crew members (12 pilots and nine air gunners), most of whom had fallen in combat with Hurricanes between 10 and 21 May (the period covered by this account), were eventually released by the French. This action naturally angered the RAF and Prime Minister Churchill in particular, who told the House of Commons that:

'...they would be used to bomb this country and thus force our airmen to shoot them down for the second time over.'

Which, in many cases, they did. But that is another story.

SELECT BIBLIOGRAPHY AND SOURCES

(Figures in brackets indicate chapters in which quotes have been used)

Primary Sources

PRO Air 41/21: '*Attack on France and the Low Countries*' (AHB/11/117/5(A) (1,2,4,5, 6,7,8,9,10,11,12,13,14)
PRO Air 50/1: 1 Squadron Combat Reports (4,5,9,10)
PRO Air 2/4097: 1 Squadron Reports (3,4)
PRO Air 27/1: 1 Squadron ORB (5,6,7,10,11)
PRO Air 50/4: 3 Squadron Combat Reports (2,6,7,10,11,12)
PRO Air 50/9: 17 Squadron Combat Reports (3,9,10,11,13)
PRO Air 50/16: 32 Squadron Combat Reports (10,11,12)
PRO Air 50/31: 73 Squadron Combat Reports (11)
PRO Air 50/33: 79 Squadron Combat Reports (3,6,9,10,12)
PRO Air 50/36: 85 Squadron Combat Reports (2,11,12)
PRO Air 27/703: 85 Squadron ORB (2,4,7)
PRO Air 50/37: 87 Squadron Combat Reports (2,3,11,12)
PRO Air 27/712: 87 Squadron ORB (2,4,8)
PRO Air 50/43: 111 Squadron Combat Reports (10,11)
PRO Air 27/866: 111 Squadron ORB (10)
PRO Air 50/62: 145 Squadron Combat Reports (10,11)
PRO Air 50/63: 151 Squadron Combat Reports (9)
PRO Air 27/1315: 213 Squadron ORB (10)
PRO Air 50/86: 229 Squadron Combat Reports (10,13)
PRO Air 50/97: 253 Squadron Combat Reports (10,11)
PRO Air 27/1949: 501 Squadron ORB (5)
PRO Air 50/165: 601 Squadron Combat Reports (10,11)
PRO Air 50/170: 607 Squadron Combat Reports (2,3,10,11)
PRO Air 50/175: 615 Squadron Combat Reports (2,7,9,11,12)
PRO Air 50/465: 4 (Cont) Ferry Flight Combat Reports (10)
PRO Air 4/109: Logbook of the late Flt Lt R.D.G. Wight DFC (9,10, 11,12)
1/JG53 Combat Reports, via Jack Foreman (6)

Correspondence with Mr Bill Bowman (10,11,12); Air Marshal Sir Denis Crowley-Milling KCB CBE DSO DFC AFC; the late Flt Lt A.H. Deacon; Wg Cdr P.C.P. Farnes DFM (3,10); Sqn Ldr A.H.B. Friendship DFM (4,6,7,8,9); Flg Off C.E. Hampshire (7,8,10,12); Grp Capt J.A. Hemingway DFC (3); Wg Cdr J.R. Kayll DSO OBE DFC (2,5,7,11,12); Sqn Ldr K.N.T. Lee DFC (4); the late Sqn Ldr A.G. Lewis DFC (11,12); Wg Cdr P.L. Parrott DFC AFC (1,2,3,4,5,6,7, 8,9); Wg Cdr W.H.R. Whitty DFC (2,5,6,7,8,10,11); Letter from Wg Cdr W.F. Blackadder DSO to Dixon family, via Simon Muggleton (3); Letter from the late Plt Off Peter Dixon to his brother, via Simon Muggleton (7); and interview with Flt Lt T.C. Jackson conducted by Chris Shores on behalf of authors (5,8).

Logbook of the late Sqn Ldr J.R. Cock DFC, via Dennis Newton (2,5,6); Logbook of Sqn Ldr A.H.B. Friendship DFM (11,12); Logbook of the late Wg Cdr C.A.C. Stone DFC (4,7); Diary of the late Flt Lt L.S. Pilkington DFM, via Andy Saunders (3,5,6,7, 11); Diary of the late Flg Off C.W.W. Darwin, via Norman Franks (4,8,10,11,12).

Published Sources

Adams, Perry: *Hurricane Squadron* (6,8)
Arthur, Max: *There Shall Be Wings* (6,10)
Beamont, Roland CBE DSO DFC: *My Part of the Sky* (9,11)

Bekker, Cajus: *The Luftwaffe War Diaries* (2,6,14)
Bickers, Richard Townshend: *Ginger Lacey — Fighter Pilot* (6,9)
Bickers, Richard Townshend: *Home Run* (10,11)
Bingham, Victor: *Blitzed*
Brooks, Andrew: *Fighter Squadron at War*
Burns, Michael: *Cobber Kain*
Caffrey, Kate: *Combat Report*
Churchill, Sir Winston: *Their Finest Hour* (7,8,14)
De Decker, Cynrik & Roba, Jean-Louis: *Mei 1940: Boven Belgie* (2)
Deighton, Len: *Blitzkrieg* (14)
Embry, Air Chief Marshal Sir Basil GCB KBE DSO DFC AFC: *Mission Completed* (6)
Franks, Norman: *Double Mission*
Franks, Norman: *Fighter Leader*
Franks, Norman: *The Air Battle for Dunkirk*
Franks, Norman: *Valiant Wings*
Franks, Norman: *Fighter Command* (7,8,10,12)
Franks, Norman: *Hurricane at War 2* (6,10,11)
Galland, Generalleutnant Adolf: *The First and the Last* (4)
Gardner, Charles: *AASF* (2,3,5,6,7,9,11)
Gelb, Norman: *Scramble* (7,8)
Gleed, Ian DSO DFC: *Arise to Conquer* (10,11,12)
Goddard, Air Marshal Sir Victor KCB CBE: *Skies to Dunkirk* (1,9,13)
Halliday, Hugh: *242 Squadron: The Canadian Years* (10)
Hearn, Grp Capt Peter: *Flying Rebel: The Story of Louis Strange* (13)
Horne, Alistair: *To Lose a Battle* (4,9)
Johnson, Frank: *RAAF over Europe* (7)
Johnson, Air Vice-Marshal J.E. CBE DSO DFC: *Full Circle* (1)
Mackersey, Ian: *Into the Silk*
Masters, David: *So Few* (13)
Monks, Noel: *Squadrons Up!* (4,9)
Moulson, Tom: *The Flying Sword* (9,11)
Nelson, Kenneth: *Spitfire RCW*
Revell, Alex: *Vivid Air*
Richey, Paul DFC: *Fighter Pilot* (2,3,6,7,9,11,14)
Shaw, Michael: *Twice Vertical*
Shores, Christopher et al: *Fledgling Eagles*
Simpson, Allan DFC: *We Few* (10,12)
Sims, Edward: *Fighter Exploits* (10)
Stones, Donald DFC: *Operation Bograt* (2,6,10,12)
Sutton, Barry DFC: *The Way of a Pilot* (9,10)
van Ishoven, Armand: *Bf110 at War* (10)
Wallace, Graham: *RAF Biggin Hill* (11)
Watkins, David: *Fear Nothing* (2,3,4,7)
Wynn, Kenneth: *Men of the Battle of Britain*

Other Sources

Facts on File, British Newspaper Library (2,5,11)
Daily Mirror, June 1940 (8,12)
Flight, May 1940 (3,8)
Letchworth Citizen, 7 June 1940 (6)

INDEX